Pentecostal Experience

Princeton Theological Monograph Series

K. C. Hanson, Charles M. Collier, D. Christopher Spinks,
and Robin Parry, Series Editors

Recent volumes in the series:

Sammy Alfaro
Divino Compañero: Toward a Hispanic Pentecostal Christology

David L. Balch and Jason T. Lamoreaux, editors
Finding A Woman's Place: Essays in Honor of Carolyn Osiek

Paul W. Chilcote
*Making Disciples in a World Parish:
Global Perspectives on Mission & Evangelism*

Eric G. Flett
*Persons, Powers, and Pluralities:
Toward a Trinitarian Theology of Culture*

Vladimir Kharlamov
Theosis: Deification in Christian Theology, Volume Two

Mitzi J. Smith
The Literary Construction of the Other in the Acts of the Apostles: Charismatics, the Jews, and Women

Jon Paul Sydnor
*Ramanuja and Schleiermacher:
Toward a Constructive Comparative Theology*

Philip D. Wingeier-Rayo
*Where Are the Poor?: A Comparison of the Ecclesial Base Communities
and Pentecostalism—A Case Study in Cuernavaca, Mexico*

Pentecostal Experience

An Ecumenical Encounter

PETER D. NEUMANN

PICKWICK *Publications* · Eugene, Oregon

PENTECOSTAL EXPERIENCE
An Ecumenical Encounter

Princeton Theological Monographs Series 187

Pickwick Publications
An Imprint of Wipf and Stock Publishers
199 W. 8th Ave., Suite 3
Eugene, OR 97401

www.wipfandstock.com

ISBN 13: 978-1-61097-692-3

Cataloging-in-Publication data:

Neumann, Peter D.

    Pentecostal experience : an ecumenical encounter / Peter D. Neumann.

    Princeton Theological Monographs Series 187

    xii + 374 p. ; 23 cm. Includes bibliographical references and index.

    ISBN 13: 978-1-61097-692-3

    1. Pentecostalism—Doctrines. 2. Chan, Simon. 3. Macchia, Frank D., 1952–. 4. Yong, Amos. 5. Theology—Methodology. I. Title. II. Series.

BT123 N47 2012

Manufactured in the U.S.A.

To Sharon,
whose love and sacrifice made this book possible

Contents

Preface

I WAS RAISED IN THE PENTECOSTAL TRADITION, APPRECIATING THE VI-
brancy of its spirituality and openness to the experience and activity of
the Spirit in church and personal life. This spirituality also included,
among other things, an emphasis on Scripture as the authority for
Christian life and practice, and this emphasis was only reinforced when
I went to train for pastoral ministry at Eastern Pentecostal Bible College
(now Master's College and Seminary). Later I began graduate work
at Wycliffe College within the ecumenical atmosphere of the Toronto
School of Theology. There I was exposed to people and ideas from a
number of other Christian traditions, which began to help me value the
diversity of ways that Christians approached their faith and experience
of God, as well as their understanding and interpretation of Scripture. In
particular, courses with David A. Reed on Pentecostal and charismatic
theology, and Brian J. Walsh on postmodernism served to challenge me
to think more critically about the relationship between Pentecostal experience, Scripture, and the function of authority within Pentecostalism.
Still later, during my doctorate work at Wycliffe College, I was introduced to postliberal theology in the work of George A. Lindbeck and the
late George P. Schner. Through this I grew in appreciation for the ways in
which theological understanding and doctrine, and indeed experience
of God, is shaped and mediated by the traditions and (sub)cultures in
which we find ourselves.

All of these factors led me to begin asking deeper questions about
the nature of Pentecostal experience and the authority it bears within
Pentecostal theology. I knew that Pentecostals looked to Scripture as
their authority, but also that their experiences with the Spirit reciprocally influenced the ways in which they understood Scripture. Now,
however, things were becoming even more complex! It began to dawn on
me that the very Pentecostal theological and spiritual tradition in which

I had been raised actually served to shape the ways that those within that tradition were experiencing the Spirit. I had grown up assuming that experience of the Spirit was more or less direct or immediate, but now it was becoming clear that other theological and cultural factors were influencing my experience of God. Further, it appeared that these factors were operating more or less unacknowledged, but nevertheless authoritatively, within my own Pentecostal tradition and the shaping of its theology and doctrine. I began to wonder whether a more nuanced view of experience of God—one that more explicitly acknowledged the mediated nature of experience—might produce some theological fruitful results for Pentecostalism itself, in particular its ability to grow in its self-understanding and interaction with the broader ecumenical Christian community. All of this has served as impetus for the focus of this book, which is a slightly revised version of my PhD thesis (successfully defended in 2010 at the University of St. Michael's College), entitled, "Encountering the Spirit: Pentecostal Mediated Experience of God in Theological Context."

In completing an undertaking of this sort, there are a number of people who deserve acknowledgment and thanks. David A. Reed, who was my thesis director, has been a theological guide and mentor to me for many years. From him I have learned not only a greater appreciation for my own Pentecostal tradition, but also the value of patiently taking the time to really listen to what those from other traditions are saying, and how they are saying it, in order to move toward understanding. His thoughts, questions, and keen eye for detail have been extremely valuable in helping me complete this project. Harold G. Wells suggested that I should consider expanding on a paper submitted in one of his courses, comparing Pentecostal and Jürgen Moltmann's respective approaches to the experience of God. That encouragement factored significantly in the formulation of my PhD thesis (and ultimately this book). Additionally, I want to thank my friend, Randall (Randy) Holm, for reading over the manuscript of this book, and offering encouragements as well as suggesting possible directions for future explorations based on this study. I am, of course, also deeply indebted to the three Pentecostal theologians—Frank D. Macchia, Simon K. H. Chan, and Amos Yong—whose work served not only to provide respective case studies for this book evidencing a growing sophistication within Pentecostal theology, but has also inspired and challenged me to imagine new possibilities for theology rooted in the Pentecostal tradition.

The members of my family have also been immensely supportive during my doctorate work and the completion of this book. I am thankful for each one, and love them very much. My son, Nathanael, and daughter, Mikayla, are truly blessings from God (and growing up far too quickly!). Sharon, my wife, has my deepest gratitude. Her love, sacrifice, and encouragement (and patience!) has made this project possible, and I am honored to be sharing life together with her. Finally, I am immensely thankful for and overwhelmed by the graciousness of the Lord for enabling me to undertake and complete this work. It is my sincere hope and prayer that this study will serve to contribute to the building up of the church, to the glory of God.

Introduction

The Question of Experience in Pentecostal Theology

THE PURPOSE OF THIS BOOK IS TO EXPLORE THE APPEAL TO EXPERIENCE of God within contemporary Pentecostal theology. There is, of course, tremendous diversity encompassed under the catch-all term "pentecostal."[1] Veli-Matti Kärkkäinen has rightly suggested that we should speak of "pentecostalisms," rather than one pentecostalism.[2] So, at the outset it is necessary to identify whose theology we are intending to study. In an effort to simplify things somewhat, our focus will be on Classical Pentecostalism, one sub-tradition of the variety of pentecostalisms globally.[3] In brief, then, the goal here is to investigate how the appeal to

---

1. David B. Barrett highlights this diversity, citing the number of those within the Christian theological tradition sharing a pentecostal-type spirituality as being over 500 million, also crossing virtually all denominational, cultural, political, and ethnic boundaries (Barrett, "Worldwide," 313).

2. Kärkkäinen, *Pneumatology*, 89. Also see Anderson, *Introduction to Pentecostalism*, 10, cf. 9–15.

3. See Barrett, 381–83, 395–97. Barrett surveys what has come to be understood as the three "waves" of pentecostalism. Classical Pentecostals are generally those associated with denominations and movements emerging at the turn of the twentieth century, emphasizing a post-conversion crisis experience of Spirit baptism (usually accompanied by glossolalia). This first wave is to be distinguished from the charismatic movement, which emerged in the late 1950s and 1960s among mainline Protestant and Roman Catholic denominations, and the "Third Wave" (or neo-pentecostals/neo-charismatics), emerging in the 1980s. The latter wave is made up of evangelicals open to aspects of Classical Pentecostal spirituality (e.g., power manifestations and spiritual gifts), while downplaying any idea of post-conversion stage of Spirit baptism or tongues as "initial evidence" of this experience. For the purposes of this study, the capitalized term "Pentecostal" will refer to persons or ideas associated with Classical Pentecostalism, and the lower case "pentecostal" will refer more generically to the three waves overall. This study also acknowledges Oneness Pentecostalism as historically part of Classical Pentecostalism;

experience currently functions within this narrower tradition through an exploration of Pentecostal theology and spirituality in general, but even more particularly, in the works of three of its notable contemporary theologians, Frank D. Macchia, Simon K. H. Chan, and Amos Yong.

The Ubiquity of the Appeal to Experience

This is an important study for at least three reasons. First, the appeal to experience has become more or less ubiquitous in contemporary Christian theology in general. Harvey Cox, in *Fire from Heaven*, remarks that the concept of, and appeal to experience has played an increasingly significant role in Christian theology (as well as many other areas of life). He notes, for example, contemporary liberation and feminist theologies as having a particular "penchant" for experience as an authoritative resource for theological construction.[4] Cox goes on to suggest that the appeal to experience tends to become a catch-all source of authority, used to validate just about any type of ideology or claim—"virtually anyone can claim anything in the name of experience. The results are often exciting but confusing." Cox cites several theologies by way of example, each adhering to apparently contradictory positions, yet all the while mutually appealing to "experience" as an authority in support of its claims. Complicating matters further, these varying theologies may be appealing to different concepts of experience—the very term "experience" being a notoriously slippery one.[5]

That the concept of experience has become ubiquitously significant in contemporary theological dialogue is widely acknowledged, its emergence and growth in Western philosophical and theological traditions being historically linked, in many respects, to the Enlightenment and the so-called "turn to the subject."[6] This fascination with the role of experience

---

however, our focus will be on Trinitarian Pentecostalism as traditionally understood. On Oneness Pentecostalism, see Reed, *"In Jesus' Name"*; and "Oneness Pentecostalism," 936a–44b.

4. Cox, *Fire from Heaven*, 304.

5. Ibid., 313. We will readdress this issue in chapter 1; however, for discussion concerning definitions of "experience," see Gelpi, *Turn to Experience*, 1–7; Maddox, "Enriching Role," 107–27; Hart, "Introduction," 1–3; Boeve, "Theology and the Interruption," 12; Rossi, "Authority of Experience," 271–72; and Lane, *Experience of God*, 7–8, 12–13.

6. Boeve, "Theology and the Interruption," 11, 13–14, 24–26; Hart, "Experience of

in theology was elevated significantly by Friedrich Schleiermacher in the nineteenth century,[7] and continued to evolve in the twentieth century,[8] in the latter half becoming associated with the growing debates and skepticism surrounding foundational epistemology.[9] Schleiermacher's appeal to an interior, immediate, self-conscious experience of God as foundational for theological knowledge has been met with considerable doubt concerning the trustworthiness of interior appeals, as well as the universal applicability of appeals to experience in general.[10]

Experience as an authoritative appeal, then, is connected to the realm of theological epistemology; experience is frequently called upon to justify theological claims and beliefs.[11] Francis Schuessler Fiorenza observes, however, that the postmodern critique of foundational epis-

---

the Kingdom," 71–75; Hart, "Introduction," 3–12; Burhenn, "Philosophy and Religious," 144–60; Lane, *Experience of God*, 2; Schlitt, *Theology and Experience*, 3; and Schner, "Appeal to Experience," 42.

7. Schleiermacher is arguably the father of the modern appeal to experience in Protestant theology, locating the essence of religion in his "feeling of absolute dependence." See Schleiermacher, *Christian Faith*, 131; Brown, "Experience Skewed," 159; Hart, "Experience of the Kingdom," 72; Fiorenza, "Experience of Transcendence," 197–201, 209; Boeve, "Theology and the Interruption," 11; and Mackintosh, *Types of Modern* 42.

8. Albeit with mixed reception—some celebrating, some skeptical, concerning the role experience could or should play in theology. Cox identifies Karl Barth and George A. Lindbeck as examples of the latter (Cox, *Fire from Heaven*, 314–15; cf. Boeve, "Theology and the Interruption," 33–36). Aside from the examples previously noted by Cox, in the early twentieth-century Roman Catholicism initially expressed skepticism and disdain toward the idea of experience functioning as a theological resource. It has, however, since demonstrated considerable integration of experience in theological construction, becoming more open to immanentist conceptualizations of God's relationship to the world (specifically, by the Spirit). On this see Schlitt, *Theology and Experience*, 3–5; and Lane, *Experience of* God, 5–7. Jongeneel observes that experience of God is commonly connected to pneumatology (Jongeneel, "Preface," ix–xi). Aside from the theological epistemic issues surrounding experience, considerable interest has been generated concerning the psychology (and to a lesser extent, the sociology) of "religious" and "mystical" experiences. On the psychology of religious experience see Wulff, "Phenomenological Psychology," 183–99. On the sociological aspects of religious experience see Poloma, "Sociological Context," 161–82.

9. Boeve, "Theology and the Interruption," 11–39; Burhenn, "Philosophy and Religious," 144–60 (esp. 151–59); Fiorenza, "Experience of Transcendence," 184–88; Kelly, "Not One," 146–52; Schlitt, *Theology and Experience*, 27–30.

10. Fiorenza, "Experience of Transcendence," 197–201, 209; Kelly, "Not One," 144–46; cf. Rossi, "Authority of Experience," 274–76.

11. Hemming, "Are We Still," 159; Brown, "Experience Skewed," 160.

temology has challenged the "transcendent" authority of the appeal to experience, largely due to its assertion that experience is contextually mediated—enmeshed in the language and culture in which the appeal to experience occurs.[12] One inference from this is that there is no such thing as raw, pure, or "innocent" unmediated experience.[13]

The recognition of this mediation—that human experience is determined, or interpreted, by and through a particular context—is widely acknowledged; but there is not consensus concerning the extent to which language and culture determines experience. As David Brown notes, theologians skeptical of the appeal to experience tend to "overdetermine" the linguistic and cultural context, whereas others may choose to view God as informing theology (revealing Godself) through all sorts of general human experience (including "religious experiences").[14] So, while the *mediatedness of experience* is generally acknowledged, there is disagreement among theologians as to *how* (i.e., the extent to which) the nature of mediation applies when it comes to the appeal to experience of God.[15] Should accent be placed on the possibility of experience of God mediated through the world and various common human experiences? Or, should the accent of mediation fall on the particular "cultural-linguistic" (or "faith") context, raising suspicion as to the reliability of experience as a revelatory resource for theology?[16] Especially in the latter case, the mediatedness of experience also raises doubt concerning the possibility of God being experienced in such a way that could interrupt (or surprise), so as to introduce radical change or reform within a

12. Fiorenza, "Experience of Transcendence," 184–88, 209. Also see Paloma, "Sociological Context," 178; George Pattison, "What to Say," 192; Kelly, "Not One," 144–48; Schlitt, *Theology and Experience*, 27–30; Burhenn, "Philosophy and Religious," 149–58; Boeve, "Theology and the Interruption," 13–14, 24–39; Voiss, "Thought Forms," 242–43; and Hess, "Religious Experience," 301.

13. Fiorenza, "Experience of Transcendence," 187, cf. 185–87. Also see Burhenn, "Philosophy and Religious," 155–57; Hart, "Experience of the Kingdom," 81; Nieto, *Religious Experience*, 104–6; Hess, "Religious Experience," 301, 312–13; Lane, 10–11, 13–17, 20–22; Paloma, "Sociological Context," 178; and Pattison, "What to Say," 192.

14. Hart identifies the former as "non-correlationists" and the latter "correlationists" (Hart, "Introduction," 5–7; cf. Boeve, "Theology and the Interruption," 13–39).

15. This issue is further complicated by contextual theologies, which emphasize the historical particularity of experience, and then appeal to this contextual experience as a hermeneutical lens for constructing theology. On the justification of such a contextual appeal, see Voiss, "Thought Forms," 241–56.

16. The "cultural-linguistic" concept is derived from Lindbeck, *Nature of Doctrine*, 18; cf. Fiorenza, "Experience of Transcendence," 185–87.

particular Christian (or other) theological framework. The above questions demonstrate the appeal to experience to be a significant and lively topic in contemporary Christian theology.

Pentecostalism: An Experiential Tradition

The second reason for this study is that Pentecostalism is widely understood to be an experiential tradition; experience of God (the Holy Spirit) is intricately woven into Pentecostal identity and praxis. Cox again is helpful here, describing Pentecostalism as "the experiential branch of Christianity *par excellence.*"[17] He observes that Pentecostals talk about experience "a lot," and persistently emphasize personal experience as "a *sine qua non* of spirituality and the indispensable touchstone of faith."[18] Cox suggests that part of the appeal of Pentecostalism globally is its conviction "that the Spirit of God *needs no mediators,* but is available to anyone in an intense, *immediate,* indeed *interior* way."[19] So, Pentecostal spirituality should best be understood as experiential, as opposed to doctrinal; in practice, experience functions as an authority along with Scripture and reason (although the extent of authority it should receive remains an unresolved matter).[20]

In sum, Cox claims that Pentecostalism can be defined by two key features: experience and Spirit. Both of these features are central to Pentecostal identity and self-understanding, and yet both remain rather imprecisely defined. Pentecostals need to remedy this ambiguity in order to clarify their own self-understanding, and their role in the world toward bringing liberation, as well as to avoid falling into "fundamentalism."[21] To this end, Cox makes two suggestions. With regard to "Spirit," Pentecostals need to recall that early Pentecostalism always identified the

---

17. Cox, "Some Personal Reflections," 30 (italics original).

18. Cox, *Fire from Heaven,* 312, 310 (italics original).

19. Ibid., 87 (italics added). Cox suggests elsewhere that the attraction of Pentecostalism is due to its "promise of an unmediated experience of God . . ." (Cox, "Foreword," 9).

20. Cox, *Fire from Heaven,* 71, 313.

21. Ibid., 313–19. Here Cox advocates what he terms "experientialism" as the way forward for Pentecostalism and religions in general, over against "fundamentalism" (ibid., 300–309). In doing so, he seems to be approaching his analysis of Pentecostalism from a religious studies point of view, which can tend to appeal to a more imprecise transcendental notion of God.

Spirit as the eschatological Spirit of the biblical narrative, bringing hope for the future and liberation in the present.[22] With regard to experience of God, early Pentecostalism always understood this to be an encounter with this same Spirit. Cox also, however, begins to hint at something else here. He suggests that experience should be thought of not so much as a source, but *as a means* by which the "Source" (God) becomes known. Experience makes known spiritual reality; it does not create it.[23] What Cox appears to be implying (albeit imprecisely), and significant for this study, is that experience of God has a *mediated quality*—it is a way, or a means by which God becomes known. Understood in this sense, Cox may be hinting that Pentecostals need to reflect more seriously concerning the *mediated quality* of their experience of God.

The above observations of Cox are helpful because he has concisely identified a number of key issues regarding Pentecostalism and experience of God. That Pentecostals consider experience of the Spirit to be part of their core identity is hardly a matter of contention. As mentioned, experience of the Spirit is widely considered an integral part of Pentecostal spirituality,[24] leading some critics to highlight this as a weakness of the movement,[25] and at times even causing some Pentecostals to downplay this aspect of their identity.[26] As Randall Holm notes, however, "Pentecostals are increasingly addressing unapologetically their experiential disposition as not only being a legitimate, but an essential expression of their faith."[27] Further, in line with Cox's assessment, there is growing awareness of the limitations of attempting to define Pentecostalism by particular doctrines or theology; and some are

22. Ibid., 316–19. Cox advocates that Pentecostals should recover some of their emphasis on eschatology to invigorate their political involvement in the world.

23. Ibid., 316–17.

24. See Spittler, "Spirituality," 1097a; Spittler, "Maintaining Distinctives," 134; Anderson, "Pentecostals Believe," 54–56; Kärkkäinen, *Pneumatology*, 87–98; Anderson, "Global Pentecostalism," 214; Anderson, *Introduction to Pentecostalism*, 14, 196–97; and Clark and Lederle et al., *What Is Distinctive*, 36–40.

25. See Bruner, *Theology of the Holy Spirit*, 20–22, 82.

26. Stephen E. Parker notes this trend among some, linking it with Pentecostals' attempt to locate themselves within North American evangelicalism (Parker, "Led by the Spirit," 24–40; see also Stephenson, "Epistemology and Pentecostal," 1–8). Examples of downplaying the role experience as influencing Pentecostal theology can be seen in the works of Assemblies of God (USA) theologians, such as Higgins, "God's Inspired Word," 83; and Railey and Aker, "Theological Foundations," 44.

27. Holm, "Varieties of Pentecostal," 1.

instead advocating experience as perhaps being a more fruitful unifying element. Allan Anderson states, "Pentecostalism is more correctly seen in a much broader context as a movement concerned primarily with the experience of the working of the Holy Spirit and the practice of spiritual gifts. Because Pentecostalism has its emphasis in experience and spirituality rather than in formal theology and doctrine, any definition based on the latter will be inadequate."[28]

But if experience is explicitly granted such a central place in Pentecostal self-understanding, this implies experience does (and should) occupy a fundamental role in Pentecostal theological construction. In other words, since (as Cox observed) experience functions as an authoritative theological resource for Pentecostals, it would seem necessary that Pentecostals work to clarify what is meant by experience and its relationship to theology and doctrine. What is clear, at least, is that experience and theology are interconnected for Pentecostals, since Pentecostals do not simply accept appeals to experience at face value as being of God. What Pentecostals do recognize as "adequate" experience is shaped by their already held theology and values[29]—precisely because they believe that experience of God is *an encounter* with the Spirit identified in the biblical narrative (and in particular the book of Acts).[30]

At this point, to help better locate our subject matter, it is useful to highlight some of the contemporary literature concerning Pentecostalism and experience. Throughout the 1990s, and continuing into the present, there appears to be a more conscious effort on the part of Pentecostals to reflect on the role of experience of God in connection to their theology and spirituality. Among the examples, Stephen E. Parker traces how Pentecostals have historically defended the role of experience in their theology (fearing they may have underemphasized its significance at times), and argues for the importance of experiential spirituality in

---

28. Anderson, *Introduction to Pentecostalism*, 14. Also see Warrington, "Experience," 1–4.

29. Clark and Lederle et al., 44.

30. "Encounter" is a common way of describing the way Pentecostals think about experience of the Spirit. See Cartledge, *Encountering the Spirit*, 19–20; Smith, "Faith and the Conditions," 88–91; Anderson, *Introduction to Pentecostalism*, 187–88; and Yun, "Metaphysical Construct," 1–8. Pentecostals generally understand their experience of the Spirit as being patterned in Acts. On this privileging of Lukan narrative, see Menzies and Menzies, *Spirit and Power*; Stronstad, *Charismatic Theology*; and Stronstad, *Prophethood of All Believers*.

developing a practical Pentecostal theology of decision-making.[31] Steven J. Land has also argued that Pentecostal spirituality needs to be viewed as experiential, with the Spirit of holiness and power shaping human affections within an apocalyptic eschatological framework.[32] Daniel Albrecht has provided a helpful depiction of Pentecostal experiential spirituality gleaned from a social-scientific analysis of Pentecostal corporate worship.[33] Randall Holm and Koo Dong Yun have highlighted the pragmatic character of experience in Pentecostal spirituality,[34] and others, such as Kenneth J. Archer, and Paul W. Lewis have also attempted to identify experience as integral to Pentecostal hermeneutics and scriptural interpretation.[35] Further, the theme of the 2007 annual meeting of the Society for Pentecostal Studies was, "The Role of Experience in Christian Life and Thought: Pentecostal Insights," producing a number of academic papers pertaining to this subject.[36] This brief survey indicates that the function of experience in Pentecostal theology is clearly a live issue and merits further analysis, particularly in regard to how contemporary Pentecostal theologians are wrestling with the matter of the mediated nature of experience of God. Concerning this latter point, however, no major study currently exists; and it is hoped that this book will help fill this gap.

Pentecostalism: Emerging from Adolescence

The third reason for this study, closely related to the above, is that Pentecostalism is arguably maturing into adulthood, and needs to clarify aspects of its identity—including its theology of the experience of God. Approaching the close of the twentieth century several key Pentecostal voices were raised suggesting Pentecostalism was at a "crossroads" in its journey towards maturity.[37] William D. Faupel, Cheryl Bridges

31. Parker, "Led by the Spirit," 24–40.

32. Land, *Pentecostal Spirituality*.

33. Albrecht, *Rites in the Spirit*. Also see Albrecht, "Anatomy of Worship," 70–82; Albrecht, "Pentecostal Spirituality: Looking," 107–25; and Albrecht, "Pentecostal Spirituality: Ecumenical."

34. Holm, "Paradigmatic Analysis," 5–8.

35. Archer, *Pentecostal Hermeneutic*; Lewis, "Towards a Pentecostal." Also see Stronstad, "Pentecostalism, Experiential," 1–32.

36. See bibliography for examples.

37. Cox, for example, suggests that Pentecostalism is at a crossroads needing to choose between fundamentalism and experientialism (Cox,. *Fire from Heaven*, 309).

Johns, and John Christopher Thomas, in their respective presidential addresses to the Society for Pentecostal Studies during the 1990s, each highlighted this point in different ways, sharing a similar concern that while Pentecostals have something valuable to contribute to the broader church and world, in order to successfully do so they must wrestle with the question of their own identity.[38] Johns proposed that Pentecostalism is in the midst of transition, moving from adolescence into adulthood,[39] stating, "[M]odern Pentecostalism, especially in North America, may be described as experiencing a turbulent adolescence characterized by a search for new identity, which is often leading to fads, clubs, and cliques. In addition, Pentecostals have approached this task of self-definition based on a corporate sense of shame. This shame-based identity has resulted in an acute self-consciousness; the movement always sees itself through the lens of an 'imaginary audience.'"[40]

In light of this, she states that there is "an urgent need for Pentecostalism to grow up," and suggests that two paths lie before Pentecostals as they move toward maturity. Borrowing categories from psychologist David Elkind, she identifies the first path as "growth by substitution," in which Pentecostals might compose a "patchwork identity" for themselves by imitating other Christian traditions—the most readily accessible being evangelicalism (especially in North America). Taking this path, however, will result in little internal stability, leading to insecurity and potential neuroticism.[41] The second option, and the one Johns hopes Pentecostals will choose, is "the path toward maturity through growth by integration."[42] This path calls for serious self-reflection and understanding, and a willingness to accept how Pentecostals are alike and dislike other Christian traditions. The first path, Johns fears, will lead to stagnation, but the second to new life and vitality.[43] Faupel echoes

38. Faupel, "Whither Pentecostalism?," 9–27; Johns, "Adolescence of Pentecostalism," 3–17; Thomas, "Pentecostal Theology," 3–19. Also see Nichols, "Search for a Pentecostal," 57–76. Nichols suggests constructing a unique Pentecostal theology based on Barth's emphasis on the 'otherness' of God.

39. Johns, "Adolescence of Pentecostalism," 4; cf. Thomas, "Pentecostal Theology," 3–5.

40. Johns, "Adolescence of Pentecostalism," 9.

41. Ibid., 10.

42. Ibid., 11.

43. Ibid., 4; cf. Faupel, "Whither Pentecostalism?," 27. Faupel also fears Pentecostalism is becoming "increasingly rationalistic and sterile."

Johns' concerns, suggesting that Pentecostals need to see themselves as more than simply a subgroup of evangelicalism, and embrace a distinct, more courageous self-understanding. The proposed solution, again, is for Pentecostals to develop their own unique mission, hermeneutic and agenda.[44] The call here is clearly for Pentecostals to take the path to maturity by developing a theology shaped by its own distinct identity and spirituality. Only in doing so will Pentecostals be able to offer themselves freely and confidently to others in a global, ecumenical environment.[45]

Thomas is optimistic about the development of a unique Pentecostal identity and theology. As evidence of this he points to what he discerns as four phases of Pentecostal scholarship. The first three phases have evolved from an initial generation of scholars, who simply happened to be Pentecostals, *participating in* theological graduate work, to Pentecostal scholars *writing about* their tradition, to Pentecostals *using the perspectives of their tradition* to inform their theology and research. This fourth generation, however, is now in a position to "read, assess, and critique academic works by Pentecostal scholars, an opportunity largely impossible just a few short years ago." The willingness of this fourth phase of Pentecostal scholars to dialogue in meaningful ways with those outside the Pentecostal tradition *from* a Pentecostal perspective is evidence to Thomas that "the inferiority complex of previous generations is beginning to disappear and with it the courage to construct Pentecostal theological paradigms from the ground up is beginning to emerge."[46] There is evidence, then, that Pentecostalism is maturing toward a more healthy, integrated identity and self-understanding, allowing it to become a contributing "adult" voice within the church and world.

Integrating the Media of Scripture, Tradition, and Reason

At this point the three threads of experience, Pentecostal theology/spirituality, and Pentecostal maturation can be brought together. If Pentecostalism is truly maturing and coming of age with regard to constructing a unique theological perspective, then it must remain true

44. Faupel, "Whither Pentecostalism?," 25–27. Advocating a similar way forward see Robeck, "Taking Stock," 60.

45. Johns, "Adolescence of Pentecostalism," 17; Robeck, "Taking Stock," 60; Land, *Pentecostal Spirituality*, 29. Land also speaks of Pentecostals as being in adolescence, needing to discover their unique identity.

46. Thomas, "Pentecostal Theology," 5; cf. Land et al., "Editorial," 3.

to its experiential spirituality, while at the same time be able to wrestle with the complexities of the concept of experience of God, including its *mediated quality*. Further, and in particular, being involved in a global, ecumenical environment will necessitate that Pentecostals grapple with and integrate the traditionally understood forms of mediation by which the Spirit has provided the church resources for Christian life and theology—namely, Scripture, tradition, and reason.

These media are highlighted in Richard Bauckham and Benjamin Drewery's edited work, *Scripture, Tradition and Reason: A Study in the Criteria of Christian Doctrine*, in which they argue that the three resources in the title form "the 'threefold cord' of all informed reflection on the Christian faith." The goal of their book is to explore the relationship between these three strands, highlighting how they mutually relate to and inform one another.[47] In other words, Scripture, tradition, and reason never function independently; rather, all three are always present—whether it be in the transmission of Scripture and the formation of the canon, the passing on of church teachings, or discerning if and how discoveries from outside the church and traditional theology might inform theological thought.[48] Concerning these media, Pentecostals have always understood themselves to be the people of the Bible, but have been more skeptical concerning ecumenical traditions and "man-made creeds";[49] and their relationship to "reason" has been rather ambiguous. If Pentecostalism is to demonstrate its maturity and function as an adult dialogue partner among the Christian traditions, it will need to take seriously this "threefold cord" by which the church has traditionally understood the Spirit to be mediating resources for theology and spirituality.

The methodological approach being adopted here is supported by recent voices within Pentecostalism that suggest the so-called "Wesleyan quadrilateral"[50] (of Scripture, tradition, reason, and experience) as

47. Bauckham and Drewery, *Scripture, Tradition, and Reason*, vii.

48. There are three key chapters in the book, each focusing on Scripture, tradition, and reason respectively, surveying how the other two criteria have informed the primary one being studied: Bruce, "Scripture," 35–64; Bauckham, "Tradition," 117–45; Pailin, "Reason," 207–38. Bruce traces the impact that tradition and reason have had upon the transmission and formation of the biblical canon. Bauckham addresses the ways Scripture and reason have informed Christian tradition. Pailin demonstrates how the authority of Scripture and tradition came to be viewed quite differently under the influence of Enlightenment rationalism.

49. Faupel, "Whither Pentecostalism?," 21.

50. This term was coined by Albert C. Outler (Bevins, "Pentecostal Appropriation,"

a potentially valuable framework on which to construct Pentecostal theology.[51] Pentecostalism has historical roots within Wesleyanism, and arguably shares some of Wesley's experiential and soteriological emphases[52] (although Wesley might be uncomfortable with aspects of Pentecostal "enthusiasm").[53] Wesley's consideration of experience as a valuable resource for theology is congruent in many respects with Pentecostal emphasis in this regard, including his accent on the inner witness of the Spirit and tendency to favor empirical method.[54] Further, however, Wesley's belief that experience was insufficient (and dangerous) without the resources of Scripture, tradition, and reason, serves to demonstrate that the Spirit's work is only inadequately discerned or understood without these other three components informing the process.[55] Acknowledging the benefits of following Wesley's quadrilateral,

---

3). For a fuller discussion of the four resources/criteria of Wesley's quadrilateral, see Thorsen, *Wesleyan Quadrilateral*, 75–154.

51. Most explicitly see Bevins, "Pentecostal Appropriation," 2–13. Also see Moore, "Toward a Psychological," 2–5; Coulter, "What Meaneth This?," 53; Robinson, "Pentecostal Hermeneutic," 3; Lewis, "Towards a Pentecostal," 16; and Maddox, "Enriching Role," 107–27. Maddox argues that experience deserves a fresh look as a resource for Christian theology in general based on Wesley's appeal to experience.

52. See Dieter, "Wesleyan-Holiness Aspects," 55–80. For other traditions influencing the emergence of Pentecostalism in the twentieth century see Menzies, "Non-Wesleyan Origins," 81–98; and Leggett, "Assemblies of God," 113–22. On Pentecostalism's connection to Arminianism and Wesley's more synergistic approach to salvation (influenced by the Eastern fathers) and sanctification, see Coulter, 51, 54–55; and Maddox, *Responsible Grace*, 65–93.

53. See Gunter, *Limits of 'Love Divine,'* 118–37. Gunter notes that Wesley was criticized at times by his contemporaries as being an "enthusiast" (a pejorative term at the time), but that Wesley worked to carefully distinguish himself from popular conceptions of "enthusiasm," referring to himself as an "improper enthusiast." Also see Oden, *John Wesley's Scriptural Christianity*, 88b–89a; and Maddox, "Enriching Role," 119.

54. Maddox, "Enriching Role," 117–21. Maddox is careful to define "experience" for Wesley as not only being inner (private) confirmation of the Spirit's work. The Spirit's work was also confirmed and discerned through public consultation with other Christians. But "public" could also refer to an appeal to common, daily life experience, which Wesley used to confirm such doctrines as inherited depravity and the freedom of the human will. This latter emphasis demonstrates Wesley's leanings toward empiricism (i.e., more practical and pragmatic) as opposed to rationalism. Wesley, however, did not restrict knowledge to being gained only through the five physical senses, but also to a more spiritual inner sensibility as well. On this latter point see Oden, "John Wesley's Scriptural Christianity," 85b.

55. See Thorsen, *Wesleyan Quadrilateral*, 76–78. Thorsen argues that Scripture served as Wesley's primary theological resource, supplemented by tradition, reason, and

then, a mature Pentecostal theology needs to demonstrate an ability to both recognize and integrate the experience of the Spirit through these traditional, interrelated media of Scripture, tradition, and reason.

A brief caveat is necessary here concerning the term "reason." Bauckham insightfully notes that church tradition has always been informed by reason in its doctrinal development, but that what might be considered "reason" is always (also) mediated within a given culture or historical setting. "Reason," then, can quite easily come to mean that which is "common sense" in any given time or culture, or even become a technical term of a particular philosopher or philosophical school.[56] To acknowledge the former and to avoid becoming trapped in specialized philosophical terminology, Bauckham suggests that it is better to "think more broadly of Christianity's relation to its *context*."[57] More specifically, a Wesleyan understanding of reason, according to Robert L. Moore, is that which pertains to scientific and empirical wisdom from the broader culture.[58] It is this more contextual and empirical definition of reason that will serve us in this study.[59]

The Central Argument: Pentecostal Maturation and Mediated Experience of God

The central thesis being proposed in this book is that there is growing recognition, appreciation, and integration of the mediated nature of the experience of the Spirit in the construction and development of Pentecostal theology, and that this is evidence of maturation within Pentecostalism. Pentecostals are acknowledging more explicitly the need to reflect on the meaning and role of experience in theology. Further, as was noted earlier pertaining to Wesley's quadrilateral, Pentecostals are becoming more willing to openly reflect on the threefold cord of

experience. Also see Maddox, *Responsible Grace*, 36–47.

56. Immanuel Kant's nomenclature of "pure" and "practical" reason is an example of "reason" being used as a technical philosophical term (see Ameriks, "Kant, Immanuel," 460a–66b).

57. Bauckham, "Tradition in Relation," 140 (italics original).

58. Moore, "Toward a Psychological," 3; cf. Thorsen, *Wesleyan Quadrilateral*, 107–28.

59. It also needs to be said that at times "context" is used interchangeably with "experience." Contextual theologies tend to use "experience" in this way, meaning something along the lines of the perspective gained from living in and from a particular situation (whether the situation be social, political, racial, or gender focused).

Scripture, tradition, and reason as being mediations of the Spirit, and intricately connected to Pentecostal experience, theology and spirituality.[60]

Specifically, the unique focus here will be to demonstrate evidence of this maturation in regard to reflection on mediated experience of the Spirit in connection with Scripture, tradition, and reason in the works of three Pentecostal theologians—Frank D. Macchia, Simon K. H. Chan, and Amos Yong. Each of these writes from a Pentecostal perspective, and qualifies as being a third or fourth generation Pentecostal theologian according to Thomas' model.[61] All have published major works as well as numerous articles and essays, and acknowledge that experience of God needs to be understood in a more qualified, mediated sense. At the same time, Macchia, Chan, and Yong also attempt to preserve traditional Pentecostal emphasis on experience of the Spirit as being *encounter* or *interruption*. Further, while all these theologians would appeal to every strand of the threefold cord, each can also be viewed as accenting one of the three traditional media of the Spirit—Macchia accenting Scripture (more broadly, "Word"), Chan, the Christian tradition, and Yong, reason (insight from the context of the broader world, including non-Christian religions and secular sciences). As previously mentioned, at present, no major Pentecostal fourth-generation study exists concerning the function of the appeal to experience in contemporary Pentecostal theology, and this, in large part, is what makes this study unique.

60. The 2005 Society for Pentecostal Studies (SPS) annual meeting was themed, "That Which We Have Received We Now Pass On: Spirit, Word, and Tradition in Pentecostalism." Further, in 2001 a philosophy stream was added to the annual meeting, serving as evidence of a growing acknowledgment that Pentecostals need to incorporate these areas into their theological development. The theme of the 2008 SPS annual meeting (joint with the Wesleyan Theological Society) focused on the relationship between theology and science. It should be acknowledged that the charismatic stream of pentecostalism would probably already be more comfortable with the mediated emphases of experience of the Spirit through Scripture, tradition, and reason. But this book is an attempt to explore how those from within the Classical Pentecostal stream are wrestling with these issues.

61. At the time of writing, Macchia and Yong are both credential holders with the Assemblies of God (USA), and Chan holds credentials with the Assemblies of God, Singapore.

Implications of Exploring the Pentecostal Appeal to Experience

The significance of this study is further demonstrated by several inter-related implications that should emerge through an exploration of the Pentecostal appeal to experience in theology. First, this investigation holds potential to help Pentecostals grow in their own self-understanding and confidence in their theologically unique identity, as well as the perspective they bring to broader Christianity. As Pentecostals are able to perceive evidence of theology bearing fruit as it is constructed using explicitly Pentecostal values and perspectives, this should provide motivation to overcome adolescent insecurities and attempts to withdraw from interaction and dialogue with other traditions. In other words, Pentecostals will be more confident to engage with the broader Christian tradition—demonstrating more adult-like qualities, convinced they have something unique to offer.

Second, and on the other hand, this exploration should cause Pentecostals considerable pause in their popular, and sometimes naïve, appeals to experience of the Spirit as justification for belief and practice. The history of Pentecostalism is tainted with charges (and evidence) of triumphalism, elitism, and schism (often within its own ranks).[62] An appreciation for the mediated nature of experience of the Spirit should introduce a healthy humility and acknowledgement of the contextuality in which the development of Pentecostal doctrine and practice emerges. This acknowledgement may even lead to more openness toward taking a new look at rearticulating some Pentecostal doctrines to be more meaningful in the broader Christian tradition and world.

Third, related to the above, Pentecostals should also be able to develop an appreciation of the broader Christian tradition—considering, for example, how the Spirit actually works through tradition. This will hopefully enable Pentecostals to acquire a greater openness toward ecumenical dialogue (arguably, in keeping with some aspects of early Pentecostal identity).[63] Through dialogue it is also hoped that there will be a reciprocal appreciation for the Pentecostal tradition, including its emphasis on encounter with the Spirit. An openness toward Pentecostal

---

62. See Spittler, "Maintaining Distinctives," 122–24; Anderson, *Introduction to Pentecostalism*, 12, 208; and Land, *Pentecostal Spirituality*, 222.

63. See Robeck, "Taking Stock," 39–45.

ways of experiencing the Spirit may introduce, for other Christian traditions, fresh means by which the Spirit is able to "interrupt," and bring reformation and transformation to the church globally.

Fourth, acknowledging experience of the Spirit as mediated opens new ways of discerning the Spirit's activity in the church, world, and individual life. Yong is explicit in this emphasis, suggesting innovative (sometimes controversial) ways for discerning the work of the Spirit in the world—including the possibilities of discerning the Spirit in other religions and secular sciences, and using these as possible resources for rearticulating Christian theology.

Placing Pentecostal Theologians in Ecumenical Dialogue

In keeping with the above goals, the approach being used here will be to explore the major theological emphases of our three Pentecostal authors—Macchia, Chan, and Yong—while drawing out the ways in which the theology of experience of the Spirit functions within their respective projects. Special attention will be given to noting how the idea of mediated experience of God factors into their theologies, and the implications of their projects for Pentecostal theology and spirituality will be highlighted. As a means toward this exploration, however, the Pentecostal appeal to experience needs to be placed in a broader theological context. Since the work of Macchia, Chan, and Yong is to serve as demonstration of Pentecostalism moving toward maturity (adulthood), we need to place these theologians in dialogue with the broader Christian tradition to see how Pentecostalism is demonstrating an ability to both *inform and be informed* by other theological traditions.

There are two issues that immediately arise when it comes to initiating such a dialogue. The first concerns the guests who will be invited to participate, and the second concerns the topic of conversation. With regard to the guests, Pentecostal Harold D. Hunter suggests a helpful rule of thumb for organizing ecumenical conferences. He believes it important to invite participants from four streams of Christianity: Roman Catholic, Orthodox, Protestant, and Pentecostal. Since Macchia, Chan, and Yong serve as our Pentecostals, we need also to make sure the three other streams are represented.[64] With regard to the topic of conversa-

---

64. Hunter, "'Full Communion,'" 1. Hunter also suggests participation from five continents, but we will limit ourselves here to having at least heeded him on the importance

tion, this will be guided by the focus of our thesis—namely the appeal to experience of God as it functions within theology. Further, since experience of God (in Christian and Pentecostal theology) has traditionally been understood to be experience of the Spirit, pneumatology will more broadly serve to help direct the conversation, while highlighting how experience of the Spirit is worked out in these various theologies.

Bringing the topic of conversation and the principle of "four streams" together, we can begin to distribute our dialogue invitations to theologians who both represent some aspect of their tradition (although even within the streams there is by no means agreement on the topic of experience and Spirit), and at the same time have something distinctive to say about experience of the Spirit. This also does not mean that these theologians all hold a positive view concerning the importance of the appeal to experience (it should not surprise us if some are suspicious of such things), but simply that each of the voices selected will have something meaningful to contribute to the conversation. While many invitations could be sent out, controlling the scope of this project demands that a limited number of theologians be included. The selection process was based on the criteria that a theologian must be somewhat contemporary (working at least within the twentieth century), represent elements of their respective tradition, and (most importantly) be able to contribute something unique to the conversation concerning the experience of God.

The following, then, will serve as dialogue partners with our Pentecostal theologians: from the Roman Catholic stream, Yves Congar, Elizabeth A. Johnson, and Donald L. Gelpi; from the Orthodox stream, Vladamir Lossky and Sergius Bulgakov; and from the Protestant stream, Jürgen Moltmann, James H. Cone, and Robert W. Jenson. It should be noted that this selection attempts to introduce some diversity even within the varying streams to include feminist, liberation, and postliberal voices. More could also be said here as to the distinctive contribution each brings to the conversation (and so why each was included), but that would entail getting ahead of ourselves. That each of the above brings something unique and valuable to the table will become (it is hoped) apparent in the upcoming chapters. So, while there are obviously other

---

of hearing from the main Christian theological traditions.

possibilities for theological dialogue partners, this sampling would seem sufficient for a lively and meaningful conversation.[65]

Each theologian from the three streams, then, will be provided opportunity to "speak" concerning the subject of the experience of God. Further, in order to help better identify the perspective and approach of each of these various theologians concerning this subject, we will employ a helpful continuum for understanding the appeal to experience, proposed by Roman Catholic Jesuit theologian, George P. Schner (1946–2000). Later, these voices can be brought, where appropriate, into dialogue with our Pentecostal theologians.

This entire study and dialogue, however, needs to be placed in the broader framework of understanding the appeal to experience in theology, and also how Pentecostals have (and are) approaching this issue. While some of this has been introduced above, there is still need to flesh out some of the central issues surrounding the concept of experience in general, including, among other things, the challenge of defining the concept "experience" and its relationship to theological epistemology (an appeal to justify belief or doctrine). Concerning Pentecostalism, there is need to demonstrate how experience of the Spirit (best understood as "encounter," as we shall see) has functioned within Pentecostal theology and spirituality, as well as how Pentecostals have wrestled with the traditional threefold media of the Spirit: Scripture, tradition, and reason.

Synopsis

To orient the reader to what lies ahead, I offer the following by way of synopsis. Chapter 1 will attempt to accomplish two things. First, it will flesh out some of the ambiguities and challenges that emerge when exploring the concept of experience, and the appeal to experience as an authority for theological construction. As mentioned, George P. Schner will be an especially helpful resource for this section, providing a continuum by which to locate various appeals to experience as they function in contemporary theology. The second part of this chapter will provide an opportunity to listen to the voices of the theologians from the three non-Pentecostal streams, and attempt to locate each on Schner's

---

65. Other significant possibilities for dialogue partners that might readily come to mind include Karl Barth and Karl Rahner, among others. Elements of these two voices, however, will be found within our selected dialogue partners.

continuum. While each of these eight voices will be summarized as succinctly as possible, in order that their positions be fairly represented and used in later dialogue, the first chapter will, of necessity, be lengthier than the others. For this reason, more pragmatic readers may want to read the second section of chapter 1 selectively, to find the summary of the particular theologian(s) in whom they are most interested. Such an approach is certainly understandable, although it will leave the reader with less background to fully appreciate the later dialogue. In any case, it is recommended that the first section of chapter 1 be read in its entirety in order to place the concept of experience of God in theological and philosophical context.

Chapter 2 will be an attempt to better understand the role of experience of the Spirit in Pentecostalism through an exploration of its relationship to Pentecostal theology and spirituality, as well as how Pentecostals have wrestled with the Spirit's mediation through Scripture, tradition, and reason. Schner's continuum will again be employed in an attempt to locate the Pentecostal appeal to experience. This chapter overall will serve to (later) help identify the ways in which our three Pentecostal theologians are demonstrating continuity with their tradition, as well as where they are revisioning Pentecostal theology. Readers less familiar with Pentecostalism may find chapter 2 to be the most valuable in this book, since it can serve as an introduction of sorts toward understanding the ethos of the Pentecostal tradition.

The third, fourth, and fifth chapters will each focus on one of the three Pentecostal theologians—Macchia, Chan, and Yong respectively—surveying their understanding of the experience of the Spirit, and drawing out implications concerning their particular emphases. Macchia will serve as our theologian accenting experience of the Spirit mediated through Word (including Scripture). Chan will serve as the Pentecostal accenting experiential mediation of the Spirit through Christian tradition. Finally, Yong will serve to emphasize experience of the Spirit through reason (drawing on voices from outside the church and traditional theology). This survey will be followed, in each chapter, by a section in which the voices of our dialogue partners from the other three streams are introduced into conversation with these Pentecostals, highlighting points of convergence and divergence, and emphasizing potential challenges and benefits that might arise from hearing one another. While this study is primarily analytical in nature (as opposed to constructive), the book's conclusion will attempt to summarize the most significant discoveries made along the way, and highlight possible implications arising from this exploration.

1

Experience of God in Christian Theology and Traditions
Challenges and Varieties

THE EXPLORATION OF THE SUBJECT OF EXPERIENCE OF GOD IS AN IM-
portant one in Christian theology due to its being an appeal to authority, as well as the ambiguity of the concept of experience itself. The
widespread use of the appeal within theology in general, and the central role the appeal occupies within Pentecostalism in particular, serve
as sufficient incentive here to flesh out the concept of experience within
theological discourse. This chapter will attempt to provide groundwork
for our broader study by first exploring the concept of experience as
it functions within general theological (and philosophical) usage. In
doing so, the ways in which the appeal to experience is understood
and functions as an authority, as well as the ambiguity surrounding
the concept itself will be examined. George P. Schner will serve as a
helpful guide in this first section, orienting us to the central issues
surrounding the appeal to experience, and suggesting a continuum on
which various types of the appeal to experience may be located. In the
second section, the appeal to experience will be explored as it is fleshed
out in the works of eight theologians, representing various Christian
traditions and approaches. These theological voices will later be used
in subsequent chapters to dialogue with our three primary Pentecostal
theologians, Macchia, Chan, and Yong.

The Ubiquity and Ambiguity of "Experience" in Theology

The ubiquity of the appeal to experience in contemporary Christian theology, already highlighted in this book's introduction, is a point worth reiterating. Schner emphasizes both the widespread use of the appeal (as an appeal to authority), as well as hinting at the ambiguity of the concept, stating:

> Somewhere in this [twentieth] century the term "experience" begins to appear with regularity in the titles of articles and books in Christian theology and makes its way into proposals for methodological and doctrinal developments. Similarly, in the common parlance of the Christian faithful, and especially of students of theology, a similar appeal to "my experience," or the experience of a particular group, has become theological common sense. When one asks about what sort of appeal it is, whether it is philosophically coherent, and whether it is appropriate to the task of Christian theology, such questions are often greeted with surprise. What could be more obvious than the appeal to experience, its inevitability, or even its momentous appropriateness at this point in the history of Christianity and its theology?[1]

Schner goes on to note that the appeal to experience, in its contemporary subjectivistic expression, is largely the outworking of seventeenth-century Enlightenment philosophy, which emphasized the turn to the subject, the autonomy of reason, and judgments being derived from personal observation.[2] The evolution of these ideas resulted in the appeal becoming highly individualistic and self-authenticating, with each person's opinion coming to be viewed as meriting a hearing.[3] Experience should, then, be understood as functioning as an authority, but frequently a very individualistic authority, raising some question as to the weight of influence it should be granted. We will return to Schner's assessment later, but at this point it would be appropriate to briefly explore the ambiguity of the concept of experience—one of the questions that Schner argues needs legitimately to be addressed before conceding to experience such a privileged role.

---

1. Schner, "Appeal to Experience," 40, cf. 43.
2. Ibid., 42; cf. Boeve, "Theology and the Interruption," 11.
3. Schner, "Appeal to Experience," 42.

Defining Experience: Wrestling with a "Weasel Word"

Donald L. Gelpi (1951–2011) is helpful in highlighting the ambiguity that often surrounds the term "experience," which he observes, "enjoys a certain pride among the weasel words of the English language . . ."[4] He cites several common-sense and philosophical uses of the term "experience." First, experience can mean "practical, cumulative wisdom acquired through more or less prolonged acquaintance with some reality or with some way of doing things."[5] Second, it may be limited to only what is perceived through "sensory cognition," which "supplies the information needed to understand and judge the world around us."[6] A third use identifies experience not with sense data, but "data of consciousness," supplying "information needed to understand one's own thought processes."[7] Experience here is still, however, "restricted to the first stage in the mind's advance to insight and judgment."[8] Koo Dong Yun, commenting on this definition, explains it to mean "*all uncritical cognition*"; any critical reflection upon experience becoming "something other than experience, e.g., understanding or judgment."[9] This form of experience consists, then, of held beliefs (cognition), but grounded in "conventional assumptions," as opposed to beliefs held by critically obtaining "accurate data,

---

4. Gelpi, *Turn to Experience*, 1–2. "No sooner does one think that one has pinned down the weasel word to a single meaning that one finds it signifying something totally different."

5. Gelpi, *Divine Mother*, 21. Gelpi repeats this list using slightly different wording in both Gelpi, *Turn to Experience* (2–3); and Gelpi, *Divine Mother* (120–21). Also see Yun, "Metaphysical Construct," 1, cf. 1–4. Yun (a self-identified student of Gelpi's) briefly surveys and expands on Gelpi's definitions of experience, providing helpful explanations and examples of these sometimes complex ideas. Yun notes this first definition is often the one used on job descriptions (e.g., requiring 'X' amount of experience).

6. Gelpi, *Divine Mother*, 21. Also see Yun, "Metaphysical Construct," 2–3. Concerning this definition, Yun notes that many philosophical empiricists, including Francis Bacon, David Hume, and John Locke, adhere to the idea that knowledge derives from sense experience. Empiricists, however, are not always in agreement even on this point, some limiting knowledge to that derived from observation of the external material world, others also granting internal mental operations and reflection as an epistemic source. Yun concedes it is sometimes difficult to categorize empiricist philosophers into any one of Gelpi's definitions, suggesting, for example, that Locke, being a less strict empiricist, can also fit under the fourth definition (to be discussed).

7. Gelpi, *Divine Mother*, 21; Gelpi, *Turn to Experience*, 2.

8. Gelpi, *Divine Mother*, 21.

9. Yun, "Metaphysical Construct," 2 (italics original).

facts, or observations."[10] As we shall see, this definition of experience arguably corresponds with that popularly held within Pentecostalism, and it is worth quoting the example Yun cites at this point: "A Christian, who reaches conclusion with this uncritical thinking, automatically accepts beliefs of his or her pastors or other church members without critical investigation. He or she simply accepts others' beliefs simply based on either one's authority or credentials. Furthermore, some people simply accept beliefs or ideas defined and endorsed by a society."[11]

A fourth understanding of experience focuses not on the object of experience, but on the "how" of epistemology, which includes the "entire spectrum of human evaluative responses," including, "[s]ensations, emotions, imagination, judgments of feeling, hypothetical rational inferences, deductions, and inductive validation or invalidation of deductive principles."[12] Fifthly, some would limit experience to refer only to "conscious acts of the mind," since, in some positivist philosophies, any pre-, or unconscious activities are ruled out as contributing epistemologically.[13] Some would also restrict experience to being applicable only to "living, sensing, or thinking beings," considering "inanimate realities" to be merely "objects of experience."[14] Gelpi does suggest a sixth understanding is possible that can include "[b]oth the what and how of knowing," in which "[w]hat one experiences stands within experience."[15] This, states Yun, is the broadest form of the concept of experience, used by philosophers such as Alfred North Whitehead, to "develop the word ['experience'] into a metaphysical category."[16] Gelpi himself takes this approach, and we will return to his construct of experience later in this chapter. At this point, however, his observations and definitions serve simply to demonstrate the ambiguity of the term and the relevancy of Schner's implied assertion that the appeal to experience (as an authority) demands that such appeals not be accepted uncritically.

10. Ibid., 2–3.

11. Ibid., 3. As an example of the latter, Yun cites those who opposed Galileo Galilei (1564–1642) due to uncritical reluctance to accept the Copernican model of planetary revolution.

12. Gelpi, *Turn to Experience*, 2; cf. Yun, "Metaphysical Construct," 2–3. Yun includes John Dewey, and to an extent, John Locke under this definition.

13. Gelpi, *Divine Mother*, 21; Gelpi, *Turn to Experience*, 3.

14. Gelpi, *Divine Mother*, 21.

15. Gelpi, *Turn to Experience*, 2.

16. Yun, "Metaphysical Construct," 3.

The Evolution of the Appeal to Experience

Schner goes on to propose a means by which appeals to experience within theological discourse may be better understood and located. Schner's intent is, as Peter Althouse notes, not to construct a concept of experience; rather, he uses experience as a metaphor for theological method and attempts to demonstrate how experience *functions* in different theological contexts by locating various types of appeals to experience on a continuum.[17] Before exploring these types, however, it is worth summarizing Schner's overall argument concerning the appeal to experience, since he concisely identifies the pertinent issues surrounding the topic in general, and in doing so helps us understand his own reasons for proposing his model. Schner, then, will serve as our primary guide through this sometimes complex landscape, providing a broader context for understanding this subject, while bringing in other voices when deemed appropriate to expand on particular points.

THE JOURNEY OF EXPERIENCE FROM PRIVILEGE TO SUSPICION

It has already been noted that the appeal to experience is also an appeal to authority, and brief reference has been made to the historical reasons for its emergence, evolution and growth. Expanding on this, Schner argues that, as a derivative of Enlightenment philosophy, "experience" increasingly came to be used as a rhetorical device, needing to be understood in its essence as an alternative appeal to authority.[18] This new experiential authority, however, was brought into serious question by the "principal expositors of suspiciousness," Nietzsche, Marx, and Freud, who exposed the sociological, psychological and philosophical determinants of appeals to experience.[19] The subsequent contributions of Heidegger and Wittgenstein raised further doubts concerning the ability of the subject to interiorly and objectively examine and comprehend the exterior world. The subject itself was now viewed as being inseparable from the world in which it exists; so the experience of the subject, then, simply becomes one authority among many, losing its place of privilege.[20]

---

17. Althouse, "Towards a Theological," 9–10.
18. Schner, "Appeal to Experience," 43; also see Maddox, "Enriching Role," 113.
19. Schner, "Appeal to Experience," 42.
20. Ibid., 42–43.

Schner, therefore, calls his readers to recognize that appeals to experience frequently serve as rhetorical counter-appeals, often misused to restrict dialogue or discredit alternative positions. At the same time, however, the appeal to experience may also function simply to indicate that one's opinion is not ideological, but the unique articulation of a particular individual or group.[21] In any case, Schner's point is that the appeal to experience is never a "disinterested appeal," and often masks the fact that experience is formed within a tradition, a particular cultural and linguistic context.[22]

The cultural-linguistic character of experience is an important one to note for our purposes, since it speaks to the issue of the mediatedness of experience of God. We will return to this issue in more detail shortly; but Schner's highly digested historical survey of experience's journey from occupying a place of privilege to suspicion deserves some commentary and qualification. First, the rise of experience to a privileged place was due in large part to the assumptions of the Enlightenment, that human experience of the world was, simply, "common." The universal applicability of experience as an epistemic authoritative resource began to be called into question during the late nineteenth and early twentieth centuries, but especially encountered criticism under the scrutiny of linguistic philosophy, which arguably provided the primary ammunition needed for the postmodern rejection of the modern project.[23]

Herbert Burhenn suggests that the relationship between language and the world has been the predominant philosophical issue since the 1960s, and is arguably the most important philosophical issue of the twentieth century.[24] In short, there has been growing consensus among philosophers of language that human experience of the world is always mediated through language—experience being bound by its linguistic

---

21. Ibid., 43–45.

22. Ibid., 45–46.

23. On postmodernism being a rejection of the modern project see Lyon, *Postmodernity*, 6–8. Lyon refers to postmodernity as being the "exhaustion of modernity," and agrees with Schner in viewing Nietzsche as a significant (Lyon argues the "single most significant") progenitor of postmodernism. While postmodernism is anti-modern, it nevertheless needs to be understood as an outworking of (and therefore inseparable from) the modern project, leading another source to label it hypermodern" (Middleton and Walsh, *Truth Is Stranger*, 54–55, cf. 7–84). On the relationship between postmodernism and modernism, also see Greer, *Mapping Postmodernism*, 5–7; Sire, *Universe Next Door*, 211–41; and Carson, *Becoming Conversant*, 87–124.

24. Burhenn, "Philosophy and Religious," 149–50.

horizon.[25] This observation gave rise to doubts concerning epistemic foundationalism, since, as Francis Schuessler Fiorenza notes, language is intricately interwoven with culture, and therefore human experience and knowledge of the world could no longer be assumed as being universally self-evident. Rather, each language and culture shapes and provides the framework by which experience is understood and knowledge acquired.[26] In this perspective, the emphasis is on knowledge being viewed as contextual as opposed to foundational—although considerable debate continues to exist, especially as to how this epistemological shift should apply to theology and the appeal to experience of God.

CURRENT DEBATE OVER THE MEDIATEDNESS OF EXPERIENCE

One way of framing the issue as it now stands is by identifying some theological approaches to experience of God as "correlationist" and others as "non-correlationist," as does Lieven Boeve and Kevin Hart;[27] or, in David Brown's words, as being characterized by "under-determination" and "over-determination" respectively.[28] Correlational theology, states Boeve, is an attempt to link the two poles of Christian tradition and the broader context in which Christians find themselves (the world) by appealing to some form of common human experience.[29] This is part of the modern theological project, aimed at demonstrating the relevancy of Christianity by grounding it in present, verifiable truth claims as opposed to face-value reliance upon handed-down traditions or doctrine.[30] Boeve states, "the truth of the faith does not reside so much in tradition or in doctrines, but in a religious lived faith experience."[31] It is this experience that is understood to precede doctrine and tradition (and which can even be used to critique these).[32] Since experience (of the empirical sort identified by Gelpi) so powerfully dictates how humans

25. Pattison, "What to Say," 192. Cf. Schlitt, *Theology and the Experience*, 27–30; and Jay, *Songs of Experience*, 4–6.

26. Fiorenza, "Experience of Transcendence," 184–88. In regard to the weakening of foundational epistemology, see Burhenn, "Philosophy and Religious," 149–58.

27. Boeve, "Theology and the Interruption," 13–24; Hart, "Introduction," 5–7.

28. Brown, "Experience Skewed," 172.

29. Boeve, "Theology and the Interruption," 13, 24.

30. Ibid., 13.

31. Ibid., 14.

32. Ibid.

are to understand the world—and (assuming) there is no other means to knowledge as reliable as empirical method—it is justifiably appealed to as the authoritative means by which God must be revealed. Hart explains, "Correlational theologies do not say that experience is the *source* of our apprehension of God but rather that it is the *medium* through which we encounter the deity."[33] God is encountered, then, via human experience. There is an assumed continuity between Christian experience in particular *and* human experience in general—this generality, or commonality, being characteristic of philosophical and theological modernity.[34] Experience, then, is what holds the possibility of bridging the Christian faith with the *common* human context.

On the other hand, theological approaches that can be considered non-correlational are those that emphasize a *radical discontinuity* between common human experience and that found within the Christian tradition (or any other faith tradition for that matter). Boeve, having highlighted the link between correlational theology and modernism, suggests that non-correlational theology should be understood as having more in common with postmodern doubts concerning modernist epistemological assumptions, including that of universal truth.[35] Thus, the postmodern understanding of experience has far more to do with the idea of "rupture with the context"—experience needing to be viewed as particular, as opposed to the modernist intuitive connect between Christian faith in humanity in general.[36]

Boeve posits Karl Barth as a prime example of a non-correlationist theologian, due to Barth's insistence that there is no neutral secular (common) experience; all experience is embedded in some form of belief system.[37] George Pattison observes this concept of the embeddedness of experience as becoming more clearly articulated in postmodern philosophy of language and religion, such as that of Steven Katz, and among postliberal theologians, such as George A. Lindbeck.[38] Pattison

---

33. Hart, "Introduction," 5 (italics original). This places Cox within this correlational approach, according to our previous discussion.

34. Boeve, "Theology and the Interruption," 24, cf. 20–24.

35. Ibid., 26.

36. Ibid., 27. On the connection between postmodern epistemology and contextuality see Voiss, "Thought Forms," 242–44.

37. Boeve, "Theology and the Interruption," 27–31; see also Hart, "Experience of the Kingdom," 75.

38. Pattison, "What to Say," 191–94.

cites Katz's 1978 essay, "Language, Epistemology and Mysticism" as an example: "There are NO pure (i.e. unmediated) experiences. Neither mystical experience, nor more ordinary forms of experience give any indication, or any grounds for believing that they are unmediated. That is to say, all experience is processed through, organized by, and makes itself available to us in extremely complex epistemological ways. The notion of unmediated experience seems, if not self-contradictory, at best empty."[39]

Lindbeck picks up on this theme of the mediatedness of experience, and expresses it through his cultural-linguistic theory of doctrine, mentioned earlier.[40] The emphasis here is on how language and culture serve *to determine* the nature and content of human experiences. In the case of non-correlationist theologians, then, experience of God in or through human experience is highly suspect, since this will always be experience that falls within a predetermined framework, conforming God's "voice" (so to speak) to the expectations of the *particular* language and culture in question. In this view, the mediatedness of experience of God undermines its trustworthiness as an authoritative source of revelation. Again, the suspicion here against God being revealed through human experience exists because there is concern that the appeal to experience might give humans "mastery"[41] over God—the particular cultural-linguistic horizon dictating what God might reveal. If revelation is to happen at all, it must be interruptive to human experience, what Hart calls "counterexperience."[42]

David Brown, while acknowledging the mediatedness of experience, believes the above view to be too over-determined—language being given too much credit in dictating how God might be experienced by humans. It also raises questions as to *how* God could possibly speak interruptively at all within a particular cultural-linguistic context (must not revelation happen in some particular context, after all?).[43] At the same time, some philosophers of religion can be viewed as being too

39. Ibid., 192.

40. See Lindbeck, *Nature of Doctrine*, 18–23, 69, 113–24. Lindbeck sees religion as bearing resemblance to language and culture. In this "cultural-linguistic" approach, church doctrine needs to be viewed through the lens of "regulative" or "rule theory," since it functions intrasystematically for a particular community and tradition, and therefore remains in the realm of second order discourse.

41. Hart, "Experience of the Kingdom," 80.

42. Ibid., 80–81.

43. Brown, "Experience Skewed," 172.

under-deterministic in their failure to recognize the contextual particu-larity of all philosophy and theology, in other words, that any experience of God (or understanding of God) is contextually mediated.[44] So, while the recognition that all experience is mediated should, in Brown's view, lead to caution as to receiving appeals to experience, he also believes that theologians such as Barth (and we could add Lindbeck) have leaned too far toward mistrust concerning mediation itself, not allowing that God could use particular mediation as a legitimate means by which to be experienced by humans.[45]

That said, what should be noted at this point is that there is growing consensus that experience in general, and appeals to experience of God in particular, need to be acknowledged as being mediated through the horizons of specific linguistic, cultural, and historical situations in which humans find themselves. At the same time, there is also some push-back from taking this to the extreme of suspicion that would deny mediated experience as a means by which God might be revealed. God must not be allowed to become an object, in which his revelation is dictated by human perspective; God must be allowed to truly be an Other to be encountered.[46] Yet must this imply that experience is not to be trusted when it comes to the appeal to experience of God?

MEDIATED EXPERIENCE: A WAY FORWARD?

Pentecostal philosopher, James K. A. Smith is helpful here, allowing for the postmodern emphasis on the mediatedness of all experience, while also making room for legitimate encounter with God through experi-ence. Smith acknowledges, on the one hand, that it is true that human experience is always shaped by its cultural and linguistic horizons; faith, in other words, is the medium of experience, "the condition of possibility for experience."[47] Yet, at the same time might not God concede to hu-man horizons, seeing as God created these horizons (or, created humans

---

44. Ibid., 160–65, 170–71. Brown cites William Alston by way of example.

45. Ibid., 172–73. Brown's proposal is that we move beyond this "all or nothing" im-passe ("all" tending to underplay the mediated nature of experience; "nothing" tending to deny value to mediation of experience), and recognize that God can be experienced through such cultural particular mediations as architecture, art, and other human arti-facts. Brown calls this an "aspectival" approach (ibid., 175).

46. Hart, "Experience of the Kingdom," 79.

47. Smith, "Faith and the Conditions," 89, 90.

to be horizon-bound creatures)? Smith thinks so, suggesting that God makes Godself to be phenomenologically experience-able, becoming a phenomenon—but on God's own terms.[48] This move advocates caution, on the one hand, being aware that the faith horizon shapes all human understanding, yet also for the possibility of the experience of God, on the other. Experience of God, however, must be understood in terms of encounter, always conceding that finite human horizons cannot contain God who remains truly other. Smith states, "As such, the experience of God is not an objectification of God that would make God an 'object' in the narrow sense; but it is an encounter in which God gives himself (in a mode of donation) to be experienced by a finite perceiver—precisely because the very conditions of encounter for finite perceivers (as created by God) demand that both experience and what Hart calls a 'counter-experience' must nevertheless be an event that takes place on a register commensurate with finitude."[49]

The appeal to experience of God should be understood, in this sense, more as a testimony to an encounter, in which "the transcendence of God [becomes] more manifest."[50] This acknowledges the particular lo-catedness of the encounter—all experience being mediated within a faith horizon—while likewise conceding that God is able to make Godself known within these horizons in such a way that is viewed as more in-terruptive than that allowed by appeals to common human experience. Implied here, then, is the possibility of direct encounter with God, yet mediated through context and therefore interpreted. This might be akin to what has been called a "mediated immediacy" in regard to experience of God—God being experienced directly, but not uninterpretatively.[51]

This approach preserves God's transcendence and otherness, while allowing that experience of God can occur, and even of a sort that would interrupt the tradition (or faith context, for our purposes, Christian) in which the experience occurs. As Boeve argues, within the biblical nar-rative of the Christian faith is found a God who interrupts, who will not be "grasped" (owned) by the narrative, but who nevertheless chooses to be revealed by, in and through it. The Christian faith tradition provides the horizon by which God may be understood and experienced, and in

48. Ibid., 90.

49. Ibid., 91.

50. Ibid.

51. Schlitt, *Theology and the Experience*, 35–36.

doing so opens itself to be encountered by this God who may very well interrupt and transform the very tradition within which God speaks. It is a faith horizon that understands God to be an interrupter![52]

"Rules" Governing Human Understanding of Experience

We can now return to Schner's discussion of the appeal to experience, and in doing so notice his leanings toward non-correlational theology while also attempting to allow for the possibility of interruptive encounter with God. Schner states that in order to appeal to experience it is necessary to appreciate the "rules" governing human understanding of experience, and suggests four philosophical models for doing so: experience as construct, intentional, derivative, and dialectical.[53] As *construct*, experience is shaped by a past history and future projections, and requires a cultural-linguistic context in order to be articulated. Because of this experience is always revisable.[54] Here Schner echoes aspects of the above discussion in which the contextual particularity, or mediatedness of experience, was emphasized. His point, however, is that as a construct, no experience of God should ever be absolutized—God cannot be contained by human horizons.

With regard to experience being *intentional*, it should be understood as never being merely a private matter.[55] Human consciousness, Schner maintains, is social, mediated, and linguistic in character, and therefore experience is *of* something, or *aimed toward* something other.[56] On this point Schner does note that a distinction needs to be made between experience as a philosophical category, and experience as feeling and/or intuition, which need to be understood as two distinct

---

52. Boeve, "Theology and the Interruption," 37–39.

53. Schner, "Appeal to Experience," 46; Gelpi, *Turn to Experience*, 139, cf. 139–48. Gelpi provides a summary of Schner's essay and uses it as a test framework for his own philosophical construct of experience (to be explored later in this chapter).

54. Schner, "Appeal to Experience," 47.

55. The term "intentional" is being used in its technical philosophical sense here, indicating that any appeal to experience always "tends toward" an other. Louis P. Pojman explains intentionality as referring to "the directedness (or *aboutness*) of mental states. Consciousness is often directed at an object, its content—objects of desires, fear, belief, and appearances" (Pojman, *Philosophy*, 195; italics original).

56. Schner, "Appeal to Experience," 47; cf. Lane, *Experience of God*, 17.

epistemological moments.[57] But accented here is the idea that outside of a cultural-linguistic context the experiencing subject is not able to make sense of feeling and intuition.[58] Words, or linguistic units, are not free-floating, disconnected from an intended reference. Therefore, appeals to experience are intentional in this sense, directed at a referent.[59]

Tied closely to the above, understanding experience as *derivative* helps reiterate that no experience is strictly personal (private); rather it is received historically and within a communal tradition (or, we might add, a faith horizon).[60] Again here the mediated nature of experience is assumed. Finally, as *dialectical*, Schner stresses that experience is always unstable, always limited and perpetually in a dynamic, never crystallized, state.[61] This final characteristic makes room for the possibility of encounter and interruption.

Schner believes these four rules enable us to call into question two common phrases often used in theological argument. First, the appeal to "common human experience" must be viewed as either being empty, or as a thinly veiled prescription for how humans ought to live. Instead, it needs to be recognized that the human experience is not "common," but is dependent on language, history, and culture. At best, the only universal commonality between humans is that human beings experience things.[62] Second, the phrase "religious experience" is also questionable, since no experience can be disconnected from the rest of life. Therefore, this phrase is better understood as referring to a religious aspect of experience.[63]

---

57. Schner, "Appeal to Experience," 47–48.

58. Wessel Stoker argues for religious experience of God as being "trans-intentional," therefore rational, and yet more immediate and "non-reflective." Here he appears to be siding with Schleiermacher (Stoker, "Rationality of Religious," 292, cf. 292–98).

59. Pattison, "What to Say," 192.

60. Schner, "Appeal to Experience," 48.

61. Ibid., 48–49; Althouse, "Towards a Theological," 12.

62. Schner, "Appeal to Experience," 49–50.

63. Ibid., 50–51. On the category of "religious experience" being potentially misleading (since it assumes some sort of universal type into which all religions fall) see Boeve, "Theology and the Interruption," 34; and cf. Poloma, "Sociological Context," 178. For a helpful attempt to define "religious experience" see Nieto, *Religious Experience*, 103–31.

Schner's Typology for Locating Appeals to Experience of God

At this point, Schner suggests five typologies on a "continuum of broad possibilities for the meaning and use of the notion 'experience.'"[64] As the options on this continuum are explored here, some parallels concerning the previous discussion of correlational versus non-correlational theology should become apparent; however, Schner broadens the scope of possibilities. At opposite ends of this continuum, then, are "objectifications of experience in a theological anthropology" and "radical loss of self in the transcendent." Between these lie three other "moments."[65] He does suggest, however, that these two ends "might well join one another from opposite directions," (a point that will prove significant for at least one of our theologians being surveyed later in this chapter).[66] At one end, then, is the "appeal transcendental" (exemplified in Thomism and Kantian philosophy) in which "experience" serves as a term for foundationalist philosophy, and which assumes a transcendental dimension to all experience. While this type functions well for religious apologetics, at the same time, since it appeals to all people, it suggests that all may have a common experience of God—something Schner deems unlikely given the cultural-linguistic embeddedness of all human experience. Schner also ironically notes that the secular application of this perspective can also be used to deny anything religious or theological by demanding positivistic criteria for all experience of God.[67]

The next moment on the continuum is the "appeal hermeneutical" in which the "appeal to experience is marked by modes of suspicion." This appeal emphasizes the finite nature of human experience and thus virtually limits (or eliminates) the appeal to common human experience. In doing so, however, it also undermines its own ability to maintain this skeptical stance, since its own motives and determinants for its appeal also become fair game for suspicion.[68] For this reason, Schner does not see this as fruitful ground for theological method and construction.

The "appeal constructive" (which Schner sees as being exemplified in Barth) is the third (and central) moment on the continuum, described

---

64. Schner, "Appeal to Experience," 51.

65. Ibid., 51–52.

66. Ibid., 51.

67. Ibid., 52–53.

68. Ibid., 53–54.

as being one in which "experience is invoked as the moment of transformation," and is an "interruptive" force in the community.[69] While attempting to preserve historical tradition and communal identity, room
is also made for the possibility of transformation. It is this moment that
Schner finds most promising for constructing Christian theological discourse. It is worth quoting Schner at length on this point.

> The appeal constructive is a dual appeal to possibility and neces-
> sity. It is possible through experience to change one's life, and to
> accomplish change it is necessary for experience to interact with
> already operative determinants. What is appealed to as experi-
> ence must be capable of bearing necessity in itself, and yet be a
> "possibility," neither simply structurally inevitable nor radically
> disparate from the context into which it is brought. Experience,
> then, is not unqualifiedly the "source" of theological construc-
> tion, nor is it incapable of being normative as in the appeal
> hermeneutical. It can be known and articulated, as the appeal
> immediate or mystical will not readily admit, and it does not
> collapse into a theory of human nature in order to establish its
> normativity.[70]

Here it should be observed that Schner sees far more promise in
non-correlational theological approaches than the correlational approaches explored earlier. Put another way, Schner is both exemplifying
caution toward appeals to experience of God, while remaining open to
the possibility of God being encountered and interrupting within particular faith contexts. Experience, in this sense, is invoked in order that
the Christian faith tradition might consider change and reformation.
As the community interacts with elements of experience, these experiences are subsumed into the broader theology, eventually becoming no
longer "interruptive," but part of the tradition as a whole.[71] "Experience
passes into habit, an appeal to what challenges passes into an appeal to
the tradition."[72] This occurs because God, not humanity, is the revelatory
agent of experience.[73] The community and tradition, then, function as

---

69. Ibid., 54.

70. Ibid. For the sake of transparency, I also find this moment the most attractive due
to its attempt to remain faithful to a historical community (tradition) and openness to
community reformation. Of course, other "appeals" might claim the same!

71. Ibid. 54.

72. Ibid., 55; cf. Althouse, "Towards a Theological," 14.

73. Schner, "Appeal to Experience," 55.

both the medium for revelation, as well as the stable (and often oppos-ing) reference point in which the experience is to be evaluated.[74]

The fourth moment on the continuum is the "appeal confessional." This appeal agrees with the appeal constructive in allowing experience to become normative, but it downplays relativity to a greater degree.[75] Schner refers to this appeal as being a "naïve" appeal in a sense that, while not necessarily being unaware of criticism, it tends to close itself off from forms of suspicion in order to preserve the community and to promote a continuation of similar experiences.[76] Thus, this appeal exhibits itself primarily in first order discourse such as preaching, and in devotional or evangelistic literature.[77] The weakness of this moment is that it tends to tie the transcendent so closely together with the community that it limits questions, often becomes fideistic or fundamentalistic, and usually only has the community as its primary audience.[78] This "moment" roughly corresponds with Gelpi's third definition of experience noted earlier.

The final moment on the continuum is the "appeal immediate or mystical." This is an appeal to experience that is by definition indescrib-able or ineffable, and yet which needs to be articulated if it is to be of any value to the community.[79] Schner indicates that at this point experience is no longer constructed, intentional, derivative and dialectical; in essence it is *an appeal to experience before experience* in which "the radically sub-jective is left as it is."[80] Because of this, experience is often represented symbolically, with or without words. On the one hand, these experiences are not testable, carrying an "apodictic weight in an argument." Yet, on the other, communities usually have complex traditions for evaluating such experiences. While the "appeal mystical" calls for confidence in an experience, the "appeal immediate" is often granted authority due to the

74. Ibid.

75. Ibid.

76. Ibid., 56; cf. Althouse, "Towards a Theological," 15.

77. Schner, "Appeal to Experience," 56; cf. Althouse, "Towards a Theological," 15.

78. Schner, "Appeal to Experience," 56.

79. Ibid., 57.

80. Ibid. Also see Nieto, *Religious Experience*, 133–42. Nieto attempts to differenti-ate "mystical" from "religious" experience by emphasizing the ineffability and timeless-ness characterizing testimonies of the former. On mystical experience also see Lane, *Experience of God*, 18–20; Poloma, "Sociological Context," 166–68; Pattison, "What to Say," 191; and Wulff, "Phenomenological Psychology," 183–99.

force of the experiencing subject itself (e.g., because "I say so.").[81] Schner also notes, therefore, that despite the attempt to reach beyond community, these experiences are not very useful as an appeal unless grounded within a tradition.[82]

Noteworthy here is Schner's careful, technical use of the term "mystical," in contrast to its more popular usage (which is found at times in descriptions of Pentecostal experience of the Spirit). In particular, mystical experience is characterized as being that which is, by definition, noncommunicable (ineffable). It is for this reason that Schner cites these types of experiences as, in a sense, being *prior to* "experience" in the way he is using the term. Again we encounter the word "experience" being used, even in the same sentence, to refer to quite distinct epistemological moments. For Schner, then, experience is that which is communicable within the context of a cultural-linguistic community—meaningful to others and to the experiencing subject, based on the pre-existent horizon of meaning through which experience is interpreted. To reiterate, there is no uninterpreted, raw, or innocent experience that can be appealed to as a neutral, unbiased authority—experience, in this sense, only occurs mediated within a defined community or tradition.

In the next section, Schner's continuum will be used as a means by which to locate the various appeals to experience of the theologians invited to our ecumenical conversation. This is by no means a simple task, since some appeals to experience tend to be more dynamic or fluid, not settling easily on any one "moment" on Schner's continuum. Despite this, however, Schner's framework does provide a helpful way to locate these appeals, and to this we now give our attention.

The Appeal to Experience in Christian Theological Traditions

The following survey will explore the appeal to experience as expressed by theologians from various Christian traditions. Congar, Johnson, and Gelpi will represent the Roman Catholic tradition; Lossky and Bulgakov, Eastern Orthodoxy; and Moltmann, Cone, and Jenson, the Protestant

---

81. Schner, "Appeal to Experience," 58. On the forcefulness of private mystical or religious experiences, and yet the difficulty in using these as evidence for Christian faith claims, see Pojman, *Philosophy*, 94–105.

82. Schner, "Appeal to Experience," 57–58.

stream.[83] One theme that will help focus and guide our exploration here is the person and work of the Holy Spirit, who is generally considered to be the one through whom experience of God occurs (although there is hardly consensus as to the how, where, when and why in this regard, as we shall see). Summarizing the theology of experience of God for each of these writers for a project of this sort presents something of a challenge. Some readers will find these surveys to be overly terse (omitting particular elements or nuances of a particular theologian's broader work), while others may find this overview of eight theologies of experience to be exceedingly protracted. In what follows, however, I have attempted to strike a balance in which sufficient space is given to each theologian in order to present their perspective concisely and fairly, and to enable them to be useful as dialogue partners in the later chapters with our three Pentecostal theologians.

Yves Congar and the Inseparability of Spirit and Word

Yves Marie-Joseph Congar (1904–1995) was a Roman Catholic Dominican priest and theologian,[84] who, according to Donald Gelpi, represents a more classical approach to pneumatology within the Roman Catholic tradition.[85] While this may be the case, Congar is by no means unprogressive in his attempt to expound the role of the Spirit in the Church[86] and Christian life, drawing on the resources of the Second Vatican Council to do so. While Congar takes seriously the ecclesiastical institution, he also desires to respond to contemporary challenges and criticisms facing the Church through a renewed emphasis on the Spirit. So, on one level, Congar's work on the Spirit (and how God is experienced) may be understood as an effort to affirm the Church as institution, while at the same demonstrating theologically why fresh thinking is needed on such issues as the roles of laity and clergy in Church life,[87]

---

83. The criteria for this selection was outlined in the introduction to this book.

84. "Congar, Yves Marie-Joseph," 327.

85. Gelpi, *Divine Mother*, viii.

86. Because Congar's focus is the Roman Catholic Church, "Church" is capitalized in this subsection.

87. Congar, *Word and the Spirit*, 58–62, 78–84.

Pentecostal/charismatic expressions of spirituality,[88] and the Spirit's work outside of the Church and in the cosmos in general.[89]

In brief, Congar believes a fresh understanding of the interrelationship between the Son and Spirit holds the key that will enable the institutional Church to be enriched by recognizing a more dynamic operation of the Spirit in the ecclesia.[90] Congar states, "If I were to draw but one conclusion from the whole of my work on the Holy Spirit, I would express it in these words: no Christology without pneumatology and no pneumatology without Christology."[91] He aims, then, to demonstrate how the missions of Spirit and Son may be understood dynamically together, and how this impacts the life of the church, and for our purposes, experience of God.

Congar believes it is possible "to reach the eternal [immanent] Trinity only by way of the economic Trinity,"[92] and so he gives special attention to the divine missions of Word and Spirit in Scripture and creation.[93] Scripture, he argues, intricately connects Word and Spirit. This can be seen from the close association of the two in Old Testament prophecy (in which proclaimed word was enabled by the Spirit), and in the concept of "Wisdom," which some early Christian writers frequently associated with both Word and Spirit, so closely were these concepts linked.[94] This close relationship is also seen in the New Testament, especially in Johannine literature.[95] "Scripture, then, from Genesis to Revelation . . . bears witness to the intimate connection between Word and Spirit!"[96]

The theological stress gleaned from this scriptural witness is that the Father is the "Source," the "Sender" of Word and Spirit;[97] they together, "issue from his mouth."[98] So, "Starting with the Father, words and

88. Congar, *I Believe*, 2:161–88.

89. Congar, *Word and the Spirit*, 122–29.

90. Ibid., 78. Congar states explicitly that Church as institution and charism are not in opposition.

91. Ibid., 1.

92. Ibid., 4, 104.

93. Congar, *I Believe*, 2:7–8, 3:139–40; Congar, *Word and the Spirit*, 104–5.

94. Congar, *Word and the Spirit*, 5–16.

95. Ibid., 17.

96. Ibid., 19.

97. Ibid., 18.

98. Ibid., 15.

the Spirit are always joined."[99] The Father is the source unseen,[100] and in order to enter into dialogue with an other (the creature), he sends his Word, enabling the Father to express "himself outside himself."[101] By words a person "makes known his or her thoughts and feelings to another by signs"; and in this way, word functions as "both distance and bond."[102] In the historical divine missions it was through the "Logos-Image-Wisdom that everything was (created),"[103] and through the Word the unseen Father makes himself "known" and "visible in the world's history."[104] This Word is the historical Christ, the "Logos who was in God and who was God manifested historically."[105]

But word alone is not sufficient for divine communication—it needs to be received and appropriated by faith. So Congar states, "The Word is therefore effected in and by the faith that receives it. It is here, theologically, that the Spirit intervenes."[106] The Spirit enables belief in the Word;[107] and since the triune persons, manifest in the divine missions (economy), reveal the immanent Trinity (or "eternal Trinity"),[108] we are able to infer that the Spirit unites the communication of Father and Son.[109] The Spirit is the one who perfects, or completes communication—both within the triune life and between God and the world.[110] The Spirit is the "bond of unity within God [and] also between God and creation." As the completion of communication, then, the Spirit enables God to exist "outside himself."[111] Thus, biblically and theologically, Word and Spirit are bound together—the "two hands of the Father" in the divine mission.[112]

---

99. Ibid., 18.

100. Congar, *I Believe*, 3:139–40.

101. Congar, *Word and the Spirit*, 10.

102. Ibid., 9; cf. Congar, *I Believe*, 3:12.

103. Congar, *Word and the Spirit*, 10.

104. Ibid., 11.

105. Ibid., 12, cf. 11.

106. Ibid., 12.

107. Ibid., 12–13.

108. Congar, *I Believe*, 3:11–12.

109. Ibid., 3:148.

110. Ibid.

111. Ibid., 3:149.

112. Congar, *Word and the Spirit*, 61.

While intricately linked, Congar insists that Word and Spirit are still distinct, fulfilling different aspects of the divine mission. The Logos is the objective Word, while the Spirit creates the capacity to receive and obey the Word of the Father, whether this be written or spoken.[113] Thus, the Spirit operates practically in the Church to illuminate the meaning of Scripture and enable reception of the Word preached.[114] The Church (as Christ's body) bears the Word, and is the "Interpreter and guardian of the Scriptures."[115] In this sense the Church serves as locus for the Spirit, who operates within the body of Christ to bring truth and complete the reception of the Word toward salvation. The Church ought not, however, become complacent, for it too may be confronted by the Spirit.[116]

Here Congar challenges the Roman Catholic magisterium and ordained clergy to recognize that the Church offices operate only within the broader context of the "People of God, which represents the fullness of spiritual gifts."[117] Clergy need to acknowledge that the dynamic operation of the Spirit involves more than structure and hierarchy—the Spirit operates in God's People as a whole. Congar gives this ecclesiastical point considerable attention as he wrestles to both preserve and justify Church hierarchy by emphasizing the role of Word, while at the same time attempting to integrate the freedom of the Spirit into ecclesiastical life. At times he seems to subordinate the Spirit's role to that of the Word, but at others demonstrates the Word's reliance on the Spirit. Exemplifying the former emphasis, Congar states, "The presence and activity of the Spirit sometimes takes striking forms, the most spectacular of all perhaps occurring at the first Pentecost . . . *Usually, however, the Spirit is an inner whispering and even silence.* It is the word that is expression and inspiration."[118]

So, while linking Word and Spirit, Word tends to occupy a predominant role here; and elsewhere this same theme is reiterated. Jesus, Congar states, "is the fullness of the Word of God." As for the Spirit, he is

113. Ibid., 21–23.

114. Ibid., 25.

115. Ibid., 27–28.

116. Ibid., 33, cf. 30–33. Here Congar is sympathetic to the concerns of the Protestant Reformers, Luther and Calvin, who feared that too close an identity between Church and Spirit (with hierarchy emphasized to the detriment of the freedom of the Spirit) would make the Church blind to internal error.

117. Ibid., 33, 34–35.

118. Ibid., 35 (italics added).

"totally relative to Jesus."[119] Again, with regard to Church structure, "The Word is the form and the Spirit is the breath. . . . The Spirit, however, is the Spirit of *Jesus Christ*. He does no other work but that of *Jesus Christ*. There is no time of the Paraclete that is not the time of Jesus Christ . . ."[120]

What does this mean with regard to the experience of the Spirit? Aside from enabling faith and reception of the Word (as mentioned), the Spirit is experienced in other ways as well. The Spirit is *present* personally in disciples of Christ (individually and corporately), enables prophetic ability in the Church to bear witness to the gospel, and also empowers Christ's body to wrestle against evil powers in the world by reassuring "that the world is wrong."[121] In all this the Spirit is working, but always remains in a sense "without a face and almost without a name. He is the wind who is not seen, but who makes things move."[122]

In other places, however, Congar works to loosen ecclesiastical restrictions often placed on the Spirit. He acknowledges, for example, the Spirit's activity within various revival movements in Christian history outside of Roman Catholicism, including (more recently) the Pentecostal and charismatic movements.[123] He also states that the Spirit may operate not only through the mediation of Church structures and sacraments, but also at times in "immediacy."[124] Thus, the Church should be careful to make room for "personal initiative" among individual believers who may be experiencing the leading of the Spirit.[125] Private revelations also must be considered a valid possibility, as well as prophetic ministry, which (while mainly occurring within the ecclesia) may also function outside the ecclesial community—even directing a prophetic word toward the Church![126] After all, since the Spirit blows where it wills, "We cannot simply be satisfied with discerning that Spirit on the basis of what

---

119. Ibid., 44.

120. Congar, *I Believe*, 2:34–35 (italics original).

121. Congar, *Word and the Spirit*, 45–46.

122. Congar, *I Believe*, 3:144.

123. Congar, *Word and the Spirit*, 49–51. Elsewhere Congar attempts to wrestle with specific issues arising out of the charismatic movement, such as the meaning of "charismatic" and the operation of the charisms of tongues, prophecy, and healing (Congar, *I Believe*, 2:161–88).

124. Congar, *Word and the Spirit*, 52–53.

125. Ibid., 53–55.

126. Ibid., 55–58, 62–72.

we already know about Jesus from the Scriptures and the traditions of the churches."[127]

To elevate the importance of the Spirit's mission overall, then, Congar takes a fresh look at Jesus' earthly mission. He argues that whereas classical theology tended to focus only on the Spirit's involvement at Christ's assumption (Incarnation), there were in fact successive stages in the Spirit's descent upon Jesus during his earthly life and ministry.[128] Christ's assumption was the first of three decisive events, or moments, "when Jesus became—and was not simply—proclaimed as the Son of God in a new way . . ."[129] The two other moments are Jesus' baptism, in which he was anointed for messianic ministry, and his resurrection and glorification.[130] These three distinct events (assumption, baptism-anointing, and resurrection/glorification) effectively introduce a change in Jesus' consciousness in regard to his Sonship.[131] Congar is careful to avoid adoptionism since, "He became Son of God not from the point of view of his hypostatic quality or from that of his ontology as the incarnate Word, but from that of God's offer of grace and the successive moments in the history of salvation."[132] The significance of this "pneumatological Christology" is that it implies (with regard to salvation history) that the "Word proceeds . . . from the Father and the Spirit," and this has significant ecclesiological implications.[133]

Congar's pneumatological Christology implies that the Word, the form and structure of the Church, is a product of the Spirit. Further, Word and Spirit need to be viewed as "co-instituting" principles in the Church.[134] The Spirit does not simply animate the Church institution, but must be viewed as being able to renovate the Church, even as the Spirit operates in and through the existing forms.[135] Nevertheless, Congar is reticent to allow that the Spirit might *identifiably* be at work outside the

127. Ibid., 66. Congar does distinguish, however, between "prophetism" and faith, the latter of which is explicit faith in Jesus and may be found only in the Church.

128. Ibid., 85–87; Congar, *I Believe*, 3:166. Congar cites Aquinas as an example of a classical emphasis.

129. Congar, *I Believe*, 170, cf. 92; Congar, *Word and the Spirit*, 85–100.

130. Congar, *I Believe*, 3:167–69; Congar, *Word and the Spirit*, 88–91.

131. Congar, *Word and the Spirit*, 92.

132. Ibid; cf. Congar, *I Believe*, 3:170–71.

133. Congar, *Word and the Spirit*, 93.

134. Ibid., 78–84; Congar, *I Believe*, 2:7–12.

135. Congar, *Word and the Spirit*, 82–83.

ecclesia, denying that there is a "Free sector" in which the Spirit operates alongside the Church.[136]

But while perhaps not being able to positively identify how the Spirit is at work outside the Church, Congar does make some allowance for this possibility (albeit somewhat ambiguously in places). Since the Spirit is the *Spiritus Creator*, it also functions in the cosmos in general, guiding it toward liberation.[137] The Spirit secretly directs the salvific work of God in the world; so it is possible that the kingdom of God may be found even where people "do not explicitly speak of God or Jesus."[138] At the same time, the Church remains the "illuminated zone," so to speak, and Congar is quick to provide boundaries.[139] The Spirit's work is not autonomous, but always linked to Christ's mission;[140] and the Spirit's ultimate goal in history is toward "the Constitution of the body of the sons of God in Jesus Christ . . ."[141] So, "We simply do not know the frontiers of the Spirit's activity in this world, nor the ways in which he acts. We can only be sure they're related to Christ, whose spiritual body is formed with man by the Spirit."[142]

Locating Congar's Appeal to Experience

Congar's work exemplifies theological wrestling to preserve ecclesial identity through tradition (in this case, Roman Catholic) while attempting at the same time to deal with issues of relevancy. His "pneumatological Christology" and "Christological pneumatology" emphases demonstrate the give and take required to remain in such a tension. For this reason, on Schner's continuum, Congar seems to exemplify what we might call a "traditional 'appeal constructive,'" acknowledging the weight granted to

---

136. Ibid., 61. Congar notes that this is a shift in his thinking from his earlier work, *The Mystery of the Church* (1953). Interestingly, in *I Believe in the Spirit*, he seems a bit more reluctant to abandon the idea of a "free sector" than in *The Word and the Spirit* (Congar, *I Believe*, 2:11).

137. Congar, *Word and the Spirit*, 122, 124. Briefly, and without explanation, Congar indicates that he accepts aspects of Marxist and Hegelian eschatology in regard to history being "the acquisition of freedom or liberation" (ibid., 125).

138. Congar, *I Believe*, 2:222.

139. Ibid., 223.

140. Congar, *Word and the Spirit*, 60.

141. Ibid., 126.

142. Ibid. Congar also states, "It may be possible to say where the church is, but not possible to say where it is not."

the Roman Catholic historical confession in his work. In other words, his desire to build on the changes introduced in the Second Vatican Council, and to move the Church toward fuller recognition of the Spirit's work in all its members, does demonstrate considerable constructive tendencies. But on the other hand, his adherence to the confessional appeal (while by no means naïve) also appears to dominate in a number of cases, leading him to view the Spirit's activity, for the most part, as "whispering" behind the Word (i.e., institution). We locate Congar's appeal, then, as an "appeal constructive," but in dynamic tension with the "appeal confessional."

Elizabeth A. Johnson and Women's Experience of God

In, *She Who Is*, Elizabeth A. Johnson, a feminist theologian within the Roman Catholic tradition,[143] sets out an innovative proposal to reform speech about God within classic Christian theology. Christian theology, she claims, has often been dominated by androcentric and patriarchal metaphors, as well as Hellenistic philosophical categories, which have contributed to the domination and oppression of women throughout history.[144] Since speech helps form the primary symbols by which communities develop frames of reference for understanding themselves, their values, and the world,[145] what is needed is fresh speech about God—"a good word about the mystery of God recognizable within the contours of the Christian faith [that] will serve the emancipatory praxis of women and men, to the benefit of all creation, both human beings and the earth."[146] Johnson's goal is explicitly not a reverse sexism or the elimination of gender differences, but the transformation of unjust systems within the world toward the formation of a liberated "new community," in which all people, male and female, will flourish.[147]

To this end, Johnson draws upon what she considers to be neglected female imagery and symbols found in the biblical and classical Christian theological traditions, as well as the experience of women in history, in order to reform speech about God and contribute to religious and

---

143. See Johnson, *She Who Is*, 11, 17.

144. Ibid., 3–5, 19–22, 23–28, 33–41. *She Who Is* will primarily guide our discussion throughout this subsection.

145. Ibid., 3–5.

146. Ibid., 8. These ecological concerns are also outlined in Johnson, *Women, Earth*.

147. Johnson, *She Who Is*, 30–31, cf. 17–19. See also Johnson, *Women, Earth*, 24.

societal renewal.[148] Johnson explains, it is not that female imagery for God is superior to male imagery, but rather the current historical situation in which sexism, androcentrism, and patriarchy dominate makes it necessary to accent female metaphors when speaking of the divine mystery in order to truly bring glory to God.[149] In fact, if speech about God is not renewed, she is concerned that it could lead to a loss of belief in God altogether. "If the idea of God does not keep pace with developing reality, the power of experience pulls people on and the god dies, fading from memory."[150]

Johnson's above reference to the "power of experience" is telling. She is convinced that human encounter and interaction in everyday historical reality has a powerful psychological and social influence upon conceptions of God. For this reason, she "appeals to women's experience" as an important resource (among others) toward a feminist liberation theology.[151] This project entails demonstrating "the hidden dynamic of domination" in Christian theology and tradition, utilizing resources outside of the Christian tradition, and ultimately reconstructing "new articulations of the norms and methods of theology."[152] But the overarching criterion by which she judges the merits of her discoveries (and all theology), "is the emancipation of women toward human flourishing."[153] This criterion, then, functions with a great deal of authority in Johnson's program, and indicates that women's experience largely serves as her theological point of departure.

Johnson believes the historical experience of the emancipation of women is, in fact, an experience (a revelation) of God that can be expressed through human speech.[154] Thus, the experience of women in history serves as a fundamental resource for Johnson's theology.[155] She

148. Johnson, *She Who Is*, 42–47, 59–120.

149. Ibid., 15, 45–47, 54–57. Thus, such a project is necessary not only to contribute to women's emancipation, but also for the honor of God, which is bound up with "human happiness" and liberation (ibid., 14).

150. Ibid., 15.

151. Ibid., 29; cf. Johnson, *Women, Earth*, 23–28.

152. Johnson, *She Who Is*, 29, 30; cf. Johnson, *Women, Earth*, 10–22.

153. Johnson, *She Who Is*, 30.

154. Ibid., 75. Johnson asserts that all speech about God is historically bound, and so the "unfathomable mystery of God is always mediated through shifting historical discourse" (ibid., 6).

155. Ibid., 61–75.

does acknowledge a plurality of women's experience (there is, therefore, no *one* feminist theology); however, there are certain experiences that are common to feminist theologies, among them, "fundamental to the emancipatory speech about God in feminist liberation theology [is] the experience of conversion."[156] By "conversion" she means the "awakening" of women "to their own human worth," in a dialectic of recognizing and saying "no" to all forms of sexist repression and confirming a "solidarity of sisters" with women in history.[157] Most importantly, this awakening "can be interpreted . . . as a new experience of God, so that what is arguably occurring is a new event in the religious history of humankind."[158]

In arguing for experience of God in women's emancipatory experience in history, Johnson relies on Karl Rahner's transcendental anthropology, as well as J. B. Metz's emphasis on experience of God as being communal and liberative.[159] Most explicitly, she draws on Rahner to assert that experience of God occurs through experience of oneself (and community), since, "Human beings are dynamically structured toward God."[160] Johnson expands:

> Accordingly, the experience of God which is never directly available is mediated, among other ways but primordially so, through the changing history of oneself. Rather than being a distinct and separate experience, it transpires as the ultimate depth and radical essence of every personal- experience such as love, fidelity, loneliness and death. In the experience of oneself at these depths, at this prethematic level whence our own mystery arises, we also experience and are grasped by the holy mystery of God as the very context of our own self-presence. In fact the silent, nonverbal encounter with the infinite mystery constitutes the enabling condition of any experience of self at all.[161]

Because of the intrinsic connection between the holy mystery and the self, "Personal development of the self constitutes development of the experience of God."[162] In this sense, to experience oneself, then, is to experience God. Combining this with Metz's historical and commu-

---

156. Ibid., 61–62.
157. Ibid., 62–63.
158. Ibid., 62.
159. Ibid., 65–66.
160. Ibid., 65.
161. Ibid.
162. Ibid.

nal experiential emphasis, Johnson argues that the appeal to women's experience in history is experience of the divine.[163] She states, "Because the mystery of God is always and only mediated through an experience that is specifically historical, the changing history of women's self-appraisal and self-naming creates a new situation for language about the divine mystery, . . . one that takes female reality in all its concreteness as a legitimate finite starting point for speaking about the mystery of God."[164]

Aside from women's experience, the resources of Scripture and the classical theological tradition also provide justification for a reinterpretation of God, although these need to be deconstructed in order to root out the sexist language of domination.[165] Within the scriptural tradition, support for the validity of referring to God using female imagery is found in the Old Testament terms "Spirit" and "Shekinah," as well as other various maternal references to God.[166] Of greatest significance, however, is the female symbol of Wisdom/Sophia found in Hebrew wisdom literature.[167] Sophia is "a female personification of God's own being in creative and saving involvement in the world. The chief reason for arriving at this interpretation is the functional equivalence between the deeds of Sophia and those of the biblical God."[168] Sophia serves, then, as a metaphor accenting the nearness of the transcendent God.[169]

Within the classical theological tradition, a resource is found in the emphasis on the "incomprehensibility of God" and the "analogical nature of religious language."[170] Johnson applauds the move within early

163. Ibid., 66.

164. Ibid., 75.

165. Ibid., 76–120. Johnson justifies the application of a feminist hermeneutic to the Bible, for example, by an appeal to the Second Vatican Council's assertion that biblical revelation is granted for the "sake of our salvation." In other words, it is revelation for the purpose of redemption, and not for other aspects of life, such as politics or science. This allows for Scripture to be selectively gleaned for texts that emphasize liberation, while not taking androcentric and patriarchal texts as normative (ibid., 78–79).

166. Ibid., 82–86, 100–103.

167. Ibid., 86–100; cf. Johnson, *Women, Earth*, 51–57.

168. Johnson, *She Who Is*, 91. Johnson suggests extra-biblical female deities, such as Isis, as being a possible influence upon the key concept of Wisdom/Sophia.

169. Ibid. Johnson's use of Sophia should be distinguished from that of Bulgakov, as we shall see. While both use Sophia as a concept to emphasize God's immanence, Johnson does not develop this into a theology of essence as does Bulgakov, but instead chooses to emphasize this name as a metaphor for God's nearness.

170. Ibid., 120, cf. 104–20.

Christian theology to find common ground with the Greek philosophical tradition concerning the notion of divine "inaccessibility to human comprehension . . . rooted in the idea that the one ultimate origin of all things must be totally different from the everyday world of multiplicity and change."[171] God's hiddenness, then, is not due "to some reluctance on the part of God to self-reveal in a full way, nor to the sinful condition of the human race . . . Rather it is proper to God as God to transcend all similarity to creatures, and thus never to be known comprehensively or essentially as God."[172] As a result, humans are only able to speak of God by way of analogy.[173] Because all creation exists and is sustained by God, this relationship with creation means that speech about God is meaningful, but that ultimately "words are but pointers to the origin and source of all."[174] Words may speak truthfully of God, but are always limited; and so "many [new] names for God" are needed, thereby justifying the place of female metaphors for God.[175]

Based on women's experience and female metaphor, Johnson advocates a fresh approach to speaking of the Trinity as Spirit-Sophia, Jesus-Sophia, and Mother-Sophia.[176] She also notes that women's experience of God has not typically occurred within ecclesiastical boundaries (where they have more often than not experienced oppression).[177] Instead, this has occurred in the "field of the Spirit,"[178] the universal presence of God working in every part of creation.[179] Therefore, Johnson argues that a starting place for Trinitarian theology legitimately begins with women's experience in history and with Spirit-Sophia.

We will only make note of two other key emphases within Johnson's program emerging from the above. First, she views Spirit-Sophia as being the means by which experience of God occurs, and through whom

---

171. Ibid., 107.

172. Ibid., 105. It is precisely on this point that Jenson (as we shall see) believes Christian theology has sometimes erred. Jenson and Johnson's theology of revelation and experience diverge considerably here.

173. Ibid., 109.

174. Ibid., 114.

175. Ibid., 117–20.

176. Ibid., 121–87.

177. Ibid., 122.

178. Ibid.

179. Ibid., 123.

God is mediated.[180] Experience of the Spirit occurs potentially in and through every aspect of creation, being mediated through the "natural world," personal and interpersonal relationships, and in the "macro systems that structure human beings as groups."[181]

> If we ask more precisely which moments or events mediate God's Spirit, the answer can only be potentially *all* experience, the whole world. There is no exclusive zone, no special realm, which alone may be called religious. Rather, since Spirit is the creator and giver of life, life itself with all its complexities, abundance, threat, misery, and joy becomes a primary mediation of the dialectic of presence and absence of divine mystery. The historical world becomes a sacrament of divine presence and activity, even if only as a fragile possibility. The complexities of the experience of the Spirit therefore, are cogiven in and through the world's history: negative, positive, and ambiguous; orderly and chaotic; solitary and communal; successful and disastrous; personal and political; dark and luminous; ordinary and extraordinary; cosmic, social, and individual.[182]

The work of the Spirit, then, must not be relegated to the "subjective side of the event of revelation, or to the emotional aspects of human experience.[183] Instead the Spirit must be recognized as "vivifying," and "renewing and empowering" creation toward healing, and opposing all forms of injustice.[184] Spirit-Sophia also "graces" all religious communities, so that, "No people are devoid of the inspiration of the Spirit."[185] A renewed appreciation of Spirit-Sophia can also help Christian theology emphasize God's "indwelling nearness" in the world without being "bound by it," God's taking sides with the oppressed in situations of injustice, and the reality of relationship between God and creation.[186]

The second emphasis emerging from Johnson's description of the Spirit's activity is a proposal for a theological rearticulation of the inner

---

180. Ibid., 124–49.

181. Ibid., 125, 126, cf. 127.

182. Ibid., 124 (italics original); cf. Johnson, *Women, Earth*, 57–60.

183. Johnson, *She Who Is*, 129. Here Johnson distances herself from the revelational theology of Barth, as well as criticizing Pentecostals and charismatics for their overemphasis on emotion in worship.

184. Ibid., 133–39.

185. Ibid., 139, cf. 139–41.

186. Ibid., 147–48.

life of the Trinity, which will in turn affect the way in which values and models for humanity are derived theologically. In brief, Johnson advocates that the triune persons be understood in a more social and relational sense than has been classically emphasized.[187] The images typically used for the Trinity (Father, Son, and Spirit), as well as the traditional way of speaking of the internal divine structure (processions) have been stereotypically male and hierarchical.[188] A feminist relational model of the Trinity is able to replace processional models with a concept of "sequence" that "does not necessitate subordination" in the triune life. In general, a feminist rearticulation of the Trinity will emphasize its "Mutual relations," "Radical equality," and "Community in diversity."[189]

But this relationality within the Godhead also helps explain God's relationship to creation.[190] God is connected to creation in a real way; indeed, is in communion with it. Sophia-God relates to the historical world from "overflowing graciousness."[191] For Johnson, this means that while the world exists dependent on God in a way that God is not dependent on the world, nevertheless, "God is in the world" and the world is in God.[192] So, the way to avoid both classical theistic dualism and pantheism (identifying God and the world) is through a "dialectical theism" or "panentheism" in which God penetrates the world so all can exist in God.[193] This understanding of God's inner life and (derivatively) relationship to creation provides further theological justification for the appeal to women's experience of God in history.

187. Ibid., 196.

188. Ibid., 193–95.

189. Ibid., 216–18, 218–19, 220–22. Here Johnson demonstrates reliance on and affinity with Moltmann's doctrine of Social Trinity (cf. ibid., 195, 207–8).

190. Ibid., 224–27.

191. Ibid., 228.

192. Ibid., 230, cf. 228–33.

193. Ibid., 231–32. Johnson claims that this approach differs from some other feminist theologies that appeal to pantheism. Johnson rejects this as having emerged from women having had to submerge and lose themselves in institutions and social structures dominated by hierarchy and patriarchy. She finds panentheism far more empowering and liberating for women. She also finds it more conducive to justifying ecological sensitivities. On this latter point especially, see Johnson, *Women, Earth*, 41–51, 57–60, cf. 5–9, 61–68.

LOCATING JOHNSON'S APPEAL TO EXPERIENCE

Johnson's Christian feminist liberation theology does demonstrate considerable constructive elements, but at the same time exemplifies characteristics of two other points on Schner's continuum. In regard to her emphasis on women's experience in history and suspicion of aspects of classical theology and biblical tradition, and especially due to her fundamental criterion for discerning the Spirit's work by means of evidence of liberative effect (for women in particular), she may be located at the "appeal hermeneutical." But Johnson's reliance on Rahner's transcendental anthropology, and her strong panentheism, also converges with the "appeal transcendental." There is no doubt considerable oscillation between these two points for Johnson, but her emphasis on Wisdom/Sophia and the transcendence of human experience, would seem to place her closer to the "appeal transcendental" in regard to the means by which humans experience God and by which she develops her theology.

Donald L. Gelpi and the Triadic Construct of Experience

The contribution of Jesuit theologian, Donald L. Gelpi (1951–2011), is somewhat unique among the other approaches in our survey, for although he writes within the Roman Catholic tradition,[194] he attempts to develop a theology of experience based in North American pragmatic philosophy, drawing on philosophers such as Charles Sanders Peirce and Josiah Royce, among others.[195] He believes that many other theological approaches to the experience of God have failed to produce workable models largely due to their reliance on metaphysical di-polar constructs of experience. "A di-polar construct," explains Gelpi, "describes experience as the subjective interrelation of concrete percepts and abstract concepts."[196] Such a construct, however, is unable to explain "ordinary human experience" or the "graced transformation of natural human

194. See "Donald L. Gelpi, S.J."

195. Gelpi, *Divine Mother*, x; Gelpi, *Turn to Experience*, 5ff., 13, 16–17, 29ff.; and Gelpi, *Experiencing God*, 18–51. It should also be noted that Gelpi is at least partly motivated to explore the possibilities of experience with God due to his involvement in the Roman Catholic charismatic movement. On this see Gelpi, *Experiencing God*, 11–12; Gelpi, *Divine Mother*, 3; and Gelpi, "Response," 27–30.

196. Gelpi, *Turn to Experience*, 3. In his book Gelpi analyzes four theological approaches to experience that utilize the di-polar construct, identifying their inadequacies. He looks at Schillebeeckx, Liberation theology, Process theology, and Transcendental Thomism.

experience by Christian faith" through the work of the Holy Spirit.[197] Citing Royce, Gelpi explains that in a di-polar construct of experience "all knowledge takes place exclusively between one's ears . . . [and is] purely a subjective process that, as a construct, lacks the categories to interpret the basic human experience of communication." Further, this "cannot account philosophically for the social character of knowing."[198] Obviously this poses problems for the possibility of experience of God, due to the strong spirit/matter dichotomy often inherent in this construct.[199]

Gelpi proposes to overcome this challenge through a "triadic, realistic, communitarian construct of experience," which "defines experience as a process made up of relational elements called 'feelings.' It discovers three generic variables in the higher forms of experience: evaluations, actions, and tendencies."[200] This rather dense statement requires some exposition. For Gelpi, human experience cannot be restricted to two poles, but is better understood triadically. Within human experience are found "three shifting and interrelated realms," as opposed to simply perception and abstraction.[201] First, "We respond evaluatively to ourselves and to our world. Our evaluative responses range from concrete sensations to abstract conceptions."[202] Human evaluation includes both perceptions and sensations,[203] and can in fact be construed as a "continuum stretching from sensation to abstract inference."[204] This realm of evaluation is also referred to by Gelpi as the "experiential realm of *quality*."[205]

Another variable, or interrelated realm, under the rubric of experience is "actions." Says Gelpi, "Besides responding evaluatively to reality,

197. Ibid.

198. Ibid., 13. Gelpi notes that the di-polar construct of experience is rooted in philosophical nominalism, which he defines as "any denial of real generality in things," in contrast to the realism advocated by Charles Sanders Peirce. Peirce "regarded the whole of post-Cartesian, Western philosophy as nominalistic" (ibid., 5).

199. Ibid., 137. Gelpi notes that this is a problem in Schillebeeckx's construct of experience, which excludes God from experience since God is not concrete and sensible (ibid., 15–16).

200. Ibid., 126; cf. Gelpi, *Divine Mother*, 39. Gelpi draws on Peirce and Royce for this triadic construct.

201. Gelpi, *Divine Mother*, 23.

202. Ibid.

203. Ibid., 24.

204. Ibid., 29.

205. Ibid., 23 (italics added), cf. 23–25; Gelpi, *Turn to Experience*, 126–27.

we also interact decisively with persons and things we encounter. We bump into them, and they bump back. Let us call the realm of decisive action and reaction the experiential realm of *fact*."[206] This is the realm of "action and reaction" or "decisions." *Facts* make "experience concrete," by effecting "this rather than that." They shape the social environment by establishing "links between interacting selves."[207] Thus, in experience we have the interaction of realms of quality and fact, evaluation and decision (action).

However, selves involved in the reacting/responding cannot simply "be reduced to the evaluations and decisions they generate."[208] This is because these selves are also experienced by other selves, and are more than simply "concrete acts or particular evaluations."[209] The self also contains autonomy and develops "habitual tendencies to react or respond in certain ways," which, states Gelpi, can be understood as the "experiential realm of *law*."[210] Gelpi explains, "Each self endows its own evaluations and decisions with significance by linking them to one another in intelligible habits. When we understand actions and evaluations, we perceive the self that performs them. For each self abstracted from its actions and evaluations is a general, habitual impulse to react decisively or to respond evaluatively in a specific way."[211]

The three "feelings," then, within this construct of experience are *qualities*, *facts*, and *laws*. Further, each of these experiential realms is able to be transformed by the Spirit (to whom Gelpi refers as the "Holy Breath").[212] But to the point, in this construct the self is constituted by the process of the interaction of these three relational realms—the self *is* experience.

---

206. Gelpi, *Divine Mother*, 23 (italics added).

207. Ibid., 35.

208. Ibid., 23.

209. Ibid., 36.

210. Ibid., 23 (italics added).

211. Ibid., 36. On self and the development of habit, see 36–39.

212. Ibid., 23. In *The Divine Mother*, Gelpi chooses to refer to the Spirit as "Breath" based on a translation of the Hebrew, *Ruah*. He also refers to the Spirit using female terminology in this particular work, and believes there is ample support for this in Scripture and tradition. He insists, however, that this does not apply sexuality to the Spirit (Gelpi, *Divine Mother*, 9–11). We will follow Gelpi's use of feminine pronouns for Spirit in this subsection.

> Each self is the sum total of its history. Each self's history is the sum total of its experience. As a consequence, each self is its experience. It does not *have* experiences. When I say, "I have experiences," I distance myself linguistically from the experiences I say I have, as though I enjoy some kind of reality apart from them. In point of fact, I sum up all that I experience. I am the cumulative product of my experience. Whatever I am is the totality of my experience. The persons and things that have changed me have become part of me, flesh of my flesh, bone of my bone, just as I in changing them have become part of them.[213]

The self as an experience has broader societal application, for it implies an "inexistence" between self and the world. "Because I am an experience, not only do I exist in my world but my world as felt, as experienced, exists in me. To say my world exists in me simply means that it makes me to be the kind of self I am. When it impinges on me and I respond to it, we exist in one another because we experience one another."[214]

The above construct is able to provide a framework for understanding how it is that humans experience God, and further, as a means by which to better understand the three "mysteries" of Christian theology, namely, the Trinity, the Spirit's indwelling of the church, and the Incarnation.[215] Concerning experience of God, "We experience both the Lordship of Jesus and the Fatherhood of God in the enlightenment of Their Holy Breath." Toward understanding experience of God, then, Gelpi asserts, "pneumatology holds the key."[216] Further, by taking into account the historical missions of the Holy Breath and the Son, it can be seen that the triadic construct of experience may also be applied to God, and in doing so help shed light on the inner life of the Trinity.[217]

First, with regard to the historical mission of the divine Breath as recorded in both Old and New Testaments, she is always "experienced as a gracious enlightenment, [and so] ought to be perceived as the mind of God."[218] Based on the divine Breath's activity within human history (bringing enlightenment in many forms, especially in the life and ministry of the person of Jesus), it can be inferred that "The divine Pneuma

---

213. Ibid., 41–42 (italics original).
214. Ibid., 42 (italics original).
215. Gelpi, *Turn to Experience*, 149ff.
216. Gelpi, *Divine Mother*, 45.
217. See Gelpi, *Turn to Experience*, 150; and Gelpi, *Divine Mother*, 60, 74.
218. Gelpi, *Divine Mother*, 45, cf. 45–60.

is then the mind (*nous*) of the Christian Godhead. She is the mind common to both Father and Son. Through Their union with the Breath They share an identity of conscious divine life."[219]

The mission of the Son is not to be confused with that of the Breath.[220] The Logos is not "the conception of the divine mind so much as the one through whom the Father speaks and acts . . . [,] the spoken Word of God who reveals to us simultaneously both the reality of the Father and His mind, who is the Holy Breath."[221] Further, while the Breath may have had other "missions" prior to the coming of Jesus, her mission now is "mediated by the incarnation," and consequently is experienced "explicitly as the Breath of the Son and of the Father Who sent Him."[222] Again, the missions of Breath and Son reveal the distinction between persons as well as the interpersonal relations within the Godhead.[223] This introduces, as implied above, a measure of particularity with regard to salvation history, for "the missions are the only place where the relationship of the divine Persons to one another is revealed to us."[224] Through experience of the Spirit we are given access to the triune God's reality.[225]

The historical divine missions, then, enable identification of the variables operative in human experience (*qualities*, *facts* and *laws*) as also being operative in the divine life. Thus, says Gelpi, "We can then conceive of the Christian God as an experience: not, of course, as a finite spatio-temporal experience, but as the supreme exemplification of experience, as that experience than which none greater can be conceived, as the experience of all experiential reality. Since, moreover, experienced realities stand within the experience that grasps them, not outside of it, it follows that all reality exists in God."[226]

This implies that not only are human selves (as experiences) "inexistent," but that God and creatures are also "mutually inexistent."

219. Ibid., 59, (italics original), cf. 60.

220. Ibid., 65.

221. Ibid., 66.

222. Ibid., 70.

223. Gelpi, *Turn to Experience*, 150.

224. Gelpi, *Divine Mother*, 74.

225. Ibid., 83. Elsewhere Gelpi states, "apart from the incarnation, an experienced encounter with the Holy One will probably not disclose the triune character of God's inner life. Only the historical missions of the divine persons does that" (Gelpi, *Turn to Experience*, 152).

226. Gelpi, *Turn to Experience*, 150–51; cf. Gelpi, *Divine Mother*, 90.

Experiences exist always and only within experience, and so the "world . . . stands within the divine experience. It exists in God." On this basis, Gelpi believes that the connection between God and the world must be understood as *relationally panentheistic*. This panentheism does not advocate the world as being identical with God, "or the body of God." Rather, "The world is simply what God experiences." Yet God and the world remain "distinct realities," and so the world "is not the only thing He experiences. For God also experiences Himself." But nevertheless, "a world experienced by God exists in God."[227]

So, just as on a human level experience occurs within experience (socially, in relationship with other selves), so too does human relationship with, and experience and knowledge of God occur by means of social interaction—this is not a di-polar operation.[228] Explains Gelpi, "We enter into social relationships by interaction. When we interact socially, we grasp intuitively and inferentially the other selves with whom we interact. If God chooses to interact with a triadic human experience, then the human experience touched by God will perceive the divine reality as a transcendent, autonomous, personal tendency to act in specific ways, i.e. as a personal self. The Judeo-Christian tradition calls that autonomous divine self the Holy Spirit."[229]

Because God is an experience, and the Spirit the "mind" of the triune life, God is intelligible and may be revealed in human experience, able to be "felt and received," both directly and sacramentally. Direct experience is possible when God "touches us without created intermediaries"; for example, in "moments of solitude [where] the human heart can expand to a sense of the divine presence." Alternatively, sacramental perception of God occurs "when He touches us in the words and deeds of persons he has graciously transformed."[230]

This transformation may also be understood as "conversion," which is an important concept for Gelpi. Conversion is not limited here to a religious understanding, and can occur naturally, in everyday ways not

227. Gelpi, *Divine Mother*, 95. Gelpi notes that a number of American thinkers have been attracted to panentheism, among them Jonathan Edwards, Josiah Royce and William James. He also distinguishes his panentheism from that of process philosophy, as well as that of Jürgen Moltmann. Among other reasons, Gelpi is reluctant to commit to the "dialectical understanding of creation which Moltmann defends" (ibid., 101n.9).

228. Gelpi, *Turn to Experience*, 14.

229. Ibid., 16–17.

230. Gelpi, *Divine Mother*, 94.

immediately prompted by the Spirit. In this "generic sense [conversion] is the decision to assume personal responsibility for the quality of one's subsequent development in some area of human experience."[231] Conversion, then, can occur in a number of dimensions of life: affective, intellectual, socio-political, moral, speculative, and religious.[232] It is only the last of these (in its Christian form) in which the Spirit is explicitly or directly active: "religious conversion transforms and transvalues the other forms of conversion and endows them with ultimate meaning and purpose."[233] The New Testament provides ample witness to the ways the Spirit "converts" Christians in their experiences, including providing gracious illumination, a sense of commission (being sent as witness), forgiveness ("purification"), inspiration to bear prophetic witness against the forces that crucified Jesus, liberation, application of the atonement, sanctification and a variety of charisms.[234]

Aside from experience of God, Gelpi also demonstrates how the triadic construct helps reveal the personhood of the Holy Breath, and provides an analogous social model for understanding the perichoretic relationship within the Trinity without loss of the autonomy of the divine persons.[235] He also sees promise in the triadic model for providing a more "dynamic interpretation of the hypostatic union," and for interpreting the reality of the church as the community enlivened by the Holy Breath.[236]

LOCATING GELPI'S APPEAL TO EXPERIENCE

Locating Gelpi's appeal to experience is somewhat less of a challenge in some respects, since he is familiar with Schner's continuum and proposes that his own triadic construct of experience falls closest to the

231. Ibid., 33.

232. Gelpi, "Response," 31, 36, cf. 31–36; Gelpi, *Divine Mother*, 33.

233. Gelpi, *Divine Mother*, 33; "Response," 36. For example, Christian religious conversion transforms affective, intellectual, moral, and socio-political "conversions" into Christian hope, faith, charity, and opposition to injustice respectively.

234. Gelpi, *Divine Mother*, 73–74, 198–202. Gelpi elsewhere also says every Christian ought to experience a "Pentecostal moment when gospel living matures into charismatic service of the Christian and human communities" (Gelpi, "Response," 36).

235. Gelpi, *Divine Mother*, 103–24, 125–50.

236. Gelpi, *Turn to Experience*, 152, cf. 152–56.

"appeal constructive."[237] This is because the triadic model avoids the fallacies of di-polar constructs, including becoming trapped in hermeneutical and epistemological suspicion. Gelpi can acknowledge the "interpreted character of human experience"; but rather than this being a barrier to knowledge of reality, a triadic construct "recognizes that through evaluation and interpretation we become present to our world and it to us."[238] God interacts with us and yet remains distinct and so can always confront us. On the other hand, Gelpi's attention to the Spirit's mission as presently defined by the Son, and emphasis on Scripture and ecclesial tradition indicates that he preserves sufficient roots upon which to construct a theology of experience, while yet allowing him to move theologically into the future, not becoming restricted by fundamentalism, in which only tradition can mediate experience of God.[239]

Vladimir Lossky and Eastern Orthodox Mystical Theology

In *The Mystical Theology of the Eastern Church*, Eastern Orthodox theologian Vladimir Nikolaevich Lossky (1903–58)[240] argues for the inseparability of Christian dogma and mysticism as the necessary elements in moving humanity towards God's intended goal, which is deification (or *theosis*).[241] Lossky uses the term "mystical theology" to descriptively encompass what he considers to be the appropriate "doctrinal attitude" leading to union with God through access to the divine mystery.[242] Since Christianity's foundational doctrine, the Trinity, is both a theological revelation and yet also an "unfathomable mystery," therefore, he argues, both "theology and mysticism support and complete each other."[243] Mystical experience finds its grounding, then, in theology (which is public), while the Church is also able to encourage personal experience

---

237. Ibid., 146.

238. Ibid. See also Gelpi, "Response," 36–40. Gelpi's use of Peirce allows for a fallibilistic epistemology that avoids traditional metaphysics demanding a priori universal and necessary knowledge. Gelpi's metaphysic is thus potentially universal, but not necessary—always open to verification and revision.

239. Gelpi, *Turn to Experience*, 147.

240. See "Lossky, Vladimir Nikolaevich," 787.

241. Lossky, *Mystical Theology*, 9–11.

242. Ibid., 7.

243. Ibid., 8.

of God among its members.[244] Personal mystical experiences may be "secret" (ineffable), says Lossky, but mysticism is not ultimately private, since it is integral to theologizing.[245]

Mystical theology, then, necessarily begins in "darkness"; God's nature is "unknowable," and "absolutely incomprehensible."[246] This truth, Lossky explains, is what the Church has historically defended (in the councils), and must strive to preserve over against theological approaches that attempt to comprehend God through the intellect (or the senses).[247] "If in seeing God one can know what one sees," he states, "then one has not seen God in Himself but something intelligible, something which is inferior to Him."[248] Such positive, or *cataphatic*, theology can never ultimately lead to true knowledge of or participation in the divine, since God is always beyond human understanding.[249] The divine mystery demands adopting an *apophatic*, or negative, theology, which is another way of describing what Lossky means by "mystical theology."[250] He states,

> It is by *unknowing* . . . that one may know Him who is above every possible object of knowledge. Proceeding by negations one ascends from the inferior degrees of being to the highest, by progressively setting aside all that can be known, in order to draw near to the Unknown in the darkness of absolute ignorance. For even as light, and especially abundance of light, renders darkness invisible; even so the knowledge of created things, and especially excess of knowledge, destroys the ignorance which is the only way by which one can attain to God in Himself.[251]

Knowing God comes paradoxically, through an "awareness of the incomprehensibility of the divine nature," which "corresponds to experience: to a meeting with the personal God of revelation."[252] The

244. Ibid., 9. Since Lossky has the Eastern Orthodox Church in view, we will capitalize "Church" in this subsection.

245. Ibid., 21.

246. Ibid., 25, 28.

247. Ibid., 32, 48; Lossky, *Vision of God*, 10.

248. Lossky, *Mystical Theology*, 25.

249. Ibid., 25, 39. Lossky states that the cataphatic method is at best only moderately helpful, and only insofar as it leads us towards the recognition of the incomprehensibility of God (ibid., 39, 41).

250. Ibid., 28.

251. Ibid., 25 (italics original).

252. Ibid., 34.

goal of theology, then, is pursuit of "an experience which passes all understanding."[253] This is the apophatic way, which may include moments of "ecstasy," but which is not limited to such. This way is, rather, "an expression of that fundamental attitude which transforms the whole theology into a contemplation of the mysteries of revelation."[254]

For Lossky it is important to understand that the goal of apophatic theology is the Trinity; not God's nature or essence, or even a person. The Trinity is that which transcends all of these concepts.[255] God's threefoldness is the starting point, the ineffable "base of all theological contemplation," not deducible from any other principles.[256] Contrary to the Latin approach, which begins "from one essence in order to arrive at the three persons," Eastern Orthodoxy safeguards the divine mystery, says Lossky, having as its point of departure the "concrete," "the three hypostases," and "seeing in them the one nature"[257]

Consistent with his tradition, Lossky asserts that the unity of the Godhead is preserved through the Father's monarchy (which is one reason the East has rejected the *filioque*).[258] The three hypostases indwell one another, but work by "a single will, a single power, a single operation."[259] What distinguishes the hypostases, then, is "relation of origin."[260] The Father is the source from which Son and Spirit proceed in different (ineffable) modes; thus, to say that the Son is begotten and that the Spirit proceeds "is sufficient to distinguish them."[261] This theological approach is necessarily apophatic, since the origin of relation is "above all a negation, showing us that the Father is neither the Son nor the Holy Spirit; that the Son is neither the Father nor the Spirit; that the Holy Spirit is neither the Father nor the Son."[262] While ineffable, yet so too, "The Trinity is, for

253. Ibid., 38.

254. Ibid., 42.

255. Ibid., 44.

256. Ibid., 47–48.

257. Ibid., 52. Lossky believes the Latin approach tends to obscure the "reality of God in Trinity" due to its giving itself over to a particular and unbiblical "philosophy of essence" (ibid., 64).

258. Ibid., 58–62. The Father is the "unique source of Godhead and principle unity of the three . . ." (ibid., 62).

259. Ibid., 53.

260. Ibid., 54.

261. Ibid., 55.

262. Ibid., 54.

the Orthodox Church, [also] the unshakable foundation of all religious thought, of all piety, of all experience. It is the Trinity we seek in seeking after God . . ."[263]

But another mystery emerges here, according to Lossky, for Scripture also identifies the Trinity as being both accessible and yet inaccessible.[264] The Bible speaks both of the inability of humans to "see" God and live, while also affirming the possibility of seeing God in beatific vision.[265] Mystical theology "cannot accommodate itself to a transcendent God," since Christians are promised union with God in deification. But even less so is it "able to envisage a God immanent and accessible to creatures,"[266] since the Trinity is fundamentally incomprehensible and "is an absolute stability."[267] For Lossky, there is no movement or evolution within the Trinity, and no direct access into the essence of the Godhead, which would introduce more than three hypostases into the divine life; humans cannot participate in God's essence or hypostases.[268] "Nevertheless," he asserts, "the divine promise cannot be an illusion: we are called to participate in the divine nature. We are therefore compelled to recognize in God an ineffable distinction other than between His essence and His persons, according to which He is, under different aspects, both totally inaccessible and at the same time accessible."[269]

Here Lossky draws on the theology of Gregory Palamas (1296–1359), who affirms God as both communicable and incommunicable.[270] To speak of (not comprehend) this mystery, the Eastern Church distinguishes "between God's essence and His energies," the latter being exterior manifestations of the Trinity.[271] Explains Lossky,

263. Ibid., 65.

264. Ibid., 68; Lossky, *Vision of God*, 9–20.

265. Lossky, *Vision of God*, 9, 22–26. On the former point Lossky cites, for example, the inability of Moses to see God's face (Exod 33:20–23) and the assertion in 1 John 4:12 that no one has ever seen God (among other references). On the latter, he cites Jacob's wrestling with God (Gen 32:24–30), and 1 John 3:1–2 and 1 Cor 13:12 as the key texts in the New Testament.

266. Lossky, *Mystical Theology*, 68.

267. Ibid., 45.

268. Ibid., 45–46, 70.

269. Ibid., 70.

270. Lossky, *Vision of God*, 127, cf. 124–37.

271. Lossky, *Mystical Theology*, 71; cf. Lossky, *Vision of God*, 10, 127–28.

God's presence in His energies must be understood in a realistic sense. It is not the presence of a cause operative in its effects: for energies are not effects of the divine cause, as creatures are; they are not created, formed *ex nihilo*, but flow from the outpourings of the divine nature which cannot set bounds to itself, for God is more than essence. The energies might be described as that mode of existence of the Trinity which is outside of its inaccessible essence. God thus exists both in His essence and outside of His essence.[272]

The energies are not contingent on creaturely existence, "just as the rays of the sun would shine out from the solar disk whether or not there were any beings capable of receiving their light." Yet, "the created world does not become infinite and coeternal with God because the natural processions, or divine energies, are so."[273] Human experience of God, including deification, is participation *in the energies* of the Trinity, but *not the essence* of divine life.

Within Lossky's mystical theology the human vocation has always been to attain union with God, to unite creation with the divine.[274] Humanity was created in God's image and likeness, perfect, yet not deified. So, the divine goal has always been to unite the human and divine natures (deification), and grace (by the divine energies) has always been operating to this end.[275] God's image is primarily exemplified in human personhood but not human nature, personhood accenting the freedom to not be determined by nature.[276] Personhood also implies that the deification process has always required two wills: the divine will granting grace, and the human will obediently submitting to this process. Thus experience of God involves human participation.[277] The introduction of sin into creation (by human free will) did not alter the human calling, but did introduce death into creation, and limited the operation of

272. Lossky, *Mystical Theology*, 73 (italics original).

273. Ibid., 74. Lossky later insists also that creation is contingent on God's will and denies its co-eternality. He does this partly in reaction against sophiology, such as that exemplified in Bulgakov (ibid., 93–96).

274. Ibid., 117, 110.

275. Ibid., 126, 117.

276. Ibid., 120, 122.

277. Ibid., 127–28.

uncreated grace (the energies) to having only external effect upon, and not within, humans (until Pentecost).[278]

Lossky indicates that Christ's mission—his assumption, death, and resurrection—is that which provided the way to overcome the "triple barrier of sin, death and nature."[279] This work enables the reunification of humanity with divine *nature*.[280] Further, the Spirit's work at Pentecost complementarily introduces "the possibility of fulfilling the *likeness* [of God] in the common [human] nature."[281] The work of Christ and Spirit are thus inseparable. Pentecost, however, while made possible by the Incarnation, should not be understood as simply its "continuation"; it is, rather, the "sequel" or "result" of the Incarnation.[282] Pentecost is the Spirit's "personal coming, when He appeared as a Person of the Trinity, independent of the Son as to His hypostatic origin, though sent into the world 'in the name of the Son.'"[283] Pentecost and the Insufflation (John 20) together serve to constitute the Church, the new body of humanity, formed by Christ, and filled by the Spirit.[284]

As such, for Lossky the Church should be "regarded as the sphere wherein the union of human persons with God is accomplished. . . . It is therefore necessary to be united to the body of Christ in order to receive the grace of the Holy Spirit."[285] While the Spirit may be viewed, in some sense, as sustaining all creation, the Spirit's activity of conferring divine

278. Ibid., 130, 132–33. Separation from God, then, is not only a matter of nature but also will (ibid., 135).

279. Ibid., 135. Christ's assumption united divine and human natures, death overcame sin, and resurrection conquered death (ibid., 154).

280. Ibid., 159, 166.

281. Ibid., 166–67 (italics added).

282. Ibid., 159. Indeed, "Pentecost is thus the object, the final goal, of the divine economy upon earth."

283. Ibid., 168. This distinction is explained further: "The one [Christ] lends his hypostases to the nature, the other gives His divinity to the [human] persons. Thus, the work of Christ unifies; the work of the Spirit diversifies. Yet, the one is impossible without the other" (ibid., 167).

284. Ibid., 166, 156. Lossky differentiates between the Insufflation and Pentecost as two distinct "communications" of the Spirit to the Church. The first is a "functional" giving of the Spirit to the Church as a whole as a "bond of unity." The second is a "personal coming" to each believer (thus "personal") within the Church (ibid., 167, 168).

285. Ibid., 177. It is thus through the Spirit that the Trinity dwells within and confers energies upon humanity. While the Spirit confers uncreated grace, the Spirit is to be distinguished from the energies (ibid., 171–72).

energies (toward deification) occurs only within the Church.[286] "Thus, in relation to union with God, the universe is arranged in concentric circles about a centre which is occupied by the Church, the members of which become sons of God. . . . The Church is the centre of the universe, the sphere in which its destinies are determined. All are called to enter the Church . . ."[287]

The Church, as sphere of deification of the new humanity, will ultimately also benefit the cosmos.[288] Lossky asserts, however, that the Church is only obligated to avoid acting according to the world (system), and to continue focusing its attention on the mystery of the Trinity through apophatic mystical theology, which implies little need for attention to socio-political issues.[289] This is not to deny that God is working to renew creation and eradicate injustice, but to simply affirm and emphasize that God's means toward this end are ineffable.

For Lossky, then, the arena for experience of God is the Church, since this is where the process of deification occurs.[290] Members of Christ's body must cooperate with God's grace in this "way of union" in a cooperative synergetic process, submitting their wills to the conferring of the energies (grace) by the Spirit.[291] How grace and human freedom function together to this end is a mystery, but acceptance of this cooperative reality is necessary and fundamental. The journey toward deification must be, therefore, "personal, conscious and voluntary,"[292] involving the practice of virtues (e.g., fasting, vigils, and alms), repentance, and above all prayer.[293] In prayer one may very well experience moments of

286. Ibid., 177–78.

287. Ibid., 178.

288. Ibid., 112. On this point Lossky criticizes Bulgakov's sophiology as an "ecclesiology gone astray," since it collapses the Church into the cosmos, i.e., "the Cosmos is the Church."

289. Ibid., 246.

290. Ibid., 177. Lossky states, "It is therefore necessary to be united to the body of Christ in order to receive the grace [energies] of the Holy Spirit."

291. Ibid., 196, 200–205. Lossky states, "If God has given us in the Church all the objective conditions, all the means that we need for the attainment of this end, we, on our side, must produce the necessary subjective conditions: for it is in this synergy, in this co-operation of man and God, that the union is fulfilled. This subjective aspect of our union with God constitutes the way of union which is the Christian life" (ibid., 196).

292. Ibid., 207.

293. Ibid., 196–97, 204–6, cf. 206–12. Prayer is especially accented, since the move to union with God is toward personal relationship.

ecstasy, but these are not the goal; rather "the fruit of prayer is divine love" toward God and fellow humans.[294]

Lossky's mystical theology, which began with "darkness," concludes with a mystical vision of God in "Light." Scripture, he claims, portrays God as "Light," implying that God "cannot remain foreign to our experience."[295] God incomprehensible will be made visible to the deified. While this beatific vision ultimately belongs to the eschaton, nevertheless, some may attain, "even in this life," a vision of this "uncreated light," a "visible quality of the divinity, of the energies or grace in which God makes himself known."[296] This is a "mystical experience [surpassing] at the same time both sense and intellect," and is not "comprehensible to those who have not had it."[297] But even without such an experience, Christians in "proper spiritual health" should in general find themselves consciously aware of the Spirit's presence (via the energies) operating in their life, moving them toward union with God.[298]

LOCATING LOSSKY'S APPEAL TO EXPERIENCE

Lossky's appeal to experience occurs in dynamic tension between the "appeal confessional" and the "appeal immediate and mystical" (as is perhaps already evident in the term "mystical theology"). The confessional element is evident in his accent on the Church as "the centre of the universe," the locus of the missions of both Son and Spirit, and the sphere in which the divine energies actively move believers toward deification.[299] This is further exemplified in viewing the Church's duty and mission as contemplation and preservation of the mystery of the Trinity, while giving considerably less emphasis to socio-political affairs outside the ecclesial arena. The "appeal mystical," is demonstrated by Lossky's emphasis on God's incomprehensibility to human intellect and senses, while yet acknowledging private and ineffable moments in which the divine may be beheld. This mystical experience is, however, not without content; for it is not experience of a nameless transcendence, but of

---

294. Ibid., 212.

295. Ibid., 218.

296. Ibid., 220, 221; cf. Lossky, *Vision of God*, 130–33.

297. Lossky, *Mystical Theology*, 221, 231.

298. Ibid., 225, cf. 171–72.

299. Ibid., 178.

the revealed Trinity, and occurs within the particularity of the Eastern Orthodox theological tradition.

Sergius Bulgakov and Experience in Creaturely Sophia

Sergius (Sergei) Nikolaevich Bulgakov (1871–1944) was a Russian Orthodox priest and theologian,[300] who, while (in his words) affirming all the dogmas of the Orthodox Church, interprets all theology and the world sophiologically. For Bulgakov, sophiology is more than a particular doctrine within theology. Rather, "The sophiological point of view brings a special interpretation to bear on *all* Christian teaching and dogma, beginning with the doctrine of the Holy Trinity and the Incarnation and ending with questions of practical everyday Christianity in our own time."[301] Sophiology serves, then, as an overarching framework for understanding the "relation between *God* and world, or, what is practically the same thing, between *God* and *humanity*."[302]

The need for a renewed understanding of the relationship between these two "worlds" (divine and creaturely), and revealing where Bulgakov begins his appeal to experience, is his observation of the existence of two seemingly incompatible poles in relation to the Christian attitude toward life. He identifies these two poles as "dualism" and "monism," or, put another way, "world-denying Manicheism" and "secularism."[303] The Church, he claims, has often been guilty of the former, having become, in Thomas Hopko's words, "caught up in cultic ecclesiasticism," distancing itself from world affairs in its pursuit of union with God,[304] and resulting in an "anti-cosmism."[305] For those unable to deny the significance of the world and nature, the only alternative seemed to be "cosmism" (secularism), in which God's existence is denied or becomes practically irrelevant.[306]

---

300. See "Bulgakov, Sergei Nikolaevich," 237.

301. Bulgakov, *Sophia*, 13 (italics original). As with Lossky, "Church" will be capitalized in this subsection, referring to the Eastern Orthodox Church.

302. Ibid., 14 (italics original).

303. Ibid., 14–15.

304. Bulgakov, *Orthodox Church*, XII.

305. Bulgakov, *Sophia*, 20.

306. Ibid.

In response, Bulgakov aims to overcome these poles, uniting the creaturely and divine worlds in "one divine-human theocosmism."[307] He begins by advocating that the consubstantiality of the Trinity has not been sufficiently examined, and deserves closer reflection.[308] To this end, Bulgakov looks to the Bible, which provides clues as to the "substance of God" based on the concepts of the "Wisdom of God" ("Sophia") and the "Glory of God" ("Shekinah").[309] He rejects theological interpretations that identify Wisdom with the Logos or any hypostasis in the Godhead.[310] Wisdom and Glory are not two created principles or properties of God, and differ "from God's personal being" while yet being "inseparably bound up with it."[311] Wisdom and Glory can be differentiated (as content and manifestation respectively), and yet "can in no way be separated from one another."[312] So, how are Wisdom and Glory related to the Trinity? Bulgakov affirms that together they *are* the substance, the essence, the *ousia* of God—"ousia stands precisely for Wisdom and Glory." The "divinity in God constitutes the divine Sophia (or Glory), while at the same time . . . it is also the ousia: Ousia = Sophia = Glory."[313]

Sophia, then, is not a "fourth hypostasis," or a reality behind the triune hypostases, but is the substance of the divine life, inseparable from it.[314] Explains Bulgakov, "The tri-hypostatic God possesses, indeed but one Godhead, Sophia; possesses it in such way that at the same time it belongs to each of the divine persons, in-accordance with the properties distinguishing each of these persons (just in the same way each possesses the one common Ousia). Ousia-Sophia is distinct from the hypostases, though it cannot exist apart from them and is eternally hypostatized in them."[315]

---

307. Ibid., 17, 20. Bulgakov was influenced here by German idealism and the sophiology of Vladimir Solovyov.

308. Ibid., 23–24.

309. Ibid., 25–26, 29–30.

310. Ibid., 26, 28.

311. Ibid., 30.

312. Ibid., 31. Bulgakov elsewhere associates these as being aspects of the Logos and Spirit's (the "Dyad's") involvement in the creaturely world in Sophia, although distinguishing these from their hypostases (Bulgakov, *Comforter*, 177–89).

313. Bulgakov, *Sophia*, 33, cf. 32.

314. Ibid., 35; Bulgakov, *Comforter*, 55.

315. Bulgakov, *Sophia*, 33–34, cf. 37–53. Elsewhere, Bulgakov states, "Divine Sophia possesses being not only for the hypostatic tri-unity but also in herself . . . She . . . is . . .

Having so established Sophia as the Ousia of the triune life in the "divine" realm, Bulgakov moves on to address Sophia's relationship to the "creaturely" realm. To begin, God's creation of the world from "nothing" implies that creation has no source but God.[316] The act of creation introduces nothing new to the divine life, nor is the world necessary for God; yet there must be a relational correspondence between the inner triune life and the power of God that sustains the world.[317] The creaturely world must, in some sense, mirror the divine world, the latter serving as the prototype for the former. Thus, the Wisdom of God is "a prototype of creation existing with God prior to the creation of the world."[318] The Trinity created the world "on the *foundation* of the foundation of the Wisdom common to the whole Trinity."[319] So, "God the Father creates the world by Sophia, which is the revelation of the Son and of the Holy Spirit."[320]

The created realm, asserts Bulgakov, is thus permeated by Sophia (Ousia), while yet remaining distinct from the life of the divine hypostases. The world "exists outside God" (distinguishing Christianity from pantheism), yet so too "Wisdom in creation is ontologically identical with its prototype, the same Wisdom that exists in God. [And so] the world exists in God . . ."[321] Again, "Nothing can exist outside of God, as alien or exterior to him," since in fact it was "nothing" from which God created the world.[322] The world, then, is related to God *panentheistically*.[323] Creation, being in God, is energized by God and no other source; yet the distinction between the divine hypostases and creation is maintained—God's personality is not the means by which God and the world exist in relationship.[324] Here Bulgakov affirms the teaching of Gregory

---

also a *spiritual* principle, the spirituality of the trihypostatic spirit. She exists inseparably from the divine trihypostatizedness but *not* indistinguishable from it" (Bulgakov, *Comforter*, 155 [italics original], cf. 53–67, 153–76).

316. Bulgakov, *Sophia*, 72.

317. Bulgakov, *Sophia*, 61–63, 73.

318. Ibid., 65.

319. Ibid., 67 (italics original).

320. Ibid., 69, cf. 71–72.

321. Ibid., 71–72.

322. Ibid., 72.

323. Ibid. Bulgakov at times refers to his panentheism as a "pious" pantheism (Bulgakov, *Comforter*, 199–200).

324. Bulgakov, *Comforter*, 200. Bulgakov not only speaks of the hypostases as

Palamas concerning the "uncreated energies" that penetrate creation and are "nonhypostatic."[325] Unlike Lossky, however, he attributes the fact of God's energy in creation, giving "life to the world," to the *substance* of divinity in creation.[326]

Bulgakov states that in "creating the world . . . God communicates to it something of the vigor of his own being, and, in the divine Sophia, unites the world with his own divine life. Insofar as the creature is able to bear it, God communicates Sophia, the creaturely Sophia, to creation."[327] The mediation between the divine and creaturely worlds occurs, then, not by the divine hypostases, but by the divine Ousia. "Sophia unites God with the world as one common principle, the divine ground of creaturely existence." So, Sophia exists in "two modes, eternal and temporal, divine and creaturely."[328] The "creaturely Sophia" grounds creation, characterizing it with "becoming, emergence, development [and] fulfillment," as Sophia, through the Logos and Spirit, moves creation toward union with God.[329]

The fact of creaturely Sophia has implications, for Bulgakov, concerning the operation of grace, the activity of God, in and among human beings. The soteriological goal of the (human) creature in the Eastern Orthodox tradition is deification, and grace is granted for the creature to synergistically participate to this end.[330] But unlike (Western) Roman Catholic theology, grace is not to be categorized as "natural" or "supernatural."[331] Rather, the presence of creaturely Sophia means that for humans, made in God's image, grace does *not* operate in a *coercive or mechanical* way.[332] Instead, "the natural sophianicity of creation constitutes the general condition of its reception." It is in fact the divine image

---

persons, but at times the Trinity as "Hypostasis" (Bulgakov, *Sophia*, 52; cf. Bulgakov, *Comforter*, 55). Lossky criticizes Bulgakov on this and other aspects of his sophiology (Lossky, *Mystical Theology*, 62 n. 1, 80, 96, 112).

325. Bulgakov, *Bride of the Lamb*, 309, cf. 5, 75.

326. Bulgakov, *Comforter*, 200.

327. Bulgakov, *Sophia*, 73.

328. Ibid., 74.

329. Ibid., 72, 75. Bulgakov distinguishes the operation of the "spirit of God" (God's essence—Sophia) from the activities of the Holy Spirit in this regard, although these are intricately related (Bulgakov, *Comforter*, 153–76).

330. Bulgakov, *Bride of the Lamb*, 294, 296–97.

331. Ibid., 295.

332. Ibid., 298.

in humans, "man's sophianicity," that "makes him open to sophianization" (deification).[333] Humans thus have a natural receptivity to grace
and an ability to participate toward deification by virtue of existence in
the creaturely Sophia.[334] By nature, then, humans are (in some sense)
"theandric."[335]

Due to the fall, thinks Bulgakov, the presence of Sophia has been
darkened and needs to be awakened.[336] Through the Incarnation and
Pentecost, both enabled by Sophia's simultaneous existence in divine
and creaturely modes, sanctification is again made possible.[337] The
Incarnation unites the worlds of creature and God, and the Spirit is
poured out in order to "elevate humanity . . . all the way to the heights of
divine inspiration . . ."[338]

As might be expected, for Bulgakov, the locus of the Spirit's activity
is the Church, the "Body of Christ, which lives with the life of Christ,
[and] is by that fact the domain where the Holy Spirit lives and works."[339]
It is through the Church that "we participate in the divine life of the Holy
Trinity, it is life in the Holy Spirit by which we become children of the
Father . . ."[340] It is the Church that is fully "theandric" in character, and
"Divine-humanity *in actu*."[341] In the Church, both divine and creaturely
Sophia "mutually permeate one another and are entirely, inseparably and
unconfusedly united."[342]

Within the Church, then, the way of sanctification and deification are fully made available. Cooperation of the creature is necessary
toward this end, and "in striving toward union with the divine life, a
creaturely being cannot fail to encounter God *personally*, so to speak;
and this encounter is not a hypostatic union of two natures but an encounter or union of hypostases, divine and creaturely."[343] With regard

333. Ibid., 300.

334. Ibid., 299.

335. Bulgakov, *Sophia*, 85.

336. Bulgakov, *Bride of the Lamb*, 300.

337. See Bulgakov, *Sophia*, 88–96, 98–102.

338. Ibid., 100.

339. Bulgakov, *Orthodox Church*, 2.

340. Ibid., 3.

341. Bulgakov, *Sophia*, 134 (italics original).

342. Ibid., 134.

343. Bulgakov, *Bride of the Lamb*, 303 (italics original). The sophianic nuances in
this description are quite notable here, accenting the link between divine and creaturely

to participation toward deification, Bulgakov identifies prayer as the act that best exemplifies and moves the sanctification process along, since (sophianistically) the "union of natures is embodied in prayer."[344] Elsewhere Bulgakov also notes the importance of openness to interior (yet objective) ineffable mystical experiences that further the unification process as being fundamental to Orthodox spirituality. Here, prayer is again held up as the key means by which to acquire the power of the Holy Spirit in the Christian life.[345]

But how does Bulgakov's sophiology impact Orthodox ecclesiology with regard to experience of God? We have already noted the Church's grounding in divine Wisdom, and ecclesiology's link to Christology—the Church is both Christ's body and the temple of the Spirit (through the Incarnation and Pentecost).[346] The Church "in the world," therefore, "is Sophia in process of becoming, according to the double impulse of creation and deification . . ."[347] Further, within the Church, the sacraments serve as the "regular channel of communication with God." But these "are by no means the only channel in such a sense that would exclude all others."[348] The boundaries of the Church, as it were, are not always well defined,[349] nor should it be identified solely with any "specific ecclesiastical organization," keeping in mind its sophianic and mystical nature.[350] The issue of the "Church and the churches," then, is left unresolved.

Even more ambitiously, however, Bulgakov asserts that the boundaries of the Church are to be viewed as expanding into the cosmos. The efficacy of the Incarnation and Pentecost "are universal," implying a sense in which, "all humankind is the body of Christ," and meaning the Church should "keep silent" in regard to the salvation of those outside its ecclesiastical boundaries.[351] Since the Church is also "Divine-humanity

---

realms.

344. Ibid., 303.

345. Bulgakov, *Orthodox Church*, 145–49. Of special importance is the "Prayer of Jesus" ("Lord Jesus Christ, Son of God, have mercy on me a sinner."), which, due in part to the power of the name of Jesus to bring deification, may be prayed (progressively) on oral, mental/psychic, and finally (ineffably) spiritual levels.

346. Bulgakov, *Sophia*, 134–35; cf. Bulgakov, *Orthodox Church*, 7.

347. Bulgakov, *Sophia*, 136.

348. Ibid., 138.

349. Bulgakov, *Orthodox Church*, 7; cf. Bulgakov, *Bride of the Lamb*, 313.

350. Bulgakov, *Bride of the Lamb*, 310–12.

351. Ibid., 313.

in history and develops through history [it] is inseparable from the life of humankind in time." Further, given that humanity is "lord of creation," the Spirit's work in the Church also extends to the realm of nature (the cosmos).[352] "Nature is not alien to the Church; it belongs to it."[353] The Church in its essence, therefore, has a "social mission" leading it "to extend its solicitude to, and accept responsibility for, the redemption not only of the individual personality, but also of social life."[354] Where appropriate, then, the Church must resist social and political forces that oppose God.[355]

In addition, says Bulgakov, the Spirit's activity is not restricted to the Church, since the Spirit is inseparable from (although not identical with) the creaturely Sophia. Through creaturely Sophia matter is able to receive the Spirit, who is the life-force in every aspect of creation, working kenotically, and influencing creation without affecting it in a mechanistic or coercive manner.[356] A social and even natural evolution, of sorts, then, is enabled by Sophia through the Spirit.[357] With regard to revelation, "pagans" too may experience Sophia as the "world soul," and even have "mystical experiences although they do not contain a true revelation of God." Non-Christian religions, then, "are not empty *sophianically*."[358] All humans, by virtue of their "sophianicity" and the working of "spirit" have a "capacity for" or "faculty of inspiration," by "the source of all inspiration, the Holy Spirit." This inspiration, while "not a *direct* Revelation of God Himself about God Himself," is nevertheless a "manifestation of spirit" and "precondition" for the realization of "Divine inspiration" and true revelation.[359]

352. Bulgakov, *Sophia*, 140, cf. 139–41.

353. Ibid., 141.

354. Ibid., 143, 144.

355. Ibid., 144–45.

356. Bulgakov, *Comforter*, 220–21, cf. 219–27. Thus, even God's enemies, the demonic, live and have being by the Spirit.

357. Bulgakov, *Sophia*, 144; Bulgakov, *Comforter*, 207–8. The teleology of natural evolution is guided by the Logos.

358. Bulgakov, *Comforter*, 214 (italics original).

359. Ibid., 216 (italics original). Bulgakov differentiates here, it will be noted, between "spirit" and "Spirit," the former referring to a common human spirit enabled, ultimately, by creaturely Sophia and the Holy Spirit.

LOCATING BULGAKOV'S APPEAL TO EXPERIENCE

Bulgakov's appeal to experience is challenging to locate due, on the one hand, to his commitment to Eastern Orthodox dogma and tradition; and on the other, to his ambiguity as to the scope of the revelatory influence of Sophia outside of the Church. His emphasis, for example, on the universal applicability of the Incarnation and Pentecost, enabled by creaturely Sophia, at times is reminiscent of the "appeal transcendental." His talk of encounter somewhat echoes the language of the "appeal constructive"; however, his qualification of this as occurring through the kenotic work of the Spirit would again indicate transcendental leanings. At the same time, his commitment to Eastern Orthodox theology and mystical tradition also demonstrates aspects of both the "appeal confessional" and "immediate and mystical." It is at this point that we need to be reminded of Schner's observation that at times the two ends of his proposed continuum may indeed meet, and perhaps Bulgakov should be taken as an instance of this.

Jürgen Moltmann and the Experience of the Spirit of Life

Jürgen Moltmann is a Protestant theologian in the Reformed tradition,[360] and an important voice to include here because he has written considerably on the subject of experience of God,[361] and has dialogued directly with Pentecostals concerning the subject of the Spirit.[362] We will focus here on his portrayal of how God is experienced in creation and history, and its effect on human understanding of God. These issues are located, however, within a broader theological framework involving his theology of history (eschatology of hope), the Trinity, creation, and the church.[363]

---

360. See Vlach, "Jürgen Moltmann."

361. See especially Moltmann, *Spirit of Life*; Moltmann, *Experiences in Theology*; Moltmann, *Experiences of God*; and to a lesser extent in Moltmann, *God in Creation*.

362. See, for example, Moltmann, *Spirit of Life*, 180–97. This work gave rise to several responses from Pentecostal theologians in the *Journal of Pentecostal Theology* 4 (1994). Also see Moltmann and Kuschel, *Pentecostal Movements*; and Althouse, *Spirit of the Last Days*. Althouse's monograph examines Moltmann's influence upon four Pentecostal theologians with regard to eschatology.

363. Moltmann also acknowledges his own life experiences, including being a prisoner in the Second World War, as having had considerable impact on his theology (Moltmann, "Autobiographical Note," 203–23).

To begin, Moltmann's theology is "eschatologically oriented," eschatology serving not as the end but the beginning of theology.[364] Eschatology serves to firmly link God to history; the future coming of God provides the conditions for time itself to exist, and history is bound up with the hope of God's coming (which will transform all history).[365] Present history is the location for experience of God's presence, and the future may be experienced now by the Spirit.[366] Thus, experience of God is historically mediated.

Concerning God, Moltmann posits a doctrine of Social Trinity, emphasizing the interpenetration of the divine persons (*perichoresis*).[367] Further, the redemptive activity of the Economic Trinity affects the life of the Immanent Trinity, the latter experiencing the suffering (and joys) of humanity and creation.[368] This is supplemented by a panentheistic doctrine of creation in which "all things are created by God, formed 'through God,' and exist in God."[369] In formulating this belief, Moltmann appeals to a Kabalistic doctrine of "*zimsum*," in which "creation is fashioned in the emptiness of God ceded for it through his creative resolve."[370] Into this "God-forsaken space" ("*nihil*") God gives his life-giving Spirit

---

364. Moltmann, "Autobiographical Note," 222, cf. 208; Moltmann, *Theology of Hope*, 16.

365. Moltmann, *Coming of God*, 26.

366. Ibid., 13, 22; cf. Moltmann, *Spirit of Life*, 103. A. J. Conyers explains: "Moltmann tilts the axis of classical transcendence from a vertical orientation that directs faith toward a supernatural, superintending deity, to a horizontal orientation that directs faith toward the future—a future anticipated as the coming of God" (Conyers, *God, Hope, and History*, 6).

367. Moltmann, *Trinity and the Kingdom*, viii, 19–20, 88–90, 129–78; Moltmann, *God in Creation*, 16–17; and Moltmann, "Trinitarian History," 636–43. Drawing on Eastern Orthodoxy, Moltmann rejects "monotheistic" hierarchical concepts of the Godhead as well as unidirectional "sending" frameworks.

368. Moltmann, *Trinity and the Kingdom*, 21–30, 47–60, 75–83, 129–77; Moltmann, *God in Creation*, 145–53; *Crucified God*, 239–40. God suffered in Christ's crucifixion and does so now by the Spirit in creation.

369. Moltmann, *God for a Secular Society*, 102. Cf. Moltmann, *Spirit of Life*, 211; and Moltmann, *God in Creation*, 103. Moltmann does attempt to distinguish God from creation by emphasis on God's determination to create that which is other than God (see Moltmann, *Trinity and the Kingdom*, 57–60; and Moltmann, *God in Creation*, 79).

370. Moltmann, *God in Creation*, 156 (italics original).

("*Ruach*").[371] So, all creation exists in and is animated by the energy field of the life-giving Spirit, and is the dwelling place of God.[372]

The Spirit, then, perichoretically links creation and the Godhead,[373] as well as every creature.[374] God's relationship to creation is one of "immanent transcendence," in which God may be experienced, perceived, and revered in all things.[375] The Spirit also preserves and moves creation history to its intended glorification, counteracting the *nihil* by indwelling and localizing its presence within space and time (the concept of "*Shekinah*").[376] Thus God also is a loving and suffering participant within creation history,[377] and must, in fact, experience "history to effect history," to bring it into the "*creatio nova*" (new creation).[378] So, for Moltmann, experience of God is experience of God's experience of the world.[379]

Regarding the church, it is the eschatological creation of the Spirit; and in a unique way it experiences and serves (in some sense) as the locus of the Spirit's presence, gifts, and energies. The church, however, needs to be understood as existing in the "framework" of the Spirit's history with creation.[380] The Spirit is not restricted to the church; rather, the church participates in the Spirit's mission, and in this way pneumatology subsumes ecclesiology.[381] Moltmann defines the mission of the church (and

371. Ibid., 86–87, 95–103 (italics original). Cf. Moltmann, *Spirit of Life*, 40–43; and Moltmann, *Trinity and the Kingdom*, 108–11.

372. Moltmann, "Response," 65; Moltmann, *God in Creation*, 9–11, 88–89, 150, 156–57, 190, 206. For Moltmann, the life-giving Spirit and the redemptive Spirit are emphasized as one in the same (Moltmann, *Spirit of Life*, 7, cf. 9).

373. Moltmann, "Response," 62–63; Moltmann, *Spirit of Life*, 82, 146, 157–59, 178–79; Moltmann, *Trinity and the Kingdom*, 57–59; Moltmann, *God in Creation*, 81–85.

374. Moltmann, *God in Creation*, 11–12, 212; Moltmann, *Spirit of Life*, 31ff.

375. Moltmann, *God in Creation*, 13–17; Moltmann, *Spirit of Life*, 31–38. By the Spirit "every natural creature contains an *immanent transcendence* and transcendence is immanent in every natural creature." Moltmann, "Scope of Renewal," 104 (italics original). Moltmann hopes this view will help restore a proper reverence for creation and prevent further destruction of the ecosystem (Moltmann, *God in Creation*, xiv–xv, 13; and Moltmann, *God for a Secular Society*, 90–99, 102).

376. Moltmann, "Creation and Redemption," 124–27, 130; Moltmann, "Come Holy Spirit," 72–77; Moltmann, *Spirit of Life*, 47–50; Moltmann, *God in Creation*, 87, 96–98.

377. Moltmann, *Spirit of Life*, 51; Moltmann, *God in Creation*, 96, 97.

378. Moltmann, *Church in the Power*, 64; Moltmann, "Come Holy Spirit," 77.

379. Bauckham, *Theology of Jürgen Moltmann*, 226–27.

380. Moltmann, *Church in the Power*, 33–36, 50.

381. Ibid., 64–65, cf. 198, 298. The church does not administer the Spirit, but the Spirit the church (through Word, faith, sacraments, grace, offices, and traditions). The

gospel declaration) as the proclamation of liberation within history.[382] Thus the church's call (and the way it experiences God) is to participate in the unifying of human relationships, human suffering and the joy of the approaching new creation as it moves toward its final Sabbath rest.[383]

The above survey provides the context for Moltmann's theology of revelation and experience of God. Opposed to traditional Protestant restriction of the Spirit to (merely) aiding proclamation of the Word, he instead proposes a mutual Spirit/Word relationship, and further suggests that Spirit is not bound to Word, but rather, Word is bound to Spirit. Implied here is that neither Word nor church is *necessary* to experience of the Spirit.[384] This approach aims to overcome a modernistic dualism in theology between revelation and human experience, which denies that Spirit is revealed in a sensible, experiential way.[385] If revelation and experience remain polar opposites, believes Moltmann, we are left only with inexperience-able revelations, and experiences that carry no revelatory value. Rejecting this as based in Neo-Platonic notions of time and eternity, he appeals instead to his eschatological theology of hope and pneumatological doctrine of creation, which firmly locate the Spirit within history.[386] The Spirit's immanence in creation means that revelation and experience are not contradictory but interconnected; the Spirit is therefore experienced in and through present historical reality. He explains, "By a historical experience of God we mean an experience of God which happens to people in the *medium of history* through historical events, and which is perceived in terms of time. But we mean the reverse too: We can also mean an awareness of reality as history which emerges from experiences of God like this."[387]

The Spirit's indwelling in human experience, God's immanent-transcendence, means God is *experience-able*, and that all experiences in

---

church is wherever there is a manifestation of the Spirit.

382. Ibid., 215–16. Some Pentecostal theologians have asserted their difficulty with Moltmann on this point (Stibbe, "British Appraisal," 14; and Kuzmic, "Croatian War-Time Reading," 23).

383. Moltmann, *Church in the Power*, 63–65.

384. Moltmann, *Spirit of Life*, 2–3, 8. This is because the Spirit can be experienced inwardly, being poured into human hearts.

385. Ibid., 5–7. Moltmann suggests Barth as a dialectical theologian exemplifying this dualism.

386. Ibid., 7.

387. Ibid., 39 (italics added), cf. 39–57.

creation can potentially be of the Spirit.[388] Such also enables human self-transcendence; so, "Every true experience of the self becomes also an experience of the divine spirit of life in the human being."[389] Experience and revelation of God occur, then, in historical events and the human's inner being, within an eschatological context.[390] Therefore, "There are no words of God without human experiences of God's Spirit. So the words of proclamation spoken by the Bible and the church must also be related to the experiences of people today . . ."[391]

The assumptions of modernism, argues Moltmann, have also reduced experience to being that of which one is *consciously aware*, the "active" subject being the conscious determiner of what will qualify as experience.[392] In response (and aside from "mystical ecstasies"),[393] Moltmann wants to take human passivity into account, suggesting a multi-dimensional concept of experience.[394] First, "experiences depend on *sensory impressions*."[395] The body, not simply (or even primarily) human consciousness, also affects experiences.[396] The center of determination is not the human subject, but "is to be found in the event that 'befalls' us, and in its source."[397] Experiences are, therefore, bodily, sensory, and often beyond our control.[398]

Secondly, continues Moltmann, experience involves *social relationships*.[399] Self-perception is largely mediated by others' perception and experience one's self: "We experience ourselves in the experience

---

388. Ibid., 34.

389. Ibid., 35, cf. 7.

390. Ibid., 45.

391. Ibid., 3, cf. 8.

392. Ibid., 19–20, 28–31. Thus, experiences that are "fortuitous, unique, unrepeatable, and for which there is no warrant are no longer perceived at all; they are filtered out" (ibid., 30).

393. Ibid., 19.

394. Ibid., 18–34.

395. Ibid., 19 (italics original). Not all sense impressions are labeled "experiences." The mundane activities of life are not in mind here; experiences are more lasting and affect one's personhood deeply.

396. Ibid., 19–21.

397. Ibid., 23. The "person who experiences" is not master, but is in fact "changed in the process of experiencing."

398. Ibid., 34.

399. Ibid., 23–27.

of other people."[400] Human experiences are also "shared experiences," while "exclusively individual" experiences remain private and incommunicable.[401] This dimension also accounts for "collective experiences," which shape those within a given culture or society consciously or unconsciously, and "acquire fixed form in external institutions and in psychological attitudes."[402] Thirdly, "the *religious dimension of experience*," falls beyond experiences of events and people. It is not cut off from daily life, but is "present in, with and beneath all our experiences of things, events and people"; it is a "tacit dimension" providing the "preconditions for all the various experiences of life."[403]

So, the Spirit is not experienced in other than the sensual (bodily), historical, social, and religious (preconditional) dimensions of existence.[404] The Spirit's immanence allows for potential discovery of "transcendence in every experience"; and "Every experience can possess a transcendent, *inward* side."[405] So, God's transcendence is immanently mediated within creation and history.[406] Further (and significant for Pentecostals), immanent-transcendence makes room for special, intense experiences of the Spirit without severing these from everyday life. Says Moltmann, "Given the premise that God is experienced in the experience of the world and life, it once again becomes possible to talk about special experiences of God in the contingent and exceptional phenomena which are called 'holy,' without having to declare everything else profane."[407] The above enables a spirituality of life, in which experiences of the Spirit and senses are not contrasted, Gnostic body/soul dualisms are avoided, political involvement is encouraged, and the love and relationships of life are affirmed.[408]

God's immanent-transcendence also affects, for Moltmann, the hermeneutical process by which the voice of the Spirit is discerned. Life

400. Ibid., 24, cf. 23. "[B]eing human means being-in-relationship, human subjectivity is only possible in inter-subjectivity" (ibid., 25).

401. Ibid., 25. Moltmann states that some shared "experiences actually confer community between people," and are usually transmitted by way of narrative (shared stories).

402. Ibid., 26, cf. 25–27.

403. Ibid., 27 (italics added).

404. Ibid., 27–28.

405. Ibid., 34 (italics original).

406. Ibid., 32, 34, cf. 35–36.

407. Ibid., 35.

408. Ibid., 84–98.

experiences impact theology, since these are (for those with eyes to see and ears to hear) experiences of the Spirit. Thus, theology is existential, evolving from within one's *sitz im leben*.[409] Theology must not be abstract or merely academic, but should develop out of life praxis; its method must be contextual, working in conjunction with application.[410] The Bible also factors into Moltmann's theological method here, but as *part of* the history of promise, not above or below it.[411] Experience of the Spirit is guided by Scripture, but is at the same time able to introduce fresh readings of Scripture. Directed by the Spirit, the church engages Scripture in dialectical process, taking from the text only that which cultivates life, leaving aside what would produce death.[412]

Moltmann's theology of experience also has implications for Christian spirituality, which begins with the experience of freedom and the affirmation of life.[413] The Spirit brings freedom, not just personally but also socially and politically,[414] which is a point Pentecostals have too often neglected. "Pentecostal and charismatic experiences of the Spirit become spiritualistically insubstantial and illusory without the personal and political discipleship of Jesus."[415]

Second, the Spirit is also experienced through community, the fellowship experienced between believers being integral to the Spirit's liberating work.[416] Third, experience of the Spirit comes through individual

409. Moltmann, *Experiences in Theology*, 3.

410. Ibid., xv-xviii, 5, 10–15, 28–29, 59–60. Moltmann dedicates a significant portion of *Experiences in Theology* to exploring black, Latin-American liberation, Minjung and feminist contextual approaches to theology (ibid., 181–301; also see Moltmann, *Spirit of Life*, 114–23).

411. Moltmann, *Experiences in Theology*, 130, cf. 126–27.

412. Ibid., 130–36, 144–50. Moltmann's hermeneutical theory is significantly more developed than what can be presented here. In brief, since God in Scripture is associated with liberative acts in history, liberation becomes the central criterion by which to discern the life-bringing activity of the Spirit (ibid., 28–40). In regard to religions in general, Moltmann suggests that the legitimacy of any religion lies only in its ability to promote life. So, freedom of religion also takes precedence over any particular religion itself (ibid., 21–22).

413. Moltmann, *Spirit of Life*, 99, cf. 103.

414. Ibid., 110–12.

415. Ibid., 121 (italics added). Discipleship involves the tangible resistance of injustice in the world, a renunciation of violence, and a growing love for all life and the ecosystem. Yet Moltmann also makes room for the Wesleyan emphasis on sanctification (important to Pentecostals) as inward healing (and feeling) (ibid., 154, 164–66, 171–74).

416. Moltmann, *God in Creation*, 99; Moltmann, *Spirit of Life*, 217–19; cf. Moltmann,

gift and call.[417] Every life is specifically gifted by the Spirit of life to fill the call ("*klesis*") to participate in the Spirit's mission. This *klesis*, in fact, transforms talents and abilities into what can be considered *charismata*. Since all actions in service to Christ can broadly be considered *charismata*, every Christian, then, in this sense is "charismatic."[418] There is thus no natural/supernatural dichotomy when it comes to *charismata*. Gifts are not best understood as supernatural, but as powers of the coming new creation.[419] Even certain *charismata* emphasized within Pentecostal circles (e.g., tongues and healing) need to be interpreted within this holistic framework of experience of the Spirit as not being other-worldly.[420]

The last experience of the Spirit is hope—anticipation of the future, providing the context for understanding the freedom and responsibility to which each participant in the Spirit's mission is called.[421] Freedom, community, and gifts find true meaning in the anticipation of the coming of God for the whole of creation. Devoid of this context, experience of the Spirit will be misunderstood and misapplied, reducing it to trivialities or to any one aspect of reality instead of holistically including all creation.[422]

Moltmann also proposes a mystical theology of experience.[423] He describes mystical experience as an intense experience of God in faith that cannot be articulated by words, and is best understood by entering into the five-stage "journey" of the mystic.[424] Stage one is "Action and meditation," an epistemological move from mere praxis to reflective the-

---

Experiences in Theology, 328–31.

417. Moltmann, *God in Creation*, 99–100.

418. Moltmann, *Spirit of Life*, 180–82 (italics original).

419. Moltmann, "Wealth of Gifts," 31, 34; cf. Moltmann, *Spirit of Life*, 183.

420. Moltmann, *Spirit of Life*, 181–86, 190–93; Moltmann, "Response," 66–67. Moltmann also includes broken aspects of life potentially as *charismata*. Thus, even physical or mental disability can be viewed as a unique *charism*. This is counter to Pentecostal/charismatic accounts of experiences of the Spirit (especially tongues and healing), which often leave little room for an appreciation or discovery of God in the midst of weakness or suffering.

421. Moltmann, *God in Creation*, 100.

422. Moltmann identifies this as a weakness of Pentecostalism (Moltmann, "Response," 62).

423. See Moltmann, *Experiences of God*, 55–80; Moltmann, *Spirit of Life*, 198–213; and Moltmann, "Theology of Mystical," 501–20.

424. Moltmann, *Spirit of Life*, 198–99; Moltmann, *Experiences of God*, 55; Moltmann, "Theology of Mystical," 502.

ology.[425] The second stage is "meditation and contemplation," in which the mystic loses herself in focus upon another object, and then contemplates how her life was transformed through this meditation.[426] The third stage is "contemplation and mystical union."[427] Here the pursuit of the direct, unmediated presence of God impels the seeker forward, and mysticism can be viewed in its narrower sense—as "*unio mystica*."[428] The fourth stage, "mysticism and martyrdom," emphasizes the mystical way as being ultimately not religious but political.[429] The final stage is the "vision of the world in God"[430]—of the Spirit filling all creation until it "become[s] the 'temple' which God himself indwells."[431] It should be noted that even Moltmann's mystical experience of God is linked to his pneumatological doctrine of creation and eschatology.

Locating Moltmann's Appeal to Experience

The broad scope of Moltmann's theology of experience makes it a challenge to locate him precisely on Schner's continuum. His work on mystical theology will at least cause us to consider whether he should be located at the appeal mystical; however, this hardly seems to be the dominant theme of his theology. What is clearer is that Moltmann's concept of experience of the Spirit is bound up with his theology of creation, in which God is related to creation panentheistically. So, while Moltmann does work to distinguish God from creation, and is open to unusual, or less common (as opposed to mundane) activities of the Spirit (e.g., tongues and divine healing), overwhelmingly his emphasis is on the Spirit as being experienced as the Spirit of life, immanent in all things. In his words, God's transcendence is an "immanent transcendence," and his activities in creation should not be viewed as supernatural. For this reason, Moltmann should probably be located closer to the "appeal

---

425. Moltmann, *Spirit of Life*, 199–202; Moltmann, *Experiences of God*, 57–61.

426. Moltmann, *Spirit of Life*, 202–5; Moltmann, *Experiences of God*, 61–68.

427. Moltmann, *Spirit of Life*, 205–8; Moltmann, *Experiences of God*, 68–71.

428. Moltmann, *Spirit of Life*, 205 (italics original). Elsewhere he states, it is a "moment of fulfilment," and "ecstasy of union," which is "dark, unknowable and inexpressible" (Moltmann, *Experiences of God*, 68).

429. Moltmann, *Spirit of Life*, 208–11; Moltmann, *Experiences of God*, 71–72.

430. Moltmann, *Spirit of Life*, 211–13; Moltmann, *Experiences of God*, 77–80.

431. Moltmann, *Spirit of Life*, 212.

transcendental," although there are moments in which he may be located at the "appeal hermeneutical" and "constructive."

James H. Cone and the Experience of God among the Black Oppressed

A theologian ordained with the African Methodist Episcopal Church, James H. Cone,[432] in his ground-breaking book, *God of the Oppressed*, outlines his rejection of the idea of a universal (transcendental) theology, arguing instead that theology is contextual. States Cone, "one's social and historical context decides not only the questions we address to God but also the mode or form of the answers given to the questions."[433] Aiming to relativize dominant traditional Euro-American ("white") theological approaches, he asserts (via Feuerbach and Marx) that theology is "*human* speech about God" and "is always related to historical situations, and thus all of its assertions are culturally limited."[434] So, "Theology is not a universal language; it is *interested* language and thus is always a reflection of the goals and aspirations of a particular people in a definite social setting."[435] No theology (including "white") is able to transcend its social environment, which functions as a "mental grid" determining the "relevant data in a given inquiry."[436] Beyond this, however, he contends that "black theology," shaped in the context (experience) of social oppression, does have a privileged understanding of God, since God's presence is to be found among the oppressed. White theology, conversely shaped in the context of oppressors, is marked by the *absence* of God's presence, and is blind to the "essence of the Gospel [being] the liberation of the oppressed."[437]

Cone acknowledges that his own life experience has been influential in helping him recognize that white theology fails to address black questions, leading him to propose black experience in the USA as a valid

432. See "James H. Cone," para. 1–4.

433. Cone, *God of the Oppressed*, 14. Johnson's feminist liberation theology may also be understood as a contextual theology, but Cone emphasizes historical and cultural particularity more so than she does.

434. Ibid., 36 (italics original).

435. Ibid. (italics original). This "means that theology is political language" (ibid., 41). Particularly in this statement Cone indicates his reliance on Karl Marx.

436. Ibid., 48.

437. Ibid., 47, cf. 42–49.

and privileged theological resource.[438] Black theology, while contextual, nevertheless has the advantage of close affinity to the biblical revelation in both content and (narrative/oral) form.[439] While abstract, speculative philosophizing has been characteristic of Euro-American theology, enslaved North American blacks had no time for such luxuries. The God of black experience was not an idea or concept to be discussed, but the liberator of the oppressed in history, encountered through the (re)telling of the biblical stories and personal testimonies.[440] Black experiences, then, both religious (e.g., sermons, prayers, and spirituals), and "secular" (e.g., folk stories, secular music, and the Blues), can serve as a starting point for developing a black theology.[441]

Along with black experiences, the Bible is also a necessary theological resource, since it provides the subject of black theology—Jesus Christ—who is intricately bound up with black experience.[442] "There is no truth in Jesus Christ independent of the oppressed of the land—their history and culture. And in America, the oppressed are the people of color—black, yellow, red, and brown."[443] The Incarnation itself, Cone believes, is a convergence of Christ with black experience, demonstrating God's solidarity with oppressed and "wretched" humanity. "And because we blacks accept God's presence in Jesus as the true definition of our humanity, blackness and divinity are dialectically bound together as one reality."[444]

The experience of black slaves convinced them, Cone argues, of God's involvement and presence in history; a view congruent with

438. Ibid., 1–4. Cone cites, among other things, his own experience of growing up in Arkansas, and encountering the "divine spirit" in the African Methodist Episcopal Church (inspiring him with "aspiration for freedom"), while at the same time living under a reality "defined" by whites, as contributing to this realization. For black descendants of the slave trade, still facing the daily realities of social, political, and economic injustice, the basic theological question is: "What has the Gospel to do with the oppressed of the land and their struggle for liberation?" (ibid., 9).

439. Ibid., 41, 49 (italics original). Cone states, "*the form of black religious thought is expressed in the style of story and its content is liberation*" (ibid., 49; italics original).

440. Ibid., 50–51, 55–56.

441. Ibid., 17–27. Truth is to be found in the historical particularities of black existence, and therefore there "is no truth for and about black people that does not emerge out of the context of their experience" (ibid., 16, cf. 16–28).

442. Ibid., 28–31.

443. Ibid., 31.

444. Ibid., 33.

biblical narrative of a historically involved God (unlike the so-called "god" of Greek philosophy), embroiled in Israel's historical, social, and political affairs.[445] The narrative form and content of Scripture supports the idea of black experience as an appropriate point of departure for knowing and experiencing God. After all, in the Old Testament, the history of Israel begins with the Exodus, in which "Yahweh is disclosed as the God of history, whose revelation is identical with God's power to liberate the oppressed. There is no knowledge of Yahweh except through God's political activity on behalf of the weak and helpless of the land."[446]

Similarly, the New Testament story of Jesus also demonstrates both the method and content of God's revelation. Cone highlights Jesus' baptism (with the descent of the Spirit) as demonstrating the prophetic character of his ministry, bringing *"Lordship and Servanthood together, that is, the establishment of Justice through suffering."*[447] Thus, *"The hermeneutical principle for an exegesis of the Scriptures is the revelation of God in Christ as the Liberator of the oppressed from social oppression and to political struggle, wherein the poor recognize that their fight against poverty and injustice is not only consistent with the gospel but is the gospel of Jesus Christ."*[448] So, Scripture affirms that God is revealed in the experience of the oppressed as Liberator in history, justifying belief in God's presence in the experience of American blacks. Further, asserts Cone, "Any interpretation of the Gospel *in any historical period* that fails to see Jesus as Liberator of the oppressed is heretical."[449]

Jesus' story also serves to define Christian truth. On the one hand, "Truth is more than the retelling of the biblical story. Truth is the divine happening that invades our contemporary situation . . ."[450] So, Jesus (truth) can be known and experienced in the context of oppression, through black experience.[451] "We must say unequivocally that who Jesus Christ is for black people today is found through encounter with him in

445. Ibid., 57. Thus, "To know God is to experience the acts of God in the concrete affairs and relationships of people, liberating the weak and helpless from pain and humiliation."

446. Ibid., 59, cf. 65.

447. Ibid., 68–69 (italics original).

448. Ibid., 74–75 (italics original).

449. Ibid., 35 (italics added). That this indicts white theology as heretical is a point not to be missed.

450. Ibid., 99. Cone here states, "Jesus Christ is the truth of the Christian story . . ."

451. Ibid., 100.

the social context of black existence."[452] On the other hand, truth is not exhausted by any one community's experience—Scripture is necessary.[453] The meaning of Jesus is determined, therefore, by dialectic between black experience and Scripture,[454] which reveals, "The Jesus of the black experience *is* the Jesus of Scripture."[455]

Christology, then, is fundamental to Cone's black theology. Jesus' "past identity, his present activity, and his future coming," are related to, and also help transform black experience.[456] The Jesus of history, states Cone, was a first century Jewish man who suffered oppression, and can therefore identify with the oppressed. Knowledge of Jesus' story, in fact, is what helped black slaves contend "that slavery contradicts the New Testament Jesus."[457] But, continues Cone, Jesus is not dead but raised; not a figure who *was*, but who *is*—"the *isness* of Jesus relates his past history to his present involvement in our struggle."[458] For this reason, black slaves testified to experiencing the presence of Jesus in their midst. "Through song, prayer, and sermon the community affirmed Jesus' presence and their willingness to make it through their troubled situation. Some would smile and others would cry. Another person, depending on the Spirit's effect on him, would clap his hands and tap his feet." [459] Such encounter provided a "vision from on high," a "foretaste of God's promised freedom"—in other words, hope.[460]

Black experience, however, also helps define and shape Christology. God's immanent presence with the oppressed operates dialectically.[461] Cone states, "God enters into the social context of human existence and appropriates the ideas and actions of the oppressed as God's own. When this event of liberation occurs in thought and praxis, the words and actions of the oppressed become the Word and Action of God. They

452. Ibid., 103.

453. Ibid., 101.

454. Ibid., 104–5.

455. Ibid., 103 (italics added).

456. Ibid., 122.

457. Ibid., 108.

458. Ibid., 110 (italics original).

459. Ibid., 113.

460. Ibid., 117.

461. Ibid., 111. Cone asserts that Christology must be done, then, from above and below.

no longer belong to the oppressed. Indeed, the word of the oppressed becomes God's Word in so far as the former recognize it not as their own but as given to them through divine grace."[462]

So closely, then, is Jesus associated with present black experience that Cone asserts "Jesus is black."[463] He continues, "Christ is black, therefore, not because of some cultural or psychological need of black people, but because and only because Christ *really* enters our world where the poor, the despised, and the black are, disclosing that he is with them, enduring their humiliation and pain and transforming the oppressed slaves into liberated servants. Indeed, if Christ is not *truly* black, then the historical Jesus lied."[464]

Experience of God (Christ), then, is intricately linked to the community of the oppressed and black experience. But this raises a significant question: "How do we distinguish our words about God from God's Word, our wishes from God's will, our dreams and aspirations from the work of the Spirit?"[465] In other words, how do we discern whether a particular community's experience (black or otherwise) is of the Holy Spirit? How can we know that black theology has not simply become an ideology?

Cone has argued that black theology is rooted in a more authentic experience of the Spirit than white theology, since the former emerges from the experience of the oppressed, is congruent with the witness (form and content) of Scripture, and is, therefore, truer to Jesus.[466] But he admits there is no totally objective way of answering the above questions concerning the discernment of the Spirit's presence and activity

462. Ibid., 90.

463. Ibid., 122, cf. 122–26. Cone acknowledges that Jesus' "blackness" is symbolic, and may not always function as an effective liberating Christological title. It does emphasize, however, Christ's oneness with oppressed blacks at this point in history (ibid., 125).

464. Ibid., 125–26 (italics original).

465. Ibid., 77.

466. See Ibid., 84, 86, 88. As noted, Cone believes the oppressed have hermeneutical advantage over "oppressors," whose context blinds them from hearing and seeing the truth of God's revelation and presence. "Only the poor and the weak have the axiological grid necessary for the hearing and the doing of the divine will disclosed in their midst" (ibid., 86). It is not, then, black theologians, but the oppressors (including white theologians), who need to acknowledge their ideology, which ignores God's mission to liberate the poor and oppressed.

in a given community's experience.[467] What he does propose, however, is that the Spirit's activity can be identified somewhat pragmatically; certain, practical concrete manifestations may serve as indicators of the Spirit's presence.

In *Black Theology and Black Power*, Cone identifies what should and should not be considered indicators of the Spirit's activity. "God's Spirit is not just a subjective feeling of piety or inspiration in the hearts of men," but is an active power in the world working toward moral, political and religious transformation.[468] Further, the Spirit's activity ought not to be identified "either with private moments of ecstasy or with individual purification from sin . . ."[469] It is not that Cone is closed to emotionally intense experiences with the Spirit. Moments of "ecstasy" may indeed be evoked in black worship, but these are not to serve as the criterion by which the Spirit is discerned.[470]

Instead, true encounter with the Spirit is revealed by "what happens to a man's total being, a change wherein he is now repelled by suffering and death caused by bigotry of others."[471] This is a "conversion," tangibly transforming one's thinking and actions to be solidaritous with the poor and oppressed against injustice.[472] "The working of God's Spirit in the life of the believer means an involvement in the world where men are suffering. When the Spirit of God gets hold of a man, he is made a new creature, a creature prepared to move head-on into the evils of this world, ready to die for God."[473]

Experience of the Spirit, then, may in fact not be a very pleasant encounter. Indeed, for the oppressor, the encounter with "Black Power"

467. Ibid., 93.

468. Cone, *Black Theology*, 57.

469. Ibid., 58.

470. Cone, *God of the Oppressed*, 132. "Black worship" is identified as a "liberative event" in which the presence of God is encountered. In communal worship, blacks "transcend the limitations of their immediate history and encounter the divine power, thereby creating a moment of ecstasy and joy wherein they recognize that the pain of oppression is not the last word about black life."

471. Cone, *Black Theology*, 58.

472. Cone, *God of the Oppressed*, 89, 130; Cone, *Black Theology*, 58–60, cf. 134–39.

473. Cone, *Black Theology*, 58. Cone states that God's work of reconciliation in the world is "not mystical communion with the divine; nor is it a pietistic state of inwardness bestowed upon the believer. God's reconciliation is a new relationship with *people* created by God's concrete involvement in the political affairs of the world, taking sides with the weak and helpless" (ibid., 209; italics original).

(through which the Spirit is working) may be an awful experience.[474] Further, true "conversion" may not always be connected to the church, since "the work of the Spirit is not always a conscious activity on the part of the persons through whom God works. . . . And this may mean that God is not necessarily at work in those places where the Word is truly preached and the sacraments are duly administered (as Reformation theologians defined the Church), but where the naked are clothed, the sick are visited, and the hungry are fed."[475]

So, no entirely objective criteria exist guaranteeing that one is "possessed by the Spirit . . . There's only a subjective certainty in which one knows that he is in touch with the Real . . . [,] an existential certainty . . ." Moreover, "The experience is its own evidence, the ultimate datum."[476] That said, however, for Cone the Spirit's activity is still most reliably identified by its tangible liberative effects, which include: resistance to political and social injustice,[477] willingness to endure suffering (convinced of God's solidarity with the oppressed),[478] a new dynamic ethic of the oppressed (guided not by set rules but by the liberative Spirit),[479] and the ability to better recognize the limits of one's own experience and avoid ideology.[480]

LOCATING CONE'S APPEAL TO EXPERIENCE

With regard to Schner's continuum, Cone's suspicion of transcendental theology in favor of the particularity of black experience places him largely at the "appeal hermeneutical." Interestingly, Cone does express some "confessional" elements, advocating a dialectic between Scripture and black experience (expressed in various narrative and oral forms), and this may be viewed as a somewhat "constructive" move (supplemented by the possibility of the Spirit bringing interruptive encounters). However, this black "confession" (favoring the "Jesus of the Bible"), functions in

474. Ibid., 61.

475. Ibid., 59.

476. Ibid., 60.

477. Cone, *God of the Oppressed*, 139–44.

478. Ibid., 169–78.

479. Ibid., 180–99. Cone includes the possibility of violence within appropriate ethical behavior (ibid., 180, 199–206).

480. Ibid., 93–98.

contrast to the historical church community and confession (the "Jesus of theology"). Further, Cone's version of the biblical Jesus is *quite* shaped by twentieth-century black experience, exemplified in (potential) openness to violence as part of his theological ethics (noted above). Cone admits that historically Jesus did not condone violence; however, he argues, Jesus' words and actions are to be viewed as *a sign, not an example,* for ethical behavior today.[481] Yet earlier we noted Cone's assertion that Jesus' past cannot be separated his presence today,[482] and that Jesus' history, in fact, enabled black slaves to recognize that Jesus was on their side. Cone's ethics, then, appears to indicate his willingness to quite radically reinterpret the meaning of Jesus in light of contemporary black experience (context). For that reason, he likely serves as our closest representative of the "appeal hermeneutical," while acknowledging "confessional" and "constructive" elements.

Robert W. Jenson and the Identity of the Triune God

Lutheran theologian, Robert W. Jenson,[483] has relatively little explicitly to say concerning experience of God compared to almost all the other theologians in this chapter. In *The Triune Identity*, however, he makes an important assertion that summarizes his position concerning how God is to be experienced in creation:

> Throughout the church's history, two experiences of spirit have struggled to interpret the Spirit. The one is of unidentifiable dynamism that simply seizes us for the future—any future, whatever future is on its way—and just, and only apparently paradoxically, so is immediately self-authenticating in experience. It is to this experience that "enthusiastic" movements in Christianity, from Montanism to congregational "human potential" groups, have covertly appealed—covertly because overt appeal means departing from christological confession. It is the same experience which in secularized form is the empty freedom of existentialism and of the debased American slogan "It's a free country." The other experience has a very different phenomenal structure; spirit here is always the spirit-of someone, Lincoln's spirit or the spirit of '76 or the team's spirit. When this structure is allowed to

481. Ibid., 204.

482. Ibid., 111.

483. See Jenson, "Interview with Robert W. Jenson," para. 1.

rule our interpretation of the Spirit, as it must if we are to agree with Scripture, the Spirit is always specifically Jesus' spirit and the Father's.[484]

Here Jenson highlights two antithetical approaches to experience of God. In the first, Spirit is an "unidentifiable dynamism"; whereas the second links the Spirit to a particular historical confession concerning Jesus. Also raised is the issue of how one can know whether one is being seized by the Holy Spirit or by some other identity or group interest (ideology). Jenson's position is that "Spirit" has a particular identity (as Spirit of the Father and Son), and that the identity of the Trinity is revealed only through particular historical events (through Scripture), and preserved through the Christian community.[485]

This method of understanding the Trinity is developed in contradistinction to the Hellenistic approach to theology, which Jenson believes has negatively impacted Western Christianity.[486] In brief, ancient Hellenic religion associated the realm of divinity with timelessness, in contrast to the world and mortals, which are subject to time's destructive movements.[487] Timelessness and impassibility (along with other negative atemporal predicates, such as "invisible," "intangible," and "immutable") were assumed to be essential to divine nature, which by definition could not be affected by the temporal world.[488] As Christianity and Hellenism encountered one another, the assumption of God's timelessness and impassibility found its way into Christian theology,[489] and the church

484. Jenson, *Triune Identity*, 170.

485. Jenson holds in suspicion, then, everything from Pietism, Wesleyanism, and Pentecostalism to various contextual and/or liberation theologies. Elsewhere Jenson bemoans approaches to theology that tend to simply identify the gospel with "whatever is 'justifying' or 'healing' or 'liberating' or whatever such value the theologian finds her or himself affirming" (Jenson, *Systematic Theology: Triune*, 12).

486. Ibid., 8–10. Jenson gives considerable attention to the historical unfolding of the influence of Hellenism (see Jenson, *Triune Identity*, 57–102).

487. Jenson, *Triune Identity*, 58; Jenson, *Systematic Theology: Triune*, 94.

488. Jenson, *Triune Identity*, 60, cf. 59–61. For Hellenism, divine nature is distant and removed (hidden) from history and temporal reality, only able to be accessed by means of the mind. Among the results emerging from this theology came the need to search for that which could serve to mediate between the temporal and eternal—"beings of a third ontological kind between time and Timelessness, to bridge the gap." Further, Jenson notes that in order to speak of the Trinity in meaningful ways, the genre of myth was employed, in which temporal images were applied to the eternal (ibid., 61).

489. Ibid., 61–65. Jenson calls this the "Christianizing of Hellenism," since the apologists and theologians integrating these two approaches to theology were Hellenists

(especially in the Western tradition) has continued to wrestle with the implications throughout its history.[490]

Scripture, however, argues Jenson, tells the story of a God identified in, through, and by history. God is not distinguished by certain (assumed) predicative attributes, but by particular events.[491] In the Old Testament, "To the question 'Whom you mean, 'God'?' Israel answered it, 'Whoever got us out of Egypt.'"[492] Thus, "In the Bible the name God and the narration of his works thus belong together. The descriptions that make the name work are items of the narrative. And conversely, identifying God, backing up the name, is the very function of the biblical narrative."[493] The New Testament functions similarly. "To the question 'Who is God?' the New Testament has one new descriptively identifying answer: 'Whoever raised Jesus from the dead.'"[494] Further, the God of the exodus and Christ's resurrection is one and the same.[495]

For Jenson, the name "Jesus," used in the New Testament, encapsulates God's mission through Christ.[496] But another proper name for God (evoked by the historical resurrection) emerges[497]—"Father, Son,

---

wrestling with their faith in Christ and the biblical witness. He notes Ignatius' early description of God as impassible already in 125 CE.

490. Ibid., 65–66, 103–111; cf. Jenson, *Systematic Theology: Triune*, 94–96. Major theological challenges evolved from a commitment to divine impassibility and the gospel witness to the fact of Christ in history. In regard to Trinitarian theology, both of the errors of modalism (which teaches that "God himself is above time and the distinctions of Father, Son, and Spirit") and subordinationism (which allows the Father to maintain his impassible status while allocating the Son to a subordinate and mediate position within time as something less than divine) emerged due to an assumption of Greek categories and predicates for the divine. Jenson believes that Christian theology in the Western tradition has been particularly impacted by Hellenic theology and traces its influence through key theologians in Christian history including Augustine and Aquinas. But he also identifies the Cappadocians (Basil, Gregory of Nazianzen and Gregory of Nyssa) as having provided some means of overcoming the Greek imposition on Trinitarian thought. Here Jenson advocates more of an Eastern Orthodox Trinitarian approach, taking the hypostases as the point of departure as opposed to the ousia.

491. Jenson, *Triune Identity*, 5ff.; Jenson, *Systematic Theology: Triune*, 63–74.

492. Jenson, *Triune Identity*, 7.

493. Ibid.; *Systematic Theology: Triune*, 43–44.

494. Jenson, *Systematic Theology: Triune*, 44; cf. Jenson, *Triune Identity*, 8.

495. Jenson, *Triune Identity*, 8; Jenson, *Systematic Theology: Triune*, 44–45.

496. Jenson, *Triune Identity*, 9; cf. Jenson, *Systematic Theology: Triune*, 45.

497. Jenson, *Triune Identity*, 42.

and Holy Spirit."[498] This name is "a very compressed telling of the total narrative by which Scripture identifies God . . . ; in it, name and narrative description not only appear together, . . . but are identical."[499] Christians identify God by this name (connected to the biblical narrative), states Jenson, or else are not part of the true Christian community. In short, "Israel's and the church's God is thus identified by specific temporal actions and is known within the temporal communities by personal names and identifying descriptions thereby provided. Nor does Scripture contain permission to transcend these relations at any height of spiritual experience, even though craving to rise above such temporal and 'limiting' modes of experience is endemic in religion."[500]

"Religion" (Hellenic approach to theology) attempts to transcend historical identifiers to find revelation of God. The gospel, however, is incompatible with this approach, says Jenson, being an event in history and "an unconditional promise of [future historical] fulfillment."[501] God is not found *behind* history, hidden by qualities inherent in the divine nature. Rather, there "is no way or need of getting to God past what happens to Jesus in time . . ."[502] The Hellenization of theology has also introduced differentiation between the so-called missions and processions of God—the economic and immanent Trinity—allowing discussion of the triune life apart from salvation history.[503] Such is irreconcilable with the account of God in the Hebrew Scriptures.[504] God's relationship to creation requires articulation in a historical framework, in which "the 'immanent' Trinity is simply the eschatological reality of the 'economic.'"[505]

498. Ibid., 9; *Systematic Theology: Triune*, 45.

499. Jenson, *Systematic Theology: Triune*, 46.

500. Ibid.

501. Jenson, *Triune Identity*, 26.

502. Ibid., 26, cf. 17–18, 21–24. Elsewhere Jenson states: "It is itself a particularity of Israel's and the church's God that he so insist upon his particularity, a component of his identity that he can be definitively identified." This is contrary to the "standard religious attitude" that the "principle of individuation . . . cannot finally apply to deity" (Jenson, *Systematic Theology: Triune*, 47). For a fuller discussion of Jenson's understanding of creation and time, see Jenson, *Systematic Theology: Works*, 29–48.

503. Jenson, *Triune Identity*, 125f., 138–40.

504. Ibid., 40. Jenson argues it is precisely Hellenic theology, and not the Old Testament, that introduced obstacles to understanding the Trinity. This is because Greek interpretation of the divine was grounded in metaphysical categories, whereas the Hebrew understanding of God has always been through historical events (ibid., 34–40).

505. Ibid., 140.

God's identification within the historical biblical narrative means "God" should be understood as a predicate,[506] not referring to some immaterial substance, but to the "mutual life of Father, Son, and Spirit."[507] Further, this "being of God is not a something, . . . but a *going-on*, a sequentially palpable event, like a kiss or a train wreck."[508] Hence, the hypostases of Father, Son, and Spirit is prior to the fact that "God is."[509] "There is one event," says Jenson, "God, of three identities. Therewith my proposed basic trinitarian analysis."[510]

Distinguishing divinity, then, is not "timelessness" over against "time," but "Creator" over against "creature"; thus no mediator (in the Hellenic sense) is required.[511] States Jenson, "'Creator'/'creature' names an absolute difference but no distance at all, for to be the Creator is merely as such to be actively related to the creature. Each of the inner-trinitarian relations is then an affirmation that as God works creatively among us, so he is in himself."[512] So, divine nature is not eternal, but "temporal infinity"; God is identified historically, but not bound by time.[513] So, "To be God is, in this interpretation, always to have future."[514]

Experience of this God, then, is possible because, in creating the world and history, "room" was made in the triune life for an other, and time is the realm in which creation exists and God can be experienced.[515]

506. Ibid., 113. This is reverse of the idea that God has predicates, i.e. characteristics or attributes necessary for maintaining the title "God" (ibid., 112). Bulgakov also describes Sophia as "predicate" of the Trinity, although he differs from Jenson in regard to his understanding of God's essence (Bulgakov, *Sophia*, 52).

507. Jenson *Systematic Theology: Triune*, 214. Here Jenson is borrowing from Gregory of Nyssa's reflections on the Trinity.

508. Ibid., 214 (italics original).

509. Ibid., 215.

510. Jenson, *Triune Identity*, 114, cf. 111–14. Jenson notes that the identification of God as event is also seen in the work of Karl Barth (with whom Jenson shares similar views on this and other points), and process theology (ibid., 176–81). Jenson distances himself from the latter, however, suggesting that while process metaphysics helps us view "all reality as concretely consisting in events," in fact it does not posit God as an enduring entity, and God therefore becomes indistinguishable from the world (ibid., 180–81).

511. Ibid., 106–7.

512. Ibid., 107.

513. Jenson, *Systematic Theology: Triune*, 215–17; cf. Jenson, *Triune Identity*, 161–71.

514. Jenson, *Triune Identity*, 166.

515. Jenson, *Systematic Theology: Works*, 25, 46; Jenson, *Systematic Theology: Triune*, 226.

God is therefore knowable, not as an object, but because the creature is invited into knowledge of Godself.[516] "To be, as a creature, is to be mentioned in the triune moral conversation, as something other than those who conduct it."[517] In this sense, for Jenson, the triune life brackets creaturely life; there is no metaphysical distance from God, although the Creator/creature distinction remains firm.[518]

In creation, asserts Jenson, God's self-communication comes through creatures;[519] "if God wishes to speak to persons beyond himself, creatures are necessary for him."[520] So, God is not absent or silent in history; God's presence and speech is mediated through embodied creatures. Yet God also remains hidden.[521] This hiddenness, however, is not a metaphysical necessity; rather, "What hides God are the sins and evils with which that creation is filled."[522]

The embodied speech of God in creation is literally the Son, the Logos, the active Word of the Father.[523] The Son *is* God's speech in creation,[524] affirms Jenson, historically identified in the person of Jesus, the Word of God.[525] In Jesus, the Creator/creature divide is overcome; and so God participates historically in salvation, not only after the Incarnation, but in Israel's history as well.[526] In the Old Testament "the Lord's agency [is] intrinsically historical and therefore occurs as speech,"

---

516. Jenson, *Systematic Theology: Triune*, 224–25.

517. Jenson, *Systematic Theology: Works*, 35.

518. Ibid., 25.

519. Ibid., 156.

520. Ibid., 160.

521. Ibid., 160–61; *Systematic Theology: Triune*, 233.

522. Jenson, *Systematic Theology: Works*, 162; cf. Jenson, *Systematic Theology: Triune*, 233.

523. Jenson, *Systematic Theology: Triune*, 78, 165; cf. Jenson, *Systematic Theology: Works*, 157–59.

524. Jenson, *Systematic Theology: Triune*, 97.

525. Jenson, *Triune Identity*, 22. "God, we may therefore identify, is what happens with Jesus."

526. Jenson, *Systematic Theology: Triune*, 76–77, cf. 78, 139–41. With Barth, Jenson echoes the idea that in some sense God chooses to "unite himself, in the person of Christ, with humankind" even prior to the historical Incarnation (ibid., 140). While admitting this to be something almost beyond human ability to articulate, Jenson does insist it is possible to understand the Son as being Wisdom, the "Shekinah" and "angel of the Lord" in the Old Testament historical narrative; and as such God participates in Israel's story as the Word of God (see Jenson, *Systematic Theology: Works*, 157–60).

identified as "word."[527] "In Trinitarian Theology 'the Word' stands for God's identifying communication of himself . . . This word, as actually spoken, is *precisely* the trinitarian Logos."[528]

The Son, the Word of God, then, is *always* the (temporal, not time-less) mediator in creation, and his identity is unalterable. The crucifixion finalized Jesus' identity, while the resurrection means that the Word continues to speak in new and surprising ways. The Word, however, is not given to be altered by the church, or extracted from its narrative location. The identity of Jesus Christ is settled and not evolving.[529]

If the Son is mediator, what, then, is the role of the Spirit? Jenson argues that the Son mediates not only Creator and creation, but also Father and Spirit.[530] Relation to the Father comes through the Son, and the Spirit directs creatures to hear the Word of the Father.[531] "The Father gives and intends, the Spirit frees and witnesses, Jesus is intended and is witnessed to. And interpreting each pair personally, we get: the Father gives and intends = is Subject; Jesus is intended and is witnessed to = is Object; the Spirit frees and witnesses = is Spirit."[532] The Spirit is also God's future, whose primary role is to perfect the Father's intention, pointing to the objective Word of God, to which the creature must respond by faith.[533] God is thus experienced by hearing the Word by the Spirit, the Spirit *of Christ*, whose identity is unalterable and yet temporally unbound.

Further, Jenson-stresses that the Spirit's identity ought not to be specified "without reference to Israel and the church, without the created community whose spirit he is in fact is . . ."[534] The Spirit belongs to

527. Jenson, *Systematic Theology: Triune*, 78–79.

528. Ibid., 79 (italics added). Jenson is adamant on the particularity of the Logos/Word, and that another hypostasis of the Trinity does not act narratively to fulfill this function (ibid., 111). He criticizes Augustine as blurring the identities of the triune persons by stating that Old Testament theophanies could be the Father, Son, or Holy Spirit.

529. Ibid., 198–200. This places Jenson at considerable odds with various contextual and liberation theologies.

530. Ibid., 114. Jenson states, "The occurrence and plot of the life of God's people with God depends as a whole upon the occurrence and plot of the life of God with his people. It does so precisely as this one life is in both aspects constituted in the Father's originating, the Spirit's perfecting, and the Son's mediating of the two . . ."

531. Ibid., 109–10.

532. Jenson, *Triune Identity*, 148.

533. Jenson, *Systematic Theology: Triune*, 219–20, cf. 157. Jenson also describes the Spirit as God coming from the future.

534. Ibid., 148, cf. 87.

and is manifest in the body Christ; for since his ascension, Jesus has been embodied in the church, through whom he now speaks. "The Church speaks *about* Christ as God directly *for* God in his name . . . He is the speech of the Father; as the Father's speech to us he is embodied in the Church and therefore does not, whatever might have been, speak except by his body . . . When two or three gather as the Church to petition the Father, there he is, praying with and indeed through them."[535]

From this, Jenson argues that the church is called to preserve and witness to the gospel through adherence to Scripture, dogmatic tradition, liturgy, and the teaching office (ordained clergy). However, these elements (alone or together) cannot guarantee fidelity to the apostolic witness. The community of Christ must also trust the Spirit to sustain the church's identity over time, allowing her to maintain faithful witness.[536] Therefore, the Spirit's work is quite localized in the church, acting to bring believers into communion with the triune life.

Practically, the Spirit preserves the gospel through ordination and the teaching office, as well as enlivening the reading of Scripture, by which the church objectively hears the Son and responds through prayer to the Father.[537] As the community of the Spirit, the church is both the interpreter and prophet of Scripture.[538] However, as the Spirit's book,[539] the Bible may need, on occasion, to be defended within and against a sometimes erring Christian community.[540] Says Jenson, "It is the Spirit who makes the gospel an actual and so potent word, a 'word-event,' if one will," yet, "the Spirit's efficacy is not simply other than the Son's personal subjectivity as the one who identifies *himself* to his people . . ."[541] Experience of God, then, is mediated through the Son by the Spirit in the church. God is most explicitly experienced in the re-enactment of the gospel in the Eucharist, where the resurrected Christ is located.[542] For this reason, Jenson is somewhat agnostic as to whether knowledge or

535. Jenson, *Systematic Theology: Works*, 271 (italics original).

536. Jenson *Systematic Theology: Triune*, 4, 12, 15, 25–26.

537. Ibid., 29, 228–29.

538. Jenson, *Systematic Theology: Works*, 276.

539. Ibid., 272–76.

540. Jenson, *Systematic Theology: Triune*, 40.

541. Ibid., 175 (italics original).

542. Ibid., 203–5.

experience of God can be possessed, or at least comprehended, outside the church.[543]

LOCATING JENSON'S APPEAL TO EXPERIENCE

Concerning Schner's continuum, it is perhaps easiest to discern where Jenson is not located—namely, at the "appeal transcendental" or "hermeneutical"; and neither would the "appeal immediate or mystical" correspond easily with his emphasis on the historicity of the triune identity.[544] Jenson does evidence elements of the "appeal confessional," since he continually affirms the traditions of the church, and narrowly locates the Spirit's activity within the ecclesial realm. But even more so, he exhibits an "appeal constructive," insisting on the living aspect of the Word, which is always able to surprise and confront, and relying ultimately on the Spirit to preserve the gospel, and not the dogmatic and liturgical traditions. The Spirit is not bound by the church, even while being located within the church. So, the Spirit who is of the Father and Son, and of God's future, may enable the church to speak the gospel in fresh ways—the Spirit is dynamic and not static.

Conclusion

This chapter has attempted to survey the appeal to experience within Christian theology by examining the challenge of the concept of experience itself, as well the variety of ways the appeal functions within the works of eight theologians. Although an attempt was made to locate each theologian at a particular moment on Schner's continuum, it should be evident at this point that doing so proved to be not a simple task. Even being linked to the same ecclesial tradition did not guarantee unanimity, and it would seem that, at least within the work of these theologians, the appeal to experience is often not static, but more dynamic and fluid. That said, the purpose of our survey in this chapter has been to provide a theological context for examining the Pentecostal appeal to the

543. Ibid., 163. Jenson suggests that the response to the Logos outside the church, mediated through the creatures, has resulted only in idolatrous religion.

544. It should be noted, however, at one point Jenson does state, somewhat ambiguously, that theology cannot do without the sort of language often called "mystical," particularly in liturgical proclamation and prayer. But he quickly moves away from this point (Jenson, *Systematic Theology: Triune*, 225).

experience of God, and it is believed that a sufficient foundation and diverse sampling has been provided for our later dialogues.

Some other summary observations concerning our theologians are also appropriate at this point, and two interrelated themes in particular are worth noting.[545] First, several of those surveyed critiqued Hellenistic influences upon Christian theology, advocating that God not be viewed as impassible, but as revealed in the particulars of history.[546] Interestingly, however, while this form of historical mediation is more generally acknowledged, there was not consensus as to the form in which God's mediation in history presently occurs. Those closer to the "appeal transcendental" or even "hermeneutical" tended to interpret this mediation more generically—the Spirit serving as the historical link in God's salvific program. Those on the other side of the "appeal constructive," however, tended to accent the Spirit's historical mediation more specifically through the ecclesial community. So, while mediation of the Spirit is acknowledged in both cases, opinion as to the way in which this works itself out is not unanimous.

Second, connected to historical mediation is the question of God's relationship to the world. This not infrequently raised discussion concerning the missions of the Spirit and Son; and so exploration of the appeal to experience in theology involved reflection on these missions as well as aspects of Trinitarian theology. Closely connected, we also observed several attempts to outline some form of creation theology. At least four of our theologians advocated panentheism as a means to overcome their perceived difficulties with classical theism (and pantheism); but even here the respective panentheisms were not always defined in the same way. Consensus, it seems, is hard to come by in theology! In sum, what we have learned is that theological exploration of the experience of God is interconnected with a number of theological topics, including: the doctrine of God and historical mediation (and/or immediacy), the relation of the missions of Spirit and Son, and the theology of creation. In our exploration in the chapters to follow it would seem appropriate, then, to monitor how Pentecostals relate experience of God to these theological spheres as well.

545. A detailed comparison of those surveyed in this chapter is beyond our scope and purposes, and so the comments here have been generalized considerably.

546. Jenson was perhaps the most radical in his disassociation from Greek thought in this regard.

2

Pentecostalism and Experience of the Spirit

THIS CHAPTER ADDRESSES AN ISSUE RAISED IN THE INTRODUCTION OF this book; namely, that while Pentecostals frequently appeal to experience of God, this appeal is often left rather ambiguously defined.[1] What follows, then, is an attempt to characterize Pentecostal experience of the Spirit by surveying its significance within Pentecostal theology and spirituality. Further, we will also explore how Pentecostals, as part of their emergence into adulthood, are wrestling with the traditional mediations of the Spirit—Scripture, tradition, and reason—in relation to their experience of God.

Understanding Encounter with the Spirit through Pentecostal Theology

The Experience/Theology Tension in Pentecostalism

Experience of the Spirit has always been integral to Pentecostalism. Keith Warrington argues that experience is the "heartbeat" of Pentecostalism, without which it would not exist.[2] Mathew S. Clark and Henry I. Lederle state that experience is the point of departure for Pentecostal spirituality and faith, just as other Christian denominations might begin with doctrine.[3] "Pentecostal theology," they state, "demands more than *belief*

---

1. See Lewis, "Towards a Pentecostal," 2–9; and Parker, "Led by the Spirit," 11.
2. Warrington, "Experience," 4.
3. Clark and Lederle et al., *What Is Distinctive*, 36 (italics original).

in an experience—it demands the *experience of the experience* itself."[4] Following this line, Russell P. Spittler identifies the "most pervasive" aspect of Pentecostal spirituality as being "the worth accorded to individual *experience*," adding that "Pentecostals consider personal experience the arena of true religion."[5] Historian Douglas G. Jacobsen likewise summarizes Pentecostalism:

> In short, then, pentecostals are Spirit-conscious, Spirit-filled, and Spirit-empowered Christian believers. In contrast to other groups or churches that emphasize either doctrine or moral practice, pentecostals stress affectivity. It is the *experience* of God that matters—the felt power of the Spirit in the world, in the church, and in one's own life. Pentecostals believe the doctrine and ethics are important, but the bedrock of pentecostal faith is experiential. It is living faith in the living God—a God who can miraculously, palpably intervene in the world—that defines the pentecostal orientation of faith.[6]

Within this experiential faith context, Pentecostals primarily emphasize two vivid and transformational experiences—the *new birth* (conversion) and a subsequent post-conversion experience of *baptism with the Holy Spirit*.[7] As an old Pentecostal adage asserts, such experiences are "better felt then telt, better walked than talked."[8] Ronald R. N. Kydd explains,

> The meaning of [such a] saying is fairly clear. The experiences you can have with God are so private and yet earth-shaking that inevitably something is lost when you start talking about them; . . . when we press our experiences with God into words and sentences, we may end up with something lucid and precise, but find that part of the reality of the experience has been lost in

4. Ibid., 40 (italics original).

5. Spittler, "Spirituality," 1097a (italics original); cf. Spittler, "Maintaining Distinctives," 134. That Pentecostals highly value the appeal to experience of God is widely acknowledged. For example, see Kärkkäinen, *Pneumatology*, 89–92; Anderson, *Introduction to Pentecostalism*, 14, 196–97; Anderson, "Global Pentecostalism," 214; and Robinson, "Pentecostal Hermeneutic," 2.

6. Jacobsen, "Introduction," 4 (italics original).

7. Althouse, "Towards a Theological," 2. Althouse acknowledges that some Pentecostal groups (with stronger Holiness roots) emphasize a third experience of sanctification, occurring prior to Spirit baptism. Also see Jacobsen, "Introduction," 4, 8; and Kärkkäinen, *Pneumatology*, 95–98.

8. Anderson, "Pentecostals Believe," 56, cf. 58.

the process. . . . However, in spite of the awkwardness with the process, we have tried to talk about these experiences. In fact, we have little choice. Experiences with the Spirit are of great importance to Pentecostals. We have wanted our families and friends to share in them with us, and as a result we had to look for ways to tell them about them.[9]

What we should note, on the one hand, then, is that experience is integral to and functions authoritatively within Pentecostalism. Spittler observes, "a quoted aphorism often heard in pentecostal circles runs this way: 'The person with an experience is never at the mercy of another person with a doctrine.'"[10] Experience is an authoritative means by which God is known and the divine will revealed; as such it holds epistemological value,[11] and at times primacy over theology and doctrine.[12] Yet, on the other hand, while words falter at capturing or passing on the significance of experiences with the Spirit, Pentecostals have still endeavored to communicate their experiences theologically and doctrinally.[13] A tension exists, then, between experience and theological articulation within Pentecostalism.[14]

Further complicating the issue, the concept of experience also operates somewhat ambiguously within Pentecostalism. It is probably helpful to locate such transformative encounters as Spirit baptism as being close

9. Kydd, "'Better Felt,'" 30–31.

10. Spittler, "Spirituality," 1097a.

11. Robinson, "Pentecostal Hermeneutic," 2; Clark and Lederle et al., *What Is Distinctive*, 36–39; cf. Lewis, "Towards a Pentecostal," 1–28.

12. Warrington, "Experience," 5, 8; Warrington suggests that experience precedes theological articulation for Pentecostals. Also see Warrington, *Pentecostal Theology*, 15–16; cf. Anderson, "Pentecostals Believe," 55; and Jongeneel, "Preface," xi.

13. Notice, for example, the repetition of the (undefined) term "experience" in the Pentecostal Assemblies of Canada's (PAOC) statement on Spirit baptism: "The baptism in the Holy Spirit is an *experience* in which the believer yields control of himself to the Holy Spirit. Through this he comes to know Christ in a more intimate way, and receives power to witness and grow spiritually. Believers should earnestly seek the baptism in the Holy Spirit according to the command of our Lord Jesus Christ. The initial evidence of the baptism in the Holy Spirit is speaking in other tongues as the Spirit gives utterance. This *experience* is distinct from, and subsequent to, the *experience* of the new birth" (Pentecostal Assemblies, *Statement*, article 5.6.3; italics added). The PAOC statement does not speak for all Pentecostals; however, it does represent a classical Pentecostal understanding of this doctrine, and it is the denomination with which I am ordained and most familiar.

14. Clark and Lederle et al., *What Is Distinctive*, 35–42. They note this tension to be different for Pentecostals than for charismatics.

to what Schner referred to as being "religious aspects" of experience. Even so, such encounters cannot be generically labeled "religious experiences," and require qualification. For Pentecostals, not just any experience can be considered of God or authentically Pentecostal. As Jacobsen notes, experiences with the Spirit, such as healings or other charismata, were not unique to early Pentecostals, or sufficient to distinguish Pentecostal identity.[15] Such experiences needed to be understood in a particular way, occurring and interpreted within a broader Pentecostal theological and spiritual framework.

> There is no doubt that experience was a crucial dimension of the early pentecostal movement, but it was *experience guided by theological truth that really mattered*. Experience alone was considered dangerous. Every Pentecostal leader worth his or her salt knew that. Experiences needed to be examined and evaluated. They needed to be properly labelled and categorized so believers could know where they stood in their relationship with God and to what they should aspire. . . . The very act of becoming a pentecostal was in a certain sense a function of the theological labels one used to describe one's religious experiences. Experience alone did not make one a pentecostal. It was experience interpreted in a pentecostal way that made one pentecostal.[16]

No doubt, in contrast to more rationalistic approaches, Pentecostals had a certain theological "style" with regard to the "gravity" they allotted spirituality and experiences with the Spirit.[17] But it is not the case that early Pentecostals were not involved in careful, rational, even systematic theological articulation.[18] Pentecostals have always used words to explain their experiences, and "words taken together constitute the field of theology, and every religious movement—pentecostalism included—has

15. Jacobsen, "Introduction," 5.

16. Jacobsen, *Thinking in the Spirit*, 3 (italics added).

17. Ibid., 7 (cf. ibid., 5–8); Jacobsen, "Introduction," 2. Spittler notes this accent on spirituality underscores the limitations of theological discourse for understanding Pentecostal experience of God. He defines spirituality as "a cluster of acts and sentiments that are informed by the beliefs and values that characterize a specific religious community" (Spittler, "Spirituality," 1096b; cf. Wacker, "'Wild Theories,'" 22).

18. Jacobsen, *Thinking in the Spirit*, 7–8 (cf. ibid., 4–6). Jacobsen argues that the intent behind writing theology among early Pentecostals was not simply for practical reasons, but for the purpose of "truth-telling"—exploring the theological significance of encounters with the Spirit. Further, while early Pentecostal theologians were "amateurs" at their task (in comparison with other theological traditions), nonetheless, this should be considered formal theology.

a theology or theologies to guide it on its way."[19] Paradoxically, of course, there is a "twist"—Pentecostalism as a movement was birthed in "protest against too much reliance on words," or at least "religious words without religious experiences to back them up; it was a protest against theological hollowness."[20] What is clear, however, is that *both* theology *and* experience are deeply enmeshed and integral to Pentecostal identity.[21] There is, then, value in attempting to understand Pentecostal experience of the Spirit theologically, and a brief survey of some suggested approaches is merited.

Approaches to Understanding Pentecostal Experience Theologically

One basic approach locates Pentecostal experience of God within a two (or three) stage theological framework. Gordon L. Anderson (Assemblies of God, USA) typifies this position, speaking of experience with the Spirit as being primarily associated with two key crisis events—conversion and a post-conversion Spirit baptism (accompanied by tongues).[22] However, as Warrington observes, not all Pentecostals see things quite this way. Certainly, not all hold to tongues as the "initial evidence," and the meaning of Spirit baptism is also widely interpreted.[23] So, Pentecostal experience cannot be theologically reduced to these crisis moments.

Donald W. Dayton provides a broader attempt to define Pentecostalism theologically, suggesting that four doctrines form the *gestalt* of Pentecostalism: conversion (justification), Spirit baptism (evidenced by tongues), divine healing, and a pre-millennial return of

19. Jacobsen, "Introduction," 5. Grant Wacker, in fact, suggests that "the movement is better described by its beliefs than its practices. Contrary to stereotype, Pentecostals are deadly serious about doctrine." He quickly qualifies this, stating, "Nonetheless, a purely doctrinal definition is too thin" (Wacker, "'Wild Theories,'" 21, 22).

20. Jacobsen, "Introduction," 5; also see Jacobsen, *Thinking in the Spirit*, 354–56. Jacobsen argues that Pentecostal emphasis on doctrine led to many vehement disagreements within their ranks even from the outset.

21. Jacobsen, *Thinking in the Spirit*, 5.

22. Anderson, "Pentecostals Believe," 54. This is not to say that Anderson would necessarily reduce Pentecostalism to these crisis moments.

23. Warrington, "Experience," 2–4; cf. Coulter, "What Meaneth This?," 42. On the diversity of interpretations of Spirit baptism, see Lederle, *Treasures Old and New*; cf. Suurmond, *Word and Spirit*, 144–48.

Christic.[24] Dayton argues that these four (or five) elements of the "full gospel" are held together by the person of Jesus, who forms the center, orienting all these aspects of Christian experience.[25] Clark and Lederle also highlight this Jesus-centered approach, using it to suggest a preliminary characterization of Pentecostal experience:

> To be Pentecostal is to have experienced the power of God in Jesus. This statement may perhaps serve as a tentative definition of the Pentecostal believer. Experience in this sense is essential to Pentecost—without it there cannot be true identification with the church of the Book of Acts, either in mission or in essence. That there is a God who is involved in the lives of mere humans, and who wants to act dynamically in the lives of *all* people, is a basic tenet of Pentecostal faith. That man experiences in this power of God in Jesus Christ alone is a corollary. The old Pentecostal formula—Jesus Christ: Saviour, Healer, Spirit-baptiser, Coming King—attests to this. It is Christ who lies at the heart of the Pentecostal experience, although the power by which he is known is that of the Spirit. For this reason Pentecostals are understandably sceptical of the dialogical elements in Christianity which claim to see the Holy Spirit active in non-Christian religions. Their experience of the Spirit is experience of the Spirit of Jesus, and many in the Third World avow that "The power of God in Jesus" in their own lives has meant a radical deliverance from those spirits which are active in non-Christian religions.[26]

Among the significant points raised by Dayton, and Clark and Lederle, is that Pentecostal experience can be discerned to a large degree by its connection to the Jesus of the Bible. There is a traditional emphasis within Pentecostalism that links Spirit to Word, and which serves as a criterion of sorts for distinguishing what can and cannot be viewed as experience of the Spirit.[27] That said, Warrington notes that the four- (or five-)

---

24. Dayton, *Theological Roots*, 20–21. While some Pentecostals would add the fifth element of sanctification, nonetheless, he argues that all Pentecostals subscribe to at least these four.

25. Land, *Pentecostal Spirituality*, 18; cf. Thomas, "Pentecostal Theology," 17.

26. Clark and Lederle et al., *What Is Distinctive*, 43–44 (italics original).

27. Ibid., 44–47. Clark and Lederle claim that Pentecostals are able to avoid the dangers of subjectivism "Precisely because it is Christ who is encountered" (ibid., 45). Pentecostals will have personal and subjective encounters with God, but these will all bear some similarity because it is the experience of the same person (ibid., 46).

fold Jesus-centered model is not uniquely held by Pentecostals, and so it too is insufficient for qualifying Pentecostal experience theologically.[28]

Steven J. Land has suggested an alternative to a strictly theological understanding of Pentecostal experience, while still retaining a connection to the five-fold model.[29] He posits that Pentecostalism is best understood by its spirituality, and not merely articulated doctrinal beliefs,[30] defining spirituality as "the integration of beliefs and practices in the affections which are themselves evoked being expressed by those beliefs and practices."[31] Explains Land, "My thesis is that the righteousness, holiness and power of God are correlated with distinctive apocalyptic affections which are the integrating core of Pentecostal spirituality. This spirituality is Christocentric because it is pneumatic; its 'fivefold' Gospel is focused on Christ because of its starting point in the Holy Spirit. Underlying this correlation is a soteriology which emphasizes salvation as participation in the divine life more than the removal of guilt."[32]

Several of Land's points are noteworthy here. First, he believes that a dichotomy between power and holiness exists within current Pentecostalism, and that this can be overcome by emphasizing the affections as the heart of Pentecostal spirituality.[33] Second, he defines the affections as being apocalyptically oriented—the "soon coming King" doctrine functions as the primary motivating "vision" for Pentecostals.[34] Third, while retaining aspects of the five-fold Christocentric orientation, greater emphasis is given to a pneumatic starting point (thus, Word and Spirit relate more dynamically).[35] Pentecostal experience of the Spirit,

28. Warrington, "Experience," 2. Also see Cross, "Can There Be," 19–20.

29. Land, *Pentecostal Spirituality*, 18.

30. Ibid., 32–53; Land, "Passion for the Kingdom," 23; cf. Wacker, "'Wild Theories,'" 21–22.

31. Land, *Pentecostal Spirituality*, 13.

32. Ibid., 23.

33. Ibid., 23, 44. Land draws heavily on the historical link between Wesleyanism and Pentecostalism in making this point. On the affections as central to Pentecostal spirituality, also see Jacobsen, *Thinking in the Spirit*, 362.

34. Land, *Pentecostal Spirituality*, 59–71, 136–60; cf. Land, "A Passion," 28–46. Land re-envisions Pentecostal eschatology, arguing it should be understood not within a dispensationalist framework, but as an inaugurated eschatology in which Christ is the King, and the Spirit is now experienced as the reigning presence of God in present history (ibid., 53–55). On Land's revisionist eschatology also see Althouse, *Spirit of the Last Days*, 61–66.

35. Land, *Pentecostal Spirituality*, 183. On this Word/Spirit relationship, also see Del

then, centers on the eschatologically-oriented affections, worked out in three primary experiences—justification, sanctification and Spirit baptism (each corresponding to a member of the Trinity).[36]

Land's approach is not without its detractors. Dale M. Coulter, for example, acknowledges Land's attempt to move beyond the five-fold Christocentric model, advocating a broader Trinitarian scope. He believes, however, that Land may still be overly tied to the five-fold model, suggesting that it sounds more like Pentecostals *were* than presently *are*.[37] Alternatively, Koo Dong Yun critiques Land's emphasis on the affections as the core of Pentecostal spirituality. Emphasis on affections, he argues, better characterizes the spirituality of the Great Awakening or eighteenth- and nineteenth-century Methodism, but not twentieth-century, North American Pentecostalism, which has a far more pragmatic spirituality (a point to which we will return).[38] So, while Land's portrayal of Pentecostal spirituality and theology is helpful (and has been influential), it is not an entirely convincing representation for all.

Terry Cross offers yet another theological approach toward understanding Pentecostal experience theologically. He is not content that spirituality should be so closely equated with theology (as with Land), and argues that a better integrating principle is needed as a foundation for Pentecostal theology.[39] He views the five-fold model as too restrictive in its christocentricity, and offers instead an experiential Trinitarian rubric as the principle for theological reflection. Cross believes Pentecostals "must begin with the essential experience of the direct encounter of the Spirit in their lives." He does not, however, restrict this "encounter" to the experience of Spirit baptism. Instead, "direct encounter with the Spirit is

---

Colle, "Postmodernism," 106.

36. Land, *Pentecostal Spirituality*, 82–93. Justification (regeneration) corresponds to the Father's bringing of believers into missional fellowship. Sanctification corresponds to the Son, moving the Christian to seek the will of the Father in love. Spirit baptism is the third experience, in which the believer is equipped to do battle for the Lord.

37. Coulter, "What Meaneth This?," 40–41. This contradicts the view advocated by Land and others that the first ten years of Pentecostalism represent not its infancy but its heart. See Land, *Pentecostal Spirituality*, 13, 26, 47; and cf. Johns, "Adolescence of Pentecostalism," 5.

38. Yun, "Metaphysical Construct," 7. Yun does not, however, deny historical connections between Pentecostalism and the Holiness tradition.

39. Cross, "Can There Be," 13–14. To be fair, Land does not equate spirituality and theology either, and in fact calls for further exploration as to how these two are related (Land, *Pentecostal Spirituality*, 220).

necessary even for salvation. Therefore, this essential, common experience of believers is that we have been confronted by the God of scripture and must make a decision to follow him or not. When we decide to follow Jesus, immediately we are led into a greater understanding of God."[40] Cross emphasizes, then, that understanding of God (theology) should be shaped by experiences of God, but *also primarily* by the God being experienced (thus avoiding the anthropocentrism of Schleiermacher and Feuerbach). So, while integrating encounters with the Spirit (who is God), it is a God-centered (Trinitarian) experiential theology that serves as the framework.[41]

Coulter, however, is not convinced that Cross has sufficiently presented a *distinctly* Pentecostal theology of experience.[42] He proposes that a more fruitful approach is to explore the historical theological traditions that implicitly (and explicitly) influenced early Pentecostalism. Specifically, he believes that the influence of the Eastern fathers and Arminianism (via Wesley) deserves attention; and from these, two possibilities emerge for serving as the theological core of Pentecostalism. First, Coulter explains, Pentecostalism has a "dynamic view of revelation as an ongoing enterprise where the Spirit continuously speaks to the church throughout its earthly existence."[43] This factor implies that Pentecostalism has more in common with Roman Catholicism and Eastern Orthodoxy than Protestantism, and this point should be sufficient to distinguish it from its Reformed-Baptistic and Wesleyan-Holiness heritage.[44] Secondly, Pentecostalism emphasizes a more synergistic soteriology, which "attempt[s] to construe sanctification as being causally linked to salvation to such an extent that it impacts the justification of the individual believer."[45] In short, Coulter believes that experience alone is insufficient to distinguish Pentecostalism; experience needs to be understood through a particular theological core. So, while Pentecostals share theological similarities with Methodists, Roman

---

40. Cross, "Can There Be," 21, cf. 19–21.

41. Ibid., 5–6, 21.

42. Coulter, "What Meaneth This?," 39.

43. Ibid., 53, cf. 51–56; also see Althouse, "Towards a Theological," 2.

44. Coulter, "What Meaneth This?," 53–54, cf. 56–63.

45. Ibid., 54, cf. 55.

Catholics, Wesleyans, and evangelicals, they should not simply be identified with any one of these traditions.[46]

> I would contend that finding the theological core Pentecostalism must involve more than the examination of an experience of the Spirit. It must embrace the richness of the Pentecostal tradition and the complex interplay between the already-existing doctrines within its tradition. It is the complex interplay between experience, revelation and an inherited "evangelical" doctrine of Scripture that provides a distinctive insight into the Scripture principle [i.e., the way they read Scripture] and how it should function. Likewise the interaction between sanctification, Arminian views on freedom of the will and experience of the Spirit's presence and power led to a modified view of justification. These are theological distinctions and they may be offered by Pentecostals as providing insight into the truth underlying doctrinal assertions.[47]

I view Coulter's theological portrayal of Pentecostal experience as quite promising. The emphasis on Jesus and Scripture underscores Pentecostalism's strong Spirit-Word connection, while yet preventing Word-domination by accenting ongoing revelation and a more synergistic soteriology (not so dominated by forensic categories). But can even this theological articulation adequately represent all Pentecostals? Warrington reminds us that theological conceptions alone will ultimately prove insufficient for characterizing Pentecostalism because the beliefs of Pentecostals globally are simply too diverse.[48] "Pentecostals," he states, "are less defined by their doctrines, and more by their perception that God lives with them in the here and now."[49] Pentecostals expect "to touch God and to be touched by him." Theirs is "a theology of encounter—encounter of God, the Bible and the Christian community." And, "Defining [this] encounter with God is less important than encountering God in

---

46. Ibid., 43, 55–56. Coulter, along with a growing number of Pentecostal theologians, believes that Pentecostalism cannot simply be understood as being evangelicalism plus Spirit baptism and tongues. Similarly, Cross believes Pentecostals are able to offer a "main course," and not just a side dish, at the buffet of theological options (Cross, "Rich Feast," 27–47; also see Cross, "Can There Be," 10–13; Land, *Pentecostal Spirituality*, 29; and Hollenweger, "Critical Tradition," 8).

47. Coulter, "What Meaneth This?," 64 (brackets added).

48. Warrington, "Experience," 1–4.

49. Ibid., 4, cf. 5, 8.

the first place."[50] Others have also observed that this experiential emphasis is largely what has enabled Pentecostalism to adapt so readily to the
variety of cultures worldwide, resulting in the diversity of expressions.[51]

Still, Warrington admits, "Although experience is important in
Pentecostal spirituality and worship, it is important to acknowledge that
it is not experience per se, but that which is associated with God, often
related to the Spirit but centralized in Jesus."[52] Echoing our earlier observations, he qualifies Pentecostal experience as being shaped by Scripture
and Pentecostal tradition (community), and being *of* the Spirit who is
Other.[53] So, once again, we find that the experience of encounter, like
theological conceptualization, is a *necessary but not sufficient criterion* for
understanding Pentecostal experience of the Spirit. Another means does
exist, however, by which to explore Pentecostal experience—observation
of Pentecostal spirituality in practice, particularly in worship—and so to
this we now turn.

Understanding Encounter with the Spirit through Pentecostal Worship

Clark and Lederle note that Pentecostal experience is difficult to understand except through a Pentecostal point of view,[54] or, as Joel J. Shuman
describes it, a Pentecostal subcultural-linguistic framework.[55] One reason

50. Ibid., 5, cf. 6–8. Warrington acknowledges that challenges emerge from allowing experience such a central place. He cites the danger of naïveté among Pentecostals,
including the devaluing of the mind and the potential addiction to seeking ecstasy-type
experiences. But he feels these issues can be largely overcome with Spirit-led discernment, and that the benefits far outweigh the risks. Pentecostal emphasis on experience
has produced a missional ethos, and an expectation of encounter with God through
the Scriptures leading to tangible life transformation. Also see Warrington, *Pentecostal
Theology*, 20–27.

51. See Coulter, "What Meaneth This?," 46; Jacobsen, "Introduction," 1; Klaus,
"Pentecostalism," 127; and Johannesen, "Remembering," 1.

52. Warrington, "Experience," 8, cf. 5.

53. Ibid., 5; also see Plüss, "Religious Experience," 3.

54. Clark and Lederle et al., *What Is Distinctive*, 38; also see Johannesen,
"Remembering," 7. Johannesen states that becoming Pentecostal is akin to learning a
new language, and sees belief (like language) as a social faculty, not an inner mental one.

55. Shuman, "Toward a Cultural-Linguistic," 214, 220; cf. Lindbeck, *Nature of
Doctrine*, 63, 69, 80, 113–24. Shuman, building on Lindbeck's doctrinal theory, views
Pentecostalism as a subcultural-linguistic community, needing to be understood
from within that framework. Lindbeck suggests that worship and liturgy function as

for this is that Pentecostals have traditionally passed on their beliefs and practices predominantly through "narrative theology" or "oral liturgy," as opposed to "discursive theology."[56] Walter J. Hollenweger describes narrative theology as operating

> not through the book, but through the parable,
> not through the thesis, but through the testimony,
> not through dissertations, but through dances,
> not through concepts, but through banquets,
> not through a system of thinking, but through stories and songs,
> not through definitions, but through descriptions,
> not through arguments, but through transformed lives.[57]

Paul W. Lewis also argues that an "oral culture" exists within Pentecostalism, in which "theology takes place in sermons, and the testimony service is a dominant rite." Such "Oral cultures tend to be relational, communal, and tend to emphasis [sic.] the pragmatic. Further, the role of the narrative, normally important in ethical formulations and development, becomes much more important as the source of knowledge and understanding."[58]

This helps explain why Pentecostalism is difficult to comprehend when analyzed merely through theological discourse, such as found in books or journal articles.[59] An alternative, and perhaps even more fruit-

---

first-order activities of subcultural-religious communities, and as such should be viewed as making ontological truth claims. Doctrine, on the other hand, functions as second-order discourse, making propositional (but not ontological) claims about the worshipping community. Doctrine is normative, then, insofar as it bears intrasystemic faithful witness to the worship practices of the community. Important, for our purposes, is that doctrine and worship are interconnected, doctrine being reliant on community proclamation and practice.

56. Kärkkäinen, *Pneumatology*, 93–94. Also see Hollenweger, *Pentecostalism*, 269–87; Land, *Pentecostal Spirituality*, 19, 35–37, 47–53, 72, 110–13; and Suurmond, *Word and Spirit*, 3–19. Land views Pentecostal orality as a derivative of an African-American spiritual influence, what Hollenweger calls "black spirituality." The other primary spiritual heritage is Wesleyanism, from which Pentecostal emphasis on sanctification is derived.

57. Hollenweger, *Pentecostalism*, 196.

58. Lewis, "Towards a Pentecostal," 8.

59. See Smith, "Closing of the Book," 55, cf. 58. A result of oral theology within Pentecostalism, states Smith, is a "popular mistrust of theology and hesitancy to keep historical records. There is a sense of the faithful which feels that by recording and articulating, something of the freshness of the Spirit . . . is lost by being domesticated. Writing is akin to hoarding the manna, which will only rot if one attempts to retain it. Instead, one ought to wait for fresh rain from heaven each morning." He asserts, further,

ful means by which to understand Pentecostal experience is by observing Pentecostal spirituality in practice, especially in the worship service, described by Jean-Jacques Suurmond as "charismatic celebration."[60] A helpful analysis utilizing this approach is provided by Daniel E. Albrecht, in his *Rites in the Spirit*.[61] Based on his observation and study of Pentecostal worship, Albrecht identifies four qualities of Pentecostal spirituality, which he places under the broader category of "experience of God." In doing so he provides a useful framework for understanding Pentecostal experience from the perspective of worship and praxis, and this will serve to guide our discussion for the remainder of this section.[62]

Pentecostal Experience of God as "Mystical" and "Supernatural"

Albrecht's first quality of Pentecostal spirituality is "Experiencing God mystically as supernatural."[63] He believes Pentecostals can be located within the broader Christian mystical tradition, defining mysticism as "direct intuition or experience of God."[64] The Pentecostal worship service, he observes, is "designed to provide a context for mystical *encounter*, an experience with the divine. This encounter is mediated by the sense of the immediate divine presence."[65] Worship participants are

---

that evangelicalism is a text-based community, and therefore when Pentecostals are subsumed into that tradition their oral spirituality is marginalized and suppressed.

60. Suurmond, *Word and* Spirit, 22, cf. 20–26.

61. Albrecht's study focuses on three Pentecostal/charismatic congregations in northern California, belonging to three different denominations: The Assemblies of God (AG), the International Church of the Foursquare Gospel (ICFG), and the Vineyard Christian Fellowship (VCF). The AG and ICFG fall within the Classical Pentecostal designation, while the VCF can be classified as neo-pentecostal. Albrecht's study is thus broader in scope than this project, but for the most part, his observations are representative of Pentecostalism (Albrecht, *Rites in the Spirit*, 41–120).

62. Albrecht, *Rites in the Spirit*, 237–51. He views the Pentecostal worship service as the "heart of Pentecostal spirituality," and labels it as "ritual" in that it is a means of expressing attitudes, beliefs and values appropriate to Pentecostalism. "Rites" designates the particular segments of what might take place in a worship service (ibid., 239). His summary of Pentecostal experience of God is repeated in condensed form in Albrecht, "Pentecostal Spirituality: Ecumenical," § I.B.

63. Albrecht, *Rites in the Spirit*, 238–43.

64. Ibid., 238–39, cf. 185–86. Albrecht borrows this definition from Evelyn Underhill.

65. Ibid., 239 (italics original). Also see Miller and Yamamori, *Global Pentecostalism*, 138. They observe that the task of a worship leader is to help the congregation to "feel"

led through various "rites," such as praise, prayer, or laying on of hands, toward "mystical-type experiences of God," including dreams and visions.[66] In a worship service, Pentecostals expect and actively respond to the presence of God in their midst. Albrecht explains, "When a worship leader says, 'let's enter into the presence of the Lord,' it is not heard as mere rhetoric. The congregation expects to have a keen awareness of divine presence."[67]

Significant here is Albrecht's accent on the concept of *encounter* for describing Pentecostal experience of God—Pentecostal experience is of the Spirit who is *Other*. He also asserts that this encounter is mediated by a "sense" of the immediacy of God's presence, although he does not explicitly clarify what this means.[68] This could be taken to denote a mediation of the Spirit through human affections (feelings and intuitions). Conversely, it might also refer to the influence of the various external rites upon the participating individuals and congregation overall, opening worshippers to particular religious-type experiences. In the latter case, this would mean that Albrecht is elevating the significance of external forms (rites and rituals) in serving to help meditate experience of God, as opposed to merely an inward seeking for God's Spirit. Based on Albrecht's overall focus, I think a combination of both is likely implied—outward forms (rites) shape the worship atmosphere toward the heightening of certain emotions and intuitions, which in turn reinforce and help interpret (give meaning to) the rites themselves.

In any case, Albrecht advocates that *belief in* direct encounter with the divine presence locates Pentecostalism to some extent within the Christian mystical tradition. He further supports this, while acknowledging Pentecostals' typical extroverted worship expression, by highlighting an element sometimes overlooked. He states, "Often in

---

the presence of God.

66. Albrecht, *Rites in the Spirit*, 239; cf. Suurmond, *Word and* Spirit, 24.

67. Albrecht, *Rites in the Spirit*, 239; cf. Albrecht, "Pentecostal Spirituality: Ecumenical," § I.B.

68. Albrecht, *Rites in the Spirit*, 186, cf. 185. Albrecht labels this aspect of Pentecostal worship the "Mode of Transcendental Ecstasy," in which "ritualists believe that they are having an experience, performing rites or manifesting behavior that is directly influenced by their God." There are moments in which Pentecostal worshippers "believe that the Holy Spirit has to some extent infused them or acted upon them. Such experiences are perceived as being direct (mystical) experience of the divine." Such comments evoke echoes of our discussion in chapter 1 concerning suggestions of "mediated immediacy" or "direct mediation" of experience of God.

the overall worship service, the celebrative mode melts into the mode of *contemplation* in which an even more salient sense of the divine is felt."[69] This contemplative mode, Albrecht describes as "a sense of openness to God, a deep receptivity"; and it is therefore an *active passivity*, a waiting for the Spirit to act or respond (to worshippers) within the ritual context.[70]

What Pentecostals anticipate in this "mystical" atmosphere is an encounter with the Spirit who is omnipresent, but who also will break in (so to speak) supernaturally.[71] Experience of God's presence is encounter with the God who is transcendent and wholly other. So, while Pentecostals may emphasize an "immanent sense of the divine,"[72] Albrecht clarifies: "The Pentecostal realm envisions a world subject to invasions by the supernatural element. Pentecostals teach adherents to expect encounters with the supernatural. For the Pentecostal the line between natural and supernatural is permeable, but the *two categories are radically separate*."[73]

The Spirit, of course, is not restricted to the congregational worship setting, and may touch even the mundane aspects of life—yet in every case it is best to interpret this encounter as an invasion of the supernatural. Central to the Spirit's invasive action, says Albrecht, is the crisis experience of Spirit baptism, understood as a "divine 'overwhelming' of the human person."[74] This interpretation also emphasizes Pentecostalism's "fundamental binary opposition or distinction of human/divine."[75]

The above discussion deserves some clarification, since I think that only with qualification can the term "mystical" be applied to Pentecostals, although Albrecht is not alone in doing so.[76] Others, however, are averse

---

69. Ibid., 240 (italics added), cf. 183–84. On Pentecostal prayer also see Miller and Yamamori, *Global Pentecostalism*, 144–46.

70. Albrecht, "Pentecostal Spirituality: Looking," 118, 119.

71. Albrecht, *Rites in the Spirit*, 240.

72. Albrecht, "Pentecostal Spirituality: Ecumenical," Introduction.

73. Albrecht, *Rites in the Spirit*, 241 (italics added).

74. Ibid., 241–42. Albrecht acknowledges that not all waves of pentecostalism describe these experiences using the language of "Spirit baptism," but the idea of being overwhelmed by the Spirit is a common theme.

75. Albrecht, "Pentecostal Spirituality: Ecumenical," § I.A.1

76. For example, Cox describes Pentecostal Spirit baptism as "mystical encounter," and their worship as "populist mysticism," although he notes that Pentecostals tend to almost exclusively emphasize experiences of joy in worship; rarely making room for

to identifying Pentecostalism with mysticism, believing Pentecostal experience provides a corrective "against the complacency and introversion of pietism and mysticism."[77] Albrecht's use of "mystical" is a way of labeling the Pentecostal belief that worshippers can, in some sense, directly experience God, and to accent the sometimes under-noticed contemplative elements in Pentecostal ritual. "Mysticism," for the purposes of this description of Pentecostal spirituality, is not being used here in its stricter more technical sense (as per Schner's earlier definition), which emphasizes ineffability and the loss of self in the divine.[78] Pentecostal encounters with the Spirit may be difficult to describe theologically, but they are not ineffable—they are publicly shared, evaluated and passed on (usually) through oral means.[79] It would seem, then, that Albrecht is using the term "mystical" in a less technical sense.

Further, notwithstanding the contemplative elements in their worship, Pentecostals are not primarily known for being inward-focused, as is often associated with mysticism.[80] Even Pentecostal contemplation is an *active* waiting, anticipating the Spirit's intervention and activity,

---

more negatively-toned experiences (such as suffering or spiritual "dryness") more common in traditional mysticism (Cox, *Fire from Heaven*, 70, 315). Wacker is reluctant to call Pentecostals mystics, although occasionally, "the longing to touch God bordered on mysticism, a craving to be absorbed into the One . . ." (Wacker, *Heaven Below*, 11). Also see Cargal, "Beyond the Fundamentalist-Modernist," 186; Cartledge, "Attending to Experience," 4–7; Coulter, "What Meaneth This?," 46; and Kay, "Pentecostal Experiences," 5.

77. Clark and Lederle et al., *What Is Distinctive*, 46; cf. Lewis, "Towards a Pentecostal," 4, 7.

78. On differentiating "mystical" from "religious" experiences, see Nieto, "Religious Experience," 103–42. He argues that religious experiences always preserve a sense of awareness of time, whereas mystical experiences lose such external locators. Pentecostal testimonies of experiences with the Spirit usually preserve these external locators, and so would tend to fall within the category of "religious experience" (although not generic) as opposed to mystical.

79. See Lewis, "Towards a Pentecostal," 4–5. Lewis strongly contends that Pentecostal religious experience needs to be differentiated from notions of ineffability and other such descriptions of mystical experiences, because Pentecostal encounters with the Spirit are defined by and articulated within a particular subcultural expression of Christianity. Further, these experiences work themselves out in concrete expressions, such as "*charismata*, missiological endeavors, [and] participatory worship," which can be tested and verified by leaders and community (ibid., 7; italics original).

80. Overwhelmingly, external worship expressions characterize Pentecostalism. See Plüss, "Religious Experience," 4–7; Jacobsen, "Introduction," 6; Hudson, "Worship," 189; Miller and Yamamori, *Global Pentecostalism*, 136–38; Armstrong, "Embrace Your Inner Pentecostal."; and Suurmond, *Word and Spirit*, 21–25.

which might very well manifest in some tangible form (e.g., healing, prophecy, etc.). Albrecht actually does qualify his "mystical" label, noting that Pentecostals maintain a natural/supernatural dichotomy, tending them toward an overly individualistic and reductionistic spirituality. Pentecostals often reduce the Spirit's activity to the sensible or tangible, and often to manifestations that are overtly physical and emotional (e.g., tears or laughter). Without this type of "evidence," Pentecostals are less confident the Spirit is being experienced.[81]

In light of the above, a Pentecostal concept of the Spirit's immanence in creation and history should likely be understood to mean "the Spirit-who-is-Other being *present* in these contexts," accenting the transcendence and invasiveness of the Spirit. This is why the term "encounter" is so appropriate for describing Pentecostal experience of God. It is, says Jean-Daniel Plüss, "an encounter of the other, [and] as such it relates to the otherness of God and yields meaning that goes beyond human experience." In other words, encounter with the Spirit provides revelation of something other than what is immanently found in everyday human life, and by doing so it provides transformative power, so central to Pentecostal spirituality.[82]

Pentecostal Experience of God as Communal

The second quality of Pentecostal worship identified by Albrecht is "Experiencing God in a communal context."[83] He summarizes:

81. See Miller and Yamamori, *Global Pentecostalism*, 145–47; and Hudson, "Worship," 196–97. Hudson observes that Pentecostal worship (particularly song lyrics) can tend to accent the Spirit's work as triumphalistic and focused on immediate individual personal transformation. There is little attention given to the process of change that occurs among most believers; and times of doubt, or feelings of God's absence, are rarely integrated into Pentecostal theology and worship.

82. Plüss, "Religious Experience," 3. Also see Tarr, "Transcendence," 195–222. He argues that Pentecostals in the academy must not give into the temptation to surrender the typical Pentecostal emphasis on God's transcendence for immanence.

83. Albrecht, *Rites in the Spirit*, 243; cf. Suurmond, *Word and Spirit*, 22–25. Albrecht's first two qualities share noticeable similarities with Suurmond's description of five characteristics of "charismatic celebration." The first, is "an oral liturgy which is not set down on paper and therefore is accessible to people who have little or no literary training." Second, "narrative theology and testimonies" evoke an "existential conviction of 'what God can do for you' and the corresponding story of 'what God has done for me.'" Third, since the Spirit works through all believers, "there is maximum participation at the level of prayer, evaluation and also the making of resolutions." Fourth, "space

"Pentecostal spirituality is rooted in a communal experience of God typified by its encouragement of democratic-participatory forms, and by its stress on the media of biblical symbols, oral exchange, and kinesthetic/music."[84] He admits, this communal element is usually overshadowed by an individualistic tendency. "There is truth in the characterization that Pentecostals are individualists. The essential mystical quality of their experience lends itself to a certain focus on the personal/individual dimensions of spirituality."[85] Nevertheless, he stresses that community plays a "determinative" role in shaping Pentecostal spirituality.[86]

The rites and rituals of Pentecostal worship provide opportunity for strong social bonding, says Albrecht, and invite high participation from all congregants.[87] Worship is a corporate "event, an experience" evoking expectation that something will happen specifically to each individual.[88] However, individual encounters with the Spirit *occur within* and are *connected to* the community. Plüss concurs; Pentecostal experience of God is relational, formed in community and therefore "typically ecclesial in

---

is made for intuitive communication, for example in the form of dreams and visions." Fifth, "body and soul are experienced as one whole in the charismatic celebration." Here, the Pentecostal liturgical practice of prayer for healing is cited, which is intended not only for the physical body, but also for the social/political spheres of life, and ultimately points to the healing of all creation. Suurmond suggests all these characteristics contain "an element of play," akin to what would be involved in "a good game" (having rules, yet serving no utilitarian end). He believes that characterizing charismatic worship as "play" emphasizes the dynamic relationship between Word and Spirit, in contrast to the Logos/institutional dominated tendencies in historic Western Christianity (ibid., 27–97).

84. Albrecht, "Pentecostal Spirituality: Ecumenical," § I.B.2.

85. Albrecht, *Rites in the Spirit*, 243.

86. Albrecht, "Pentecostal Spirituality: Ecumenical," § I.B.2. Also see Miller and Yamamori, *Global Pentecostalism*, 129–59; and Plüss, "Religious Experience," 4–7.

87. Albrecht, *Rites in the Spirit*, 244–45; cf. Albrecht, "Pentecostal Spirituality: Ecumenical," § I.B.2. Albrecht cites participatory worship as being partly responsible for attracting and retaining worshippers, since it provides opportunity to corporately experience God while allowing for individual expression. He adds that Pentecostal emphasis on lay leadership and participation has had a democratizing effect on congregational life, exemplified historically in women being allowed to occupy key roles as preachers, teachers, evangelists and missionaries. Albrecht does observe, however, that Pentecostal churches more rooted in the American evangelical tradition tend to "display less openness to women's roles in leadership." On women's role in Pentecostalism, also see Cox, *Fire from Heaven*, 123–38; Archer, *Pentecostal Hermeneutic*, 18–19; Holm, "Paradigmatic Analysis," ch. 7; Land, "Passion for the Kingdom," 21; and Lewis, "Reflections of a Hundred," §§ 2–3.

88. Clark and Lederle et al., *What Is Distinctive*, 43.

nature. It is in the context of the church, the body of Christ, that the Spirit of God enables, legitimates or questions a believer's experiences."[89]

Within this "participatory communal experience," Albrecht identifies three primary media that shape Pentecostal liturgy. First, Pentecostals relate and communicate to one another with "biblical symbols," using them as a criterion to evaluate doctrines and practices, frequently asking, "Is it biblical?"[90] The second medium is "orality," and the third, "kinesthetic/musical." Music and bodily expression are fundamental elements in Pentecostal worship. "Pentecostals seek to worship their God with their whole being. They have intuitively presented their bodies, their physicality, as instruments of worship. They seek to move with the Spirit, but not as incorporeal selves. Pentecostals experience God as embodied people propelled by the Spirit and by their songs."[91] James K. A. Smith notes this holistic, physical emphasis is also demonstrated through prayer for healing and physical touch (e.g., laying on of hands in prayer).[92]

Pentecostal "orality" is interrelated with this holistic spirituality. Albrecht identifies an important expression of this as "testimony," which merits further brief attention. Grant Wacker observes that "early Pentecostals assumed that their personal faith stories bore normative implications for others," and therefore designated ample time in worship services for the sharing of their spiritual journeys.[93] The role of testimony cannot be overestimated as having enabled the passing on of Pentecostal beliefs and values, serving as a more effective medium than formal theological discourse.[94] Scott A. Ellington explains, "Because our knowledge

89. Plüss, "Religious Experience," 3. Also see Miller and Yamamori, *Global Pentecostalism*, 133; Warrington, "Experience," 5; and Del Colle, "Postmodernism," 112–16.

90. Albrecht, *Rites in the Spirit*, 245, 246. Also see Wacker, *Heaven Below*, 70–76.

91. Albrecht, *Rites in the Spirit*, 246–47. Also see Cox, *Fire from Heaven*, 139–57.

92. Smith, "Teaching a Calvinist." See also Armstrong, "Embrace Your Inner Pentecostal"; Suurmond, *Word and Spirit*, 24–25; Kärkkäinen, *Pneumatology*, 170–72; and Miller and Yamamori, *Global Pentecostalism*, 29–34. Kärkkäinen notes that in African Pentecostalism spirituality affects all aspects of life, including worship, politics, healing, and even farming.

93. Wacker, *Heaven Below*, 58, cf. 58–69. Testimonies also reported inspired dreams and visions (see Suurmond, *Word and* Spirit, 24).

94. See Wacker, *Heaven Below*, 58–79; Hollenweger, *Pentecostalism*, 196; Alexander, "What Doth the Lord," 20; Land, *Pentecostal Spirituality*, 72, 110–13; and Suurmond, *Word and* Spirit, 22. As we will see in chapter 4, however, Chan believes that oral

of God is relational and not merely informational, theology can be better expressed orally, because that is the primary mode of relational communication among ordinary people in the community of faith . . . Testimony and oral expression lend themselves to the understanding and knowing of the God with whom we are in an active relationship, and it requires no 'special knowledge' or expertise in order to participate actively in the search to know God."[95]

Plüss further points out that testimonies are more effective than creeds or formal faith confessions in making encounters with the Spirit an accepted part of Pentecostal worship and spirituality. Unlike creeds, which orient worshippers to the past, testimonies invite the present engagement of the listeners, and hold potential for future transformation.[96] Creeds do not invite testing, whereas testimony requires it. Testimonies are not taken at face value to be true, but must fall within the commonly held beliefs of the congregation.[97] These observations highlight the reliance of Pentecostal experience upon a cultural-linguistic framework.[98] Pentecostal experience is not as individualistic as might be assumed—it is communally formed.[99]

Pentecostal Experience of God as Empowerment for Mission

Albrecht's third quality is "Experiencing God as empowering Spirit and commissioning Lord," which more clearly reveals the Pentecostal view of the nature and purpose of encounter with the Spirit. God's personal presence is manifest among believers, and this presence comes with

---

theology is losing its effectiveness in traditioning Pentecostal values, and so other means are needed to fulfill this role.

95. Ellington, "Pentecostalism," 26–27, cf. 38.

96. Plüss, "Religious Experience," 9. Testimonies are thus more engaging than sermons. "In other words, because testimonies can be questioned and because they call upon a personal reaction by the hearer, they are inviting rather than moralizing in character."

97. Ibid; also see Johannesen, "Remembering," 5.

98. See Cartledge, "Testimony to the Truth," 601–5. He notes that the very nature of testimony reinforces the idea that beliefs are socially mediated within a cultural-linguistic framework.

99. Plüss, "Religious Experience," 9. He notes that testimony expresses diversity and unity simultaneously—the uniqueness of the individual being received into the broader community.

power.[100] Albrecht explains, "The manifestation of power (e.g., in healing or other 'signs and wonders') has sacramental quality for Pentecostals. In the manifestations of power God *proves God's interest in the affairs of humankind* in specific ways. The experiences of power reflect *very personal experiences*, an *individual experiencing* a personal God. For example, the event of Spirit baptism is normally experienced as profoundly personal and intimate. The sense of personal intimacy continues in the 'Spirit-filled life.'"[101]

The distinctive Pentecostal emphasis on an experience of Spirit baptism is quite personal, and often linked to a deepening of one's relationship to Christ, "making Jesus more real."[102] But its primary *purpose* is empowerment, enabling believers to engage in kingdom service more effectively—power is intricately linked to an aim, a commission. States Albrecht, "Pentecostals experience God as the commissioning Lord. The One who empowers, they believe, also calls and sends. Empowerment seeks more than self edification. Instead, Pentecostals recognize in their sense of empowerment a calling to assist others. They understand the commission of Jesus to serve the world as their commission . . . and they believe that the Spirit enables them to accomplish the mission . . ."[103]

Albrecht notes that Pentecostals do attempt to apply this commission to societal problems, albeit rather simplistically. But "nonetheless, they do in their own way seek to positively affect society by sharing good news in word and deed. The result has been a disproportionate level of involvement in missionary, evangelistic and other service ventures."[104]

100. Albrecht, *Rites in the Spirit*, 247, cf. 248. It is not insignificant that the experience of the Spirit's power often occurs in the act of praying for others (or being prayed for), and often involves the laying on of hands. Wacker observes that in praying for one another early Pentecostals expected to experience "the transfer of divine energy from one specially gifted believer to another" (Wacker, *Heaven Below*, 94). This emphasis on physical contact is also highlighted by Smith, "Teaching a Calvinist"; and Miller and Yamamori, *Global Pentecostalism*, 143–44.

101. Albrecht, *Rites in the Spirit*, 247 (italics added); cf. Albrecht, "Pentecostal Spirituality: Ecumenical," § I.B.3.

102. Albrecht, "Pentecostal Spirituality: Ecumenical," § I.B.3.

103. Albrecht, *Rites in the Spirit*, 248, cf. 247. Also see Miller and Yamamori, *Global Pentecostalism*, 2, 29–34, 142. Miller and Yamamori report (globally) examples of what they term "Progressive Pentecostals," who apply Spirit empowerment to ministries directed at social transformation, noting that encounter with the Spirit in worship often serves as impetus.

104. Albrecht, *Rites in the Spirit*, 248. On the connection between encounter with the Spirit and Pentecostal missional impulse also see Plüss, "Frog King," § 6; Plüss, "Religious

Pentecostal encounter with the Spirit, then, is largely intended to benefit not self, but others.

Pentecostal Experience of God as Creativity

Albrecht describes the fourth quality in this way: "Pentecostals experience God as creative; and consequently, they live out a creative spirituality." Pentecostals exhibit a "self-taught inventiveness," and ability to improvise in worship and all of life.[105] The Spirit is experienced creatively by Pentecostals "as liberating, empowering, and gifting," bringing a "sense of intimate connection to God," and a "perception of being personally attached to God and [His] supernatural resources."[106] Confident of their commission and connection to the Spirit's creativity and power, Pentecostal spirituality is often expressed in "entrepreneurial form," marked by "pioneering innovation, adaptability, and pragmatic action."[107]

Wacker confirms this characterization, arguing that the success of Pentecostalism (meaning its ability to proliferate) has been due to two deep impulses: primitivism and pragmatism.[108] Primitivism was evidenced in early Pentecostals' longing for direct contact with the divine, but their simultaneously held practical instincts meant they were never purely primitivists. States Wacker, "[A]t the end of the day pentecostals proved remarkably willing to work within the social and cultural expectations of the age. . . . [This] ability to figure the odds and react appropriately, made them pragmatists to the bone."[109] This primitivism at times led Pentecostals to deny their own pragmatic disposition. They had a tendency to try to "eliminate the natural side of every equation,"

Experience," 6; and Del Colle, "Postmodernism," 101. Del Colle suggests that a number of contemporary Pentecostal theologians have gravitated to postliberal theology (as opposed to fundamentalist evangelicalism on the one hand, or liberalism on the other), since it allows them to engage in theological construction and still maintain an accent on Christ's uniqueness, which is necessary to preserve the Pentecostal missional impulse.

105. Albrecht, *Rites in the Spirit*, 249.

106. Albrecht, "Pentecostal Spirituality: Ecumenical," § I.B.4.

107. Albrecht, *Rites in the Spirit*, 250.

108. Wacker, *Heaven Below*, 9–10, cf. 11–14. Also called, "idealism versus realism, or principle versus practicality."

109. Ibid., 13–14, cf. 12.

avoiding crediting practical decisions for their successes.[110] It was precisely this primitivism/pragmatism combination, however, that allowed for their survival and spread. Wacker asserts, "Pentecostals' primitivist conviction that the Holy Spirit did everything, and that they themselves did nothing, bore grandly pragmatic results."[111] This pragmatic instinct still permeates Pentecostalism today, and will be revisited in our upcoming discussion of Pentecostal experience and reason later in this chapter.

Summarizing and Locating Pentecostal Experience

At this point it is appropriate to summarize some of our discoveries so far. We have learned that Pentecostals emphasize encounter with the Spirit, understood within a framework shaped by particular theological beliefs and spiritual practices (a subcultural-linguistic context). So, to what are Pentecostals appealing when they speak of experience of the Spirit? Clark and Lederle helpfully suggest some criteria for determining whether an experience is of the Spirit, and further, is genuinely (adequately) "Pentecostal."[112] Most of the elements discussed so far in this chapter are taken into account in their working summary. They suggest that Pentecostal experience: 1) includes salvation (i.e., conversion) and a transformed moral life,[113] 2) is "Dynamic and observable,"[114] 3) leads to a deeper commitment to Christ,[115] 4) affects one's "lifestyle" toward "freedom,"[116] 5) leads one to become more committed to the mission of Jesus (since this is the purpose of Spirit baptism),[117] and 6) includes "emotion," in that the encounter with the Spirit involves the whole physi-

---

110. Ibid., 13.

111. Ibid., 14.

112. Clark and Lederle et al., *What Is Distinctive*, 44, cf. 51–63. A related issue concerns discernment of the Spirit's activity in the world in general. This is a major theme in Amos Yong's work, as we shall see. On discernment also see King, "Searching for Genuine," 1–8.

113. Clark and Lederle et al., *What Is Distinctive*, 51–53.

114. Ibid., 53–55.

115. Ibid., 55–56.

116. Ibid., 56–58.

117. Ibid., 58–60. Any experiences detracting from this mission are to be rejected, including "hypnotism, occultism, mysticism (particularly in the extrovert mission-consciousness of Pentecost), mass hysteria and emotionalism, brain-washing, indoctrination, and many other similar phenomena which have an experiential aspect" (ibid., 60).

cality of a person.[118] They add that none of these criteria are adequate in themselves, since the discernment of the worshiping congregation is also required to identify the Spirit's activity.[119]

In light of the above criteria and description of Pentecostal experience, it is appropriate at this juncture to propose a possible location for Pentecostalism on Schner's continuum of the appeal to experience. Peter Althouse has helpfully attempted to do just this, suggesting that Pentecostals be located within the "appeal confessional" due to their emphasis on oral, proclamational theology.[120] Pentecostal testimony and theology is by and large unreflective, not focusing on debate but declaration, and therefore exhibits the naïveté of the appeal confessional. At the same time, Althouse suggests that this appeal only arises in dialogue between the constructive and mystical appeals, the relationship between these three moments being "more dialectical than Schner wants to allow." He concludes, "The appeal to experience in Pentecostalism is an appeal confessional, which attempts to articulate the encounter with God in a devotional way."[121]

118. Ibid., 60–63. This is to be distinguished from emotionalism. Stephen E. Parker also provides a helpful more general definition of "experience" that highlights the conscious, psychological, and physiological components of moments identified as "experience." He states, "experience refers to a complex conscious, affective, physiological phenomenon, involving both cognitive awareness of external events and internal physiological, affective and conscious reactions to such events" (Parker, "Led by the Spirit," 11).

119. Ibid., 63. Also see Plüss, "Religious Experience," 10–11; and Cox, *Fire from Heaven*, 319.

120. Althouse, "Towards a Theological," 3–8, 16–18. This is in contrast to locating Pentecostalism in mysticism, or even as sharing Schleiermachian theological sentiments. Rather, the fact that Pentecostals testify about their experiences with the Spirit in a meaningful way is evidence that these experiences are not ineffable, and therefore not technically "mystical," as we noted earlier.

121. Ibid., 18. A few implications from Althouse's observations are worth noting. First, his placement of Pentecostalism at the appeal confessional is quite similar to Yun's explication of Gelpi's third definition of experience (noted in chapter 1); namely, experience as somewhat empirically grounded, yet pre-critical and unreflective, tending to take as authoritative the word of certain influential leaders or the tradition as a whole. As "confessional" Pentecostal theology has tended to remain on a first-order level, resistant to second-order reflection and evaluation. This study, however, aims to demonstrate that Pentecostalism is showing signs of moving beyond first-order naïveté, in particular in its acknowledgement of the mediated nature of experience (which by definition requires second-order theological reflection). Second, the very nature of the appeal confessional is that it is a public, communal appeal to experience, and not as private as might be assumed (as we have seen). Third, Althouse has rightly emphasized "encounter" as the key

Althouse's characterization helps to confirm that, while Pentecostals emphasize the immediacy of encounter with the Spirit, nevertheless, such occurs within a confessional (subcultural-linguistic) context. In other words, Pentecostals already *tacitly* accept that authentic Pentecostal experience of the Spirit is mediated through Scripture and Pentecostal confession (tradition). The guiding argument of this book, however, is that Pentecostalism is also demonstrating its maturation by a growing willingness to more explicitly acknowledge and integrate a mediated understanding of experience of the Spirit into theological reflection. So, while we have observed some evidence of this, there is need to further explore the relationship of Pentecostalism to the traditional theological media of Scripture, tradition, and reason.

Pentecostal Experience and Scripture

Of the three resources of the Spirit's mediation to be explored, the one that assimilates most readily with Pentecostal experience is Scripture. Gordon L. Anderson suggests two beliefs that, in his view, hold all Pentecostals together: "a doctrine of the experiential nature of the believer's relationship to God," and a commitment to the authority of Scripture.[122] Although not debating the *fact of* scriptural authority, however, there is presently less consensus among Pentecostals concerning the relationship between the text of Scripture and experience of the Spirit.

Stephen E. Parker provides a helpful historical overview of some of the issues pertaining to Pentecostal experience in relation to Scripture. He explains that an emphasis on experience, and a traditional reliance on testimony to articulate their beliefs, exposed Pentecostals to accusations that their experience preceded their theology and hermeneutics. In other words, some detractors argued Pentecostals were reading their experiences (in particular, Spirit baptism with tongues as initial

---

term with which Pentecostal experience of the Spirit should be understood—it is experience of an Other. Finally, his observation of a dialectical movement between the various "moments" on Schner's continuum for Pentecostals was also evident in the theologians explored in chapter 1.

122. Anderson, "Pentecostals Believe," 54. Pentecostals have always emphasized biblical authority, influenced by Protestant traditions in this regard. On this see Lewis, "Towards a Pentecostal," 9–11; Miller and Yamamori, *Global Pentecostalism*, 148; Albrecht, "Pentecostal Spirituality: Ecumenical," § I.B.2; and Wacker, *Heaven Below*, 70–72.

evidence) into the biblical text.[123] Gordon D. Fee, although himself a Pentecostal, alleged, "In a sense, the Pentecostal tends to exegete his or her experience."[124] Parker summarizes, "such charges implied that there was not only an unreflective and uncritical quality to Pentecostal 'experience,' but that experience itself was an illegitimate place to begin theological reflection."[125]

Some Pentecostals, perhaps to be more accepted by evangelicals, responded by downplaying experiences with God and/or attempting to demonstrate how such experiences could be supported through scriptural exegesis.[126] Parker traces how Pentecostals addressed the challenges raised, for example, by Frederick Dale Bruner's *A Theology of the Holy Spirit* and James D. G. Dunn's *Baptism in the Holy Spirit* (both published in 1970) with alternative exegetical approaches supporting a Pentecostal doctrine of post-conversion Spirit baptism.[127] During the 1980s Pentecostals gave considerable attention to the study of hermeneutics,[128] including whether there exists a distinct Pentecostal

123. Parker, "Led by the Spirit," 24–26. Parker's 1992 PhD dissertation focused on demonstrating experience as a valuable element in constructing a Pentecostal theology of discernment and decision-making.

124. Fee, *Gospel and Spirit*, 86. Also see Bruner, *Theology of the Holy Spirit*, 20–22, 82. Bruner is very critical of Pentecostals in this regard. Wacker, however, argues to the contrary, that many early Pentecostals did not pursue the experience of Spirit baptism until after they had become convinced that it was a biblical truth (Wacker, *Heaven Below*, 80).

125. Parker, "Led by the Spirit," 26.

126. Ibid., 27, cf. 24–40; see also Parker, "Led by the Spirit," 29. For examples of contemporary AG theologians downplaying experience as an authority see Railey and Aker, "Theological Foundations," 44; and Higgins et al., *Introduction to Theology*, 33–47. Parker also notes that some Pentecostal historians worked to show how Pentecostal experience could be grounded in church history. Stanley Burgess and Cecil Robeck are exemplified as attempting to argue for the existence of charismatic gifts throughout church history. On this latter point, also see Kydd, *Charismatic Gifts*.

127. For a Pentecostal point by point response to Dunn, see Ervin, *Conversion-Initiation*.

128. In a 1993 issue of *Pneuma* dedicated to the topic, Murray W. Dempster stated that up to that time no other subject had dominated the Pentecostal academic world more so than that of hermeneutics (Dempster, "Paradigm Shifts," 129). Throughout and following the 1980s, the literature on hermeneutics has continued to grow. For example, see Ervin, "Hermeneutics," 11–25; Sheppard, "Pentecostals and the Hermeneutics," 5–33; Sheppard, "Pentecostals, Globalization," 289–312; Stronstad, "Pentecostalism, Experiential," 1–32; Johns, "Some New Directions," 145–67; McGee, "Early Pentecostal Hermeneutics," 96–118; Robinson, "Pentecostal Hermeneutic," 1–10; Autry, "Dimensions of Hermeneutics," 29–50; Byrd, "Paul Ricoeur's Hermeneutical," 203–14; Cargal, "Beyond the Fundamentalist-Modernist," 163–87; Dempster, "Paradigm Shifts,"

hermeneutic.[129] Some, like Roger Stronstad and Robert P. Menzies, utilized redaction criticism to argue that the Luke-Acts narrative provides didactic (not simply historical) material, and can therefore be used to support Pentecostal theology and experience.[130] Whether they have been successful in making their case is still open to debate.[131]

In any case, Parker observes that while the adoption of evangelical historical-grammatical hermeneutical methods helped Pentecostals become more accepted among evangelicals, it also more or less limited Pentecostal dialogue partners to the latter. Further, downplaying the significance of experience in the hermeneutical process hindered Pentecostals from exploring more dynamic and subjective possibilities as existing between text and interpreter.[132] Parker states, "the de-emphasis (even devaluing) of experience has contributed to a concomitant lack of attention to focusing on Pentecostal practices as a locus for Pentecostal theological construction."[133] While this move has helped Pentecostals

---

129–35; Israel et al., "Pentecostals and Hermeneutics," 137–61; Harrington and Patten, "Pentecostal Hermeneutics," 109–14; Cartledge, "Empirical Theology," 115–26; Clark, "Pentecostalism's Anabaptist Roots," 194–211; and Poirier and Lewis, "Pentecostal and Postmodernist," 3–21.

129. Parker, "Led by the Spirit," 30–32. See also Wacker, *Heaven Below*, 72–76; and Lewis, "Towards a Pentecostal," 1–28.

130. See Stronstad, *Charismatic Theology*; Stronstad, *Prophethood*; Stronstad, "*Charismatic Theology* Revisited," 101–22; and Menzies and Menzies, *Spirit and Power*. Also see Turner, *Power from on High*, 20–79. In brief, Stronstad and Menzies argue that evangelicals have typically prioritized the Pauline epistles as providing the primary didactic content for Christian theology and doctrine, while New Testament narratives (in particular, the books of Luke and Acts) have served to more or less illustrate the truths found in the epistles. Thus New Testament narrative material has been read through a Pauline "lens," importing Pauline theology into Lukan narratives. One result has been, for example, the assumption of Pauline definitions of Spirit baptism (cf. 1 Cor 12:13) into Luke's narrative. By utilizing redaction criticism, however, it is proposed that Luke writes theologically, and presents a charismatic pneumatology distinct from that of Paul's soteriological pneumatology. Luke's stories, then, deserve to be appreciated didactically (Luke *intends* to teach his readers something about the Spirit). This is significant for Pentecostals, since their theology of Spirit baptism is derived from Luke-Acts.

131. Stronstad and Robert P. Menzies emphasize that only once Luke and Paul have been heard on their own terms can they be synthesized in order to develop a biblical theology. A criticism, however, on this point has been that neither Stronstad or Menzies has adequately accomplish this synthesis. They have more-or-less bifurcated Luke and Paul, leaving two canons—one Pentecostal and one evangelical. Macchia attempts to overcome this (see chapter 3).

132. Parker, "Led by the Spirit," 33–35.

133. Ibid., 39.

avoid some unwanted extremes, Parker argues, it has also negatively led to a stifling of Pentecostal spirituality. What is needed, he suggests, is a "theological method that would allow retention of the focus on experience while satisfying the criteria for a critical theology."[134]

In the early 1990s, some Pentecostals began to emphasize more explicitly the value and contribution of experience to the hermeneutical process. Several questioned the evangelical hermeneutical criterion of author intentionality (with its ties to modernist epistemological rationalism), echoing Parker's concerns that this might prove antithetical to Pentecostal spirituality.[135] What was proposed (again, by some) was greater openness to experiential, subjectivistic readings of Scripture, often relying on aspects of postmodern epistemology.[136]

The Pentecostal contribution to hermeneutics, then, involves not only a prioritizing of the Luke-Acts narrative, but even more so a belief in the Spirit's ongoing revelatory activity in the church and reading of Scripture. Ellington argues, unlike evangelicalism, which attempts to *demonstrate* scriptural authority through rationalistic criteria, Pentecostals *assume* Scripture to be authoritative, and find this to be verified by the Spirit's activity in the daily lives and testimonies of Christian believers. So, Scripture is rightly viewed as the primary authority for Pentecostals; however, their *concept of biblical authority emerges in conjunction with Pentecostal experience of the Spirit*—the two cannot be disconnected.[137]

Among the suggestions for integrating Pentecostal experience and Scripture reading, perhaps most comprehensive to date has come from Kenneth J. Archer in his monograph, *A Pentecostal Hermeneutic for the Twenty-First Century: Spirit, Scripture and Community*.[138] It is

---

134. Ibid., 50, cf. 49.

135. For example, see Archer, *Pentecostal Hermeneutic*, 133–48; Cargal, "Beyond the Fundamentalist-Modernist," 182–86; Coulter, "What Meaneth This?," 56–63; Stephenson, 6–8; Lewis, "Towards a Pentecostal," 9–14; and Ellington, "Pentecostalism," 16–38. Parker's work was published too early to take into account this hermeneutical shift within Pentecostalism.

136. See Dempster, "Issues Facing Pentecostalism," 261–62; Byrd, "Paul Ricoeur's Hermeneutical," 203–14; Israel et al., "Pentecostals and Hermeneutics," 137–61; Cargal, "Beyond the Fundamentalist-Modernist," 163–87; and Sheppard, "Biblical Interpretation," 121–41. The influence of Paul Ricoeur and Hans-Georg Gadamer is notable in a number of these works.

137. Ellington, "Pentecostalism," 19; Wacker, *Heaven Below*, 73.

138. On this also see Cartledge, *Encountering the Spirit*, 116–31; and Wacker, *Heaven Below*, 72–76.

worth reviewing some of his points here, since Archer exemplifies the growing sophistication in Pentecostal hermeneutical method, while also providing a helpful summary of the development of Pentecostal hermeneutics in the twentieth century. Archer's goal is to "articulate constructively a contemporary Pentecostal hermeneutical strategy," but grounded in the ethos of early Pentecostalism.[139] To this end, he characterizes early Pentecostalism as "paramodern,"[140] and as utilizing a hermeneutical strategy distinct from both "modernistic Fundamentalism and Liberalism."[141]

In the wake of German higher criticism, in the early nineteenth century, American Protestants moved in three notable directions with regard to biblical authority and hermeneutics. Modernist liberals opted for an "experiential foundationalism," in which biblical authenticity was found in "personal experience."[142] Conservative fundamentalists attempted to ground biblical authority in scientific or historical claims, relying on "Common Sense Realism," but also assumed a modernistic epistemology.[143] In contrast,

> The Wesleyan Holiness movement and the Pentecostals forged a third route. From a paramodern perspective, they affirm both the objective nature of Scripture and the importance of personal experience as a means to reaffirm the supernatural inspiration of Scripture. Hence, the Holiness tradition and Pentecostals located the inspirational work of the Holy Spirit in both the past written document (Scripture) and in their present experience with Scripture. Inspiration was not limited to the Scripture in the sense that it was a past document containing no errors, but it also included the present ability of the Scripture to speak to the community. The community experienced the Spirit through reading and living according to the Scripture. Fundamentalists, on the other hand, located the inspirational work of the Spirit in the past written document (Scripture) only.[144]

139. Archer, *Pentecostal Hermeneutic*, 1, cf. 2.

140. Ibid., 29–34. "Paramodern" implies that Pentecostals were influenced by modernity, and yet were not subsumed into this worldview entirely. We will explore this in greater detail in our upcoming section on reason.

141. Ibid., 1–2.

142. Ibid., 39.

143. Ibid., 40, cf. 40–57, 63; cf. Wacker, *Heaven Below*, 75.

144. Archer, *Pentecostal Hermeneutic*, 40.

Pentecostals shared a hermeneutical approach, says Archer, already utilized within the Holiness movement. Both emphasized "the practical and ethical understanding of Scripture," being "more concerned with living faithfully and responsibly with God and less concerned about articulating a cognitive intellectual understanding of God" (as was typical among fundamentalists). Further, "The Pentecostals said yes to both the authority of Scripture and the authority of experience. This puts Scripture and lived experience into a creative dialectical tension. Pentecostalism's lived experience was coloring their understanding of Scripture and Scripture was shaping their lived experiences."[145]

This early Pentecostal emphasis, however, should not be confused with that of Protestant liberalism. States Archer, "The Pentecostals, like the Liberals, were very concerned about religious experience as authenticating Christianity. But unlike the Liberals, who talked about 'religion of the heart' and experiencing God through the divine elements in the natural, Pentecostals would point to the supernatural signs of divine intervention taking place in their worship services (tongues and healing). Hence, early Pentecostals were generating religious experience, whereas the Liberals were simply talking about it."[146]

With the above in mind, Archer explains that Pentecostals read Scripture, "through the marginalized Wesleyan Holiness eyes from a restorationist revivalistic perspective."[147] This approach was based in what Archer labels a premodern "Bible Reading Method,"[148] adopted directly from Wesleyan and Keswickian predecessors,[149] and geared toward applying the Bible to immediate needs (as opposed to a rigid literalism).[150] "[This] was a commonsensical method that relied upon inductive and deductive interpretative reasoning skills. Once the biblical data was ana-

---

145. Ibid., 63. Thus, early Pentecostals viewed themselves as being "scripturally sound and at odds with both liberal theology and Protestant orthodoxy." They could not embrace modernity, and yet at the same time their emphasis on divine healing and the Holy Spirit distinguished them from fundamentalists (ibid., 22).

146. Ibid., 63.

147. Ibid., 22.

148. Ibid., 65, cf. 65–93; cf. Archer, "Early Pentecostal," 32–70.

149. Archer, *Pentecostal Hermeneutic*, 75.

150. Ibid., 69. Reiterating our earlier observations, Archer states, this was a "Praxis-driven 'Jesus-centrism' Christianity" (ibid., 73), or a "Jesus-ology" of sorts, in which Jesus served as the hub of a web of central narrative convictions made up of the five strands of the five-fold gospel (ibid., 117–18).

lyzed, it was then synthesized into a biblical doctrine. Harmonization was the acceptable and necessary way to synthesize all the biblical data on a particular subject."[151]

So, contrary to fundamentalists who read the Bible "as a past revelatory document," Pentecostals "read the Bible as a presently inspired story."[152] This allowed Pentecostals to support such doctrines as Spirit baptism and initial evidence (not to mention the Oneness Pentecostal position of water baptism in the name of Jesus only).[153] What distinguished first-generation Pentecostal use of the "Bible Reading Method," however, was a unique theological framework that served to form what Archer calls their "Central Narrative Convictions."[154] Pentecostals viewed themselves as a restorationist movement, typified through a "latter rain" motif.[155] In this view, the first outpouring of the Spirit occurred at Pentecost, followed more or less by hundreds of years of church apostasy (especially exemplified in Roman Catholicism).[156] Pentecostals, however, were participating in the prophesied fulfillment of the second ("latter") rain outpouring of the Spirit, returning apostolic faith, power, and authority to the church.[157]

This, combined with their "primitivistic impulse," led Pentecostals to interpret Scripture and church history through the lens of the book of Acts, and enabled them to "eclipse Modernity and return to a premodern era," in which the "supernatural was normal rather than abnormal."[158] Further, explains Archer, simultaneously reinforcing this approach was Pentecostal "oral-aural" interaction with Scripture.

151. Ibid., 74. This method was a modification of the proof-text type of approach. It was "thoroughly popularistic, thus a 'precritical,' canonical and text centered approach from a revivalistic-restorational biblicist perspective" (ibid., 75).

152. Ibid., 69. Pentecostals were unlike modernists and fundamentalists in their assumption that God was actively involved in the physical realm. Yet with the fundamentalists they viewed the Bible as sacred revelation, and believed the Bible stories had occurred historically just as recorded. Pentecostals were influenced by modernistic historiography, and yet believed that the "truthfulness of Scripture was discovered relationally, personally and experientially more so than 'scientifically'" (ibid., 70–71).

153. Ibid., 75–91.

154. Ibid., 114–18, cf. 94–126.

155. Ibid., 12–14, 97–98. Also see Wacker, "Playing for Keeps," 203–7; Althouse, *Spirit of the Last Days*, 9–60; and Faupel, "Function of 'Models,'" 54–64.

156. Archer, *Pentecostal Hermeneutic*, 102, 112–13.

157. Ibid., 101–3, cf. 117.

158. Ibid., 110–14, 117, 124; cf. Wacker, "Playing for Keeps," 196–219.

Personal testimonies of Pentecostals often referenced Bible stories and terminology. Contemporary events were not infrequently interpreted through scriptural narratives, and conversely, Scripture was interpreted through Pentecostal life experiences.[159] As a result, "From Modernity's perspective, Pentecostals constantly blurred the exegetical boundaries of what the text meant to each of the original hearers and what the text meant to contemporary readers."[160] Hermeneutically, then, Pentecostals were distinguished from not only Protestant liberalism and conservative fundamentalism, but also from their Wesleyan and Keswickian relatives.[161] Archer summarizes, "Pentecostals were convinced that God was breaking into their world, and so they babbled. In their babbling they protested modernity along with cessationist Christianity and were able to create an intense experiential eschatological counter-culture Christian community. Interestingly, their narrated hermeneutical approach which emphasized the importance of a controlling story and the immediacy of experiential meaningfulness, has much more in common with the (Premodern) New Testament writers [sic.] approaches than the Historical Critical approaches of Modernity."[162]

Archer argues, however, that after the 1920s, Pentecostals more or less abandoned earlier hermeneutical approaches in an effort to be accepted by fundamentalist evangelicals, and began to adopt more of the concerns and methods of modernism.[163] This transformation was compounded as Pentecostals entered the academy and became further "evangelicalized," adopting historical critical approaches to exegesis. In this shift from a paramodern to modern approach, the role of experience became relegated to verifying, rather than informing the hermeneutical

159. Archer, *Pentecostal Hermeneutic*, 118–20; cf. Wacker, "Playing for Keeps," 201–2.

160. Archer, *Pentecostal Hermeneutic*, 120; also see Suurmond, *Word and* Spirit, 22–23. Suurmond refers to this as a "charismatic exegesis," which includes "a playful interaction between the text of the Bible and the present situation, in which the story of scripture is interwoven with that of the community. Conversely, the believers recognize themselves in the text. The story is best suited for expressing communal experiences in a way which not only encourages the building up of the community but also makes these experiences accessible to newcomers."

161. Archer, *Pentecostal Hermeneutic*, 125.

162. Ibid., 126.

163. Ibid., 64. Also see Lewis, "Reflections of a Hundred," § 3; and Holm, "Paradigmatic Analysis," 54–70.

process.[164] Archer views this "assimilation of Pentecostalism into Evangelicalism as destructive to Pentecostal experiential identity and doctrine,"[165] and therefore joins what he identifies as a growing minority, advocating that experience and the active role of the Spirit should be more central in Pentecostal hermeneutics so as to preserve Pentecostal values and spirituality.[166]

To this end, Archer proposes a "triadic" strategy for Pentecostal hermeneutics, involving the Pentecostal community, Scripture, and the Spirit.[167] This proposal is informed by narrative criticism, semiotics, and reader response criticism, and also calls for a greater recognition of the Spirit speaking through the community and not simply to individuals.[168] Further, since Pentecostals cannot (and should not) remain paramodern, he suggests postmodern hermeneutical strategies as being more suitable than modernistic historical critical approaches for sustaining Pentecostal spirituality.[169] Only a distancing from rationalistic approaches can preserve the two elements—experience and Spirit—necessary for a hermeneutic appropriate for Pentecostalism. Pentecostals believe the Spirit still speaks today, and this demands an approach to Scripture rooted in a particular experiential worldview.[170]

Archer explains this approach: "Thus the supernatural experiential worldview of Scripture, which helped to create Pentecostalism, helps also to sustain the Pentecostal view of God. That is, an understanding of God who is greater than and beyond creation yet in and among his people. Signs and wonders provide evidence for this understanding. Therefore, the Pentecostal/Charismatic experiences helped people to identify with the charismatic experiences of biblical characters creating

---

164. Archer, *Pentecostal Hermeneutic*, 131, 141–42.

165. Ibid., 142, cf. 131–48. Archer discusses the Pentecostal responses to Bruner and Dunn noted earlier, as well as William W. Menzies' emphasis on Lukan vs. Pauline pneumatology as important moments within the development of Pentecostal hermeneutics. However, he feels that the Pentecostal attempt to utilize the "authorial intent" criterion will likely never resolve doctrinal disagreements between Pentecostals and evangelicals.

166. Ibid., 142, 154–55.

167. Ibid., 159–91.

168. Ibid., 158–84.

169. Ibid., 146–47.

170. Ibid., 144, 147. At the same time he carefully adds that any claim to experience of the Spirit contrary to Scripture must be repudiated, since the Bible has always been the primary Pentecostal authority.

an existential bond of 'shared experience' which reinforces the community's identity as the eschatological people of God."[171] So, while utilizing contemporary hermeneutical strategies, Archer believes these must be congruent with the early Pentecostal ethos to preserve what is essential to Pentecostalism.[172]

In sum, then, Pentecostals need to be understood as "people of the Book," Scripture being a medium with which Pentecostals readily associate experience of the Spirit. The above survey helps identify the important dialectic between Scripture and experience that has operated within Pentecostalism from its emergence. Rationalistic approaches that downplay the role of experience in the hermeneutical process are becoming viewed by many as being detrimental to Pentecostal spirituality. Conversely, approaches integrating the experience of the Pentecostal community and encounters with the Spirit are being viewed as truer to the early Pentecostal ethos, and more conducive for sustaining Pentecostalism as it matures into adulthood.

Pentecostal Experience and Tradition

In contrast to the way in which Pentecostals have, from the start, accepted the compatibility of Scripture with experience of the Spirit, is the view they have held concerning ecclesial and theological tradition as a mediation of the Spirit.[173] In short, church tradition with its institutions, creeds, and discursive theology was viewed as a human creation, functioning to restrict and constrict the freedom and experience of the Holy Spirit. Jacobsen states, for Pentecostals, "theology done in a traditional way . . . had lost touch with the Spirit and become dry and brittle, and incapable of conveying the living truth of God's love to anyone."[174] Pentecostals

---

171. Ibid., 144.

172. Ibid., 147.

173. Gordon D. Fee identifies five different senses of "tradition": 1) the oral tradition of the first century church, 2) early church consensus, 3) an authoritative office (i.e., Roman Catholic), 4) various Christian streams as traditions, and 5) our own set of life experiences and the setting which makes up our personal history (Fee, *Gospel and Spirit*, 67–70). Pentecostals more generally tend to view tradition as referring to the second through fourth senses, so this will serve as the scope of the term for our purposes. The fifth sense refers more to aspects that will be covered concerning the Pentecostal relation to "reason."

174. Jacobsen, *Thinking in the Spirit*, 2. See also Smith, "Spirit, Word," 14.

always opposed "man-made creeds and dead rituals," affirms Cox.[175] Instead, spirituality was to be biblical, practical, and experiential.[176]

Their high view of Scripture, combined with primitivism,[177] led Pentecostals to see a clear distinction between the true apostolic faith and the humanly-devised traditions and theologies that had developed in the course of church history.[178] This was not, then, a rejection of orthodoxy, but a rejection of traditionalism, "creedalism," and "orthodoxism."[179] Anything deviating from what Pentecostals understood as scriptural was viewed with suspicion. Randall Holm explains, "Emulating out of a predominantly Holiness, Wesleyan background, Pentecostals, from the beginning, affectionately maintained a high view of Scripture. However, the measure of their commitment did not lie in any careful articulation of their belief, rather it was expressed through their vehement denunciation of anything that appeared to usurp the sufficiency of Scripture.

---

175. Cox, *Fire from Heaven*, 75. Also see Faupel, "Whither Pentecostalism?," 20, 21; Anderson, "Pentecostals Believe," 55; Robeck, "Taking Stock," 53; Warrington, "Experience," 1, 5, 8; Land, "Passion for the Kingdom," 24; Jacobsen, *Thinking in the Spirit*, 357; and Archer, *Pentecostal Hermeneutic*, 73.

176. Jacobsen, *Thinking in the Spirit*, xi. Jacobsen agrees that Pentecostals have always understood "that there is a difference between being religious and being spiritual, and Pentecostals generally have opted for the more spiritual side of that divide." Yet he also warns against erecting a dichotomy in this regard, stating, "Religion is embodied in doctrines, creeds, and formal liturgies, while spirituality finds better outlet in poetry, song, and dramatic performance. This distinction is helpful, but if argued too forcefully it deconstructs itself. Ultimately there is no such thing as pure spirituality or pure religion; they need each other. Spirituality needs religion to keep it from simply dissipating into thin air, and religion needs spirituality to keep it from becoming hollow."

177. See Miller and Yamamori, *Global Pentecostalism*, 148. They define Pentecostal primitivism as the assumption that "first-century Christianity is normative above all other periods of Christian history." Also see Archer, *Pentecostal Hermeneutic*, 110–14; Johns, "Pentecostalism and the Postmodern," 89; McKay, "When the Veil," 35; Jones, "Culture, Context," 1; and Poirier and Lewis, "Pentecostal and Postmodernist," 4.

178. Lewis, "Reflections of a Hundred," § 2. It is for this reason the term "apostolic" became a popular label, identifying Pentecostalism in contrast to what was merely tradition. Wacker states, "They yearned physically to enter the apostolic world, to breathe its air, feel its life, see its signs and wonders with their own eyes." This is why they frequently gave biblical names to their events and organizations (Wacker, *Heaven Below*, 72). The title of the official Azusa Street newspaper, *The Apostolic Faith*, is evidence of this very point. For Pentecostals the history of the church was filled with apostasy, in large part contributing to the diminishment of miracles, spiritual gifts and experience of the Spirit in general. See Archer, *Pentecostal Hermeneutic*, 112–13, 117; and Robeck, "Emerging Magisterium?," 214.

179. Faupel, "Whither Pentecostalism?," 20–21.

Among those variables held suspect, Pentecostals frequently included church traditions, institutionalism, creeds and doctrines."[180]

As primitivists, Pentecostals firmly believed they were restoring the true apostolic faith, the "full gospel," to the world.[181] One anonymous early Pentecostal declared, "We believe in unity with Christ's people everywhere, *in the word of God. It is the old-time apostolic assembly,* the same old teaching of 1900 years ago. It is new to the world in these last days, but *its teaching and doctrine is old as the New Testament.*"[182] For early Pentecostals, the experience of the New Testament apostles was now being restored and in some respects replicated in their midst, confirmed especially by the experience of Spirit baptism accompanied by the biblical sign of tongues.[183] Conversely, the lack of such experiential manifestations in other church traditions undermined their credibility for Pentecostals, and demonstrated their distance from authentic apostolic faith.

Thus, ecclesial institutions, and not just creeds, were held suspect by Pentecostals. In view of Christ's imminent return, Pentecostals had

180. Holm, "Paradigmatic Analysis," 49. Also see Kärkkäinen, "Authority, Revelation," 110; Higgins et al., *Introduction to Theology*, 42; and Lewis, "Reflections of a Hundred," § 2. Lewis here states that the emergence of Oneness Pentecostalism (1914–16) was due to a primitivistic emphasis on the book of Acts and a rejection of church tradition. In short, Oneness groups highlighted the fact that water baptism in Acts occurred in the name of "Jesus only." This called traditional Trinitarian doctrine into doubt, being viewed as a humanly introduced error and deviation from the apostolic faith.

181. Archer, *Pentecostal Hermeneutic*, 22, 110–11, 113, 117; Wacker, *Heaven Below*, 76–77; Robeck, "Taking Stock," 54. Early Pentecostalism's low view of church history acknowledged only a few bright lights as being valuable for Pentecostal spirituality. Early Pentecostal leader, William Seymour states, "All along the ages men have been preaching a partial Gospel. A part of the Gospel remained when the world went into the dark ages. God has from time to time raised up men to bring back the truth to the church. He raised up Luther to bring back to the world the doctrine of justification by faith. He raised up another reformer in John Wesley to establish Bible holiness in the church. Then He raised up Dr. Cullis who brought back to the world the wonderful doctrine of divine healing. Now He is bringing back the Pentecostal Baptism to the church." Seymour, "The Pentecostal Baptism Restored," *The Apostolic Faith*, 1.2 (Oct. 1906).

182. Author unknown, "Questions Answered," *The Apostolic Faith* 1.11 (Oct. 1907–Jan. 1908) (italics added). It is noteworthy that the Scripture verse printed directly below *The Apostolic Faith* header on the front page of each issue was Jude 3, "Earnestly contend for the faith which was once delivered unto the saints." Other references to the importance of adhering to apostolic (scriptural) doctrine include: Seymour, "Christ's Messages to the Church," *The Apostolic Faith* 1.11 (Oct. 1907–Jan. 1908); and Author unknown, "Shall We Reject Jesus' Last Words?" *The Apostolic Faith* 1.2 (Oct. 1906).

183. Wacker, "Playing for Keeps," 203–5; Fee, "Baptism in the Holy Spirit," 87–99.

little time for human organization and bureaucracy.[184] Such things only served as obstacles, impeding believers from getting down to the business of evangelism.[185] Simultaneously, however, Pentecostals also exhibited a strong desire for Christian unity and blamed institutionalism for division in the church.[186] William Seymour, the leader of the Azusa Street revival from 1906 to 1908, typifies this desire, stating, "we are not fighting men or churches, but seeking to *displace dead forms and creeds and wild fanaticisms with living, practical Christianity.* 'Love, Faith, Unity' are our watchwords, and 'Victory through the Atoning Blood' our battle cry."[187]

Spittler views this desire for Christian love and unity as revealing that there have always been "ecumenical impulses" among Pentecostals.[188] Cecil Mel Robeck Jr. likewise agrees that early Pentecostal Pioneers were almost universally committed to Christian unity, adding "Pentecostals are ecumenical, we just don't know it."[189] At the same time, this desire

184. Clark and Lederle et al., *What Is Distinctive*, 40–41; Wacker, "Playing for Keeps," 209–10. Wacker refers to this as an "antistructuralist impulse," related to Pentecostal primitivism.

185. Land, "Passion for the Kingdom," 25.

186. Anderson, "Pentecostals Believe," 55. Pentecostals were quite aware of the denominational schisms that existed during the emergence of their movement. This provided justification for their distrust of church institutions and humanly constructed organizations committed to the project of church unity. Also see Yong, "Pentecostalism and Ecumenism," § 2.

187. Seymour, "'The Apostolic Faith' Movement" *The Apostolic Faith* 1.1 (Sept 1906) (italics added). Articles in *The Apostolic Faith* were often published anonymously and frequently left untitled. However, Seymour served as editor at this time and it is likely these were his words (cf. Archer, *Pentecostal Hermeneutic*, 73).

188. Spittler, "Maintaining Distinctives," 128. Also see Irvin, "'Drawing All Together,'" 26. Irvin here notes, "The movement that spread from Azusa Street in 1906 prefigured important themes and commitments that would come to characterize the ecumenical movement as well. Prominent among these were a challenge to the divisions among Christian churches of the world and a call for the unity of people across boundaries of race, gender, class and language."

189. Robeck, "Taking Stock," 37, cf. 39, 41–44. Robeck states that almost without exception early Pentecostals believed that their movement would provide the answer to Jesus' prayer for unity (John 17:11, 22). He also observes that Pentecostals have frequently involved themselves visibly with other Pentecostals and Christians. At the same time they have resisted (especially in North America) being involved with certain formal ecumenical expressions, most notably the World Council of Churches. This openness to unity and inclusivity for all Christian traditions (with the exception of Roman Catholics) is also noted in Lewis, "Reflections of a Hundred," §§ 4–5; Irvin, "'Drawing All Together,'" 44ff.; Clark and Lederle et al., *What Is Distinctive*, 19; and Shaull and Cesar, *Pentecostalism and the Future*, 96.

for unity was held in tension with a resistance to human organization, meaning that early Pentecostal ecumenism needs to be understood somewhat differently from that of such organizations as the World Council of Churches (WCC).[190] Exhibiting this tension, one early Pentecostal woman expressed,

> If this movement stands for anything, it stands for unity of mind. It was raised up to answer the prayer of Jesus: "That they might be one, as the Father art in me and I in thee." What is the matter with the world today? Here is a little selfish sect and there a denomination by itself. They do not love one another as God would have them. Let us honor every bit of God there is in one another. Let us honor the Holy Ghost to teach men to get them out of their error.[191]

Denominations formed, it was believed, as the result of (merely) human effort—a "hunting for light. They built-up denominations because they did not know a better way."[192] True Christian unity, however, was something that could only be created by the Spirit, and this was just what the Spirit was thought to be doing among early Pentecostals. The Spirit enabled Pentecostals to transcend the limits of human organization. [193] "The Pentecostal movement is too large to be confined in any denomination or sect. It works outside, drawing altogether in one bond

---

190. See Yong, "Pentecostalism and Ecumenism," §§ 2–3; Kärkkäinen, "Pentecostals as 'Anonymous Ecumenists'?," 51; and Robeck, "Taking Stock," 44. Robeck here notes that the term "ecumenism" was often thought of pejoratively among Pentecostals (especially in North America), while "unity" was a term that held positive overtones.

191. Anna Hall, "Honor the Holy Ghost," *The Apostolic Faith* 1.2 (Oct. 1906).

192. Author unknown, "The Church Question," *The Apostolic Faith* 1.5 (Jan. 1907). Further, to identify the Pentecostal movement with any institution or denomination was a sure-fire way to quench any revival. An example of this is found in an early Pentecostal testimony in which a "leading Methodist layman" expressed his thanks to God that the Pentecostal revival did not start in a Methodist church, "but in a barn" (a reference to the Azusa Street meetings being held in a former livery stable). If it had started in the church, this individual was convinced that the "poor colored people and Spanish people would not have got it" (i.e., not have been allowed to participate in the revival due to denominational, class and racial discrimination) (Author unknown, "Bible Pentecost: Gracious Showers Continue to Fall," *The Apostolic Faith* 1.3 (Nov. 1906)).

193. Robeck, "Taking Stock," 39; Kärkkäinen, *Introduction to Ecclesiology*, 74–75. Kärkkäinen notes here that Pentecostals tended to describe their church organizations as "fellowships," and not "denominations," in order to emphasize the necessity of the living, active, and tangible presence of the Spirit.

of love, one church, one body of Christ."[194] All believers, regardless of race, gender, class, age,[195] or denomination were welcome to embrace Pentecostal experience of the Spirit, but this experience could never be subsumed under any tradition or institution.[196]

This Pentecostal antithesis between Spirit and institution (or, more broadly, "tradition") meant that the latter was not readily regarded as an authority.[197] Holm states, "For early Pentecostals, it was anathema to talk of an Institutional Word. Theirs was a movement without a human leader. Jesus Christ, mediated through the Word (Bible) and Spirit, was their only leader. The Holy Spirit, unleashed through the Latter Rain would be sufficient to guide them into truth and provide church unity."[198] Jackie David Johns concurs; Pentecostals have been, and in

194. Author unknown, *The Apostolic Faith*, 1.1 (Sept. 1906).

195. As evidence of the transcendence of Pentecostalism, *The Apostolic Faith* often highlighted the diversity of nationalities, races, classes, genders, and even ages of those participating in the movement. For example, one article reports the Pentecostal revival as having been experienced in places such as Hawaii, Norway, England, Sweden, India, China, Germany, Ireland, Australia and Liberia (Author unknown, "Pentecost Both Sides of the Ocean," *The Apostolic Faith* 1.6 (Feb.–Mar. 1907)). Other articles highlighted the participation of children in the revival. For example, Author unknown, "Little Children Receive the Holy Ghost," *The Apostolic Faith* 1.2 (Oct. 1906); and Author unknown, "A Children's Meeting," *The Apostolic Faith* 1.9 (June-Sept. 1907). On diversity also see Plüss, "Religious Experience," 11–12. Plüss writes, "Pentecostalism is by virtue of its fast growth and global nature predisposed to think in terms of diversity. There is *no such thing as a normative Pentecostal experience or a singular Pentecostal point of view*. The experience of being filled with the Holy Spirit may be a common theological notion, but it is *played out in diversity*. In all likelihood the *experience of diversity* will be a decisive factor in promoting Christian cooperation and ecumenical discussion" (italics added). Plüss advocates, then, for both a plurality of experience *and* theology within Pentecostalism. He views this not as a deficiency, but a strength inherent in the movement, allowing for possibilities of ecumenical fellowship.

196. One notable deviation from the typical Pentecostal openness to unity was their outright rejection of Roman Catholicism. *The Apostolic Faith* not infrequently refers to Roman Catholicism in negative tones, and as a religion needing to be forsaken. One testimonial, for example, states: "A young man who a year ago was in the chain gang, is now baptized with the Holy Ghost and preaching everywhere. He was a Catholic but *God took Romanism out of him*" (Author unknown, *The Apostolic Faith* 1.1 (Sept. 1906); italics added). Robeck notes that Roman Catholics have typically taken the brunt of criticism among Pentecostals. This attitude was no doubt a carryover from their roots in the Holiness movement (Robeck, "Taking Stock," 40, 57; cf. Irvin, "'Drawing All Together,'" 34–36).

197. Kärkkäinen, *Introduction to Ecclesiology*, 77.

198. Holm, "Paradigmatic Analysis," 118.

many ways continue to be, "resistant to bureaucratic authority."[199] While Pentecostals have gone on to create their own denominations, this move needs to be viewed as being somewhat counterintuitive.[200] Holm puts it succinctly, "Pentecostals are not necessarily anti-institutional, they just do not like institutions."[201]

To summarize thus far, "tradition" for Pentecostals has often been viewed pejoratively. Tradition—whether theological, liturgical or institutional—has generally not *consciously* factored into Pentecostal experience of the Spirit, and deep suspicion of tradition continues among many Pentecostals. Maintaining such a posture, however, is not without weaknesses. For example, Holm insightfully observes that the suspicion of anything institutional has (at least in the case of his denomination, the Pentecostal Assemblies of Canada) led to the unacknowledged disguising of bureaucratic denominational processes (such as the election of leaders) using spiritualized language. He states, "The moment a this-worldly structure is clothed in other-worldly attire, closure is enacted, accountability is denied and any future change or modification is handcuffed."[202] In other words, unacknowledged bureaucracy may in practice bear even more authority than an acknowledged one!

Another weakness is the propensity of Pentecostals to embrace elitist or triumphalist attitudes, enabling theological disparities to quickly escalate into outright schism.[203] If one's own movement is viewed as the location of the "full gospel" (in contrast to other church traditions), without acknowledging the development of "tradition" (doctrinal and organizational) in that same movement, then any divergence of opinion among members can hastily be interpreted as deviation from the apostolic faith. Wacker notes that among early Pentecostals being one

199. Johns, "Pentecostalism and the Postmodern," 90–91.

200. Hollenweger, *Pentecostalism*, 424.

201. Holm, "Paradigmatic Analysis," 288.

202. Ibid., 159. Holm explains, "For example an antiquated voting procedure which denies a transparent evaluation of potential candidates in an attempt to remain true to the will of God has rendered simple elections a breeding ground for underground murmuring, and coercion—the two characteristics they wish to avoid."

203. Robeck, "Taking Stock," 54; Spittler, "Maintaining Distinctives," 122–24. Spittler views attitudes of triumphalism and elitism as resulting from Pentecostals becoming enamored with their own successes and growth, as well as their doctrine of Spirit baptism, which they believed distinguished them from other 'have-not' Christians. On the issue of the initial evidence doctrine creating a "two-tiered" Christianity, also see Fee, "Toward a Pauline Theology," 105–20.

in spirit usually meant conformity in doctrine; there was little room for diversity of opinions, and doctrinal issues quickly led to division.[204] Jacobsen likewise states that the early Pentecostal ethos made it difficult to accommodate differences. "Hence, theological creativity led to division, and division slowly led to the institutionalization of doctrinal and denominational differences, so much so that by the 1920s . . . many pentecostals were no longer talking to each other."[205]

A final weakness is that Pentecostals fail to recognize that they have emerged from and been shaped by other historical Christian traditions, and have developed their own unique theological and organizational traditions (including a liturgy, as Albrecht has aptly demonstrated).[206] As previously noted, this lack of self-understanding has arguably led Pentecostals to uncritically embrace theological emphases (e.g., aspects of evangelical theology) potentially detrimental to Pentecostal spirituality.[207] Failure to acknowledge the existence and development

204. Wacker, *Heaven Below*, 76–79; cf. Lewis, "Reflections of a Hundred," §§ 2–3. Concerning the propensity of Pentecostals toward schism, Lewis points out that even before what he terms the "Period of Entrenchment and Adaption" (1929–67), Pentecostals already had subdivided into three main groups: Holiness Pentecostals (emphasizing Wesleyan sanctification), Baptistic Pentecostals (emphasizing a more Calvinistic sanctification), and Oneness ("Jesus only") Pentecostals. The entrenchment years also contained other internal challenges with the emergence of the "Latter Rain" movement and the rise of a number of prominent and often controversial healing evangelists. On the early debate over sanctification, see Leggett, "Assemblies of God," 113–22; and Anderson, *Vision of the Disinherited*, 153–75. Aside from doctrine, others point out that racism on the part of white Pentecostals also served to harm the inclusive spirit of early Pentecostalism (Clemmons, "True Koinonia," 48; Irvin, "'Drawing All Together,'" 30; Robeck, "Taking Stock," 46–47). More recently, attempts have been made to repair the damage done by racism. In 1994 the Pentecostal fellowship of North America (PFNA) was dissolved largely due to its white dominance and was replaced by a racially integrated Pentecostal / Charismatic Churches of North America (PCCNA) (Hollenweger, *Pentecostalism*, 39).

205. Jacobsen, *Thinking in the Spirit*, 354–55.

206. Nineteenth-century Wesleyan and Holiness spirituality is perhaps the most readily available example of Pentecostal reliance on a tradition. See Hollenweger, "Critical Tradition," 8; Archer, *Pentecostal Hermeneutic*, 14–17, 22; and cf. Lewis, "Towards a Pentecostal," 9. Lewis here argues that Pentecostals have created their own "Pentecostal paradigm," which can be understood as "a conglomeration of understanding related to what might be called 'the Pentecostal tradition.'"

207. See Archer, "Pentecostal Way," 4; Lewis, "Towards a Pentecostal," 15–16; Lewis, "Reflections," § 3; Hollenweger, "Critical Tradition," 8; Tarr, "Transcendence," 196, 202–9, 214–15; Cargal, "Beyond the Fundamentalist-Modernist," 182–86; Smith, "Closing of the Book," 58–59; and Robeck, "Taking Stock," 54–55. More will be said concerning the

of a Pentecostal liturgy has led to certain rituals becoming accepted (and even fossilized) prior to adequate theological reflection or evaluation.[208] Similarly, Faupel notes that the current doctrinal statements of Pentecostal denominations sound a lot like the "man-made" creeds they had previously scorned.[209] Doctrinal statements in themselves are not the problem. The danger occurs when such statements begin to tacitly function with an authority that cannot be challenged—and such can more readily occur when the existence of an evolving tradition is not acknowledged within a movement.[210] Robeck strongly argues, for example, that the doctrines of Spirit baptism and initial evidence function in this way within the Assemblies of God, USA (AG), being enforced by an unofficial "magisterium" of sorts, through its General Presbytery and Doctrinal Purity Commission.[211]

This devaluing of tradition can also mean that the vast resources available within the historical church traditions may readily be ignored (or despised), rather than serving to aid Pentecostals as they wrestle with various emerging theological and practical issues. In response, there is a growing call for Pentecostals to acknowledge the important role of tradition (both of their own and other Christian streams), and have greater appreciation for the resources it offers.[212] In particular, some are urging

epistemological reasons for the tension between Pentecostalism and evangelicalism in the following section.

208. Hudson notes that Pentecostals have sometimes prided themselves as being superior to liturgical Christian traditions, while failing to recognize their own liturgy (Hudson, "Worship," 187; cf. Johns, "Pentecostalism and the Postmodern," 95).

209. Faupel, "Whither Pentecostalism?," 23. Cf. Lewis, "Reflections of a Hundred," §3; and Lewis, "Towards a Pentecostal," 9.

210. Kärkkäinen argues that while Pentecostals hold Scripture over tradition, their doctrine of "initial physical evidence" is not solely based on Scripture, and so is akin to a Roman Catholic doctrine (Kärkkäinen, "Authority, Revelation," 110). Holm also discovered, in his analysis of the PAOC, that not a few credentialed clergy had trouble differentiating between the authority of Scripture and that of the denomination's *Statement of Fundamental and Essential Truths* (Holm, "Paradigmatic Analysis," 44).

211. Robeck, "Emerging Magisterium?," 217, 224, 228, 238–39, 249–51. Using the example of tongues as initial evidence, he demonstrates how recent AG publications have editorialized the testimonies of some early Pentecostals to make them sound more in line with the current AG Statement of Faith. He concludes that the AG has a growing but unacknowledged "magisterium" of sorts, and that such revisions demonstrate the authority of tradition in operation within this particular denomination.

212. Ibid., 214; Land, "Passion for the Kingdom," 42–43; Lewis, "Reflections of a Hundred," § 5. The growing awareness of the importance of tradition is also evidenced by the theme of the 2005 annual meeting of the Society for Pentecostal Studies, entitled,

Pentecostals to mine the resources of Roman Catholic and Orthodox theology, arguably already evident within Pentecostal spirituality via Wesley.[213] Closely related is a growing call to ecumenical fellowship, in part to enable Pentecostals to gain better self-understanding.[214]

One helpful resource for understanding Pentecostalism's evolving relationship with the broader Christian tradition and ecumenical fellowship is provided by Veli-Matti Kärkkäinen, who outlines five stages in the history of Pentecostal/ecumenical relations.[215] He identifies the first stage as "The Original Vision of Christian Unity," which refers to the early Pentecostal "ecumenical impulse," discussed earlier.[216] During the second stage, "Instead of unity, the main purpose came to be survival and competition with others."[217] Responding to rejection from other churches, Pentecostals began to ridicule the lack of spiritual enthusiasm and cessationist theology found in other denominations.[218] Growing

---

"That Which We Have Received We Now Pass On: Spirit, Word, and Tradition in Pentecostalism."

213. Coulter, "What Meaneth This?," 52–55; Bevins, "Pentecostal Appropriation," 16–18; Moore, "Toward a Psychological," 1–5.

214. Land, "Passion for the Kingdom," 42–44. Cf. Lewis, "Towards a Pentecostal," 16; Plüss, "Frog King," § 8; Bevins, "Pentecostal Appropriation," 16–17; and Coulter, "What Meaneth This?," 40.

215. For a similar four stage overview of the historical relationship between Pentecostalism and ecumenism see Hollenweger, *Pentecostalism*, 355–56; and Lewis, "Reflections of a Hundred," §§ 2–5.

216. Kärkkäinen, "Pentecostals as 'Anonymous Ecumenists'?," 40–42. Here Kärkkäinen highlights the early Pentecostal "ecumenical impulse" previously discussed. It is worth also noting that, according to Irvin, the practice of tongues among early Pentecostals symbolized that people of all languages and ethnicities were the object of the outpouring of the Spirit. The sign of tongues served to intensify missional fervor, and in this way functioned not so much as a boundary-marker (as in later Pentecostalism), but as a symbol of inclusivity that could transcend the traditional ecumenical approach of "inclusion through forced adherence to linguistic and cultural forms" (Irvin, "'Drawing All Together,'" 51).

217. Kärkkäinen, "Pentecostals as 'Anonymous Ecumenists'?," 43. Kärkkäinen does not provide any exact dates for this development, however, Lewis suggests the Pentecostal "Period of Formulation" as being from 1901–29. He then proposes 1929–67 as a "Period of Entrenchment and Adaptation," and this roughly seems to correspond with Kärkkäinen's outline (Lewis, "Reflections of a Hundred," §§ 2–3).

218. Kärkkäinen, "Pentecostals as 'Anonymous Ecumenists'?," 42. Kärkkäinen states, "partially because of some extremes in their worship, and partially because of the rigidity of some of the older denominations. The more Pentecostals became marginalized by the establishment, the more there arose among Pentecostals prejudices toward other Christians, especially the Roman Catholic Church. Finally this led to exclusivism."

intolerance toward other Christian traditions led Pentecostals to encourage like-minded believers to abandon other denominations and join Pentecostal churches.[219] Ironically, during this period of survival Pentecostals informally aligned themselves doctrinally with fundamentalist and evangelical groups, and the enemies of these new unlikely allies became the enemies of the Pentecostals—namely mainline Protestant and liberal churches, including those involved in more formal ecumenical endeavors.[220]

During the third stage, identified by Kärkkäinen as "A Vision of 'Spiritual unity,'" Pentecostals began to redefine Christian unity as being more of an invisible than visible reality (largely due to their exodus from visible denominations). The WCC was rejected by Pentecostals, since it appeared to them to be a human attempt to do the work of God.[221] Yet at the same time Pentecostals began to involve themselves more formally with other believers, so long as they corresponded with their "viewpoint." Here Kärkkäinen cites the Pentecostal acceptance into the National Association of Evangelicals (USA) in 1947, and the Pentecostal Fellowship of North America in 1948.[222]

The fourth stage was, "The Emergence of an Ecumenical Perspective." The appearance of the charismatic movement in the 1950s forced Pentecostals to rethink their suspicion of mainline Protestant

219. Clark and Lederle et al., *What Is Distinctive*, 19; Robinson, "David Du Plessis," 148. The doctrine of initial evidence also took on more exclusivistic overtones. Land suggests that the accent on tongues as evidence of Spirit baptism arose largely due to the rejection of Pentecostals by other Christians. While glossolalia had always served as evidence of Spirit baptism for early Pentecostals, its meaning became far narrower. Rather than a sign that barriers between people were being broken down, it became a doctrine that tended to create division between Christians (Land, "Praying in the Spirit," 88, 91).

220. Kärkkäinen, "Pentecostals as 'Anonymous Ecumenists'?," 43.

221. Ibid., 43, 44. Pentecostal suspicion of formal ecumenical endeavors was likely encouraged by their new fundamentalist allies who shared this sentiment. On this see Spittler, "Maintaining Distinctives," 128–29; Lewis, "Towards a Pentecostal," 16; Robeck, "Taking Stock," 56; and Hollenweger, "Critical Tradition," 441.

222. Kärkkäinen, "Pentecostals as 'Anonymous Ecumenists'?," 44–45. Cf. Faupel, "Whither Pentecostalism?," 25; Johns, "Adolescence of Pentecostalism," 6; Lewis, "Reflections of a Hundred," § 3; Land, "Passion for the Kingdom," 42; Robeck, "Taking Stock," 55, cf. 41–43; and Tarr, "Transcendence," 204. Tarr views this move as having been highly damaging, resulting in the loss of signs, wonders and the miraculous among Pentecostals. Robeck notes that even as Pentecostals began to cooperate with such ecumenical organizations, they were rejecting human attempts to make unity visible. They apparently did not view their own organizations as being human creations, but rather as being brought about by the work of the Spirit.

denominations, as well as the Roman Catholic Church. Pentecostals began to view this renewal (albeit slowly and cautiously) as a sovereign work of the Spirit.[223] Finally, Kärkkäinen identifies the fifth stage as the "Roman Catholic-Pentecostal dialogue: an exercise on the frontiers of ecumenism."[224] The Roman Catholic-Pentecostal dialogue began in 1972, and continued in four basic phases through 1996. This was a significant dialogue, states Kärkkäinen, since it involved the two largest Christian groups in the world, both of which are not members of the WCC (with some exceptions within broader Pentecostalism).[225] This willingness of Pentecostals to dialogue ecumenically has also been extended to Wesleyan and Orthodox traditions.[226]

Within Pentecostalism, then, there can paradoxically be seen both suspicion of tradition, and also an ecumenical openness that, despite considerable internal repression, appears to be emerging again. Why this current openness to other Christian traditions and to the resources of tradition itself? No doubt the original ecumenical impulse, and especially the impact of the charismatic renewal (with its challenge to Pentecostal elitist attitudes), have played an important role.[227] However, one other theological trend is worth noting. There is growing recognition among Pentecostals that biblical authority is connected to the community of faith—that one's understanding of Scripture is *mediated through* the community in which one finds oneself.[228] Mark J. Cartledge notes that progressively more Pentecostal scholars are moving toward a positive view of "the testimony of tradition," connected to a cultural-linguistic theory of truth.[229] In this view, belief is socially mediated, and theology cannot but be tied to some sort of tradition. He states, "While tradition may have a negative connotation, it is now widely accepted that we all do our theology from some kind of position or tradition, that is a cultural-linguistic context. Tradition, which is living, open to change

223. Kärkkäinen, "Pentecostals as 'Anonymous Ecumenists'?," 45–47. One Pentecostal who was very involved in ecumenical relations during this period was David du Plessis (Robinson, "David Du Plessis," 143–55).

224. Kärkkäinen, "Pentecostals as 'Anonymous Ecumenists'?," 47.

225. Ibid., 47–48, cf. 42–50. Also see Kärkkäinen, "Trinity as Communion," 209–30.

226. Lewis, "Reflections of a Hundred," § 5.

227. Robeck, "Taking Stock," 54.

228. Ellington, "Pentecostalism," 28–29; cf. Smith, "Closing of the Book," 68–70.

229. Cartledge, "Testimony to the Truth," 604; cf. Del Colle, "Postmodernism," 101.

and transformation, nevertheless provides a platform from which to speak, act and judge."[230]

Schner also, while not speaking for Pentecostals, helps articulate the attraction of this cultural-linguistic approach for explaining the interrelationship between experience and tradition:

> [On] the one side they say, since what you say is not my experience, it is not authoritative. On the other side they say: Since what you say is not in keeping with authority [i.e., church tradition], it is not authentic experience. But the tables can be easily turned. The appeal to experience is in fact an appeal to authority: "my" experience authorizes (gives authority) to me, is the basis on which I choose what to do and say. And, the appeal to authority is in fact an appeal to experience: you must do as I say because what I tell you is what I know (what I experience) to be true, or more broadly I merely remind you of what has always been true (is the common accumulated experience, the wisdom, of the community).[231]

The reluctance Pentecostals have had in recognizing the authoritative function of communal tradition in favor of experience is no less an appeal to authority, since experience is only articulated within an existing tradition. Acknowledging that tradition is in many ways what allows experiences of God to occur opens the way for constructive theological discourse between experience and tradition, which in turn allows the community to avoid stagnation.[232] While there are perhaps limits as to how much Pentecostals will be willing to embrace this cultural-linguistic approach,[233] Schner's description demonstrates why many believe it holds promise for helping Pentecostals recognize tradition as an inescapable reality for better understanding the uniqueness of the Pentecostal tradition itself (and its reliance upon other Christian traditions), and for entering into positive ecumenical fellowship.

---

230. Cartledge, "Testimony to the Truth," 604. Examples of those considering or advocating such a move include Coulter, "What Meaneth This?," 62; Smith, "Closing of the Book," 68–70; and Shuman, 207–23. We will also observe this trend in Chan, Macchia, and Yong to varying degrees.

231. George P. Schner, "'New Ways," 6–7.

232. Ibid., 10.

233. Cf. Lewis, "Towards a Pentecostal," 4–5. This will be further discussed in the next section.

Pentecostal Experience and Reason

Bearing in mind our broader use of the term "reason," for our purposes here, then, it will refer to the general epistemological context in which Pentecostalism emerged—i.e., the commonly held assumptions as to what was "reasonable" or "rational" in North American culture at the turn of the twentieth century. It should also be noted that "reason," can refer to both method and content. Human reason (as method) can be employed to discover truths (content) about the world, outside of that revealed in Scripture. This extra-biblical truth (for example, scientific discoveries), once received and assimilated, can serve as an authoritative pool of knowledge and be brought into dialogue with Scripture. Here, then, the focus will be on the relationship between Pentecostal experience and reason, acknowledging both method and content, and highlighting two distinguishable yet interrelated epistemological forces that served to define what was arguably considered "reasonable" thinking during Pentecostalism's emergence and development: modernism (with its emphasis on Enlightenment rationalism and human discoveries) and pragmatism (with its emphasis on empirical method utilized practically in daily life).[234]

With regard to modernist epistemology, we noted in our earlier discussion on hermeneutics that early Pentecostals were not modernists, and in some respects were anti-modern. Clark and Lederle describe early Pentecostalism as characterized by a general "anti-intellectualism" and suspicion of the modernistic "intellectuals of the day."[235] Early Pentecostal commitment to biblical authority factored into their suspicion of modern thought, with its reliance on Enlightenment epistemology.[236] It was not that Pentecostals were irrational. They did use, as Archer

---

234. For sake of focus, we leave aside the moral/ethical cultural context in which Pentecostals found themselves. On the contrast of Pentecostal morality with the surrounding culture see Wacker, *Heaven Below*, 121–40.

235. Clark and Lederle et al., *What Is Distinctive*, 41; cf. Wacker, *Heaven Below*, 31. Wacker believes that early Pentecostals were not so much anti-intellectual as pragmatically impatient with "pointless theorizing."

236. See Archer, *Pentecostal Hermeneutic*, 197. Archer here characterizes the Enlightenment as "A seventeenth- and eighteenth-century Western movement that emphasized individual autonomy and critical philosophical reasoning. Rationalism, Skepticism and Empiricism characterized this intellectual period. Science made significant technical progress during this time. Because it replaced human reasoning with external authorities as a source of knowledge it aroused great suspicion concerning the

puts it, "Common Sense reasoning"; however, "they had not immersed themselves in modernistic academic language and thought."[237] Archer describes modernism as the "nineteenth- and twentieth-century western cultural worldview that was an intensive extension of Enlightenment beliefs. It is characterized by strong belief in human progress through scientific, rationalistic reasoning from the perspective that a person can be neutral and objective. Scientific and historical verification were the means of validating all truth claims."[238]

Human reason occupied a privileged place of authority in the modernist worldview,[239] and not a few Christians sought to demonstrate how Christianity could be compatible with modernist assumptions, resulting in both liberal and fundamentalist expressions.[240] Pentecostals, however, with their *assumption of* biblical authority, could not grant human reason the place of authority advocated by the surrounding intellectual culture.[241] Further, Pentecostal holistic spirituality and emphasis on the affections helped elevate their suspicion of reason, often viewing it as a substitute for the Spirit's power. Jacobsen affirms, reliance on human reason was viewed as a sure-fire way to quench the Spirit's activity.[242] Again, Pentecostals were not irrational (although often portrayed this way by detractors). Rather, they were, as Jackie David Johns puts it, "transrational"—truth was not the possession of reason alone; orthopathy and orthopraxis were held as equally important as orthodoxy.[243] Holm summarizes, "Pentecostals celebrated intuition over systematics, experience over creeds, spontaneity over

---

claims of traditional Christianity. The Enlightenment provides the womb for the conception of Historical Criticism."

237. Ibid., 63; cf. Wacker, "'Wild Theories,'" 28. Wacker suggests this unwillingness to submit to the spirit of "the times" is possibly one reason Pentecostalism flourished.

238. Archer, *Pentecostal Hermeneutic*, 197–98.

239. Carson, *Becoming Conversant*, 92–95.

240. Archer, *Pentecostal Hermeneutic*, 198. Both expressions, in other words, rely on aspects of modernist epistemology. On the Enlightenment influence on Bible interpretation, see Frei, *Eclipse of Biblical*.

241. They did not take the same route as the fundamentalists, who, as previously noted, attempted to demonstrate the authority of Scripture by means of modernist rationality.

242. Jacobsen, *Thinking in the Spirit*, 360.

243. Johns, "Pentecostalism and the Postmodern," 89. Also see Lewis, "Towards a Pentecostal," 17–19.

liturgy, proclamation over articulation, practicality over abstracts, affections over reasoning and discovery over apologetics."[244]

At the same time, Pentecostals were not unaffected by their surrounding epistemological context. In practice they exhibited certain elements of modernism, particularly in their penchant for informal empirical method (as we shall see). This is why Archer describes early Pentecostals as "paramodern."[245] It is worth quoting him at length on this point.

> Early Pentecostalism should not be viewed as "pre-modern" because it was born in the modernistic age. It shared characteristics of the so-called pre-modern era, but it relied upon the adaptation of modernistic language and belief to discover and articulate its practices and beliefs (plus it insisted on tangible, visible signs of the Holy Spirit's presence), even though it was in opposition to Modernity. Pentecostalism should not be viewed as "anti-modern" because it did not attempt to develop a "critical" argument against modernity, which accepted the epistemological premise of modernity, that truth and faith was based entirely upon "objective historical evidence" in the manner of the Fundamentalists. Pentecostals saw themselves as Fundamentalists, yet the "Fundamentalists" seldom welcomed Pentecostals to their councils or saw them as allies. "Paramodern" would be a better way to classify early Pentecostalism. This concept captures the fact that Pentecostalism emerged within Modernity (a historically definitive time period), yet existed on the fringes of Modernity (both in a sociological and economical sense, and by its emphasis on physical evidence for the Spirit's presence—a modernistic slant on scientific experimentation language). Pentecostalism could never accept Modernity's worldview completely, but it did utilize aspects of Modernity (like technology, language, inductive reasoning) to advance the Pentecostal cause. Pentecostalism was (and is) a protest to the central features of Modernity. The Pentecostal movement began as a Paramodern movement protesting Modernity and cessationist Christianity.[246]

244. Holm, "Paradigmatic Analysis," 282–83.

245. John Christopher Thomas also uses the term, "para-modern," to describe Pentecostals, but does not expand on its meaning (Thomas, "Pentecostal Theology," 12).

246. Archer, *Pentecostal Hermeneutic*, 33. Gerald T. Sheppard likewise notes the influence of the Modern context on early Pentecostals. Describing them as "submodern," he states, Pentecostals "ate from the crumbs that fell beneath the table at the banquet of modernity. They participated self-consciously or unwittingly on an *ad hoc* basis in the modern experiment" (Sheppard, "Biblical Interpretation," 127). Lewis similarly

On the one hand, then, Pentecostals can be distinguished from modernity, rejecting elements of its *content and values*.[247] Lewis identifies some of the "characteristics of modernity [as being] autonomous individualism, narcissistic hedonism, reductive naturalism, absolute moral relativism, and modern chauvinism." Such was where human reason (without revelation) was inevitably thought to lead.[248] Reason, then, was not *the* authority—God was. Yet, on the other hand, Pentecostals utilized some *methods* of modernity, its "language and arguments," in developing and articulating their beliefs.[249] In particular, an informal scientific empiricism is conspicuous in early Pentecostal doctrinal expression, which demanded (or assumed) that the Spirit's activity would be evidenced by observable, physical phenomena.[250] So, a tension existed—Pentecostals viewed reason with suspicion, while simultaneously adopting some of its useful elements.[251]

This tension evolved through the twentieth century as Pentecostals began to adopt evangelical methods (arguably reliant on modernist epistemology) for articulating and defending their beliefs. As noted, some have viewed this move as detrimental to Pentecostalism, fuelling current debate as to whether Pentecostal spirituality and theology is more compatible with modern or postmodern epistemology.[252] Exemplifying the latter, Lewis classifies Pentecostalism as a "non-Enlightenment en-

---

describes Pentecostals as "*ultramodern* insofar as they perpetuate the direction and endeavors of modernity" (Lewis, "Towards a Pentecostal," 17; italics added).

247. Archer, *Pentecostal Hermeneutic*, 195.

248. Lewis, "Towards a Pentecostal," 16. Lewis argues that Pentecostals continue to reject these values.

249. Archer, *Pentecostal Hermeneutic*, 71.

250. The doctrine of initial evidence is an example of this empirical bent (to be explored below).

251. In reaction to Pentecostal suspicion of reason, some are calling for Pentecostals to use reason to avoid naïve hermeneutical decisions, and to better critique the operation of spiritual gifts (prophecy in particular). See Stronstad, "Pentecostalism, Experiential," 27–28; McKay, "When the Veil," 17–40; Bevins, "Pentecostal Appropriation," 14–15; and Moore, "Toward a Psychological," 1–4. Both Bevins and Moore appeal for Pentecostals to utilize the Wesleyan quadrilateral in matters of discernment.

252. Lewis, "Towards a Pentecostal," 14–15. Murray W. Dempster summarizes the contrast between modern and postmodern epistemology as being that the latter emphasizes human knowledge as being more perspectival than objective, more social than individual, more relational than autonomous, and a rejection of metanarratives (Dempster, "Issues Facing Pentecostalism," 262; cf. Cross, "Can There Be," 1–2; and Del Colle, "Postmodernism," 97–99).

terprise," rejecting "the whole Enlightenment epistemological enterprise, and its fruit. By this, I mean the Enlightenment's emphasis on foundationalism, the mind/body problem, the quest for certainty, the epistemic usage of doubt, and the objective/subjective problem."[253] Lewis continues: "The Pentecostal sees the whole 'foundational' enterprise as fatally flawed, because it does not understand the diversity of knowledge, nor the nature of relational knowledge. In other words, the Pentecostal notes the usage of experience, tradition, empirical verification and pure rationality of reason in various aspects of Pentecostal hermeneutics and ethics. Each informs the other with a holistic relationship."[254]

Others, however, such as Robert P. Menzies, have reacted against "jumping on the postmodern bandwagon,"[255] fearing this will unmoor Pentecostals from well-reasoned theology, and potentially even lead into moral relativism.[256] He advocates holding fast to evangelical historicism, since salvation is tied to historical events and Scripture, adding, "In short . . . Pentecostalism, because of its pragmatic and experiential focus, may be easily attracted to the ahistorical vision inherent in postmodern thought. This, however, *is a weakness, not a strength*."[257] Not surprisingly, then, some of the initial optimism toward postmodernism has been tempered and qualified among Pentecostals.[258] Even Lewis, despite high-

253. Lewis, "Towards a Pentecostal," 17.

254. Ibid., 18. Others suggesting a post-critical or postmodern epistemology as being more congruent with Pentecostalism include: Cox, *Fire from Heaven*, 110; Miller and Yamamori, *Global Pentecostalism*, 142; Cargal, "Beyond the Fundamentalist-Modernist," 167–87; Del Colle, "Postmodernism," 97–116; and Sheppard, "Biblical Interpretation," 121–41. Some also highlight postmodern openness to affectivity over rationalism, and penchant for narrative over propositional proclamation as being more convergent with Pentecostal ethos and spirituality than the modernist approaches utilized by Pentecostals' evangelical and fundamentalist cousins. See Baker, "Pentecostal Bible Reading," 34–48; Smith, "Advice to Pentecostal," 1–15.; Archer, *Pentecostal Hermeneutic*, 71, 146–54; and Cross, "Can There Be," 10–13.

255. Menzies and Menzies, *Spirit and Power*, 63–68.

256. Dempster, "Issues Facing Pentecostalism," 262.

257. Menzies and Menzies, *Spirit and Power*, 65 (italics added). Robert P. Menzies is responding to Timothy Cargal's appeal for Pentecostals to adopt a postmodern epistemology. John C. Poirier and B. Scott Lewis have strongly critiqued Pentecostal buy-in to postmodern epistemology, suggesting it is built on an inadequate interpretation of the Enlightenment, and a naïve understanding of the sciences, especially concerning quantum physics (Poirier and Lewis, "Pentecostal and Postmodernist," 3–21).

258. See Cargal, "Beyond the Fundamentalist-Modernist," 187; and Del Colle, "Postmodernism," 101–8, 110, 112–16. Cargal does admit that postmodernism is not without its weaknesses. Del Colle also identifies several areas that Pentecostals must

lighting the inadequacies of the "Enlightenment enterprise" is nonetheless also reluctant to embrace postmodernism wholeheartedly, seeing it as yet too fluid and undefined.[259]

The challenge, it seems, is to avoid locating Pentecostalism solely within modernity or postmodernity, although the latter appears to have gained momentum with regard to its appeal.[260] Jacobsen insightfully highlights the paradoxical relationship Pentecostals have to both their modern and postmodern contexts:

> If Pentecostal faith is in some sense quite flexible and postmodern, it is in another sense still firmly grounded in a bedrock commitment to religious truth. Pentecostals, for all their openness to new revelation, remain solidly committed to the Bible as the word of God. For all their freedom to explore new ways of making sense of Christian faith, most pentecostals also remain linked to communities of discernment (denominations, congregations, small groups, and families) that act as hedges on unfettered spiritual creativity. And it is precisely this dual sense of freedom and groundedness that has made pentecostalism so appealing to so many people in the twentieth century. Pentecostalism represents spiritual freedom mixed with old-time religious assurance, and

---

critique concerning postmodernism. Pentecostals, he observes, emphasize "presence" (of God, by the Holy Spirit), whereas postmoderns emphasize "absence." Pentecostals, while utilizing postmodern deconstruction need to offer more constructive alternatives, since Pentecostals are not quite as ahistorical as might be believed. Further, while both postmodernists and Pentecostals have a penchant for the "oral," Pentecostals are more word-centered in contrast to the postmodern anti-word stance. Finally, Del Colle suggests the Pentecostal call to holiness was perhaps far easier in a modernistic context, since postmodernism can easily dismiss such community distinctiveness to being "an innocuous sideshow among the de-centered communities and selves . . ." (ibid., 110). Incidentally, Robert P. Menzies also emphasizes this last point, stating that while postmodernism does promote more openness to sharing experiences, it does not allow any one testimony to occupy a place of authority—it is simply one opinion among others (Menzies and Menzies, *Spirit and Power*, 65).

259. Lewis, "Towards a Pentecostal," 15. He later states, "The Pentecostal position is not necessarily sequential to the Enlightenment enterprise, nor is it pre-Enlightenment, it is just not entrapped within the Enlightenment agenda as typified by Rationalists, Empiricists and Romanticists. Further, the roots of postmodernity is World War I, whereas the Pentecostal movement developed a decade prior" (ibid., 17).

260. See Del Colle, "Postmodernism," 101. Del Colle notes that one application of postmodern epistemology is found in the postliberal theology of George A. Lindbeck and Hans Frei. In his opinion, many new Pentecostal theologians appear to be taking the path of postliberalism as an alternative to fundamentalism and evangelical theology.

that is a powerful package of faith for an age like our own that is
both leery of dogma and hungry for certainty.[261]

It is important to recognize that this modernism/postmodernism
deliberation is in many ways a debate concerning the level of authority
that reason (in its modernistic form) should be granted in the formulation and evaluation of Pentecostal theology and experience. Clark and
Lederle correctly suggest that while contemporary Pentecostals may still
maintain a suspicion of modernist epistemology, it is no longer due to a
"glorification of ignorance." Instead this stems from a healthy critical realism that recognizes that modernist epistemology is laden with presuppositional baggage that may or may not be compatible with Pentecostal
spirituality.[262]

A related, equally significant issue is the pragmatic tendency within
Pentecostalism, which underscores the influence of the North American
epistemological context upon the emerging movement.[263] Like those
around them, Jacobsen points out, Pentecostals were "hungry for certainty," and sought this out through an inherent empiricism that assumed physical reality and daily life interactions as a tacit authority of
sorts, shaping their theology. But this pragmatism also helps distinguish
Pentecostalism from other aspects of modernism, in particular, the latter's penchant for abstract rationalism.

It has been observed that parallels exist between the emergence of
Pentecostalism and empirically-oriented, North American philosophical
(and popular) pragmatism.[264] This is not, as Holm notes, to suggest the
latter as a historical antecedent to Pentecostalism, but simply to observe

261. Jacobsen, *Thinking in the Spirit*, 363–64. He states that the reason early
Pentecostal theology caught on was that it had the ability to "ring true to people's life
experiences and the experiences of their communities. Today we might call that kind
of theology postmodern, meaning that it acts like it can freely mix and match ideas
and insights from many different sources and paste them into a new collage of faith at
will. In many ways, that is exactly what happened in some first-generation Pentecostal
theology."

262. Clark and Lederle et al., *What Is Distinctive*, 41.

263. We briefly noted this characteristic earlier in this chapter under Albrecht's discussion of Pentecostal creativity.

264. Jacobsen believes there is a parallel between Pentecostalism and the rise of the
"empirical movement in American theology, a precursor of process theology" (Jacobsen,
Thinking in the Spirit, 359). On this also see, Yun, "Metaphysical Construct," 5–8;
Hamilton, "Experiential Construction," 6–7; Smith, "Spirit, Word," 1–16; and Cartledge,
"Testimony to the Truth," 599–601.

that both were fertilized in the same epistemological *context*.[265] So, says Lewis, "partially due to the zeitgeist at the formulation of Pentecostal thought, Pentecostal thought has been fundamentally pragmatic."[266] That pragmatism, as a method, served as a "reasonable" authority of sorts within early Pentecostalism, and continues to do so, is argued by a number of voices, including Koo Dong Yun, Randall Holm, and Ken Smith, among others.

Yun calls North American Pentecostals to become more aware of this often unarticulated pragmatic bent, since he believes it explains Pentecostal theology and spirituality more accurately than an overemphasis on the affections (as espoused by Land).[267] "Pragmatism," he states, "is more embedded in the American culture than we want to admit."[268] He continues: "One should not forget that the American Pentecostal movement in the twentieth century sprang from the American soil (or horizon). A doctrine cannot be rightly understood without locating it in its context. Pentecostalism emerged around during the same period in which American pragmatism became popular and conspicuous. Accordingly, no one can disavow the pragmatic influence on the emergence of Pentecostalism because pragmatism robustly penetrated the American culture. In other words, no religion is exempt from cultural influence."[269]

The Pentecostal understanding of what is true, argues Yun, has far more in common with the pragmatism of William James than that of abstract Enlightenment rationalism (although both are linked to modernity).[270] Ken Smith concurs, Jamesian pragmatism "mesh[ed] well with the Pentecostal temperament."[271] William James (1842–1910) drawing on the pragmatic philosophy of Charles Sanders Peirce (1839–1914),[272] developed the idea that truth was that which was "good," and

265. Holm, "Paradigmatic Analysis," 32.

266. Lewis, "Towards a Pentecostal," 7.

267. Yun, "Metaphysical Construct," 7–8. As an Asian, Yun suggests he may be more attuned to this element than North Americans.

268. Ibid., 5.

269. Ibid., 7.

270. Ibid., 5–6.

271. Smith, "Spirit, Word," 14.

272. Ibid., 7. Cf. Cartledge, "Testimony to the Truth," 599–600; Johns, "Pentecostalism and the Postmodern," 83; and Yun, "Metaphysical Construct," 6. Peirce argued that the meaning of a thought or idea is found in what it intends to produce.

what was "good" was that which worked, or was useful.[273] In other words, James focused truth value on the end result, insisting that truth could not be found in theories that had not been subjected to real world experimentation and empirical verification.[274] Holm states that James reacted to what he viewed as "tender-minded" reliance on metaphysical foundationalism, in favor of a "tough-minded" approach that allowed brute facts to dictate the value of theory.[275] Yun affirms this; for James, truth was not found in abstract propositions. Rather, truth was "concrete and consequential," and had "cash value." Therefore, truth requires verification—preferably by sense data, although indirect observation is also acceptable.[276]

Pragmatism and experimental (empirical) method is notable within Pentecostal theology and practice in its refusal to submit to abstract theological systems, and insistence upon tangible verification with regard to the Spirit's activity. Pentecostals, observes Jackie David Johns, simply assume that creation is an "open system," in which God is a frequent participant.[277] This allowed them to embrace the empiricism of the day (albeit in popular form), since God was expected to be tangibly discernable within creation. Jacobsen states, Pentecostalism "was thoroughly empirical from the very beginning of the movement. Pentecostals were interested in discovering what God was actually doing in the world, rather than being interested in what traditional theology said God was supposed to be doing."[278]

Rationalism, creeds and institutions tended to 'close' the system, which was unacceptable to the Pentecostal temperament. An emphasis on verifiability can be found in both Pentecostal doctrinal formulation and decision-making—Pentecostals expected demonstrable results in

---

273. Johns, "Pentecostalism and the Postmodern," 83; Cartledge, "Testimony to the Truth," 600.

274. Smith, "Spirit, Word," 7–8.

275. Holm, "Paradigmatic Analysis," 28. Therefore, states Jackie David Johns, "pragmatism used the scientific method as a tool for problem solving rather than the method for discovering absolute truth." Further, this introduced the "seeds of an open system," and a challenge to the Enlightenment worldview (Johns, "Pentecostalism and the Postmodern," 83).

276. Yun, "Metaphysical Construct," 6.

277. Johns, "Pentecostalism and the Postmodern," 89, cf. 83.

278. Jacobsen, *Thinking in the Spirit*, 360.

their relationship with God.[279] Tongues speech, for example, served to empirically validate both their experience and doctrine.[280] Jacobsen states, "A commitment to empiricism was also implicit in the assertion that the baptism of the Spirit had to be signified by an outward, visibly observable, action such as speaking in tongues."[281] Even the description of tongues as the "initial *physical evidence*" of Spirit baptism borrowed terminology from the empirical sciences.[282]

But even before the initial evidence doctrine became institutionalized, tongues served another purpose, further demonstrating Pentecostal pragmatism. Early Pentecostals understood Spirit baptism as having been given to empower believers for mission and evangelism. So, almost all early North American Pentecostals (including the influential Charles Parham) assumed that tongues, as xenolalia, would enable missionaries to minister effectively in foreign cultures without having to take the time to learn new languages.[283] As Allan Anderson observes,

279. While physical manifestations (signs, wonders, healings, etc.) can function as tangible assurance for the believer of God's presence and commitment, the lack of such might too readily be interpreted as indication of the Spirit's absence. This is why Wacker says that while early Pentecostals insisted theologically that the Spirit was a person, sometimes in practice the Spirit seemed to be reduced to an impersonal power (Wacker, *Heaven Below*, 89).

280. Yun, "Metaphysical Construct," 6–7. Yun states, "I assert, moreover, that even pragmatism itself was a resultant of the age where modern science was dominating. Classical Pentecostals were consciously or unconsciously affected by the scientific method of natural sciences. This scientific method taught that one formulated a hypothesis based on empirical observation, and this hypothesis should have been verified through various experiments by observable sense data. The scientific method was mainly rooted in scientific materialism. This scientific materialism, an extreme form of empiricism, taught that knowledge can only be procured by the scientific, sense data, and the ultimate reality consisted in matter only. In other words, the reality of truth should only be verified by tangible data. This reductive, scientific method was embedded in the American culture, and being influenced by this attitude, classical Pentecostals were perhaps looking for that verifiable sense data, namely, glossolalia or speaking in tongues."

281. Jacobsen, *Thinking in the Spirit*, 360.

282. Others have also noted this connection between pragmatic empiricism and the Pentecostal doctrine of Spirit baptism. See Holm, "Paradigmatic Analysis," 169–72; Sheppard, "Biblical Interpretation," 127; Lewis, "Towards a Pentecostal," 18; Jacobsen, *Thinking in the Spirit*, 360; and Archer, "Early Pentecostal," 37.

283. Yun, "Metaphysical Construct," 8; Holm, "Paradigmatic Analysis," 176–78; Anderson, "Burning Its Way," 5–6. Xenolalia is a language unknown to the speaker, but assumed to be a known human language being used somewhere on earth. Irvin explains that while, for the most part, the tongues of Azusa Street were originally understood to be xenolalia, even still, tongues were allowed to be uttered even when no person present

however, as Pentecostal missionaries arrived on foreign soils, it became overwhelmingly *evident* that they could not speak the language(s) of the nationals. Eventually, this reality challenged the predominant view, leading to a theological revisioning of the purpose of tongues.[284] Rather than understand tongues as xenolalia, this encounter with reality caused most Pentecostals to begin viewing tongues as glossolalia.[285]

In this case, the theological meaning of tongues was altered, based not on the authority of Scripture, but that of pragmatic reasoning and informal empirical observation.[286] Grant Wacker affirms, "pentecostals freely admitted that good sense and sound judgment represented a kind of authority that could not be gainsaid."[287] Further, just as the doctrine of xenolalia was abandoned because it did not "work," the glossolalia "evidential construct" proved highly effective for perpetuating Pentecostalism, serving to empirically justify that this particular doctrinal construct was correct. Holm summarizes: "The course of the pragmatics changed from saying, 'the Holy Spirit is alive and well because I have experienced it,' to 'our evidential construct is true because the Pentecostal church is alive and growing.'"[288]

Holm has argued extensively that pragmatism "plays a determining role as an evolving a priori or prejudice" within Pentecostalism.[289]

---

was able to interpret them. There were, as such, a "surplus of tongues" at the meetings, thus making room for all nations symbolically (Irvin, "'Drawing All Together,'" 51–52).

284. Anderson, "Burning Its Way," 6–8. He notes that a number of Pentecostal leaders, notably Alexander Boddy, helped influence this revisioning.

285. Glossolalia is a language unknown to the speaker, and yet not necessarily a real human language. The apostle Paul's reference to the "language of angels" could be used to support this possibility (see 1 Cor 13:1).

286. Allan H. Anderson does go on to state that despite this change of interpretation for the purpose of tongues, "Pentecostal missionaries [nevertheless] got on with the job in a hurry," since the coming of Christ was imminent. "Reflection *about* the task was not as important *as action* in evangelism" (Anderson, "Burning Its Way," 13; italics added). Holm suggests that this move toward the formulation of and focus on propagating the "initial physical evidence" propositional construct was also due to a loss of "apocalyptic urgency," as it "became apparent that the end was not so imminent" (Holm, "Paradigmatic Analysis," 215, cf. 205–10).

287. Wacker, *Heaven Below*, 85; cf. Barnes, "Experience as a Catalyst," 1–8. Barnes explores the influence of pragmatism in the life of early Pentecostal leader, F. F. Bosworth.

288. Holm, "Paradigmatic Analysis," 215.

289. Ibid., 26–27, cf. 23–26. Holm's PhD dissertation sought to demonstrate the pragmatic "impulse" in PAOC decision-making through a historical case study of the denomination's decisions concerning the doctrine of Spirit baptism and tongues, the

A strength of this pragmatic theology and spirituality is demonstrated through Pentecostal "tough-mindedness," and ability to adapt to a changing world, particularly in the use of various technologies and techniques.[290] However, this attitude of "if it works, then it is probably justified," is not without its weaknesses. Holm observes that when Pentecostals were faced with difficult decisions,

> As if on cue, an unrestrained praxis-orientated pragmatism was willing to step in and assist any unresolved predicament. The questions, "Are people being saved?" and "Is the church growing?" became two predominant adjudicating criteria. It was not a question of the "end justifying the means" as if the means were otherwise questionable from the start. From a Pentecostal perspective, the end often divinized the means. For instance, if it was God's will that churches grow numerically, ipso facto growth meant God's favour and was the sign of a healthy church. Unfortunately in such situations, questions of impropriety were sometimes set aside. Conversely, if the church declined in size, or if the pastor and his family were overwhelmed with difficulty from day one, dark questions were inevitably raised concerning their calling, methods, or ability to govern a church.[291]

Yet Pentecostal pragmatism is not unrestrained. Pentecostals are, as Holm puts it, "mild-mannered" pragmatists, largely due to the role Scripture occupies in their worldview.[292] Their insistence on biblical authority provides boundaries—Scripture is authoritative and should be considered "reasonable."[293] Therefore, it is probably more accurate

---

role of women in ministry, and the issue of remarriage. Holm observes how the pragmatic a priori became progressively more explicit with the evolution from emphasis on orthopathy (1906–25), to orthodoxy (1925–50), to orthopraxis (1950–). Holm labels these periods respectively as "apocalyptic/intuitive," "accommodational," and "techno-efficacious" paradigms. This chronological division is similar to that of Lewis, who suggests the following four stages: "The Period of Formulation (1901–29)," "The Period of Entrenchment and Adaptation (1929–67)," "The Period of Challenge (1967–84)," and "The Period of Reformulation (1984–present)" (Lewis, "Reflections of a Hundred," §§2–5).

290. Holm, "Paradigmatic Analysis," 111–14.

291. Ibid., 161–162. Holm's remark is based on his study of the PAOC. Others suggest that pragmatism has made Pentecostals susceptible to "gimmickry" (Hudson, "Worship," 202), and dubious hermeneutics (Wacker, *Heaven Below*, 84).

292. Holm, "Paradigmatic Analysis," 32; cf. Johns, "Pentecostalism and the Postmodern," 90.

293. Miller and Yamamori, *Global Pentecostalism*, 148; Higgins et al., *Introduction to Theology*, 42.

to characterize Pentecostals as practical, as opposed to philosophical, pragmatists.[294]

Ken Smith has identified several areas in which Pentecostals and philosophical pragmatists, such as William James, differ. While it is true Pentecostals emphasize the freedom of the Spirit, they do not share James' teleology, believing instead that God has a specific destiny planned for human history, culminating in the return of Jesus. Further, Pentecostals would insist that God does not exist to fulfill human purposes—he is not "useful" in this sense; rather humans exist for God's pleasure.[295] Most important, however, is Smith's observation that Pentecostals would find James' "sublimation of divine transcendence to human immanence" incompatible with their worldview.[296] Jackie David Johns supports Smith's view here, arguing that the Pentecostal worldview is holistic and "God-centered," meaning, "All things relate to God and God relates to all things, [however,] this fusion of God with the phenomenological *does not collapse God into creation.*"[297] There is always a preservation of God's transcendence in the Pentecostal worldview, and this is supported by their emphasis on apocalyptic eschatology, as well as their insistence on moral separation from the world.[298] The Spirit is encountered, and so confronts humans to make "reasonable" decisions. But this is quite different than the idea that the Spirit operates immanently through human rationality. The Spirit's transcendence must not be collapsed into immanence.[299]

The traditional Pentecostal worldview emphasizes the transcendent-immanence of the Spirit, and this needs to be kept in mind as Pentecostals engage themselves in dialogue with the physical and social sciences in the attempt to discern the Spirit's work in and through

294. Lewis, "Towards a Pentecostal," 7. He distinguishes Pentecostals from Richard Rorty and John Dewey.

295. Smith, "Spirit, Word," 14–16.

296. Ibid., 15, cf. 11. Smith identifies James' view of God's immanence as pantheistic.

297. Johns, "Pentecostalism and the Postmodern," 89 (italics added).

298. Ibid., 89, 91. It seems to me that the emphasis on transcendence in the Pentecostal worldview is due in part to the Pentecostal penchant for the book of Acts, in which almost without exception the work of the Spirit is described using external metaphors (e.g., the Spirit "came upon" or "fell upon" believers, etc.).

299. See Tarr, "Transcendence," 196. Tarr suggests that Pentecostal scholars must re-embraced a strong sense of God's transcendence in order to preserve Pentecostal spirituality and identity.

these fields.[300] Further, while many Pentecostals in the academy have found the cultural-linguistic emphasis within postliberal theology to be a potential ally, this framework must be qualified. Lewis is helpful in this regard, noting that Lindbeck's theory states that "doctrine, ethics, and religious experience are limited to the community of the cultural-linguistic grouping." However, says Lewis, "This understanding seems to suffer from a Feuerbachian limitation and limits the Divine by reducing religious experience and theology to anthropology without the Divine ability of immediately impacting the individual apart from the cultural-linguistic group." He continues, "The problem with this position is that it does not adequately account for a living God who directly interacts with the present world. Since this is a basic tenet of Pentecostal belief, I cannot wholly accept the cultural-linguistic approach, yet, there is little doubt of the decidedly important and normal aspects of the cultural-linguistic limitations. This approach should be seen as normal without being normative . . ."[301] Lewis further adds that Pentecostal experience of God is not mystical; "rather it is enigmatic—which seems to be contrary to the natural order, but is fundamentally within the natural order. So, whereas Pentecostal experience is basically predicated by a cultural-linguistic tradition while not being mystical, *God can overcome a cultural-linguistic tradition*, thus, the resulting Pentecostal experience is *pragmatic* and supposed to be normal."[302]

Pentecostal pragmatism as "reason," then, can serve to challenge the status quo of what is "rational" or "reasonable." In sum, while there has always been an uneasy tension between Pentecostals and reason (in particular, certain elements of modernist rationalism), there has also been an evolution in the Pentecostal rationale for distrusting reason, influenced more recently by postmodern epistemological critiques. Further, there is a very real sense in which Pentecostals have embraced elements of their epistemological context, evidenced in their popular empirical pragmatism. Yun states, "The central primary category of Pentecostal experience is not 'affection.' Rather, it is a 'verifiable actuality' accompanied by inner

300. There is growing interest in exploring the relationship between Pentecostalism and the sciences. The 2008 annual meeting of the Society for Pentecostal Studies was themed, "Sighs, Signs, and Significance: Pentecostal and Wesleyan Explorations of Science and Creation."

301. Lewis, "Towards a Pentecostal," 4.

302. Ibid., 8 (italics added).

affection."[303] This important qualification helps us better appreciate the nature of Pentecostal theology, spirituality, and experience.

Conclusion

This chapter has attempted to characterize Pentecostal experience of God by surveying aspects of Pentecostal theology and spirituality in practice (in particular, through worship), and how Pentecostals have understood this experience in relation to the traditional Christian theological media of Scripture, tradition, and reason. Without rehearsing all the particulars discovered above, several general observations can be made, relevant to this book's overall argument concerning Pentecostalism's maturation being evidenced by a growing openness to a mediated concept of experience of the Spirit. First, for experience of God to qualify as "Pentecostal," it must include a robust emphasis on what we have noted as "encounter" with the Spirit. In other words, Pentecostals need to preserve a sense of divine immediacy—that they are, in some sense, directly encountering God. It is doubtful that any theology of experience of God that does not accentuate this element could be rightly called "Pentecostal."

Second, Pentecostals do not simply accept any such encounter as being of the Spirit. They qualify this (albeit not always consciously) within a Pentecostal sub-cultural-linguistic framework, shaped in part by the traditional media of the Spirit—Scripture, tradition, and reason. With the exception of Scripture, the influence of these media is not always explicitly acknowledged; nevertheless, both tradition and reason have always been at work, in some shape or form, helping to mold the Pentecostal understanding of what can be considered authentic experience of God.

Third, there is also growing evidence that Pentecostals are becoming more aware of the role of Scripture, tradition, and reason in shaping their experience of God, and a willingness to appreciate and integrate these media into their own self-understanding and theological development. In other words, Pentecostals are exhibiting signs that they are moving from the naïveté of Schner's "appeal confessional" towards an "appeal constructive"—acknowledging the mediated nature of experience of the Spirit and beginning to wrestle with the implications.

303. Yun, "Metaphysical Construct," 8.

A maturing Pentecostal theology, then, needs to acknowledge the ways in which experience of God is mediated, while simultaneously upholding the belief in the immediacy (or directness) of encounter with God. Despite our emphasis on the need for greater acceptance of a mediated concept of experience of God, Lewis' above noted assessment is important—cultural-linguistic theory may be a helpful way for Pentecostals to understand "normal" experience of God, but it must not be entirely allowed to dictate and define encounters with the Spirit. In the upcoming chapters we will be exploring the ways in which an appreciation of the mediated nature of the experience of God is being integrated into the work of three Pentecostal theologians—Frank D. Macchia, Simon K. H. Chan, and Amos Yong—as a way of demonstrating the maturation of Pentecostalism theologically. As we do so, we also need to be looking for evidence that the Pentecostal emphasis on encounter with the Spirit is being preserved.

3

Frank D. Macchia

Experiencing the Spirit through the Word

BY WAY OF REMINDER, OUR GOAL IN THIS BOOK OVERALL IS TO DEMON-
strate the maturation of Pentecostal theology through an exploration of
a growing appreciation within Pentecostalism of the mediated quality of
experience of God. This, and the subsequent two chapters, will explore
the work of three Pentecostal theologians who exemplify evidence of this
maturation, all acknowledging and integrating, in different ways, a mediated concept of experience of the Spirit into their work. Each of these,
further, will be used to accent one of the three traditional media of the
Spirit—Word (a broader theological category that includes Scripture),
tradition, and reason.[1]

Frank D. Macchia, serves as our first Pentecostal theologian in this
regard.[2] He values his Pentecostal heritage, and believes it has an impor-

---

1. Admittedly, Macchia, Chan and Yong all enter into some discussion of Scripture
(Word), tradition, and reason, but for our purposes we are accenting one mediation
for each, based on their primary contribution to Pentecostal theology. We broaden our
scope to Word here (from simply Scripture) in order to preserve theological focus in the
project overall, as opposed to simply concentrating on Macchia's use of Scripture. Such
is also consistent with the Pentecostal belief into ongoing revelation, and factors into
Macchia's theological project, as we shall see.

2. Macchia holds credentials with the Assemblies of God (USA), and presently is
Professor of systematic theology at Vanguard University of Southern California. He has
authored several books, as well as numerous essays and articles, and served as a former
editor of *Pneuma*. His work often attempts to bring issues pertaining to Pentecostalism
to the forefront, exploring these critically, and often placing Pentecostalism in dialogue
with other Christian traditions. The Vital Theology website reports, "He has been active
in various ecumenical settings, including the International World Alliance of Reformed
Churches/Pentecostal dialogue and the Faith and Order Commission of the National

tant contribution to make to the broader Christian world. Of the two main sections in this chapter, the first will explore Macchia's theology of experience of God, accenting the ways in which Word (including but not restricted to Scripture) mediates the presence of the Spirit. In doing so we will highlight how this enables Macchia to revision Pentecostal theology in fresh ways, with a view toward overcoming some areas of theological weakness in his own tradition. The second section will then use several theological themes raised by Macchia as a means by which to place him into conversation with our theologians from chapter 1, drawing attention to areas of convergence and divergence, and including ways that Pentecostal theology might enrich the other traditions.

Macchia and Pentecostal Experience of the Spirit

In *Baptized in the Spirit*, arguably Macchia's most comprehensive effort to outline a Pentecostal theology,[3] he begins by recounting a personal experience as a young Bible College student. After reading the book of Acts, and being impressed by the reality of God in the experience of the early Christians, he states, "I felt God grip me—God was calling me to lifelong ministry." Shortly thereafter, while praying with some other students, he recounts, "I felt a fountain well up within me. It grew stronger and stronger until it burst forth with great strength. I began to pray in tongues."[4] He describes this Spirit baptism experience, as "overwhelming," and a "God intoxication."

> I do not refer here to a drunken state but rather a consciousness wholly taken up with God so that one feels especially inspired to give of oneself to others in whatever gifting God has created within. It is essentially an experience of self-transcendence motivated by the love of God. *Experience is certainly culturally mediated* and will vary in nature from person to person, from context to context. But I simply cannot imagine this clothing with power unless some kind of powerful experience of the divine presence,

---

Council of Christian Churches (USA)."

3. Macchia's more recent book, *Justified in the Spirit*, is also a weighty and comprehensive theological work from a Pentecostal perspective. But it is narrower in its focus—namely, the doctrine of Justification viewed through the lens of Spirit baptism (on this see especially Macchia, *Justified in the Spirit*, ch. 7). *Baptized in the Spirit*, then, provides the broader scope and foundation for Macchia's latter work on justification.

4. Macchia, *Baptized in the Spirit*, 13, cf. 11–13.

love, and calling is involved, one that loosens our tongues and our hands to function under the inspiration of the Spirit.[5]

That Macchia begins his book with this story is significant in several ways. For one, it helps distinguish his value of experiences of encounter with the Spirit—he sees no incompatibility between theology and experience. In it, he also shows his Pentecostal colors, identifying this experience with inspiring vocational empowerment (and does so in a genre true to his Pentecostal heritage, namely, personal testimony). But also significant for our purposes is his acknowledgment of the mediated nature of experience of the Spirit (in this instance culturally-shaped), while seeking at the same time to speak of this type of experience as transcending historical, cultural and linguistic frameworks.

Pentecostals and the Authority of Experience: A "Mixed Blessing"

Elsewhere, in an important article, "Christian Experience and Authority in the World: A Pentecostal Viewpoint," Macchia outlines in more detail his position on the relationship between experience and theology. He affirms that Pentecostals value an "intense experience of God that is extraordinary and deeper than merely rational or cognitive 'illumination' of the Word of God." Further, Pentecostals do not tend to dichotomize experience of God and revelation (i.e., Scripture), and "would thus agree with Moltmann's dissatisfaction with the conflict between a theology of experience (à la Schleiermacher) and a theology revelation (à la Barth)."[6] So, he argues, it is important to find a way to reconcile the experience/revelation dichotomy often found in Christian theology.

To this end, Macchia notes that "the revelation of God in Scripture and proclamation that functions authoritatively to guide faith [must do so] in continuity with the revelation implied in the varieties of human experience of God." Citing Rahner, he acknowledges there must be some sort of correlation "between the 'inner word' of experience and the 'outer word' given in and through the church as revelation."[7] The significance, however, is that in order for the church "to have authority in the world

---

5. Ibid., 14 (italics added).

6. Macchia, "Christian Experience," 10a.

7. Ibid., 10b.

that is meaningful, its message and ministry will need to strike the chord of human experience effectively."[8] Pentecostals, because of their emphasis on experience of God, and openness to a wide expression of charismata through all believers, are uniquely positioned to connect the message of the church (the gospel) with the world, and contribute to its reception.[9]

Defining the nature of Pentecostal experience, however, is no simple task; and Macchia is aware that the concept of experience (in particular "religious experience") has undergone an evolution of sorts in recent centuries. He notes that the tendency of Western modernity to identify experience with conscious cognitive awareness gave way to recognition of the "depth" of human (non-rational) religious consciousness,[10] and more recently to more holistic ways of understanding religious experience.[11] Such "holistic experiential theology," says Macchia, is exemplified in liberation theologies (including feminist approaches), in which particular "counter-cultural" groups are able to "distinguish God from mainstream cultural and linguistic symbols," on the basis of "revolutionary experiences of God."[12] This assumes "an ambiguous depth of experience of God possible that is only inadequately expressed in our symbols or interpretive frameworks."[13]

While appreciating the move from modernistic rationalism, Macchia believes that this approach is difficult to maintain in light of postmodern critiques, such as Lindbeck's, which accentuate human experience as *deriving from* particular "symbol systems" or "cultural and linguistic frameworks."[14] Therefore, it is "difficult to conceive of a religious experience apart from a symbolic framework that includes deeply and corporately held doctrinal concepts, which function not only to express but also to cradle such experience."[15] Lindbeck's approach, then,

---

8. Ibid., 10b–c.

9. Ibid., 10c.

10. Ibid., 11a–b. Macchia cites Friedrich Schleiermacher, Rudolf Otto, Paul Tillich, and William James as contributing to this shift.

11. Ibid., 11b. Macchia describes this as a moving beyond a focus on religious consciousness, to a "fully 'charismatic' understanding of experience in which a limitless variety of gifts are used by the Spirit to encounter and to change us in all dimensions of our existence."

12. Ibid., 11b–c. Here we can note similarities to Schner's "appeal hermeneutical."

13. Ibid., 11c. Elizabeth A. Johnson is a good example of this approach.

14. Ibid.

15. Macchia, *Baptized in the Spirit*, 54; cf. Macchia, "Christian Experience," 11c.

calls into question such transcendental "depth" understandings of religious experience, influencing Macchia, in part, to appreciate the mediated elements of experience of God.[16]

Yet, Macchia is not satisfied that Lindbeck's approach is fully compatible with a Pentecostal understanding of experience of God.[17] He argues that Lindbeck only allows doctrinal changes to occur within cultural-linguistic frameworks out of practical necessity in response to contextualization.[18] But such a view is insufficient for Pentecostals, who view "religious experience [as] most fundamentally affected by God's presence and action. Our religious experience is to be experience of God and not most fundamentally of our interpretive frameworks!"[19] So, the cultural-linguistic approach, while helpful, does not fully account for transformative Pentecostal encounters with the Spirit. Rather, explains Macchia,

> symbols function in dialectical relationship with the presence of God through the Holy Spirit. As such, it is not only changing contexts for lived experience that accounts for the transformation of symbols but even more fundamentally the presence of God that calls forth renewed impulses within believers in relation to new contexts. In other words, since God's Spirit is ultimately at the root of all genuinely religious experience, there is a depth to experience that causes all symbols to remain "broken" (R. C. Neville) and destined for change. And there is the possibility that "the Spirit can move" and grace be "magnified" to the point that we are thrown upon the depth and ultimate horizon of our experience and dramatically reminded of the provisional and relative nature of even our most cherished systems of interpretation.[20]

According to Macchia, then, Pentecostal experience of the Spirit involves the interruption and transformation of human lives and conceptual frameworks, and such encounters need to be granted more weight than Lindbeck might allow. At the same time, he affirms that Pentecostal experience of God *is shaped* by various theological factors. For example,

---

Macchia also appreciates that Lindbeck's understanding of experience is holistic as opposed to simply cognitive or rational.

16. Macchia, "Christian Experience," 12a.

17. Ibid., 11c–12a.

18. Macchia, *Baptized in the Spirit*, 55; cf. Macchia, "Christian Experience," 12a.

19. Macchia, "Christian Experience," 12a.

20. Ibid., 12b–c.

at its heart, Pentecostalism operates with the assumption that Christian life in general is pneumatologically experiential and transformational (explaining why experience is granted such an authoritative role).[21] Further, within this experiential context, Pentecostals are shaped by a non-Western (holistic, non-rational) spirituality, an emphasis on communal charismatic empowering (accenting lay ministry), and a restorationism tied to a strong apocalyptic eschatological emphasis.[22]

Acknowledgement of this theological framework for Pentecostal experience indicates Macchia's awareness that Pentecostals, while open to transformational encounters with the Spirit, also (dialectically) interpret these experiences within their own symbol system. In short, experience of God *is mediated, but qualified* by the above observations. Further, however, Macchia believes that Pentecostal intuitive acceptance of experience of God as authoritative (within the above framework) has been somewhat of a "mixed blessing."[23] Negatively, for example, their "eschatology from above" tends to produce an otherworldly, dualistic understanding of God's work in the world.[24] "In such a symbolic framework Christian experience tends to be set in relation to the world as an alien place with threatening forces of darkness that incarnate themselves in cultural trends and movements."[25] Positively, however, this apocalyptic emphasis can also echo healthy postmodern critique of "any and all universal and tyrannical human solutions or offers of salvation in the world today."[26] Moreover, a charismatic communal emphasis has encouraged participation of laity in Christian ministry, and Pentecostals do demonstrate some holistic and this-worldly tendencies, exemplified in their emphasis on bodily healing.[27] But even here, the results are mixed—heal-

21. Ibid., 12c.

22. Ibid., 13a–b.

23. Ibid., 14b.

24. Ibid., 13c. Macchia also views early Pentecostal bifurcation of sanctification and empowerment, as well as their crisis spirituality (inherited from the Holiness movement) as having contributed to an "otherworldly spirituality that latches onto pragmatic strategies for success," while tending to remain disconnected from this-worldly attempts to heal broken social or political situations. Such crisis spirituality can also lead to attitudes of elitism among those who have attained "higher" stages (experiences) (see Macchia, *Baptized in the Spirit*, 31–36).

25. Macchia, "Christian Experience," 14a.

26. Ibid., 14b.

27. Ibid., 14a–b. Macchia here also mentions the Pentecostal penchant for pragmatism as evidence of a 'this-worldliness.' He notes negatively, however, that these prag-

ing being restricted (generally) to the individual physical body, rather than applied also to social transformation, which Macchia believes is very important.[28]

Revisioning Pentecostal Experience by Broadening Spirit Baptism

It is Macchia's conviction that Pentecostals do have much to offer to the church and world because of their experience(s) with the Spirit, but that they are operating out of a theological deficiency leading to the afore-mentioned weaknesses. Among other things, Pentecostals have typically emphasized Spirit baptism as primarily being a personal experiential reception of power for charismatic vocational ministry, which can quickly degenerate into simply viewing Spirit baptism as a sort of "raw power."[29] A more robust integrating theological framework is therefore needed in order for Pentecostals to better understand their encounters with the Spirit, so that they might not only begin to heal the fractures existing within Pentecostalism itself,[30] but also the broken relationships between the churches, ultimately becoming a more effective channel of redemption to the world.[31] To this end, Macchia proposes that the metaphor of Spirit baptism might serve as this "organizing principle of a Pentecostal theology," and expounds on this theme in *Baptized in the Spirit*.[32]

Macchia is not alone in desiring a more integrative Pentecostal theology, often with the goal of furthering ecumenical relationships.[33] He acknowledges the value of the Christological focus of Donald Dayton's four-fold Jesus-centered model, the eschatological focus of D. William Faupel and Steven Land, and Walter J. Hollenweger's emphasis

---

matic tendencies often lead "Pentecostals to easily adopt cultural forms or trends if these prove expedient to the missionary efforts."

28. Ibid., 14a.

29. Macchia, *Baptized in the Spirit*, 18, cf. 31–32. Macchia asks, "Is [Spirit baptism] a raw power without content or guidance other than pragmatic needs and considerations?"

30. Ibid., 17–18. Pentecostalism fractured early on (as noted in chapter 2) over disagreements concerning sanctification, and the Trinity (Oneness controversy), among other things.

31. Macchia, "Kingdom and the Power," 110.

32. Macchia, *Baptized in the Spirit*, 17.

33. Macchia, "Kingdom and the Power," 111.

on Pentecostal oral theological method.[34] He finds all these approaches somewhat unsatisfactory, however, due to what he perceives in each of them as a de-emphasis on Spirit baptism, which is the "crown jewel of Pentecostal distinctives."[35] A theology that is truly Pentecostal, he argues, must allow for the central place of Spirit baptism. Further, such a focus will enable Pentecostals to better contribute toward healthier ecumenism among the churches, while simultaneously challenging other Christian traditions concerning aspects of experience of the Spirit.[36]

Macchia develops this conviction based on a study of the biblical usage of the Spirit baptism metaphor. He summarizes elsewhere how this conviction emerged:

> Two things strike me as I read the New Testament use of the verb to "baptize" in the Spirit. First, Spirit baptism is the most distinctive belief about Jesus shared by all the New Testament writers. All four Gospels begin by announcing Jesus as the coming Spirit Baptizer. John links Jesus' role as Spirit baptizer to his divinity . . . Second, what strikes me further as I look at the New Testament teaching about baptism in the Spirit is that the metaphor functions in the New Testament in a way analogous to how it functions among Pentecostals globally, namely, with a certain amount of fluidity and multi-dimensionality. The overall rubric that seems to tie all of the conceptions together in the New Testament is eschatology, namely, the inauguration of the Kingdom of God through the bestowal of the Spirit.[37]

Each of these two points merits brief explanation, and we will do so by examining them in reverse order (actually the tact taken by Macchia in *Baptized in the Spirit*). First, Macchia observes that within the Christian theological traditions, Spirit baptism has been associated primarily with one of three particular dimensions of Christian experience. Reformed and evangelical (Word) traditions typically associate Spirit baptism with regeneration and entry into the church.[38] While an important emphasis,

34. See Ibid., 112–13; Macchia, *Baptized in the Spirit*, 26–45, 49–50, cf. 49–57; and Macchia, "Baptized in the Spirit," 26.

35. Macchia, *Baptized in the Spirit*, 20. Cf. Macchia, "Kingdom and the Power," 110; and Macchia, "Baptized in the Spirit," 26.

36. Macchia, *Baptized in the Spirit*, 22.

37. Macchia, "Baptized in the Spirit," 23–24.

38. Macchia, "Kingdom and the Power," 114–15; Macchia, *Baptized in the Spirit*, 64–72. Here Macchia cites Karl Barth, James D. G. Dunn, Gordon D. Fee, and Russell P. Spittler as emphasizing this position, although the latter three are open to dramatic

this position neglects the significance of experiences "of the kingdom of God in power" subsequent to conversion, calling believers to mission.[39] Further, it also tends to disconnect Spirit baptism from sacramental initiation rites, such as water baptism.[40]

Within sacramental traditions, Macchia observes, some, like Kilian McDonnell and George Montague, have attempted to reconnect Spirit baptism to "water baptism or the sacramental rites of initiation (baptism/confirmation and eucharist)."[41] In this view, the "sacramental grace given in Christian initiation will eventually (either at the moment of initiation or later) burst forth in experiences of charismatic power."[42] Macchia appreciates this openness to charismatic experiences, but is unconvinced that Spirit baptism is simply the outworking of a "'material' deposit of grace." Such does not sufficiently account for the fullness of meaning implied in the New Testament, part of which is an emphasis on Spirit baptism as an experience that introduces *something new* into Christian life.[43]

As for Pentecostals, they have emphasized Spirit baptism as a conscious empowerment for vocation into prophetic Christian witness.[44]

---

charismatic experiences.

39. Macchia, *Baptized in the Spirit*, 70. He states this position underemphasizes "Spirit baptism as an eschatological gift of the ever-new participation in the life and mission of God."

40. Ibid., 66, cf. 66–72; Macchia, "Kingdom and the Power," 114.

41. Macchia, "Kingdom and the Power," 116; cf. Macchia, *Baptized in the Spirit*, 72. Macchia notes that Pentecostal theologian Simon Chan is attracted to this position.

42. Macchia, *Baptized in the Spirit*, 73, cf. 72–75, 77, 152–53; Macchia, "Kingdom and the Power," 116–17. This view can speak of a later "release" of the Spirit within Christian life. Macchia also sees "release" as a possibly helpful description of Pentecostal experience, but qualifies this, as we shall see. Also see Macchia, "God Present," 37, 38.

43. Macchia, *Baptized in the Spirit*, 74. He here states, "Can grace both emerge from what is granted in the Christian initiation *and* confront this from beyond with something genuinely new? . . . Are we not talking about the gift of the living, eschatological Spirit, who constantly calls us to new frontiers of spiritual renewal? Can not the Spirit who indwells us still come to us in a way unprecedented since the new birth in Christ is itself unprecedented and continues to be such? I believe so" (italics original).

44. Ibid., 75–76; Macchia, "Kingdom and the Power," 117. Macchia highlights Pentecostal New Testament scholars, Roger Stronstad and Robert P. Menzies (noted in chapter 2) as having attempted to preserve the empowerment emphasis of Spirit baptism for Pentecostals by highlighting Luke's charismatic pneumatology (in contrast to Paul's soteriological pneumatology). While this has been helpful, Macchia is not convinced that Luke's pneumatology excludes soteriological elements. Further while Stronstad and Menzies have emphasized the distinctions between Luke and Paul, they have not suf-

This is a healthy, much needed supplement in the church,[45] believes Macchia, since it calls believers to recognize that they are not only converted to God, but need to experience a "second conversion" of sorts, accenting the church's call to serve in the world.[46] This emphasis, however, combined with traditional Pentecostal crisis-stage spirituality, has led to a bifurcation of this empowerment from the soteriological work of the Spirit in regeneration, initiation, and sanctification.[47] Significant for this chapter, this dichotomy (especially with regard to sanctification) has inclined Pentecostals toward viewing the Spirit's work, in some respects, as being disconnected from the work of Christ, thereby introducing a separation of Word and Spirit.[48] This separation has made it easier for Pentecostals to embrace a triumphalistic and otherworldly spirituality, at times even adopting elitist attitudes, since it detaches love (the process

---

ficiently attempted to reintegrate these into a coherent comprehensive pneumatology, which has inadvertently contributed even further to the fracturing of the charismatic from the soteriological works of the Spirit, opening the way to an otherworldly spirituality (see Macchia, *Baptized in the Spirit*, 23, 26, 25, 28, 57–58; and Macchia, "Kingdom and the Power," 113, 118).

45. Macchia, *Baptized in the Spirit*, 150.

46. Ibid., 76, cf. 77, 280–82. He states, "Pentecostals see Spirit baptism as a prophetic call that draws one close to the heart of God in praise and prophetic empathy for the world but which accents the 'second conversion' by empowering one for witness in the world." This conversion imagery is drawn from nineteenth century Pietist, Christoph Blumhardt. Macchia sees this as similar to an image suggested by Moltmann, in which the Spirit first "inhales," drawing people into communion with God and others, and then "exhales" the community "vocationally and charismatically into the world" (ibid., 76–77). On this also see Macchia, "Kingdom and the Power," 118; Macchia, "Astonished by Faithfulness," 175; and Macchia, *Spirituality and Social Liberation*, 92–93.

47. Macchia, "Kingdom and the Power," 119; Macchia, *Baptized in the Spirit*, 28–33, 80. More recently, Macchia has attempted to bridge this soteriological gap even more robustly by arguing extensively that, through the lens of Spirit baptism, the biblical concept of justification can be more accurately understood as being more or less synonymous with the reception of the Spirit. Macchia states that "justified existence," then, is "pneumatic existence" (Macchia, *Justified in the Spirit*, 214, cf. 197–202).

48. See Macchia, *Baptized in the Spirit*, 31, 80–83. Macchia does note that this separation of sanctification and power was not true of all early Pentecostals. Some early Pentecostal literature spoke of Spirit baptism as "a baptism in the love of God," and William Seymour argued that the primary evidence of Spirit baptism is love (ibid., 81). Macchia states that Pentecostals were able to separate Spirit baptism and sanctification only by defining the latter negatively and narrowly. He suggests defining sanctification (and love) more positively and broadly as "consecration unto God in preparation for a holy task," in order to help reconnect sanctification with Spirit baptism (ibid., 83; cf. Macchia, "Kingdom and the Power," 121–22).

of sanctification) from the Spirit's work (understood as a particular crisis experience).[49]

Macchia does not want the Pentecostal emphasis on Spirit baptism to be neglected, and affirms, "Christians at whatever level of spiritual maturity [may] find their ministries enhanced with greater power and effectiveness through an experience of Spirit baptism."[50] Without a broader pneumatological framework, however, the separation between sanctification (soteriology) and empowerment will continue to dog Pentecostalism—and Christian theology in general. "The bottom line," says Macchia, "is that Spirit baptism as an experience of charismatic power and enrichment cannot be separated from regeneration/sanctification and Christian initiation."[51]

Macchia's solution is that the Spirit baptism metaphor be broadened so as to encompass all three of the above ecclesial emphases: regeneration, initiation, and empowerment. Macchia believes that this is possible because biblically the metaphor of Spirit baptism was used by John the Baptist in relation to the kingdom of God, thus placing ecclesiological concerns within a kingdom framework.[52] The description of Jesus' baptism (Matt 3), in which he is predicted to be the future "baptizer" with the Spirit, is laced with apocalyptic eschatological overtones pointing "to final judgment and to the final sanctification of the entire creation."[53] Further, the story of Pentecost (Acts 2) continues these eschatological themes, linking Spirit baptism and God's kingdom.[54] Spirit baptism, then, functions as a rather fluid metaphor in the New Testament;[55] but encompassing all these dimensions is the framework of the eschatological in-breaking of the kingdom of God.[56] "If the fulfillment of the king-

---

49. Macchia, "Sighs Too Deep," 68; Macchia, *Baptized in the Spirit*, 30–32. Macchia sees Pentecostals in need of recovering some of Moltmann's emphasis on the "crucified God" in order to avoid triumphalism (Macchia, *Baptized in the Spirit*, 188–89, 262).

50. Macchia, *Baptized in the Spirit*, 77.

51. Ibid., 84.

52. Ibid., 85.

53. Ibid., 86, cf. 85–88; Macchia, "Kingdom and the Power," 124.

54. Macchia, *Baptized in the Spirit*, 86.

55. Ibid., 87. Macchia states, "Though there is a variety of accents, there is a consistent witness in the New Testament to the centrality of the Spirit to the realization of the kingdom of God in power."

56. Ibid., 17, 63, 84–88. Macchia differs here from Land and Faupel in that he views eschatology "as a context for interpreting Spirit baptism rather than as a component to

dom of God and not the narrow concern for Christian initiation is in view, a theology and an experience of Spirit baptism can be integrated on a higher level within the theology of the kingdom of God that has both incorporative and experiential dimensions."[57] In this context, Spirit baptism can be defined, in essence, as "a baptism in divine love,"[58] which "sanctifies, renews and empowers until Spirit baptism turns all creation into the final dwelling place of God."[59]

Based, then, on the connection between Spirit baptism and the fulfillment of God's kingdom, Macchia's second point can be expounded.[60] The "New Testament concentration on Jesus as Spirit Baptizer or Mediator of the Spirit," in his role of "imparting the Spirit to others,"[61] intricately connects Spirit baptism to the mission and identity of Jesus, demonstrating the strong link between Christ (Word) and Spirit, and enabling the Spirit baptism metaphor to be placed within a broader Trinitarian framework.[62] All of this together should impact the way in which Pentecostals (and all Christians) understand experience of God, allowing believers to locate their lives in relation to Spirit, Son and Father and the ultimate redemptive goals of the kingdom, which include all of creation. To this end, Macchia draws on Gregory of Nyssa, suggesting that "Christ is the King and the Spirit is the kingdom." In this view, "Spirit baptism is the means by which creation is transformed by this kingdom and made to participate in its reign of life. Spirit baptism brings the reign of the Father, the reign of the crucified and risen Christ, and the reign of the divine life to all creation through the indwelling of the Spirit."[63]

Spirit baptism, then, is that which ultimately enables humans and all creation to participate in the life of the Godhead.[64] To appreciate this

---

be viewed alongside Spirit baptism (and in competition with it)" (Macchia, "Baptized in the Spirit," 26).

57. Macchia, *Baptized in the Spirit*, 63.

58. Ibid., 63–64.

59. Ibid., 60.

60. Ibid., 90.

61. Macchia, "Baptized in the Spirit," 23.

62. See Macchia, *Baptized in the Spirit*, 89–154.

63. Ibid., 89; cf. Macchia, *Justified in the Spirit*, 277.

64. Macchia, *Baptized in the Spirit*, 104. Macchia states, Spirit baptism "is not only a divine attribute but the participation of the creature by God's grace in the divine nature" (ibid., 97).

point, explains Macchia, the Spirit's outpouring at Pentecost needs to be understood within the larger framework of the redemptive coming of the reign of God (lordship) to creation.[65] The Old Testament expectation for the "coming presence of God as Lord to cleanse, fill, and redeem," is fulfilled in the New Testament metaphor of Spirit baptism, which John the Baptist tied to the concept of kingdom.[66] This means that the "substance of the kingdom in Scripture is pneumatological,"[67] involving the very presence of God by the Spirit.[68] In this light, Pentecost is crucial to understanding Christian identity, and cannot simply be viewed as symbolizing only one dimension of Christian experience. Rather, Pentecost needs to be understood more widely as the coming of God to purge, bring new life and fill his people (the temple of the Spirit), empowering them for witness.[69]

This latter aspect cannot be neglected—Spirit baptism is not a "secret initiation ritual," says Macchia, but a "liberating force that reorders our lives," calling believers to service. "Spirit baptism constitutes the church and causes the church to missionize for the sake of the kingdom. But Spirit baptism also transcends the church, because it inaugurates the kingdom."[70] Pentecost, then, needs also to be appreciated eschatologically and cosmically.[71] Spirit baptism is what will bring the final transformation of creation, although aspects can be experienced now; eschatologically "the kingdom is 'now' but also 'not yet.'"[72] So, "Seen as

65. Ibid., 91–107. In the Old Testament, the reign of God (lordship) was associated with the redemptive presence and activity of God among his people; thus, "the kingdom in the Old Testament is present where God is present to exercise divine lordship redemptively in the world." When the fulfillment of divine lordship went unrealized for Israel, this gave rise to the apocalyptic hope that God's reign on earth would be achieved through the outpouring of the "divine breath," through his Messiah (ibid., 93).

66. Ibid., 93.

67. Ibid., 91.

68. Ibid., 95. He states, "The kingdom of God in the Gospels is primarily a redemptive presence."

69. Ibid., 98–101. With regard to mission, Macchia views nineteenth century Protestant liberalism's emphasis on the kingdom as "an ethical and communal reality," to be mistaken. But conversely, neither is an "apocalyptic and otherworldly" view correct. "The kingdom of God is God's act and, therefore, out of our grasp. Yet, the kingdom of God also involved human witness, fellowship, and justice in and through the church and even outside the church" (ibid., 94–95).

70. Ibid., 106.

71. Ibid., 101–2.

72. Ibid., 97, cf. 93, 98, 101–2. This also implies that Spirit baptism was in a sense

an eschatological concept, Pentecost becomes a symbol, not only of the divine breath filling and charismatically empowering God's people, but also indwelling all of creation one day."[73] The ultimate result of Spirit baptism, the "divine outpouring of the divine presence," is the bringing of all creation into the divine life and love of the Trinity.[74]

For Macchia, viewing Pentecost as the pneumatological inauguration of the kingdom also has implications for Christology. Prior to Pentecost, Jesus is the man in whom the Spirit has been bestowed without limit by the Father.[75] Christian theology, however, has not given adequate attention to the fact that the Spirit baptism of Pentecost helped reveal the identity of Jesus as Lord and Savior, ultimately enabling the church to develop its Trinitarian confession.[76] The Old Testament associates God with the concepts of Father and "mighty breath," states Macchia, but "It is God the Son as the Spirit Baptizer that became the unique link between the Father and the Spirit and, indirectly, to the doctrine of the Trinity."[77] This is because Spirit baptism identified the trajectory of the resurrection. "The resurrection alone is not sufficient to lead to a confession of Christ's ontological unity with the Father. It is also in the goal of resurrection, namely, in Jesus' becoming the one who imparts the Spirit of new life from the Father, which suggests this unity. Indeed, only God can impart the divine breath."[78]

This "Spirit Christology" helps explain how the church came to see Jesus as divine, an "object of worship," and as the One through whom "God redeems creation."[79] Further, says Macchia, the fact that "Christology is inconceivable, apart from pneumatology"[80] has impli-

---

not complete at Pentecost, but the "final outpouring . . . culminates with the Day of the Lord" (ibid., 102).

73. Ibid., 102–3.

74. Ibid., 104–5. States Macchia, "Since the kingdom of God is pneumatological in substance, it also has love, the love enjoyed between the Father and the Son and with creation, as its substance" (ibid., 105).

75. Ibid., 118.

76. Ibid., 90, 110.

77. Ibid., 110, cf. 111. Later Macchia states, "The root of Nicaea is Pentecost" (ibid., 185).

78. Ibid., 110–11; cf. Macchia, "Baptized in the Spirit," 23–24.

79. Macchia, *Baptized in the Spirit*, 109. Writes Macchia, "The Son is thus not Lord without the Spirit, just as the Son is not Lord without the Father" (ibid., 123).

80. Ibid., 127.

cations for all Christian theological traditions—"The significance of Pentecostalism may prove after all to involve more than an experiential integration of the Christian life."[81] In the above light, Spirit baptism may very well "provide Pentecostals of all backgrounds globally with a way of contributing their unique emphasis on this powerful metaphor, especially in charismatic diversity and fullness, to a robust orthodox faith that involves other Christian voices as well. I refer here to an orthodox faith that is rooted in the will of the Father as Creator, centered in the Son as Spirit Baptizer and Inaugurator of the kingdom of God, and richly directed toward the life of the eschatological Spirit in perfecting creation as the final dwelling place of God."[82]

But Macchia believes that one more step is needed to help Pentecostals in particular better appreciate the relationship between Word and Spirit (King and kingdom). Pentecost not only identifies the Son, but conversely, the Son's pouring out of the Spirit also helps define Spirit baptism. Pentecostals have sometimes separated the works of Spirit and Word, "distinguishing between the work of the Spirit in binding us to Christ and the work of Christ in baptizing us in the Spirit."[83] This, however, is a "misuse of the Trinitarian doctrine of appropriation"; it is invalid to view the persons of the Godhead as being "attached to

---

81. Ibid., 107.

82. Ibid., 112. Elsewhere Macchia states, "What I have in mind as the chief theological distinctive of the Pentecostal movement is a concentration on Spirit baptism eschatologically defined so as to leave 'breathing room' for various Pentecostal and Charismatic accents. Though the typically Pentecostal focus on empowerment and spiritual gifts will be maintained, there will be enough flexibility to the Spirit baptismal metaphor to include Paul's understanding of the metaphor as that which constitutes the unity of the church as a communion of saints, as well as in regeneration through faith in Christ. One can also view the goal of the doctrine in broadly transformationist terms. This expansion of boundaries of Spirit baptism allows Pentecostal theologians to maintain a focus on the chief theological distinctive of the Pentecostal Movement without narrowly defining that distinctive as 'empowerment plus tongues.' Also, it will allow Pentecostals to relate constructively with other ecclesiastical traditions from the standpoint of a pneumatological concentration" (Macchia, "Baptized in the Spirit," 26).

83. Macchia, Baptized in the Spirit, 114, cf. 113. This has opened Pentecostals to the charge of elitism, since they view those who have experienced the "baptism of Christ into the Spirit" as experiencing a fuller level of Christian life. Macchia does not want to lose the Pentecostal emphasis on empowerment for mission; indeed even asking whether, in some sense, Christians caught up in missional work are not, in fact, experiencing God in a fuller way. But he sees the Pentecostal way of framing the issue to be problematic and weak with regard to the Word/Spirit relationship.

stages" of Christian experience.[84] To appreciate the Word/Spirit relationship within Trinitarian context, then, Spirit baptism holds the key. States Macchia, "Biblically, it seems wise to attribute all of the blessings of the Christian life to Christ's impartation of the Spirit as the primary (and not secondary) act, which then provides the basis for the Spirit's drawing us to Christ and then, in Christ, drawing our lives into the flow of that living witness. Making Spirit baptism a more expansive category can in my view help Pentecostals construe the Trinitarian involvement of God in salvation in more biblical terms."[85]

Implied, then, for Macchia is that the Word needs to be more central to Pentecostal understanding of the Spirit's work.[86] The kingdom of God "has a *Christoformistic* goal and direction"—Christ is the King.[87] Explains Macchia, "Jesus mediates the Spirit who proceeds from the Father. In mediating the Spirit, Jesus draws believers in the communion enjoyed by the Father and the Son"[88] So, an awareness of the Son's role as "inaugurator of the kingdom of God" can help Pentecostals appreciate Spirit baptism within a "Trinitarian structure."[89] To this end, Macchia suggests two key points. First, "Spirit baptism accents the idea that the triune life of God is not closed, but involved in the openness of self-giving love."[90] Second, "Spirit baptism also accents the unique idea that

---

84. Ibid., 114. He says, "Appropriation involves the insight that persons of the Godhead have functions uniquely attributed to them. For example, of the Father is appropriated creation, of the Son redemption, and of the Spirit renewal of life. Of course, all three participate in every action in mutual working and every action involves the one God."

85. Ibid. More recently, Macchia has outlined this Trinitarian involvement in salvation in a theological primer on the topic, *The Trinity, Practically Speaking*. In brief, he argues that once it is accepted that only God saves, then the inescapable logical implication is that Father, Son, and Spirit, each of whom is attributed salvific activity in Scripture, share in the divine (triune) nature (see especially Macchia, *Trinity*, chs. 1 and 3).

86. Macchia, *Baptized in the Spirit*, 114. States Macchia, "The challenge here, it seems to me, is to affirm that Christ is the starting point and ultimate goal of our life in the Spirit and that new encounters with the Spirit of Christ are possible within this eschatological framework." Macchia also believes that Oneness Pentecostalism needs to better appreciate the Trinitarian context of the work of Christ and Spirit (ibid., 114–16).

87. Ibid., 106 (italics original).

88. Ibid., 160.

89. Ibid., 116, cf. 113–29.

90. Ibid., 116. Macchia states, "From the Trinitarian fellowship of the Father and the Son, the Spirit is poured out to expand God's love and communion to creation. This outpouring prefigures the eschatological indwelling of God in all of creation." Also see

participation in God's redemptive will is participation in God's presence. In being baptized in the Spirit, we are 'baptized into God'!"[91] The Spirit's outpouring is the expression and expansion of God's love,[92] inviting "all flesh" into personal "union with or participation in God."[93] Macchia expands, "The Trinitarian structure of Spirit baptism thus has a two-way movement: from the Father through the Son in the Spirit, and then from the Spirit through the Son toward the Father. . . . Spirit baptism involves all three. The God of Spirit baptism surrounds us and fills us. This God is thus not 'some distant and timelessly uninvolved deity,' as Robert Jenson notes, but participates in the life of creation in this divine participation."[94]

This is why, Macchia argues, Spirit baptism must be understood in the fullest sense as a baptism into divine love, which is the "substance of Christian life"; Spirit baptism is a relational concept first, but includes charismatic empowerment.[95] Pentecostal emphasis on power for mission is correct, so long as this is understood within the broader Trinitarian mission, and with a deeper appreciation for how both Son and Spirit serve as the "left and right hands of God."[96] It is only through both Word and Spirit that the Lordship of the Trinity is historically established in creation.[97] "In short, Spirit baptism in the context of the inauguration of the kingdom of God means that the Father's divine monarchy is not abstract but *mediated by the Son and the Spirit* in the redemption of the world."[98] More broadly, "The structure of Spirit baptism is thus

---

Macchia, "Pinnock's Pneumatology," ibid., 172.

91. Macchia, *Baptized in the Spirit*, 117.

92. Ibid., 116.

93. Ibid., 104.

94. Ibid., 117.

95. Ibid., 259, cf. 259–61. This divine love is not passive, for Macchia, but transformational and missional, enabling Pentecostals to understand their experience of Spirit baptism within the broader picture of God's redemptive activity. Love is that which ultimately brings victory in the world. Further, "All of the fractures that have plagued a Pentecostal theology of Spirit baptism can be healed ultimately by an understanding of love at the substance of life in the Spirit, love that fills us to overflowing as a purgative, empowering, eschatological gift of communion and new life" (ibid., 260).

96. Ibid., 119; cf. Macchia, "Signs of Grace," 207.

97. Macchia, *Baptized in the Spirit*, 125.

98. Ibid., 124 (italics added). Macchia acknowledges drawing on Barth's emphasis on the connection between the Lordship of the Trinity and the inauguration of the kingdom as Spirit baptism, as well as Moltmann's and Pannenberg's emphasis on Social Trinity. The latter emphasize that Trinitarian lordship is open to the experience

Trinitarian, in which the divine lordship or monarchy of the Godhead is mediated through Trinitarian relations."[99] It is this joint Spirit/Word mediation, within a Trinitarian, eschatological kingdom framework, that Macchia hopes will revision and transform Pentecostal experience of the Spirit in several ways.

First, the above helps mend the rift between empowerment and sanctification.[100] Spirit baptism is, ultimately, "a baptism in divine love," helping us understand that "the substance of the Christian life is God's love," found within the Triune story in which God's presence fills creation.[101] Empowerment for mission, then, while an indispensable emphasis, is not reception of raw energy, but is motivated by being drawn into God's love. "Spirit baptism," says Macchia, "is akin to a prophetic call that draws believers close to his heart in deeper love and empathy in order to help them catch a glimpse of the divine love for the world. It is this love that is the substance of the power for mission."[102]

With this understanding, secondly, Pentecostals can become more "attuned to the sighs of the Spirit that yearn" for the transformation of

---

of suffering within creation, which in turn redefines how God's omnipotence should be understood—namely as "God's limitless capacity to suffer" (Moltmann) (ibid., 127, cf. 119–27). On Macchia's preference for social analogies of the Trinity as opposed to psychological analogies, also see Macchia, "Pinnock's Pneumatology," 172.

99. Macchia, *Baptized in the Spirit*, 258.

100. See Ibid., 145. Macchia here states, "Empowerment for service is part of the inauguration of the kingdom of God in power to transform lives and to gift them for service in marvelous ways. Without this broad framework for Spirit baptism in the kingdom of God discussed above, empowerment for service can seem vacuous, as a raw energy for signs and wonders guided by little more than pragmatic considerations. For example, any separation of empowerment and the Spirit's sanctifying work is an abnormality that is sure to lead to the collapse of a person's ministry. The empowerment of the prophet always implied his or her being set apart and consecrated for a holy task." Macchia also spends considerable space arguing that justification needs to be understood as more than merely a forensic concept. He views justification as interrelated with sanctification, and coming through Christ's resurrection as much as his crucifixion. In doing so he combines Protestant and Roman Catholic emphases (ibid., 129–40). Likewise, sanctification is connected to empowerment, since this is to be understood as separation unto God in order to fulfill a calling to be faithful within the world, as opposed to escape from it (ibid., 140–44). On Macchia's redefinition of justification from a Pentecostal perspective, also especially see Macchia, *Justified in the Spirit*, chs. 4 and 7; Macchia "Justification through New Creation," 202–17; Macchia, "Justification and the Spirit," 3–21; Macchia, "Spirit of God," 167; Macchia, "Pinnock's Pneumatology," 168–70; and Macchia, "Finitum Capax Infiniti," 186.

101. Macchia, *Baptized in the Spirit*, 259, cf. 259–65.

102. Ibid., 271.

broken and unjust world.[103] Their holistic spirituality, with its emphasis on bodily healing, can (and needs to) be applied more broadly to social and political spheres,[104] including a willingness to enter into the suffering of others.[105] This will entail tempering Pentecostal triumphalism, as well as augmenting their apocalyptic, otherworldly eschatology (which sees the kingdom as ending history) with a "prophetic" eschatology that allows more room for the kingdom to be seen in history now.[106]

Thirdly, this broadening of holistic spirituality will, believes Macchia, further challenge Pentecostals to reframe their understanding of signs and wonders. While Pentecostals rightly view such as essential to Christian experience, they tend to grant precedence to "extraordinary" manifestations, alien to everyday life,[107] reinforcing an otherworldly and triumphalistic spirituality.[108] An eschatological kingdom framework,

103. Ibid., 280, cf. 279. He states that Pentecostal lack of "creation pneumatology," has left them "less attuned to the social structures and cultural realities that implicitly support poverty and racism."

104. This issue is dealt with in depth by Macchia in a study on the Blumhardts. Johann Blumhardt's emphasis on *Christus victor*, evidenced in bodily healing has obvious connections for Pentecostalism. But Johann's emphasis on active prayer (groaning) and yet passive waiting is a helpful corrective to Pentecostal triumphalism. Pentecostals need to recover this "waiting and hurrying" tension. Christoph Blumhardt expanded the scope of healing to social, political and cosmic dimensions. Macchia, therefore, hopes Pentecostals will be able to expand their already holistic spirituality, with its emphasis on bodily healing, through a revisioned eschatology and theology of creation. On this see ibid., 279; Macchia, *Spirituality and Social Liberation*, 158–72; Macchia, "Waiting and Hurrying," 1–30; and Macchia, "Spirit and the Kingdom," 1–5, 32a.

105. Pentecostal triumphalism can be tempered, Macchia believes, by a remembrance that Christ (the King) also suffered and was crucified. Drawing on Moltmann, he states, "The spirit-baptized church lays claim to no inherent privilege except the privilege to bear witness to another, namely, the crucified and risen Christ and to live the crucified life in solidarity with the suffering and oppressed of the world." Macchia, *Baptized in the Spirit*, 189, cf. 262; cf. Macchia, "Signs of Grace," 208.

106. Macchia, *Baptized in the Spirit*, 272–79. Macchia derives this emphasis on "prophetic" eschatology from the Blumhardts, and accents this in the life of Jesus, as well as a means by which Christians can become more involved in social justice (including prophetic criticism) and healing. See Macchia, *Spirituality and Social Liberation*, 159–63; Macchia, "Waiting and Hurrying," 24; and Macchia, "Struggle for Global Witness," 23–24.

107. Macchia, *Baptized in the Spirit*, 149, cf. 146–47; cf. Macchia, "Discerning the Spirit," 14.

108. Macchia, *Baptized in the Spirit*, 148, cf. 272. Concerning Pentecostal triumphalism, also see Macchia, "Sighs Too Deep," 68; Macchia, "Nature and Purpose," 9; and Macchia, "Signs of Grace," 208.

however, will allow Pentecostals to see all spiritual gifts as important (not just those that are unusual), and further that "miracles are not interruptions into reality that suspend the course of nature but rather involve all of nature as graced to some extent already by God but, in wonderful signs of future renewal, transform nature further in unprecedented ways."[109] This broadened Spirit baptism metaphor, then, should help Pentecostals to overcome neglect of attention to God the Father's role as Creator.[110]

The Charismatic Structure of the Church

Macchia's ecclesiology is also shaped by his broadening of the concept of Spirit baptism, and merits exploration because the church is, he believes, the primary place in which experience of the Spirit occurs, and where the ministry and mediation of the Word is most explicitly observed.[111] For Macchia, both Spirit and kingdom are prior to the church; however, the church is nevertheless an irreplaceable (unsubstitutable) witness, or sign, pointing to the kingdom.[112] He writes, "*Spirit baptism gave rise to the global church and remains the very substance of the church's life in the*

109. Macchia, *Baptized in the Spirit*, 147, cf. 147–49. Macchia continues, "The ordinary is not graceless, nor is it abandoned in the midst of extraordinary signs and wonders. It is taken up into the renewing presence of God so that it can function on another level and in a different sense than that which we can exhaustively, rationally explain. Miracles represent nature in the power of the Spirit reaching for a glimpse of its future renewal."

110. Ibid., 279. Writes Macchia, "Pentecostals are thus not accustomed to detecting the presence of grace in all of life reaching for liberation and redemption through the Spirit of creation. Thus neglected is the insight that social transformation can be viewed as a legitimate sign of the redemption yet to come in Christ. Also neglected somewhat are gifts of the Spirit through natural talents that function as signs of grace in ways that bear witness to the fulfillment of life in Christ."

111. Ibid., 168; cf. Macchia, *Justified in the Spirit*, ch. 9.

112. Macchia, *Baptized in the Spirit*, 192, cf. 192–98. The church is, historically, a fallen reality, as well as a pneumatological and eschatological one. This means that Spirit baptism "transcends the church," and "continuity with the kingdom" can never quite be achieved in this age (ibid., 197). Incidentally, Macchia suggests that Pentecostals have idealized the historical early church, exemplified in their primitivism and restorationism. An appreciation of the brokenness, even in the Acts church, might help temper Pentecostal triumphalism allowing them to "recognize the voice of the Spirit" within church history and among contemporary "Christian communions" (ibid., 198; cf. Macchia, "Nature and Purpose," 14). This observation may serve to illustrate that Macchia also believes the Spirit is mediated through tradition.

Spirit, including its charismatic life and mission."[113] Indeed, the reign of the kingdom is "centrally and uniquely ecclesial in nature."[114] Thus the Spirit is the "*ecclesial Spirit*, who is active redemptively to make possible communion with God and one another."[115]

As mentioned, Spirit baptism involves the Trinity opening itself to relationship with humanity and creation—but Macchia believes that this is especially true with regard to the church.[116] The Spirit brings believers into communion with God and one another, allowing the church to participate in (and express) the fellowship of the triune Godhead.[117] The concept of "*koinonia*," then, is a helpful and appropriate way to characterize the nature of the church; it is the "substance of Spirit baptism" and demonstrates itself as "the link between the kingdom and the church."[118] Asserts Macchia, "Spirit baptism thus implies a relationship of unity between the Lord and the church that is not fundamentally one of identity but rather communion."[119] The church is, therefore, the "central locus" of the Spirit's activity,[120] although "Spirit baptism [also] means that the *koinonia* of God is not closed but open to the world."[121]

113. Macchia, *Baptized in the Spirit*, 155 (italics original).

114. Ibid., 156. Here Macchia cites Simon Chan, who states the Spirit is the "church-located, church-shaped Spirit."

115. Ibid., 156 (italics original). Macchia here writes, "The Spirit in the *koinonia* and empowered mission of the church seeks to draw humanity into communion with God and to inspire a sighing for the day when all of creation becomes the temple of God's presence to the glory of God." The church and Spirit baptism are thus intricately related—the church being integral to the fulfillment of the kingdom, and "Spirit baptism is not a *super-additum* but is essential to the life of the church" (italics original).

116. Ibid., 156.

117. Ibid., 160, 162. The Spirit, in this sense, is the "go-between God" (cf. Macchia, "Nature and Purpose," 5–10). Macchia also emphasizes that anthropologically humans are essentially relational beings, which means that Spirit baptism is both a personal and communal experience. Speaking in tongues exemplifies this, being both experienced to edify the self and others (on this see *Baptized in the Spirit*, 172, cf. 168–78).

118. Macchia, *Baptized in the Spirit*, 160 (italics original).

119. Ibid., 156–57. This prevents the church from identifying itself with the kingdom (ibid., 157). Neither is the church, however, simply a voluntary gathering of believers (thus challenging Pentecostal Free Church propensities), since it is a fellowship (ibid., 167).

120. Ibid., 128.

121. Ibid., 161 (italics original), cf. 162–63. Macchia notes that Pentecostals do not typically construct their ecclesiology based on the concept of Trinitarian koinonia because they tend to be biblicists as opposed to theologians (cf. Macchia, "Nature and Purpose," 7).

But if the fellowship of God is open to the world, in what sense is the church unique? Responding to the challenge of "pluralism," that the church is unnecessary to the fulfillment of the kingdom, Macchia argues that such a view disconnects the kingdom proclamation of Jesus from the Spirit's outpouring, which is impossible since Spirit baptism serves to identify Jesus, and Jesus pours out the Spirit into the church and upon all flesh.[122] "The problem is that in disassociating the church (especially its proclamation and dogma) from the kingdom Jesus proclaimed, one needs to disassociate Jesus himself from the kingdom he proclaimed."[123] This approach is untenable for Macchia; the church is unique because Jesus is unique. This does not, however, negate the possibility of the witness of the Spirit concerning Jesus from being experienced by people outside ecclesiastical boundaries, particularly those within other religious faiths.[124]

So, it is the historical relationship to Jesus who bestowed the Spirit that makes the church unique; but what, then, is its purpose? Macchia proposes that the answer is found within the Trinitarian context explored earlier, in which "There is no Spirit without Word, nor Word without Spirit," and "Both Word and Spirit are the 'left and right hands' of the Father (Irenaeus)."[125] In the Trinitarian history of the Spirit and Word, Macchia carefully differentiates between two "anointings" of the Spirit upon Jesus in order to qualify in what sense the church represents Christ in the world. The Incarnation was Jesus' anointing as "the divine Word of the Father."[126] The church does not share this incarnational

122. Macchia, *Baptized in the Spirit*, 178, 180–82, cf. 178–90. He earlier states, "Any assumption that the kingdom proclaimed by Jesus does not lead integrally to the church and its mission reveals neglect of the biblical role of Jesus as the risen Lord to baptized in the Spirit" (ibid., 160).

123. Ibid., 182. Elsewhere, Macchia notes that Christian experience is not of experience itself but of Jesus Christ (Macchia, *Trinity*, 35).

124. Ibid., 221, cf. 127–28. Macchia credits Amos Yong as influencing his view here. He states that while Christ is "the only Lord of all creation and salvation, I also regard him as more inclusive and expansive in significance through the witness of the Spirit than many of us might wish to admit." Macchia does not explore this any further, leaving the extent of this point somewhat ambiguous. It is worth noting that in his earlier book, *Spirituality and Social Liberation*, he cites Jesus as being the bond between church and world (ibid., 168), whereas here the accent is on the Spirit in the world. Elsewhere he suggests that it might be possible that charismatic gifts are "not even confined to the universal church" (Macchia, "Beyond Word and Sacrament," 29b).

125. Macchia, "Signs of Grace," 207.

126. Ibid., 206.

anointing, which, if true, "would only serve to deify the church!"[127] The church, however, does participate in Jesus' charismatic (i.e., prophetic and vocational) anointing. Thus, "the church is sanctified and empowered by the Spirit to proliferate Christ's gracious presence in the world. Though Jesus' anointing is in a sense unique, it is also paradigmatic in its *charismatic specificity* for the church. Through the charismatic structure of the church, the church builds itself up in love as members help each other receive the grace of Christ that comes to us through gospel and sacrament. It also helps the church spread that grace to others."[128]

This approach radically alters the way that Christians should expect to experience the Spirit. The church's charismatic structure implies, for Macchia, among other things, "that the Christological foundation of the church is not only to be found in the church office, sacrament or proclamation. Christ is also present in multiple gifts and signs of the Spirit in the fellowship of the church."[129] Without this charismatic element, sacramental ecclesiologies can become "Spiritless, overly institutional, abstract and monolithic," and preaching "overly cerebral and abstract."[130] Christ is not fully experienced through church office, sacraments or preaching apart from the Spirit's charismatic work in bringing gifts to and through all believers (laity).[131] It is through the operation of the charismata, as concrete and diverse forms of grace,[132] that the church becomes a "graced community."[133] "Spiritual gifts open the church to God's grace and show forth signs of grace in a graceless world."[134]

This brings us to the place where we can explore more practically how Spirit is mediated through Word. Macchia believes that Word comes

127. Ibid., 207. Elsewhere, Macchia similarly argues that the church is not the "total Christ" (placing him at odds with Chan, as we shall see). The church and Christ share the mutual indwelling of the Spirit, but not the same identity (Macchia, *Justified in the Spirit*, 278).

128. Macchia, "Signs of Grace," 207–8 (italics original).

129. Ibid., 208, cf. 242–44.

130. Ibid., 208.

131. Ibid., 208–9.

132. Macchia, *Baptized in the Spirit*, 243.

133. Macchia, "Signs of Grace," 209. Because the church participates in Trinitarian koinonia, this implies the gifts are *"relational, interactive and governed by the love of God"* (ibid., 210; italics original). Macchia borrows this description from Michael Welker.

134. Ibid., 210. Macchia states the church is to be an "infirmary" of "wounded healers" (Macchia, "Beyond Word and Sacrament," 28a, 29b; cf. Macchia, "Signs of Grace," 205–6).

not only through Scripture and preaching, but because of the church's charismatic structure, the Word is made available to believers through various channels and people, and not only ordained clergy.[135] The means of receiving the Word are "polycentric," including Scripture, sacraments and the variety of spiritual gifts.[136] Macchia states, "For Pentecostals, revelation is not channeled only through proclamation of the Word from holy scripture. The voices of revelation in the Pentecostal community tend to be more decentralized, occurring among ordinary people through words of wisdom, knowledge, and prophecy, even among the illiterate who cannot read the Bible."[137]

That the church is structured charismatically reframes and relativizes the authority of preaching and sacraments within the dynamic and relational matrix of Word and Spirit. This charismatic structure means that the Spirit can, through the gifts, "'shock' the institutional life of the church and throw it back to the very core of its life in the presence of God, reminding it also that its existence and purposes are penultimate and relative to the coming Kingdom of God," as well as enabling healing grace to come in unexpected ways.[138] Macchia does identify the sacraments of water baptism and the Lord's Supper as means by which believers may experience the Spirit in a fuller way.[139] Most significant for our purposes, however, is how Macchia's proposal of the church's charismatic structure affects the reception of the Word through the proclamation of Scripture and the spiritual gift of glossolalia.

---

135. Macchia, "Beyond Word and Sacrament," 28b; Macchia, "Signs of Grace," 210. Macchia acknowledges that ordained clergy have a special role in bringing the Word, but the charismatic structure requires all people be involved in the edification of the church.

136. Macchia, *Baptized in the Spirit*, 225.

137. Macchia, "Spirit, Word, and Kingdom," 4b–c.

138. Macchia, "Beyond Word and Sacrament," 29a. Macchia is borrowing this idea from Karl Rahner. See also Macchia, "Signs of Grace," 213; Macchia, "Tongues as a Sign," 74; Macchia, "North American Response," 30; and Macchia, "Question of Tongues," 124.

139. Macchia, *Baptized in the Spirit*, 247–56. For example, the invocation of the Spirit at the table of communion (epiclesis) should be looked upon with expectation as an opportunity for various charismata to be manifest. Elsewhere Macchia states that sacraments, viewed as sign, can be "best understood as facilitating a kind of 'mediated immediacy' that occasions the experience of the Spirit" (Macchia, *Justified in the Spirit*, 286, cf. 282–91).

Hearing the Word through Scripture

Concerning the proclamation of Scripture, Macchia declares, "There is no way to overestimate the significance of *preaching and Scripture in channeling God's grace* to the church." Because Scripture is "breathed by the Spirit" it serves as "a living guide or measure of our worship and witness."[140] The Spirit operates (is mediated) through Scripture to bring guidance, order and freedom to the church. Thus, the Scriptures are "inspired"; however, "not in the sense of representing a static deposit of revealed truths we can systematize into idols of ink and paper," or "master and control according to our own self-serving ends."[141] Here Macchia draws on Barth's theology of revelation and Scripture, believing it to be compatible with Pentecostal openness to the ongoing revelatory work of the Spirit.[142] Barth, explains Macchia, affirmed Scripture to be both personal and verbal. The verbal quality is important,[143] but he accented the personal so that Scripture would not be viewed as a set of propositions to be manipulated.[144] Scripture is infallible, then, insofar as it bears witness to the living God, but not without qualification.[145] The Word of Scripture functions within the church's charismatic structure, and the broader context of Spirit baptism. Indeed, "The text participates in Spirit baptism,"[146] within the broad eschatological kingdom framework, in which Christ is King and Spirit the kingdom. This means that Scripture is not the church's sole authority (not *sola scriptura*); rather "Word and Spirit alone" (Word being Christ) serve as the ultimate voice of authority.[147]

140. Macchia, "Signs of Grace," 211 (italics added). Cf. Macchia, *Baptized in the Spirit*, 245; and Macchia, *Trinity*, 34 (cf. ibid., 31–37). Also see Macchia's analysis of the discussion on Scripture, revelation and the Spirit occurring in the Reformed/Pentecostal dialogue in Macchia, "Spirit, Word, and Kingdom," 3a–5b.

141. Macchia, "Signs of Grace," 211. He sees modernist fundamentalism as given to the idea of Scripture being a static deposit, which he feels is illusory.

142. See Ibid., 211–12; Macchia, *Baptized in the Spirit*, 244–46; Macchia, "Spirit of God," 160–63; and Macchia, "Reply to Rickie Moore," 18–19.

143. Macchia affirms, "The Bible is verbally inspired and does contain truths that we confess and live by" (Macchia, "Signs of Grace," 212).

144. Yong et al., "Christ and Spirit," 47; Macchia, "Signs of Grace," 211–12.

145. Yong et al., "Christ and Spirit," 55, cf. 58.

146. Macchia, *Baptized in the Spirit*, 245.

147. Macchia, "Reply to Rickie Moore," 18, cf. 19. In this view, Scripture is the "standard," but not the only means, of proclamation.

Within the church, Macchia believes, a dynamic relationship also exists between charismata and Scripture. Spiritual gifts help make the Word alive and relevant, and keep preaching from becoming overly cerebral, rationalistic and noetic.[148] At the same time, all the gifts are accountable to Scripture. Thus, "the Scriptures themselves are a universally relevant and binding gift of the Spirit to the church in order to guide the particular and diverse charismatic structure of the church in its ongoing life and mission."[149] Further, "this text and its truths are living and active, *constantly channeling the power and wisdom of the Spirit* to us by the grace of God in diverse ways in the midst of gifted interactions among the people of God."[150]

Concerning proclamation, those ordained to deliver the Word (and sacraments) need to be accountable not only to Scripture, but also to the congregation, since the Spirit works through all believers. In fact, asserts Macchia, in this charismatic structure, proclamation of the Word needs to be expanded to include the voice of the laity and a wider range of gifts by which the Spirit reveals Christ in the church. Such gifts would include verbal charisms such as prophecy, but also allow for "ecstatic and depth experiences of God," as opposed to simply "cognitive and rational responses to the Word."[151] In short, Macchia views the Word of Scripture as a crucial mediation of the Spirit, but qualified within the Spirit's charismatic activity in the church.

Hearing the Word through Tongues

For Macchia, a prime example of how Word (by the Spirit) is diversely manifest apart from proclamation of Scripture and (traditional) sacraments is the charism of glossolalia. This topic warrants a more extensive exploration here, since it demonstrates how broader elements of Spirit baptism are already being expressed within Pentecostalism (although

148. Macchia, "Signs of Grace," 211–12; Macchia, *Baptized in the Spirit*, 244, 246.

149. Macchia, "Signs of Grace," 211. Also see Yong et al., "Christ and Spirit," 27, 30, 40, 42, 61. Macchia believes that the Spirit also reveals God's will through church dogma and traditions, and sees experience of the Spirit as a link between the ancient and contemporary church. Yet dogma and tradition need Scripture as an "alien" voice, bringing challenge when needed. He admits to being a "restorationist" at heart, despite his love for the Roman Catholic Church and tradition.

150. Macchia, "Signs of Grace," 212 (italics added).

151. Ibid., 212; Macchia, *Baptized in the Spirit*, 246.

not always acknowledged), and it is an area in which Macchia has made considerable creative contribution in his revisioning of Pentecostal theology. Glossolalia is a gift not only near and dear to the hearts of Pentecostals, but according to Macchia, it combines elements of proclamation and sacrament, functioning as a sacramental sign, "an audible means of making God present."[152] Just as physical elements function as locators of God's presence within sacramental traditions, tongues function in this way within Pentecostal contexts, but with a twist.

First, for Pentecostals, glossolalia signifies encounter with God. Writes Macchia, "Beneath the dogma of tongues-as-evidence was the assumption that tongues symbolize an encounter with God that may be termed 'theophanic,' or as spontaneous, dramatic and marked by signs and wonders."[153] This Pentecostal "theophanic spirituality" (in contrast to the "incarnational" spirituality of sacramental traditions) accents the Spirit's freedom.[154] Indeed, tongues were, in a sense, "formed in protest" to institutional formalization and liturgy.[155] Secondly, however, tongues are not always spontaneous but occur within the context of Pentecostal ritual,[156] and link God's presence to a tangible phenomenon.[157] Since Pentecostals, "make a *visible/audible* phenomenon an integral part of their experience of the Spirit," Macchia asks, "Does this not sound more 'sacramental' than 'evidential'?"[158] This sacramentalism inherent within Pentecostalism leads Macchia to state, "For quite some time I have been convinced that *Pentecostals do not merely advocate direct and unmediated*

152. Macchia, "Tongues as a Sign," 62, cf. 61–76. He views "sign" as a richer, more biblical term than "evidence" in describing the significance of tongues for Spirit baptism (ibid., 68). Also see Macchia, "Groans Too Deep," § 1; Macchia, "Tradition and the Novum," 45; Macchia, "Struggle for Global Witness," 17; Macchia, "Discerning the Spirit," 24; and Macchia, "God Present," 42.

153. Macchia, "Sighs Too Deep," 48. Macchia states, "Of importance to Pentecostals has not been tongues *per se*, but what tongues symbolizes for them, namely, a theophanic encounter with God that is spontaneous, free and wondrous." (ibid., 49, cf. 72)

154. Macchia, "God Present," 39.

155. Macchia, "Tongues as a Sign," 64.

156. Ibid., 72. Macchia elsewhere draws on Albrecht's work (explored in chapter 2) in making this point (Macchia, *Baptized in the Spirit*, 248).

157. See Macchia, "Tongues as a Sign," 63, 69. Cf. Macchia, "Groans Too Deep"; and Macchia, "Question of Tongues," 122–23. Macchia uses Tillich's signification theory, in which sacrament is viewed as that which connects revelation and physical (including acoustic) signs. Tillich refers to this as a "kairos" event.

158. Macchia, "Tongues as a Sign," 68 (italics original).

experiences of the Spirit.[159] Rather, it is better to understand Pentecostal experience of God as a *"mediated immediacy."*[160]

In relation to Spirit baptism, tongues occupies a privileged role because it signifies the meaning of this empowering experience.[161] The significance, however, cannot be limited to the narrow, scientific meaning implied in the initial evidence doctrine.[162] Here, Lindbeck's cultural-linguist theory, in which doctrine provides the grammar for explaining (and subsequently promoting similar) experience, allows Macchia to relativize all doctrinal confessions as fallible, requiring revision.[163] But, conversely, and challenging Lindbeck, Macchia states that glossolalia demonstrates precisely that we are not restricted by cultural-linguistic environments in regard to experience because tongues symbolizes a "theophanic experience of God," a divine "self-disclosure."[164] This is why tongues can serve as a sacrament of sorts, mediating the presence of God in a physical (oral/aural) tangible way.[165] This Pentecostal sacramental (and theophanic) spirituality has implications for our upcoming ecumenical dialogue later in this chapter. At this point, however, it is worth summarizing some of Macchia's key points concerning the sacramental symbolism of tongues, since it serves as a primary and creative example of how Pentecostal experience of God is being revisioned in relation to his expanded metaphor of Spirit baptism.[166]

159. Macchia, "Tradition and the Novum," 45 (italics added).

160. Macchia, *Baptized in the Spirit*, 224 (italics added); cf. Macchia, *Justified in the Spirit*, 286.

161. See Macchia, *Baptized in the Spirit*, 172. Macchia's use of "privileged" here needs to be distinguished from the practical historical privileging of tongues by Pentecostals, which was not only based on it being mentioned in Acts in connection with Spirit baptism, but also because it distinguished them from Holiness and other revivalist groups as an identity marker. Also see Macchia, "Tongues as a Sign," 64.

162. Macchia, "Tongues as a Sign," 68.

163. Macchia, "Groans Too Deep," § 5; cf. Macchia, *Trinity*, 38. Elsewhere Macchia utilizes Lindbeck in his effort to bring together elements of Roman Catholic and Protestant doctrines of justification (Macchia, *Justified in the Spirit*, 296).

164. Macchia, "Sighs Too Deep," 54, 55.

165. This also means that tongues cannot simply be replaced with some other sign. As a sacrament, tongues demonstrates uniquely and tangibly the meaning of Spirit baptism (Macchia, "Groans Too Deep," § 2).

166. It needs to be acknowledged that much, if not all, of Macchia's work on glossolalia was published before *Baptized in the Spirit* and the development of his expanded Spirit baptism metaphor. His observations concerning tongues, however, are congruent with the framework he has developed.

First, Macchia identifies tongues as an "eschatological theophany."[167] Pentecost was the outpouring of the eschatological Spirit upon the church, involving "the transformation of language into a channel of the divine self-disclosure." This theophanic emphasis accents "the freedom of the Holy Spirit to encounter us in dramatic and unforeseen ways that change our outlook and broaden our horizons."[168] It emphasizes God's transcendence and otherness, often demonstrated in the "spontaneity and ecstasy" in Pentecostal worship.[169] Moreover, "As an unclassifiable language, tongues points us to God's final self-disclosure and, therefore, prevents us from making an idol of our worship, religious language, and theological systems."[170]

Second, proposes Macchia, glossolalia signifies God's *very* presence, reminding believers they stand "before God" ("*coram Deo*").[171] Thus, "Tongues accent the inadequacy of language in the face of the awesome mystery of God."[172] Glossolalia is an encounter with the living God, a result of God's free decision to act; it "symbolizes a divine action that is mysterious and free"—God cannot be controlled or manipulated.[173] At the same time, human involvement in glossolalia implies an openness to God and participation in God's freedom. Thus, "In glossolalia is a hidden protest against any attempt to define, manipulate or oppress humanity. Glossolalia is an unclassifiable, free speech in response to an unclassifiable, free God. It is the language of the *imago Dei*."[174] Tongues, therefore, relativizes (and democratizes) all languages, cultures and theological traditions; it serves an "iconoclastic role," functioning as an "anti-language."[175] Further, because tongues is a form of ecstasy, it

167. Macchia, "Sighs Too Deep," 55–60; cf. Macchia, "Groans Too Deep" § 4.

168. Macchia, "Sighs Too Deep," 57.

169. Ibid., 58; cf. Macchia, *Justified in the Spirit*, 97.

170. Macchia, "Groans Too Deep," § 4. This means that the potential triumphalism and otherworldliness often associated with eschatological freedom must be tempered with a recognition of the Spirit's transcendent presence in the midst of everyday broken historical existence (and including creation in the redemptive process). Elsewhere Macchia calls for Pentecostals to leave behind their historical ties to dispensational frameworks, in which the future is determined, for more open possibilities for the future of creation, including human participation (Macchia, "Sighs Too Deep," 59–60).

171. Macchia, "Sighs Too Deep," 61, cf. 60–64 (italics original).

172. Macchia, "Tongues and Prophecy," 64.

173. Macchia, "Sighs Too Deep," 60, 61.

174. Ibid., 61 (italics original). Also see "Groans Too Deep," § 4.

175. Macchia, "Tongues of Pentecost," 14; cf. Macchia, "Tongues and Prophecy," 64.

also serves as a protest against bondage to rational communication.[176] Rational reflection upon encounter with God tends to distance one from the experience, bringing it to an end. But "Tongues is a way of expressing the experience without ending it. The experience and the expression become one."[177]

Third, while glossolalia is a very personal experience, says Macchia, it nevertheless needs to be understood within the communion of the saints ("*Sanctorum Communio*").[178] The fullness of experience of God can only be realized "in solidarity with others in koinonia."[179] In this way, tongues can function to restrain unbridled Pentecostal individualism, while simultaneously engendering appreciation for the necessity and blessing of structured elements of corporate liturgy, such as the Lord's Supper.[180] It is true that the Spirit is not confined to liturgical structure. "Yet, that God does act in the midst of planned and structured rites is a sober reminder to Pentecostals that the divine reality is not restricted to, nor always present in, the unstructured and unusual. What makes something revelatory, structured or not, is whether it becomes *a transparent medium for an encounter* with the God who freely acts."[181]

Another emphasis Macchia associates with koinonia is that glossolalia signifies "differentiated unity."[182] The xenolalic tongues of Pentecost functioned historically to overcome linguistic and cultural barriers,

---

176. Macchia, "Sighs Too Deep," 64. Macchia distinguishes Pentecostal glossolalia from the trance states found in ancient Greek religions, in which there was total loss of control by the individual. He states, "Ecstasy may be a meaningful way of transcending one's situation without losing conscious control of oneself."

177. Ibid., 62.

178. Ibid., 64–67 (italics original).

179. Ibid., 65. Macchia says that tongues may be exercised corporately or privately, but even if exercised for self-edification, this should ultimately be for "the goal of reaching out to others in the body of Christ. Ultimately, there is no separation between self-edification and the edification of others" (Macchia, "Sighs Too Deep," 67; cf. Macchia, "Babel and the Tongues," 51).

180. While tongues does emphasize the "unstructured and spontaneous" elements of worship, says Macchia, nonetheless, these elements can be viewed as being related to, and elevating appreciation for, that which is structured. So, while tongues relativizes planned liturgical structures, "On the other hand, a biblical devotion to liturgies and structures can help Pentecostals gain a greater appreciation for the historical, even institutional, dimensions of our free response to God" (Macchia, "Question of Tongues," 124).

181. Macchia, "Sighs Too Deep," 67 (italics added).

182. Macchia, *Baptized in the Spirit*, 212.

symbolizing that people of every nation are being invited to participate in the divine mission.[183] The story of Acts demonstrates the inclusion of all languages, races, cultures, classes and genders in the Spirit's redemptive activity—tongues is the language of ecumenism.[184] "The unity of Pentecost is thus not abstract and absolute but rather concrete and pluralistic."[185] Pentecost can thus be viewed as both a reversal and fulfillment of Babel (Gen 11), rejecting its oppressive homogeneity, while affirming the diversity of all cultures and peoples in the fulfillment of the kingdom.[186] This means all people can be used as "prophets" for God. Indeed, the weakest, most marginalized of laity can "function as a veritable oracle of God."[187] With the goal of Spirit baptism being "all flesh" (and ultimately all creation), "Spirit baptism thus implicitly undercuts any efforts to oppress or unjustly discriminate based on differences of gender, race, social class, or physical/mental capabilities. Spirit baptism intends to grace all of creation with the dignity of being accepted, called, and gifted of God."[188]

Fourth, glossolalia links the Spirit's power to the universal Lordship of Christ the king; tongues has not only ecclesial but cosmic significance. Explains Macchia:

183. Macchia, "Groans Too Deep," § 3. This Lukan emphasis is contrasted with that of Paul in 1 Cor 14, where tongues is emphasized more as a gift for personal edification. Paul, however, also sees all gifts functioning within a broader community context.

184. Ibid. States Macchia, "It may be argued that the bringing together of Jew and Gentile in the diverse but unified praise and witness of the Spirit to the goodness of God is the central theme of Acts. Tongues, in this light, play a very important role for Luke, since they function as the most striking and outstanding involvement of God in this corporate praise and witness empowered in Spirit baptism." See also Macchia, "Sighs Too Deep," 65–66; Macchia, *Baptized in the Spirit*, 219; Macchia, "Tongues of Pentecost," 1–18.

185. Macchia, *Baptized in the Spirit*, 219.

186. See Ibid., 211–22; Macchia, "Babel and the Tongues," 36–47; and Macchia, "Unity and Otherness," 5–7. Babel here represents the tyranny and idolatry of homogeneity, which was thwarted by God's judgment by bringing confusion of language and dispersion. The dispersion of Pentecost, in contrast, demonstrates a unified, yet pluralistically diversified mission.

187. Macchia, "Groans Too Deep," § 5; cf. Macchia, "Discerning the Spirit," 15. Macchia notes that early Pentecostalism advocated inter-racial fellowship and the ordination women based on their emphasis on Spirit baptism and tongues, and laments the loss of this reality (see Macchia, "Sighs Too Deep," 65–66; and Macchia, "Babel and the Tongues," 47).

188. Macchia, *Baptized in the Spirit*, 219.

There is an important christological qualification of pneumatic experience and glossolalia here that is often neglected or misunderstood among Pentecostals. This christological qualification is more profound than the shallow and sentimental Jesus piety that is often blended with glossolalic experience among Pentecostals. It has become popular within Pentecostalism radically to separate conversion to Christ and the baptism with the Holy Spirit, as though these represent two different stages in one's spiritual growth. . . . It is not that Pentecostals have excluded Christology from their piety and theology, but the God of power experienced and described in Spirit baptism is rarely defined according to the God revealed in the incarnation, life and death of Jesus Christ. The power of the Spirit is thus defined among Pentecostals more as a triumphalistic domination of the natural order through the realm of the supernatural than as Paul's "strength in weakness" under the shadow of the cross.[189]

A stronger tie to Christology means appreciating "Christ crucified," and the "not yet" brokenness of the world and even the church.[190] Glossolalia is connected to the prayerful groans of Romans 8:26, longing for the "deliverance of the suffering creation."[191] This emphasis locates believers as participants in the global redemptive activity of the Spirit, identifying with the brokenness that longs to be healed.[192] Macchia writes, "Rather than tongues being a sign of an escape from this world into the heights of glory, they are expressions of strength in weakness, or the capacity to experience the first-fruits of the kingdom-to-come in the midst of our groaning with the suffering creation. They bring to ultimate

189. Macchia, "Sighs Too Deep," 68.

190. Macchia, "Struggle for Global Witness," 18.

191. Macchia, "Sighs Too Deep," 69, cf. 70. Macchia again relies on Johann Blumhardt for the emphasis on prayerful groaning as an active passivity awaiting redemption (cf. Macchia, "Groans Too Deep"; Macchia, *Baptized in the Spirit*, 281; and Macchia, *Spirituality and Social Liberation*, 167, 169).

192. Macchia, "Babel and the Tongues," 47, cf. 47–49. Macchia believes that tongues held more of this type of significance for early Pentecostals, who believed God was empowering even the most marginalized to launch out into global mission. This was tied to the early belief that tongues were xenolalic, and would serve as a tool for evangelistic method in foreign nations. When this did not work out practically, Pentecostals began to view tongues as glossolalic, given as evidence of a personal spiritual experience as well as for private prayer. Macchia believes that a weakness of this move was the diminished view of tongues signifying the Spirit's global mission.

expression the struggle that is essential to all prayer, namely, trying to put into words what is deeper than words."[193]

Fifth (and finally), for Macchia, tongues signifies not only a longing for new creation, but is also a sign that the new creation has already begun. In Acts, glossolalia was frequently associated with the healing and transformation of social relationships.[194] Tongues, then, like bodily healing, signifies that liberation can be experienced even today[195]—a tangible "anticipation of our final unity in diversity before the throne of grace."[196] Proposes Macchia, "Perhaps we ought to rethink what we mean by tongues as 'evidence.' This should not mean, 'You have the Spirit now!' It should mean that the Spirit has us as a visible sign of a new creation taking place in our midst and through us among others!"[197]

The significance here is holistic; liberation is not only for the soul, but mind, body and society as well. Macchia hopes Pentecostals will catch a broader vision of the Spirit's involvement in creation as a whole, not just in extraordinary 'supernatural' experiences, and will begin viewing every aspect of the Christian vocation as participation with the Spirit to bring healing to creation.[198] "This means that glossolalia and divine healing in Pentecostalism are signs that human participation is a vital part of the renewal of society and creation. Not only preaching the gospel, but medical help, social action and ecological measures can also be signs of God's presence to make all things new."[199]

In sum, Macchia's revisioning of the significance of glossolalia as the sign of Spirit baptism has considerably more breadth and depth than that typically implied by the doctrines of subsequence and initial evidence.[200] This review of Macchia's understanding of tongues has served to demonstrate how this gift functions as an expression of the

---

193. Macchia, "Groans Too Deep," § 4.

194. Macchia, "Sighs Too Deep," 70–71.

195. Ibid., 71.

196. Macchia, "Groans Too Deep," § 7.

197. Macchia, "Sighs Too Deep," 71.

198. Ibid.

199. Ibid., 72.

200. See Macchia, "Groans Too Deep," § 7. Macchia reformulates the initial evidence doctrine in this way: "The important point to the doctrine of tongues as the initial sign of Spirit baptism is that there is a depth of experience in the Spirit, the consequence of which will quite naturally be speaking in tongues, and that the experience itself does not come to full biblical expression and signification without tongues."

Word being delivered to the church by the Spirit, conveying the truth of what it means to live within Spirit baptism. In other words, understood sacramentally within the broadened metaphor of Spirit baptism and the church's charismatic structure, glossolalia exemplifies how Word mediates experience of God.

Summary

At this juncture it is appropriate to suggest a location for Macchia on Schner's continuum of the appeal to experience. Macchia may be placed at the "appeal constructive," since he preserves continuity with the Pentecostal confessional tradition, while his acknowledgement of the mediated nature of experience allows him to enter into critical self-awareness and theological reflection, enabling him to revision Pentecostal theology in fresh ways. In doing so, Macchia demonstrates evidence of maturation occurring within Pentecostalism, enabling Pentecostal theology to move away from a naïve "appeal confessional" in at least three ways.

First, he demonstrates self-awareness concerning weaknesses inherent within his own Pentecostal tradition, including otherworldliness, triumphalism, elitism, and most significantly the dichotomy between empowerment and sanctification (and soteriology in general), and suggests how these might be overcome by a broadened understanding of Spirit baptism. In the process, secondly, Macchia moves Pentecostals beyond a naïve biblicism by attempting to integrate the entirety of Scripture (not satisfied to leave Luke and Paul bifurcated), and its theological implications (e.g., eschatological kingdom context, Trinity, and the Word/Spirit relationship). His theology of (scriptural) revelation, furthermore, allows Pentecostals to remain true to their intuitions concerning the ongoing revelatory work of the Spirit, without having to abandon these for more fundamentalistic evangelical emphases. Third, Macchia shows how an appreciation of Word as mediation of Spirit, exemplified in the significance of glossolalia within the Spirit-baptized charismatic structure of the church, is able to take a key distinctive of Pentecostalism and use it to expand the meaning of Pentecostal mission. The above, moreover, allows Macchia to utilize Pentecostal theology in making a contribution to ecumenical fellowship, to which we now turn.

Macchia in Dialogue with Christian Theological Traditions

This section of the chapter will place Macchia in dialogue with the eight theologians surveyed in chapter 1 concerning the theology of experience of God. We will do our best to avoid putting words in the mouths (so to speak) of any of the theological voices being used here. Rather, the goal is simply to compare the key ideas raised in our survey of Macchia's theology of experience with that of the other theologians in an attempt to see where the authors converge and diverge, as well as whether Macchia's re-visioned Pentecostal theology can help contribute to further ecumenical dialogue. Methodologically, the following dialogue will be approached by way of themes, rather than having Macchia interact with each theologian in sequence. It is hoped that this approach will keep the conversation more lively and interactive, and it acknowledges the overlap in subject matter in the works of the theologians involved. Themes were chosen primarily in response to Macchia's main emphases, while keeping in mind that our focus is the question of how God is experienced by humans in the world. It should also be kept in mind that each voice cannot be expected to speak to each issue to the same extent, and so theologians will be brought into discussion where appropriate to their own emphases.[201]

Macchia's Goals for the Christian Traditions

As we enter this dialogue, we are helped by Macchia himself, who believes that his broadened metaphor of Spirit baptism can enrich Christian theology, contributing to ecumenical fellowship and the revitalization of all the Christian traditions. We earlier noted Macchia's reference to there being three ecclesial interpretations of Spirit baptism: Word ecclesiology, (emphasizing Spirit baptism as regeneration), sacramental (associating Spirit baptism with various initiation rites), and Pentecostal ecclesiology (emphasizing believers set apart and empowered for service).[202] Macchia's broadening of the Spirit baptism metaphor challenges all three traditions to recognize that the work of the Spirit cannot be restricted

---

201. More broadly, this also means that some theologians will be appear more prominently in dialogue with our other Pentecostal theologians in subsequent chapters.

202. Macchia, *Baptized in the Spirit*, 64–85.

to any one of the above three emphases. To this point, however, we have mainly highlighted the implications of Macchia's revisionary theology for Pentecostals. It is appropriate, now, to briefly survey how this expanded vision of Spirit baptism challenges the other Christian traditions directly.

Macchia believes an impasse exists within the Christian theological traditions concerning the ways in which the Spirit is viewed as operating in the church. Protestant churches in the Reformed tradition accent the "freedom of the Spirit in relation to the church," something Tillich describes as the "Protestant principle."[203] This emphasis, says Macchia, is held in contrast to the "sacramental principle," "which emphasizes the church as the mediator of the Spirit through visible means of grace,"[204] so as to "avoid a demonic objectification of the Spirit in sacramental means of grace."[205] At the same time, "As Tillich notes, the Protestant principle is susceptible to the danger of neglecting the role that material and audible symbols can play if they are taken up into God's free action in order to participate in the divine self-disclosure."[206] This has tended to reduce the Spirit's role to illuminating the Word (Scripture), involved only in the cognitive and noetic aspects of human experience (as noted earlier). In response, Macchia states, "To my mind, Pentecostal sacramental spirituality is unique in its effort to push beyond this impasse between the Protestant principle and elimination of the Spirit's freedom through the Spirit's 'objectification' in sacramental means of grace." Tongues serves to exemplify this combination, emphasizing both the Spirit's freedom and yet locatedness in physical phenomena.[207]

This theophanic sacramental spirituality, within the broadened understanding of Spirit baptism and the charismatic structure of the church, challenges other traditions (whether Word or sacramental) to view the Spirit as more than simply a quiet presence in initiation, or operating merely to illuminate preaching. Rather, it encourages openness

---

203. Macchia, "Tradition and the Novum," 45.

204. Ibid. Writes Macchia, "The danger of the sacramental view is an idolatrous association of the divine act with the material/audible symbols."

205. Macchia, "Question of Tongues," 122–23.

206. Macchia, "Tradition and the Novum," 45.

207. Macchia, "Question of Tongues," 123.

to, and expectation of[208] more holistic[209] manifestations of the Spirit, including experiential conscious apprehensions of being "possessed," or overwhelmed by the Spirit.[210] Such manifestations ought not to be "suppressed or ignored,"[211] for they help make the church aware, "in reality, we do not possess the Spirit, the Spirit possesses us."[212] Explains Macchia,

> I am not saying that a Christian, whose life is not rich in miraculous occurrences is substandard. That would represent a ridiculous assumption. The sanctifying Spirit manifests itself in signs that are miraculous, but the deeper signs are acts of love. I am saying, however, that a Christian should remain open to an experience of the presence of power of the Spirit that transcends cultural expectations, including those of post-Enlightenment rationalism in the West. Luke's voice in the canon calls all Christians to an experience of Pentecost that is akin to a prophetic call felt deeply like Jeremiah's experience of fire in his bones.[213]

That last sentence highlights another point that Macchia believes Pentecostals bring to the ecumenical table—namely, that "Christian initiation must include a sense that the grace of God gifts Christians for ministry and mission."[214] Mission and vocation is essential to Christian identity.[215] Bearing the above points in mind, then, we enter into our ecumenical conversation.

208. See Macchia, *Baptized in the Spirit*, 152. He notes that without this expectation, the church will not experience such manifestations as often.

209. Ibid., 276; Macchia, "Signs of Grace," 212; Macchia, "Struggle for Global Witness," 25; Macchia, "Pinnock's Pneumatology," 171.

210. Macchia, *Baptized in the Spirit*, 152.

211. Ibid., 149.

212. Ibid., 153. Thus, elsewhere Macchia states that Pentecostals remind the church that because the Spirit comes to us from "the eschatological kingdom-to-come, the Spirit will encounter people in a way that seems strange and awesome, bringing the flow of their lives to a screeching halt and calling it radically into question. In such experiences, the Spirit is the 'wholly other' because we are so far removed from the eschatological future that God has in store for us" (Macchia, "Discerning the Spirit," 14).

213. Macchia, *Baptized in the Spirit*, 150.

214. Ibid., 151. He states, in this sense, "water baptism is the "ordination service" of every Christian" (cf. ibid., 153).

215. Ibid., 152. Writes Macchia, "One enters Spirit-baptized existence at Christian initiation. But the experience of Spirit baptism connected to and following from initiation is meant to bring to conscious participation the justice of the kingdom, the growth in sanctifying grace, and the charismatic openness to bless others and to glorify God that begins in Christian initiation. These experiences are to be ongoing. We have been

God's Relationship to the World:
Immanence and Transcendence

One of the most striking similarities that emerged in our theological exploration in chapter 1 was that four of the theologians (Johnson, Gelpi, Bulgakov, and Moltmann) explicitly advocated a panentheistic view of God's relationship to creation, building the case that experience of God can occur within and through creation itself, creation existing (in some sense) within God. Each arrived at this position in different ways, and it is also notable that Moltmann, Bulgakov, and Johnson do so motivated in some respects by a desire that greater attention be given to "secular" issues, such as ecology,[216] and other social/political liberative concerns. Gelpi's panentheism, while allowing for such application, was motivated more toward providing a coherent metaphysical construct of experience in general, allowing for a robust relational epistemology.

A panentheistic view of creation emphasizes God's immanence—that God can be (or is already) experienced in that which is mundane, or even in the processes of life and history. Such a view does not necessarily exclude unusual or extraordinary encounters with God, but accents immanent experience of God as taking priority and bearing more authority with regard to theological construction. Concerning this theme, the theologian with whom Macchia has had the most explicit (published) dialogue is Moltmann. So, it is through their conversation on this subject that we can perhaps gain clues as to how Macchia's theology might speak to the emphasis on God's immanence with the other theologians as well. Macchia and Moltmann do share similar concerns on a number of matters.[217] However, the areas in which Moltmann and Macchia

---

baptized in the Spirit, we are being baptized in the Spirit, and we will be baptized in the Spirit" (ibid., 154).

216. For example, see Moltmann, *God in Creation*, 20–52; and Johnson, *Women, Earth*, 5–9.

217. Throughout *Baptized in the Spirit*, for example, Macchia frequently refers to and utilizes elements of Moltmann's theology. These include Moltmann's emphasis on Social Trinity (ibid., 117–25), the Spirit's suffering in and with creation (demonstrating God's omnipotence through his infinite capacity to suffer) (ibid., 262), holistic spirituality (ibid., 246, 276–77), the call for the church to be involved in social transformation (ibid., 45, 104, 278), and the eschatological emphasis on God ultimately filling all creation (in Macchia's case, as the goal of Spirit baptism) (ibid., 44, 95–96, 117, 271). More recently, Macchia has continued to draw on Moltmann's work in developing his theology of justification (see Macchia, *Justified in the Spirit*, 3, 71–72). Both Moltmann and Macchia have

diverge become more explicit in their interaction in several articles published in the *Journal of Pentecostal Theology* in 1994, which focused on Moltmann's pneumatology as presented in his book, *The Spirit of Life*.[218]

Macchia acknowledges his appreciation for Moltmann's accent on a pneumatology "from below,"[219] since this helps Pentecostals balance their sometimes over-emphasis on "the dramatic and miraculous work of the Spirit," resulting in a lack of "appreciation of the work of the Spirit in secular channels of liberation and healing."[220] But what Macchia perceives to be given priority in Moltmann's pneumatology, however, is the latter's emphasis on the Spirit's immanence in creation (Moltmann's "immanent-transcendence"), which undermines the "otherness" of God, and potentially the means by which to view the Spirit as acting interruptively in the world towards transformation and liberation.[221] Contrary to Moltmann's view that this "otherness" can create an irreconcilable distance between God and life (hence leading him toward panentheism), Macchia argues that the Pentecostal emphasis on "divine encounters occurring in unanticipated ways with great majesty and power, through signs and wonders such as prophetic or glossolalic utterances," actually provides the theological groundwork for social transformation. Macchia explains, "We as Pentecostals recognize the Spirit of God as near to us in all of life, even as a force that wells up from deep within and drives us toward God. The Spirit not only grips us in the depths of our beings, the Spirit also transforms our social and physical lives."[222] Here the immanence of the Spirit is acknowledged by Macchia, but while accenting the otherness and transcendence of God.

---

been influenced by the theology of the Blumhardts in viewing the Spirit as active now, working toward social and political transformation (see Macchia, "North American Response," 29; Macchia, *Baptized in the Spirit*, 196, 276–79; Macchia, *Spirituality and Social Liberation*; Macchia, "Spirit and the Kingdom," 1–5, 32; and Macchia, "Waiting and Hurrying," 1–30).

218. The *Journal of Pentecostal Theology* 4 issue was dedicated to reviewing Moltmann's *Spirit of Life* by a number of Pentecostal theologians, including Macchia and Chan among others. Althouse has also examined the interaction between Moltmann and Macchia from the point of view of eschatology (see Althouse, *Spirit of the Last Days*, 159–92).

219. Macchia, "Spirit and Life," 121.

220. Macchia, "North American Response," 29; cf. Macchia, "Spirit and Life," 121–22.

221. Macchia, "North American Response," 26, cf. 25–26.

222. Ibid., 26.

Macchia adds that Moltmann's accent on the Spirit's immanence makes it difficult to account for the "ambiguity of life; that is, life as possibly graced but also as potentially dark and destructive." Whereas Pentecostals emphasize the necessity of human cooperation in responding to grace, Moltmann, in contrast, "assumes an element of grace as part of the very definition of life itself," which makes it difficult to see how life could ever "be lost or alienated from the Spirit."[223] Macchia wants to allow more room for the possibility that humans might reject the King (Jesus) and the presence of the Spirit as the kingdom (as well as to account for evil and suffering). Grace, Macchia wants to emphasize, is conditional, whereas Moltmann seems to require that it be more unconditional (possibly influenced by his Reformed background).[224] Further, the strong emphasis on the Spirit's immanence also potentially calls into question God's freedom in interacting with humans and creation in regard to this ambiguity of life.[225]

Moltmann responds to Macchia's critique concerning this issue of immanent-transcendence, following at least two lines of thought.[226] First, Moltmann believes that while he has worked to dissolve the ontological dualism between God and creation, he preserves an eschatological apocalyptic dualism of sorts, which allows for the transformative operation of the Spirit in history. The Spirit does not come "from above" or "outside" in an ontological sense, but rather eschatologically—not "from beyond the world but rather through the risen Christ . . ."[227] Second, Moltmann believes this eschatological dualism approach will allow him to avoid the otherworldly (and sometimes triumphalistic) eschatology and spirituality that Pentecostals sometimes exhibit. The Spirit's work in the world, including through the charismata, should be viewed as the power of the coming age, thereby firmly linking the Spirit's work to creation while

---

223. Ibid., 27.

224. Macchia, "Spirit and Life," 124–25.

225. Macchia, "North American Response," 27. Also see Johnson, *Women, Earth,* 58–59. Johnson pleads a type of agnosticism concerning the ambiguity that can arise with a strong emphasis on the Spirit's immanence. She does not know how evil and suffering can exist within the Spirit's love (womb), but suggests it has to do with the mysterious process of love.

226. Moltmann is also responding to his other Pentecostal dialogue partners as well, but at times identifies Macchia in particular, providing our focus.

227. Moltmann, "A Response," 64.

being open to social and cosmic healing and transformation.[228] Here, it should be noted, there is some congruency with Macchia's attempt to correct the Pentecostal lack of a creation pneumatology.

Macchia went on to publish a further response to Moltmann, in which some of the above issues received further clarification. Reaffirmed, however, was Macchia's conviction as a Pentecostal that the transcendence and otherness of the Spirit needs to be preserved in order for the Spirit to be understood as truly bringing transformation to the world. Macchia too wants to avoid any ontological dualism and otherworldliness, emphasizing instead the eschatological newness of the Spirit's power. Explains Macchia,

> The dominant emphasis of Pentecostals is not on the Spirit *of life*, as with Moltmann, but on the Spirit as the omnipotent and strange mystery that breaks in miraculously with the sound of a violent wind. This experience brings our everyday lives to a screeching halt, calling them radically into question and transforming them in ways that are sure to seem strange to the world. I do believe that this emphasis on the strange and miraculous is important for Pentecostals. The continual "coming" or "falling" of the Spirit "over against" this world (in a sense, against us also) to empower us for praise and service is an important emphasis for a Pentecostal pneumatology that defends the eschatological freedom of the Spirit and preserves a sharp prophetic criticism of the status quo. But this eschatological emphasis alone can cause us to withdraw from the world and simply wait for God in passive resignation. Hence, we need Moltmann's focus on the Spirit working in fellowship and liberation within all of life.[229]

So, while Macchia does accent the Spirit's transcendence, he also wants Pentecostals to avoid otherworldliness and triumphalism, and finds Moltmann to be a potential ally to help counter these undesirable qualities. But Macchia also believes that Pentecostalism contains some resources within its own tradition toward overcoming these negative tendencies. He notes (in his initial response to Moltmann) that the emphasis on bodily healing serves as evidence that Pentecostal spirituality "has not precluded the Spirit's transforming work in everyday life. . . . For Pentecostals the Spirit is both free and visibly mediated in life through

228. Ibid., 63, 64, cf. 68.

229. Macchia, "Spirit and Life," 122 (italics original); cf. Macchia, "Discerning the Spirit," 14.

signs and wonders such as tongues or healing."[230] Macchia's real concern with Moltmann's pneumatology, however, is whether its focus on "the immanent presence of the Spirit in life" can sufficiently allow for "proper stress on the eschatological freedom and criticism exercised by the Spirit."[231] While Macchia agrees that Moltmann does "not explicitly identify the Spirit with the essence of life,"[232] he is yet unconvinced that Moltmann's description of the Spirit's relation to creation (e.g., speaking of "creation as 'emanation'" from the Spirit) overcomes the above mentioned problems.[233]

This dialogue can be further supplemented by emphases we already noted in Macchia's broadening of the Spirit baptism metaphor. In particular, within the eschatological framework of the kingdom, in which Christ is King and Spirit the kingdom, Macchia reaffirms that the Spirit's power and working are eschatologically located. Miracles, for example, (as noted) are not supernatural, but signs of the in-breaking kingdom. Glossolalia, in particular, serves as an eschatological theophany in this regard as well. This means that Macchia has avoided the otherworldliness emphasis so often found within Pentecostalism.

With regard to the other panentheists (Bulgakov, Gelpi, and Johnson), Macchia's challenges concerning immanentism would likely apply here as well. If the world is so embedded within God, then how can life's ambiguity (the presence of evil and suffering) be fully accounted for? Can the Spirit be distinguished from the processes of life, or truly interrupt, surprise or bring prophetic correction? Of course, each of our panentheistic dialogue partners would have her or his own way of attempting to address these challenges.

In Bulgakov's case, with his concept of the world existing in Sophia, and with Spirit as the life-force in creation enabling social evolution, it might appear especially difficult to overcome these difficulties. Certainly there could be a mutual appreciation between Macchia and Bulgakov concerning the need for the redemption of all social and political life.[234] But Macchia's accent here is on the Spirit accomplishing this in ways

---

230. Macchia, "North American Response," 29 (italics added).

231. Macchia, "Spirit and Life," 122.

232. Ibid., 123; cf. Moltmann, "A Response," 65. Moltmann argues he has sufficiently distanced himself from Hegel in this regard.

233. Macchia, "Spirit and Life," 124; cf. Moltmann, *Spirit of Life*, 228–29.

234. Bulgakov, *Sophia*, 143–45.

that are sometimes extraordinary and interruptive, as opposed to the idea of an immanent evolutionary process.[235] Conversely, Bulgakov may encourage Macchia to further look for ways in which the Spirit is at work beyond the boundaries of the church, even within "pagan" religions.[236] This is something Macchia has actually indicated as a possibility, although without fully committing himself (at least to the degree we will find in Yong). In this regard, Bulgakov's qualification that "pagan" religions do not receive direct revelation of God might be compatible with Macchia's robust connection between Word and Spirit, accenting the Spirit's mediation through Word (in various forms).

With regard to Gelpi, his strong emphasis on metaphysical immanence, the world existing in God's "mind" (*nous*) or Holy Breath, might also introduce challenges in view of Macchia's emphasis on the eschatological Spirit's interruptive and transformative work. Gelpi, however, is quite open to Pentecostal/charismatic encounters with the Spirit (such as "Spirit baptism"), viewing such through the charismatic lens of "release" of the Spirit in Christian life. Macchia too is amenable to describing empowering experiences associated with Spirit baptism as "release,"[237] but qualifies this with a strong eschatological kingdom-to-come emphasis. Spirit baptism is not simply a manifestation of an existing "deposit" of the Spirit, but a fresh encounter with the person of the eschatological Spirit. That said, Gelpi's emphasis on "conversion" (explored in chapter 1) may allow for some convergence with Macchia, which we will address shortly.[238]

In general, however, it would seem that a marked emphasis on God's immanence introduces a notable point of divergence between Macchia and the panentheists. As a Pentecostal, Macchia wants to remind the church that the Spirit baptism of Pentecost accents the otherness of the Spirit—confronting, possessing, overwhelming and transforming believers. Too strong a panentheistic emphasis may not provide sufficient room for this type of otherness.

---

235. This is not to deny that Bulgakov would allow for unusual and mystical experiences of the Spirit. Bulgakov is sometimes ambiguous as to how the Spirit's efficacy works itself out. It seems clear, however, that Bulgakov's sophiology is heavily weighted towards accenting the immanence of God within creation.

236. Bulgakov, *Comforter*, 214–16.

237. Macchia, *Baptized in the Spirit*, 77.

238. Gelpi will factor in most significantly in chapter 5 in dialogue with Yong.

God's Revelation in History (the Word)

As noted in the first chapter, Johnson's means of defending her emphasis on God's immanence stems from her own revisioning of theology using feminine language for the Godhead, and an emphasis on Social Trinity and Spirit-Sophia as the means by which God is mediated in the world.[239] She supports the latter point by appealing to an anthropology of human self-transcendence, and based on the above, sees all human experience potentially to be of God. This means that women's experience of relationships and of oppression[240] can be viewed as a vehicle of revelation, opening the way (it is hoped) to liberation and human flourishing—again, feminine imagery for God being utilized to evoke reform to this end in the Christian theological traditions. Johnson's emphasis, then, is certainly connected to the above discussion concerning God's relationship to creation; however, her focus raises theological issues concerning revelation and hermeneutics, and so we have chosen to place her here in the conversation (as opposed to in the previous subsection). Similarities with Cone's approach are quite noticeable in this regard as well, and so he may also be invited into the dialogue at this point.

Both Johnson and Cone view God as being revealed in the historical experiences of the (gender and racial) oppressed, and use this as a resource in their interaction with Scripture and the Christian theological tradition.[241] Cone adamantly believes that language can function to oppress; there is no "disinterested" speech in this regard—theology is an "interested" and political language.[242] The oppressed (blacks), however, enjoy a privileged reading of Scripture (based in black experience), leading to a more accurate language by which to speak about God—"Black theology." In a similar way, Johnson's accent is on the power of language to alter theology (for good or evil), since God is ultimately only describable symbolically. As we have seen, this allows her to modify even Scriptural

---

239. Johnson, *Women, Earth*, 41–60.

240. Ibid., 23–28.

241. We could also add Moltmann to these voices with his emphasis on hermeneutics as existential and focus on liberation; however, his main contribution to the dialogue has already been dealt with. Further, his hermeneutics are largely influenced by liberation theologies, such as that of Cone and Johnson, and so the latter will serve as our primary voices here.

242. Cone, *God of the Oppressed*, 36, 41.

nomenclature for God (e.g., "Mother-Sophia" replacing "Father") to serve broader liberative purposes.[243]

How might Macchia respond to some of these issues concerning revelation and hermeneutics raised by Cone and Johnson? First, by way of convergence, Macchia also expresses affinity with the desire for liberation of all peoples and creation. The Spirit of Pentecost is poured out for "all flesh," he affirms, and ultimately creation will be filled with God's presence and restored. In particular, Macchia is distressed with the social and political brokenness in the world and church. He bemoans the fact that while early Pentecostals demonstrated considerable openness to gender and racial equality that this has largely been lost with the institutionalization (denominalization) of Pentecostalism.[244] Macchia's interest in ecumenical dialogue,[245] and participation in the October 1994 dissolution of the Pentecostal Fellowship of North America (tainted by a history of racism) and creation of the new racially inclusive Pentecostal/ Charismatic Churches of North America, serve as evidence of both his theological and practical commitment to reconciliation.[246] Macchia would also concur that the Spirit can empower a prophetic voice against systems that are oppressive or unjust, whether they be social, political, or theological.[247]

Language—hearing the Spirit speak in new ways, and through unexpected, marginalized voices—is, then, also very significant for Macchia. The Spirit will not be dominated by any one people or group; and he views Scripture itself as functioning dynamically, rather than as a static deposit to be manipulated or used to oppress. Further, in Macchia's Spirit-baptized charismatic structure of the church, the Word is not expressed merely in the reading and proclamation of Scripture (perhaps introducing a tension here with Jenson, as we shall see), but also through a variety of charismata, especially speech gifts. The importance of testimony and

243. See Johnson, *Women, Earth*, 45–57.

244. Macchia, "Sighs Too Deep," 66. Cf. Macchia, "Kingdom and the Power," 121–22; and Macchia, "Groans Too Deep," § 3.

245. See Macchia, "Nature and Purpose," 1–17; Macchia, "Spirit, Word, and Kingdom," 1–7; Macchia, "Tongues of Pentecost," 1–18; and Macchia, "Response and Corresponding," 22–23.

246. Macchia, "From Azusa to Memphis: Evaluating," 203–18; Macchia, "From Azusa to Memphis: Where," 113–40.

247. Johnson in particular refers to raising a prophetic voice that will both disrupt and affirm to bring the flourishing of all life (Johnson, *Women, Earth*, 64–67).

other oral means for conveying and traditioning theological understanding, held mutually by Macchia and Cone, is also a connection point not to be missed. Speech receives its fullest attention, however, in Macchia's revisioning of the Pentecostal understanding of glossolalia, emphasizing this as demonstrating both the freedom of the Spirit and also the tangible presence of God. In Macchia's discussion of glossolalia, in particular, he addresses some of the concerns of both Cone and Johnson, while also introducing some points of divergence.

For Macchia, tongues-speech functions as a sign of the eschatological in-breaking of the Spirit toward liberation, but also as testimony to the fact that all languages and systems (even within the church) are broken, and in need of redemption. Tongues speech is therefore liberative and democratizing because even the most marginalized person can be empowered as an "oracle of God."[248] Macchia's emphasis here affirms the voices of all people, irrespective of gender, race, class, culture, or even age. Neither clergy, nor any theological institution or authority stands above Spirit and Word, manifest in the charismatic structure of the church, in which all God's people are called to be prophetic witnesses in both word and deed (praxis) toward bringing healing to a broken world in the power of Spirit baptism.

At the same time, Macchia's accent is on the Spirit *as* the eschatological in-breaking kingdom (accompanied and inaugurated by Christ the King), as opposed to immanently working in and through life processes (Bulgakov and Johnson). The tongues of Pentecost do not simply affirm all peoples (including the marginalized), but also that all voices can indeed be miraculously caught up into the love of God, and unified toward a common mission and goal for the kingdom. Pentecost as an eschatological event, argues Macchia, introduced not simply a reversal of the idolatrous homogeneity of Babel,[249] but also the possibility and foretaste of the unity of the eschaton *even now*. In other words, Macchia's accent is on not excluding any voices—even ones that have been oppressive—but on having all voices caught up in Spirit baptism and praise to God. Practically, of course, Macchia acknowledges that there is need to especially listen to voices that have been marginalized.[250] But he wants to

---

248. Macchia, "Groans Too Deep," § 3.

249. Macchia, *Baptized in the Spirit*, 214, cf. 211–22.

250. Macchia agrees with Moltmann, who notes that victims of oppression always have better memory than wrongdoers, and so need to be heard (Macchia, "From Azusa

open Christians to the possibility that the Spirit might bring a Word that is radically more transformative and healing than what (merely) an emphasis on the Spirit experienced (revealed) immanently through history might allow. This may indeed serve as a challenge to Cone and Johnson in this regard.

A word needs to be said here about Jenson concerning this topic of experience of God in history. As we have noted, Jenson questions any notion of God being revealed behind the story of Scripture, which records the redemptive history in which God is particularly revealed. The Trinity is connected to creation through time, not disconnected by timelessness. This leads Jenson to be suspicious of claims to experience of God not clearly tied to a particular (historical) identity—in this case, the Trinity, which mediates/communicates via the Word. For this reason, Jenson rejects viewing the Spirit as the "unidentified dynamism" guiding human (including marginalized group) experience.[251]

Macchia does exhibit an awareness of and appreciation for Jenson's concern that the Trinity be understood as being revealed historically, as was noted earlier in this chapter.[252] This is further supported by Macchia giving some credence to the postmodern epistemological insights of Lindbeck concerning the location of doctrine within cultural-linguistic frameworks.[253] This locatedness of Christian theology within the particulars of history implies a strong need for a more concrete identification of the experience of the Spirit with God's historical identity, particularly in and through Jesus (the Word)—a point with which Macchia concurs.[254] Macchia also advocates a strong emphasis on Word as the vehicle of revelation (although expanding this to include charismata), thus demonstrating some significant congruence with Jenson's emphasis on experience of God as historically located.

We also observed, however, that Macchia is not convinced that Lindbeck's cultural-linguistic theory sufficiently takes into account possibilities for the Spirit to interrupt in radically transformative ways. This is why Macchia emphasizes glossolalia as evidence that this can, in fact, be the case—tongues is an "alien" language, tangibly and concretely

---

to Memphis: Evaluating," 209).

251. Jenson, *Triune Identity*, 170.

252. See Macchia, *Baptized in the Spirit*, 117.

253. Macchia, "Christian Experience," 11c; Macchia, *Baptized in the Spirit*, 54.

254. Macchia, *Baptized in the Spirit*, 92.

expressed in the midst of a particular culture. While this does not mean that Macchia distances himself from Scripture and the historical revelation that Jenson advocates, it does call into question whether Jenson is correct in lumping the experiential emphases of liberation theologies (identified with Schner's appeals transcendent and hermeneutical) with all so-called "enthusiastic movements."[255] While Pentecostalism may practice, as Macchia notes, a spirituality of "ecstasy" (or enthusiasm) in some respects, this is not identical with the ambiguous sort of enthusiasm to which Jenson refers. As noted in chapter 2, Pentecostals clearly *always* identified their encounters with the Spirit as being encounters with the Spirit of Christ; and this linking of Spirit to Word only becomes all the more prominent in Macchia's theology of Spirit baptism.[256]

It warrants acknowledgment that Jenson's concern is that humans not be allowed to dictate the identity of the Word—Jesus' identity was sealed in his death. Jenson also does allow for the possibility that the Word might surprise us.[257] On this point Macchia's and Jenson's theology of Scripture and revelation find some congruence, since each affirms the personal nature of the Word of Scripture so as to avoid allowing any individual, institution or movement to "possess" the text, or manipulate it to self-interested ends. Macchia does, however, more so than Jenson, expand the ways in which the Word is channeled, supplementing Scripture and sacraments with the charismata, including prophecy and glossolalia. This is all accomplished by way of Macchia's unique emphasis concerning the interrelated missions of Spirit and Word in the charismatic structure of the church.

Word and Spirit

The interrelationship of Word and Spirit is a significant emphasis within Macchia's work, and can serve as another point of dialogue. Virtually every one of our eight theological conversation partners made mention of the Word/Spirit relationship to some degree.[258] Both Congar and Moltmann,

255. Jenson, *Triune Identity*, 170.

256. Cf. Macchia, *Trinity*, 35.

257. Jenson, *Systematic Theology: Triune*, 198–200.

258. We noted Congar and Gelpi's mention of the Spirit as the bond between the Father and Son (Congar using more traditional theological language, while Gelpi speaking of the Spirit as the divine "mind"). Macchia also speaks of this role of the Spirit in the Godhead, although preferring a Social Trinity model overall. Even Cone, who

in particular, shared similarities with Macchia in regard to their calling attention to the work of the Spirit in the life, death and resurrection of Jesus as a means by which to emphasize a stronger union between Word and Spirit. Their intent was to elevate the work of the Spirit, so as to keep Spirit from being subordinated to Word. This is exemplified in Congar's emphasis on both Word and Spirit as necessary for the completion of divine communication—the Word is the communication, and the Spirit enables reception (as the "two hands of the Father").[259] This emphasis is most explicit in his "pneumatological Christology,"[260] which he develops based on the Spirit's work in Jesus' assumption, baptism and resurrection/glorification. But even with these emphases, and though he shares much in common with Macchia concerning the Spirit's work in the life of Jesus, it is worth recalling that Congar still tends toward subsuming Spirit to Word (as argued in chapter 1). That said, Moltmann likewise highlights the Spirit's work in Jesus' life, advocating that Jesus first bears and then gives the Spirit, which implies Jesus' reliance upon the Spirit in the co-participation of Word and Spirit in Jesus' mission.

Macchia, however, while being appreciative of the above points, would not be satisfied that Congar and Moltmann have sufficiently drawn attention to the neglected scriptural emphases on the Spirit in the story of Jesus. Macchia's unique emphasis in this regard is on Christ as King and Spirit as the kingdom, demonstrated historically by the fact that Jesus poured out the Spirit at Pentecost, and in doing so was able to be identified as the divine Son of God. The very identity of Jesus, then, is reliant upon the Spirit. This, reasons Macchia, has significant implications, since it more robustly connects Word and Spirit together concerning their involvement in constituting the church, and providing it with its charismatic structure. Macchia actually critiques Moltmann for stressing the resurrection, and not Pentecost, as being the point at which the shift occurs from the Spirit anointing Christ to Christ giving the Spirit, since this potentially allows pneumatology to be subsumed to Christology.[261] This being the case, we might also assume Macchia

did not speak all that frequently concerning the Spirit, nevertheless advocates a strong Christological focus in his emphasis on Jesus as suffering Lord, and liberator—the Spirit presumably making the resurrected Jesus experience-able now in black communities and worship.

259. Congar, *Word and the Spirit*, 61.

260. Ibid., 93.

261. Macchia, "North American Response," 32–33; Macchia, "Spirit and Life," 125–26.

would encourage Congar to also place greater emphasis on the event of Pentecost, with its implications for Christology and ecclesiology.

Macchia's emphasis on Jesus' divinity being revealed through Pentecost might also challenge Jenson to rethink his point regarding Christ's identity being finalized in his death. Jenson does this, of course, to ensure Christ's identity is complete—not able to be manipulated by any other. Theologically and historically, however, Pentecost has shaped the church's understanding of Christ's divinity. This would not mean abandoning Jenson's point entirely, but understanding it within the fuller context of Pentecost. Such a move would still hold Word and Spirit firmly together, but would help avoid subordinating Spirit to Word. This subordination is something (bearing in mind Macchia's emphasis on the church's charismatic structure) that appears to be occurring with Jenson, who more or less restricts experience of the Spirit to the hearing of the Word in Scripture, and participation in the liturgical sacraments, which reduces the Spirit's role to more or less illumination of the Word and preservation of the gospel through the ordained teaching office. Macchia's portrayal of the Spirit/Word relationship with its foundation in Pentecost, then, has significant implications for vivifying church life.

The Church as Locus of the Spirit

It is noteworthy that the two theologians in our conversation who do accent Pentecost with regard to the Spirit's shaping of the church come from the Eastern Orthodox tradition—Lossky and Bulgakov—and both also see a link here between the Word and Spirit. Lossky and Bulgakov view Christ's Incarnation (assumption) as the bringing together of divine and human natures, thus overcoming, as Lossky puts it, the "barrier" of "nature."[262] Pentecost is the giving of divine "energies" to the church

---

Macchia also notes that Moltmann intentionally uses Pauline literature, as opposed to Luke and Acts, to develop his theology of charismata. Moltmann claims his reason for doing so was to avoid "an enthusiasm about the Spirit that goes beyond the presence of Christ." This is based on his belief that there was a diminishing Christological emphasis in the post-apostolic period in which Luke-Acts was composed (Moltmann, "Response," 66–67). Macchia is not convinced by Moltmann's argument in this regard, questioning his seeking of a history behind the text of Scripture.

262. Lossky, *Mystical Theology*, 135; cf. Bulgakov, *Sophia*, 100. A similar theme can also be seen in Jenson who speaks of Jesus overcoming the Creator/creature barrier (Jenson, *Systematic Theology: Triune*, 76–77).

(Lossky);[263] or the elevation of humanity (Bulgakov),[264] ultimately with the goal of divinization in mind. For Lossky, this means that the church is the "sphere" in which experience of the Spirit is located.[265]

Concerning this idea of the church as locus of the Spirit's work, several of our dialogue partners more or less concur with Lossky on this point, including Congar and Jenson. Macchia likewise strongly views the church as being the locus of the Spirit's work, its very existence being a necessary result of Spirit baptism. Moltmann would also see the church as the location of the gifts and energies of the Spirit, but is careful to qualify this (as does Macchia) within a larger kingdom framework. Bulgakov too, it will be recalled, situates experience of the Spirit in the church, but then expands the boundaries of the church to include the cosmos, thus blurring the lines between ecclesia and world. Cone and Johnson are less apt to want to (primarily) locate experience of the Spirit in the church. Cone at least would want to redefine what church is—namely, people participating in praxis on behalf of the oppressed for justice and liberation. Johnson does not view the (institutional) church as having been the location in which women have typically experienced the Spirit.

The matter of the degree to which the Spirit is located within the church is, of course, not unrelated to issues previously addressed concerning the immanence of the Spirit in creation.[266] But our concern here is the way in which the Spirit is experienced in-and through the church, and whether there is a means by which to help the diversity of perspectives, outlined above, find a way to come closer together. It is here that Macchia's emphasis on the Spirit-baptized charismatic structure of the church may prove to be a helpful way forward.

Macchia, again, places the church within a larger eschatological kingdom framework, which finds points of convergence with Moltmann, Johnson, and Cone's emphasis on a grander liberative work of the Spirit in history. The work of the Spirit is thus free, and not bound by institution. Yet Macchia also appreciates the sacramental, physical aspects of the Spirit's work in the church. Here we will recall his acknowledgment

263. Lossky, *Mystical Theology*, 133.

264. Bulgakov, *Sophia*, 100.

265. Lossky, *Mystical Theology*, 177.

266. A related question here is also whether the Spirit is at work in other faiths. Bulgakov, for example, mentions this, although qualifying revelation received by other religions as natural as opposed to direct. Macchia is open but cautious in this regard.

of (informal but nonetheless very real) Pentecostal corporate ritual in worship (Albrecht), and his focus on glossolalia as being sacramental in quality. Clearly he also values the sacramental traditions, calling Protestants (and Pentecostals) to a greater appreciation of these. Sacramental traditions, however, tend toward a more incarnational ecclesiology, emphasizing the church as the tangible body of Christ on earth. This emphasis was observed to be very strong in Jenson and Lossky, and Congar can likely also be included here as well (although he is more open to certain elements congruent with Macchia's charismatic structure, as we will see). Bulgakov similarly views the church in this way (calling it "theandric"),[267] but then extends the church's boundaries to the cosmos, again making it difficult to locate these precisely.

Macchia, however, believes that although it is correct to see Word and Spirit closely related to and within the church, a "church as incarnational" approach accents the wrong anointing of the Spirit upon Jesus. As discussed earlier in this chapter, he does not believe that the church shares the incarnational anointing of the Spirit upon Jesus, but rather it shares in Jesus' vocational, prophetic anointing (understanding this transfer of anointing as having occurred at Pentecost).[268] So, for Macchia, the church is both necessary and the locus of the Spirit, yet it is penultimate in the realization of the kingdom. This approach significantly broadens the scope of possibilities for the Spirit's dynamic activity in the church, including an emphasis on the Spirit's work among the laity (not only ordained clergy), through whom the church may even find itself prophetically called to reform. As Macchia reminds us, Spirit baptism is something that is experientially repeated in the churches, and not a one-time event simply transferred through the apostolic office.[269] Congar would appear to be open to this possibility as well; however, this would likely introduce more of a challenge to the ecclesiology of Jenson and Lossky.

267. Bulgakov, *Sophia*, 85.

268. Macchia, *Baptized in the Spirit*, 145. Macchia qualifies this, later stating that the church's authority is delegated, not transferred (ibid., 233).

269. Ibid., 261.

Pentecostal Theophanic and
Missional/Vocational Spirituality

This leads us to discuss one more emphasis related to Macchia's broadened Spirit baptism metaphor and the charismatic structure of the church, namely, Pentecostal theophanic, and missional/vocational spirituality. Several of our dialogue partners expressed considerable openness to the variety of charismata operating in the church, including Gelpi, Congar, and Moltmann. Lossky's and Bulgakov's emphasis on mystical, ineffable experience might also indicate openness in this regard. It may be that Macchia's sacramental theology of glossolalia (and ecstasy) would find some congruency here with Eastern Orthodoxy, with his emphasis on the limitation of human rationality to ultimately comprehend and express the fullness of meaning found in encounter with the presence of God in Spirit baptism. Experience of the eschatological Spirit is, in this sense, something beyond words, and yet by the Spirit, nevertheless, orally/aurally communicated.

More to the point, however, while Macchia has expanded Spirit baptism to encompass regeneration and initiation, he wants other church traditions to grow in appreciation for the empowering, vocational and prophetic emphasis of Spirit baptism (symbolically communicated by glossolalia). The experience of Spirit baptism in this sense is missional—a call to enter into the work of the Kingdom by the Spirit. Here, Macchia's framing this as a "second conversion" of sorts (utilizing the theology of the Blumhardts),[270] from God to the world, might serve as a helpful point of discussion. Gelpi, it will be recalled, also emphasizes conversion as the process by which human experience undergoes transformation. He also mentions religious conversion as being that which has the ability to transform all others, and this is perhaps congruent with Macchia's emphasis on the Spirit's possessing believers, transforming their lives radically, and thrusting them into kingdom service. Gelpi is amenable to such possibilities, noting that religious conversion includes expressions of prophetic empowerment and witness, although this is grounded in the immanence of the Spirit in creation, already discussed. Macchia's emphasis on the vocational empowerment element in Spirit baptism is, however, strongly linked to fellowship in the church, and so would challenge Johnson's and Cone's weaker emphasis in this regard.

270. Ibid., 280, cf. 279–82.

Finally, with Macchia's Spirit baptism emphasis we may find both a connection with and challenge to the Eastern Orthodox mystical theology and spirituality exemplified in Lossky and Bulgakov. By way of convergence we may recall Lossky's emphasis on openness to conscious awareness of God, as well as moments of "ecstasy" in prayer (and even the possibility of an ineffable beatific vision).[271] Further, humanities' vocation, for Lossky, is to unite creation with the divine (energies) through deification, requiring a synergistic (participatory) interaction between humans and God.[272] Bulgakov advocates similar themes, but with some notable differences, including a panentheistic union with God's essence (Sophia).

Such experiential and vocational emphases may very well find congruence with certain of Macchia's themes. We noted earlier Macchia's placing of Spirit baptism into a Trinitarian structure in which humanity is drawn into union with the koinonia of the Trinity. While this is not quite the same as Lossky's deification concept, it nevertheless stresses humans being caught up into relationship with God and ultimately God's complete relationship with creation when it is transformed "into the Temple of God's dwelling." The experiential elements noted above share resonance with Macchia's view of the kingdom (Spirit) as that which calls "forth powerful forms of experience and participation,"[273] as well as his accent on glossolalia as a form of ecstasy, expressing the incommunicable by the Spirit. "Tongues," states Macchia, "are the language of love, not reason."[274] There is room, then, for Macchia to advocate a mysticism of sorts as an aspect of Spirit baptism, and he notes that mystical language was even used among early Pentecostals at times to describe feelings of being overwhelmed and possessed by God.[275] He qualifies this type of "mystical encounter," however, in at least two ways.[276]

First, this type of mysticism does not imply loss of self-identity. Rather, in such experiences, "the distinction between us and God is not denied, only transcended momentarily by the Spirit as an illustration of God's solidarity with us in moments of need. In Pentecostal rhetoric,

---

271. Lossky, *Mystical Theology*, 42, 212, 220–21, 225.

272. Ibid., 117, 171.

273. Macchia, *Baptized in the Spirit*, 258.

274. Ibid., 257.

275. Ibid., 270. He cites C. H. Mason by way of example.

276. Ibid.

God takes possession of us, 'fills us' with the divine presence again and again through the renewing work of the Spirit. Spirit baptism is a kind of divine 'embrace.'"[277] Second, Macchia connects this type of Pentecostal mysticism with an eschatological hope; not one that is otherworldly or escapist, but one that propels believers to involvement in this world.[278] He believes Gerald T. Sheppard is correct in calling "Pentecostal experience 'shamanistic' for its emphasis on Spirit-possession as a deeply felt experience, except that in Pentecostal context this experience is appropriately understood as a prophetic empowerment for furthering the ministry of Jesus in the world."[279] Thus, Pentecostal mysticism brings one into relationship with God not only for ultimate unification's sake, but also for participation now with God in kingdom mission. It is with these qualifications that Macchia can speak of a Pentecostal mysticism.

There are some notable differences, then, in the way Christian spirituality is worked out between Lossky, Bulgakov, and Macchia. Lossky accents in particular that Christian vocation is worked out primarily in contemplation of the mystery of the Trinity, within the church through participation in worship (emphasizing prayer) and sacraments. Lossky does believe in the ultimate and mysterious transformation of the cosmos into union with God,[280] but toward this end human participation is not overtly advocated. So, there is little encouragement to connect spirituality to social transformation. It was precisely this disconnect between spirituality and the secular world that led Bulgakov to adopt his panentheistic sophiology. With Macchia's emphasis on Spirit baptism as vocational, however, he possibly provides a way forward for Lossky that does not require buying into the immanentism (in Bulgakov and others) that Macchia finds so problematic. The goal is similar—cosmic transformation in union with God;[281] and there is acknowledgement that

277. Ibid., 270–71. It should also be noted that Macchia's mysticism is not of the vacuous sort described in Schner's continuum, since it is clearly connected to the framework of the kingdom and the missions of Son and Spirit. Even on this point here we may find some congruency with Lossky's mysticism, which is also not empty, but functions only in relation to a particular (Eastern Orthodox) theological confession. I am indebted to David A. Reed for this latter observation.

278. Ibid., 269–70. Here Macchia advocates that Pentecostals must abandon any ties to dispensational eschatology in order to preserve an emphasis on a holistic this-worldly salvific emphasis. He identifies ties to Moltmann in this regard (ibid., 271–75).

279. Ibid., 271.

280. Lossky, *Mystical Theology*, 177.

281. Macchia, *Baptized in the Spirit*, 104. Macchia, however, does not advocate loss

the final transformation of creation requires an act of God, the return of the Christ the King. Through Spirit baptism as a "baptism into divine love,"[282] however, Macchia invites Lossky to experience the interruptive[283] eschatological Spirit *now* as a means by which to participate with the Spirit in the transformation of creation, while avoiding Bulgakov's immanent panentheism.

Conclusion

By way of summary, the above areas of conversation—God's relation to creation, self-revelation in history, the relationship of Word and Spirit, ecclesiology, and spirituality—all demonstrate that Macchia is a Pentecostal whose theology is able to engage the broader Christian theological traditions. Macchia not only exhibits a number of points of convergence with our dialogue partners in the above conversation, but also introduces considerable challenge for the churches to be open to the surprising and transformative work of the Spirit, through the "polycentric" expressions and channels of the Word that may come in unexpected and powerful ways. We have noted that Macchia's broadened metaphor of Spirit baptism as well as his accent on Word allows for these possibilities within the inaugurated eschatological kingdom of God, in which Christ is King and Spirit the kingdom. In doing so, Macchia serves as a prime example of maturation occurring within Pentecostal theology.

of the self in God (ibid., 270–71).

282. Ibid., 258.

283. Ibid., 95.

4

Simon K. H. Chan

Experiencing the Spirit through Tradition

THIS CHAPTER WILL EXPLORE THE WORK OF PENTECOSTAL THEOLO-
gian Simon K. H. Chan, focusing on the mediation of experience of
the Spirit through the Christian theological and spiritual tradition.[1]
Doing so will further support the general argument of this book, that
Pentecostalism is showing signs of theological maturation, able to listen
and contribute to the broader Christian theological community. The
method here will follow that of the previous chapter. The first section
will survey ways in which Chan attempts to integrate the mediation
of the Spirit through the broader Christian tradition with Pentecostal
theology. The second section will seek to identify aspects of convergence and divergence between Chan and our dialogue partners, so as
to further emphasize Pentecostalism's growing ability to contribute in
ecumenical conversation.

Chan and Pentecostal Experience of the Spirit

Chan wholeheartedly believes in the importance of Pentecostal expe-
rience, referring to this more broadly as the "Pentecostal reality." This
"Pentecostal reality" encompasses a "cluster of experiences which,
Pentecostals believe, distinguish them from other Christians." So, while
Pentecostals do not share consensus globally as to their distinctive

1. Chan holds credentials with the Assemblies of God (Singapore), is the Earnest
Lau Professor of Systematic Theology at Trinity Theological College in Singapore, serves
as editor of *Trinity Theological Journal*, and has authored numerous essays, and several
books.

doctrines, they do share emphasis on "a certain kind of spiritual experience of intense, direct and overwhelming nature centering in the person of Christ."[2] Such encounters (e.g., Spirit baptism) lead Pentecostals to "appropriate the work of the Spirit into their Christian lives" in a unique way, producing a distinctive type of spirituality. Chan believes, however, that Pentecostals are in danger of losing this spirituality, and need to learn better ways to preserve it.

Before exploring why Chan believes this is the case, it is important to understand that his concern is not simply for Pentecostals. More broadly, he is troubled by the state of Christian spirituality in general (specifically within Protestant evangelicalism), which has tended to bifurcate theology and spirituality (head and heart). Needed is a recovery of the lost concept of "spiritual theology" as a way of reintegrating these two elements, to produce a more holistic Christian spirituality.[3] A robust spiritual theology, Chan argues, requires three key criteria: it must be "global-contextual," "evangelical," and include a "Pentecostal-charismatic spirituality."[4]

We will return to the first two criteria later in this chapter in the ecumenical dialogue section. Concerning the third criterion, however, Chan believes that Christian history has, to its detriment, viewed "enthusiastic" spiritualities as an "aberration," and therefore unnecessary to the life of faith. The church has often neglected, ignored, or even spurned this important component, with its emphasis on the nonrational and intuitive, and the possibility of the Spirit introducing the "radically new," through an "awareness of and an openness to the 'surprising work of God,'" reminding believers that God is ultimately in control.[5] Pentecostal-

2. Chan, *Pentecostal Theology*, 7. Here Chan draws on Clark and Lederle's description of Pentecostal experience.

3. Chan wants to recover a theology that is less compartmentalized (i.e., systematic, biblical, etc.) and more holistically integrated into Christian life. He writes, "Spirituality is the lived reality, whereas spiritual theology is the systematic reflection and formalization of that reality. . . . In short, true theology arises from personal experience of God in Jesus Christ, and reflecting on the experience leads to a deeper experience or knowledge of God. . . . True theology is always doxological" (Chan, *Spiritual Theology*, 16–17).

4. On these criteria see ibid., 24–39. Chan entitles the latter the "charismatic criterion" (ibid., 37); however, we will use his term "Pentecostal-charismatic" (ibid., 39) throughout this chapter, since it accents Chan's affiliation.

5. Ibid., 37, 38. Chan adds, for hierarchical traditions like Roman Catholicism this can raise awareness that God can work "directly for the ordinary Christian right from the beginning of the Christian life." For Protestants, it challenges the sometimes rationalistic

charismatic spirituality cannot be dismissed or ignored; it is "an essential component of the Christian tradition."[6]

The "Pentecostal Reality": Necessities and Challenges

Chan is concerned, however, that Pentecostalism is losing its ability to infuse this dynamic component into broader Christianity. Pentecostals have deviated from their core values and are experiencing a "spiritual fatigue," including loss of "zeal and missionary vision." In response, Pentecostal denominations are exhibiting signs of "panic," exemplified in heightened dogmatism intended to secure self-preservation.[7] At the same time, Pentecostal adherents are too often given to chasing after new spiritual experiences, worship having become less about encounter with God and more focused on subjective feelings.[8] Combined with the growth in affluence of North American Pentecostals in particular, bemoans Chan, "the typical Pentecostal-charismatic church today is far from being a 'contrast community'; it is in fact the epitome of modern culture."[9]

Moreover, Chan believes that a key identity marker of Pentecostalism, the "initial evidence" doctrine, is "in tatters," traditional defense(s) of this belief having proven inadequate.[10] Drawing on

---

approaches taken to theology, as well as their typically "relational and ethical" understanding of "mystical union," potentially opening the way to more 'enthusiastic' aspects of spirituality. This emphasis, he argues, is not entirely foreign to Reformed Protestant tradition. Although often ignored, Calvin's location of mystical union with the beginning of Christian life holds such possibilities. Some seventeenth-century Puritans, such as John Cotton, used Calvin's pneumatology to emphasize a more conscious awareness of the Spirit (ibid., 38–39). Chan's PhD dissertation focused on Puritan ascetical spirituality (see Chan, "Puritan Meditative Tradition").

6. Chan, *Spiritual Theology*, 39.

7. Chan, *Pentecostal Theology*, 7, 8. Following Hollenweger, Chan believes the core of Pentecostal spirituality is best exemplified in the first five to ten years of the movement.

8. Ibid., 8, 9. Chan notes, for example, the recent penchant among Third Wave charismatics toward "magic" (attempting to manipulate spiritual power through prayer techniques), as well as an unhealthy adoration of mega-church leaders among Pentecostal-charismatics in general. Also see Chan, "Encountering the Triune," 224.

9. Chan, *Pentecostal Theology*, 8–9. Chan appears to have both North American and Asian Pentecostals in mind throughout his work. On Chan's hopes and concerns for Asian Pentecostalism in particular, see Chan, "Asian Pentecostalism," 29–32; and Chan, "Pneumatology of Paul Yonggi Cho," 79–99.

10. Chan, "Language Game," 81, cf. 82–83. Chan is aware of Robert P. Menzies' and

Lindbeck, Chan argues that traditional Pentecostal explanations of Spirit baptism (empowerment) and "initial evidence" were once appropriate for articulating the experiences of the Pentecostal subcultural-linguistic community—at least when such experiences were commonplace. But such explanations have proven woefully inadequate for transmitting the "Pentecostal reality" to subsequent generations, resulting in the depletion of Pentecostal experience. So, while Pentecostals desire to pass on their unique spirituality, it is becoming evident that they have been using resources ineffective for doing so. In short, summarizes Chan, the Pentecostal problem, then, is a "failure in traditioning," due to a reliance on inadequate theological constructs.[11] Pentecostals "must not be satisfied with just having an experience of the Spirit without an undergirding theology. Without a theology experience cannot be sustained for long."[12]

Chan believes this inability to tradition is directly tied to Pentecostal "lack of awareness of being part of the larger Christian tradition."[13] Pentecostals, in an effort to emphasize the Spirit's freedom, have often viewed church tradition pejoratively. But in rejecting the Christian theological and spiritual tradition (and tacitly the Spirit's mediation through this tradition), Pentecostals have unwittingly weakened their own ability to coherently and convincingly transmit the theological values and experiences they hold most dear.[14] This rejection is due to a misunder-

---

Roger Stronstad's attempts to establish a foundation for Pentecostal distinctive doctrines from an emphasis on Lukan pneumatology. He is unconvinced, however, that they have provided sufficient theological grounds for doing so, believing they have placed too much weight on a hermeneutic of "original intention," and ultimately have not (as Macchia also argued) sufficiently reintegrated Luke's pneumatology with Paul's.

11. Chan, *Pentecostal Theology*, 10. In particular, Chan identifies the doctrine of Spirit baptism as having been reduced, by Pentecostals, to an infusion of power; whereas he sees this as having broader meaning, as we shall see. Elsewhere, Chan states that Pentecostals are intuitively correct with regard to their primary theology (i.e., enacted worship and experience), but mistaken in their "explicit theology"—their systematic theology is weak (Chan, "Encountering the Triune," 216–17).

12. Chan, "Language Game," 81. Chan further believes that phenomenological analyses of Pentecostal experience are insufficient in themselves for determining the nature of the "Pentecostal reality" (Pentecostal experience). Pentecostals have always held to distinguishing theological beliefs as well, which is why Chan believes it important to carefully articulate and preserve Pentecostal beliefs theologically. He states, "I do not think that it is legitimate to call a movement Pentecostal solely on the basis of common experiences. There is, after all, no such thing as a religious experience without any theological interpretation" (Chan, "'Whither Pentecostalism?," 579, cf. 578–80).

13. Chan, *Pentecostal Theology*, 11.

14. Ibid., 22–23.

standing of how tradition functions, reasons Chan. Healthy tradition is not static but living, allowing for spontaneous development and change. Only when a tradition ceases to invite critical self-reflection (often motivated by insecurities and self-preservation) does stagnation set in. "In short, hazy theology is the bearer of dead traditionalism."[15]

Further obstacles exist concerning this idea of traditioning. Pentecostals have typically adopted an ahistorical view of experience of God (and spirituality), while tradition requires an appreciation of history.[16] Ahistoricism also tends to blind Pentecostals to the existence and influence of their own tradition(s). Asserts Chan, "The issue is not whether they have a tradition, but whether they have been effective in traditioning."[17] This situation is further exacerbated by Pentecostal propensity to view experience of the Spirit as an individual (private) matter, whereas "traditioning is by nature a communal affair."[18] Thus, lack of "critical self-reflection" has made it difficult for Pentecostals to accept the Christian dogmatic and spiritual tradition as a resource for articulating and transmitting the "Pentecostal reality."[19]

Historically, observes Chan, Pentecostals have relied on "powerful narratives" (testimony) to transmit their beliefs and experiences. But such "oral traditioning is no longer effective in a world that has rapidly moved from an oral-aural culture to print culture and from a print to visual and electronic 'sensoria.'"[20] What is needed is for Pentecostals to begin to appreciate the Christian tradition as a resource that can provide

---

15. Ibid., 17. Here we may recall Chan's characterization of Pentecostal denominations as being in a state of panic, exemplified by increasingly rigid dogmatism. This is why Chan can say, "Pentecostals do have a tradition, even if many of them are avowedly opposed to the idea" (ibid., 20).

16. Ibid., 20; cf. Chan, "Encountering the Triune," 224.

17. Chan, *Pentecostal Theology*, 20.

18. Ibid., 17.

19. Ibid., 24.

20. Ibid. Here Chan also identifies other points of weakness making it difficult for Pentecostals to appreciate the concepts of tradition and traditioning. Two are noteworthy: First, Pentecostal official statements concerning Scripture are often far more rigid (due to the influence of evangelicalism) than the way Pentecostals actually use the Bible (which Chan sees as being closer to Barth's view—"the Word of revelation exists in a dialectical relationship to the words of Scripture") (ibid., 21). Second, they also allowed their early ecumenical vision to deteriorate, leading to less openness to seeing the Christian dogmatic and spiritual tradition as a resource for theology and spirituality (ibid., 22–23).

the conceptual tools for traditioning their own spirituality.[21] Locating themselves within the broader historical Christian tradition, Chan argues, will actually help Pentecostals preserve their identity and pass on their valued experiences more effectively, even enabling the "Pentecostal reality" to be more readily received by and enrich the church universal.[22]

This may not be as big a stretch for Pentecostals as might be assumed. Chan notes that since Pentecostals already emphasize the affective aspects of spirituality, they are predisposed toward a spiritual theology that integrates head and heart, and which views theological reflection as a form of prayer.[23] A "spiritual theology" approach, then, will help preserve the "Pentecostal reality," so long as it satisfies three conditions. First, Chan submits, Pentecostals must commit to reflecting on Pentecostal beliefs and experience within the broader sphere of the Christian dogmatic and spiritual tradition. It is the Christian tradition, particularly the doctrine of the Trinity, that actually identifies (distinguishes) Christianity, of which Pentecostals are a part. Chan affirms, "Whether we are Pentecostals, Protestant, Catholic, or Orthodox we are Trinitarians."[24] Further, while Pentecostal spirituality is one important component in the Christian tradition, it is not *everything* of what it means to be Christian. "Thus Pentecostal spirituality is best understood within and sustained by the church catholic (or universal), since it is the distinctive task of the third person of the Trinity to realize the church . . . The church is where His distinctive identity is revealed."[25]

The second condition Chan posits is that Pentecostals must view the Spirit as integrally linked to, and involved in the traditioning process within, the *visible* church. Chan states, "The popular notion that

21. Ibid., 11, 24–31; cf. Chan, "Renewal of Pentecostalism," 315–25.

22. Chan, *Pentecostal Theology*, 11, 29–30. Pentecostals, states Chan, need to realize that theology actually helps preserve identity: "the creeds ensure that the church's basic identity is faithfully transmitted through history."

23. Ibid., 28–32. Chan is drawing on Steven Land's emphasis on Pentecostal affections and orthopathy.

24. Ibid., 32. Chan states, "Pentecostal spirituality is essentially affective trinitarianism" (ibid., 33). Here Chan notes that a more healthy Trinitarian theology might help Pentecostals overcome some unhealthy extremes within the movement, including a fixation on power. This problem is caused due to a failure to appreciate that the Christian tradition has emphasized the Spirit not as the focus of, but means through which, Christians worship (ibid., 33–34).

25. Chan, "Encountering the Triune," 222. Chan suggests that early Pentecostals intuitively recognized this truth, exemplified in their initial ecumenical impulse.

the Spirit is opposed to tradition could not have been further from the truth." Tradition is an ongoing work of the Spirit, requiring recognition of the historical embeddedness of dogma and spirituality, and the continuing development of doctrine. Implied here also is that the church needs to be viewed as the locus of the Spirit's activity in the world.[26]

As a third condition, Pentecostals need to reconsider *how* they worship, since it is theology and practice together that form "the primary traditioning act."[27] A more robust liturgy, in other words, is necessary to sustain a stronger ecclesiology.[28] Chan advocates a Eucharist-centered liturgy as being able to unite both the "Pentecostal-charismatic" and "evangelical" (proclamation-centered) emphases, leading to true encounter with God in worship.[29] Having briefly surveyed these three basic conditions necessary for preserving the "Pentecostal reality," in order to better appreciate Chan's emphasis on the Christian dogmatic and spiritual tradition as mediating experience of the Spirit, his second condition—namely, his ecclesiology and its relationship to the dogmatic traditioning process—requires further elucidation.

The Ontology of the Church: The Locus of the Spirit

Chan believes Pentecostalism's future (including its capacity to contribute ecumenically) depends on its ability to tradition itself, which can only be successfully accomplished by consciously locating itself within the historic Christian dogmatic and spiritual tradition. He writes, "Attitudes can be reshaped only by a strong traditioning community; essentials are discovered in the Great Tradition of the church—the 'one, holy, catholic, and apostolic' church—that all Christians profess to believe in; and only within a church that is Catholic and alive are truths traditioned and received as living faith and not as abstract ideas and propositions."[30] The

---

26. Chan, *Pentecostal Theology*, 35; cf. Chan, "Encountering the Triune," 221–22, 224–25.

27. Chan, *Pentecostal Theology*, 36.

28. Chan, "Encountering the Triune," 225–26.

29. Chan, *Pentecostal Theology*, 36–38.

30. Chan, *Liturgical Theology*, 11. Chan believes that not only Pentecostalism, but also broader evangelicalism needs to reconnect with the historical church tradition in order to ensure its survival. It is largely evangelicalism that Chan seems to have in view in *Liturgical Theology* (also see interviews with Chan in this regard: Galli, "Stopping Cultural Drift"; and Crouch, "Mission of the Trinity").

way forward, then, is through a more robust ecclesiology, prioritizing the ontology of the church, which can provide proper context for the traditioning of dogma and spirituality.

Chan's fullest development of church ontology is found in *Liturgical Theology*, where he argues that ecclesial life must be seen as "existing in perichoretic union with the triune God through the Spirit."[31] This approach is contrasted with two other interrelated trends Chan views as being exemplified in contemporary Protestantism. The first is the trend of defining the church sociologically. This trend prioritizes individuals, and the church therefore exists as a result of the coming together of believers who make up the church.[32] In this perspective, koinonia is a result of humans uniting for "a common purpose," the product of human, not divine action.[33] The second interrelated trend Chan identifies is an "instrumentalist view," in which biblical history is understood as a linear "creation-fall-redemption-consummation narrative."[34] In this view "Creation becomes the basis for understanding the nature and role of the church. The church is only a subspecies of creation and must discover the clue to its identity within the created order."[35] Put another way, "the Church derives its basic identity from creation. Christian experience becomes only a specification of a larger human religious consciousness."[36]

In some cases, Chan observes, this latter view is associated with a particular understanding of *Creator Spiritus* that universalizes the Spirit's presence out of concern for, among other things, inter-religious dialogue and participation in liberative political movements.[37] Chan believes this approach does not sufficiently preserve the identity of the Spirit (which will serve as a significant point of discussion in our later dialogue). So, in

---

31. Chan, *Liturgical Theology*, 14. Here Chan acknowledges he is following up on the trajectory of the ecclesiology of Stanley Grenz. While *Liturgical Theology* contains the fullest expression of Chan's ecclesiology, he develops similar ideas elsewhere (see Chan, "Mother Church," 177–208; Chan, *Pentecostal Theology*, 97–119; Chan, *Spiritual Theology*, 102–22; and Chan, "Church and the Development," 62–66).

32. Chan, *Liturgical Theology*, 24; Chan, "Mother Church," 177.

33. Chan, "Mother Church," 179, cf. 178. One consequence of this is the tendency of the church to view itself as existing, more or less, to meet individuals' spiritual needs (see Chan, *Liturgical Theology*, 24; and cf. Chan, *Spiritual Theology*, 37).

34. Chan, *Liturgical Theology*, 21, cf. 25.

35. Ibid., 22; cf. Chan, "Encountering the Triune," 219.

36. Chan, "Church and the Development," 62.

37. Chan, *Pentecostal Theology*, 111, cf. 110–16; cf. Chan, "Mother Church," 196–208.

contrast to the sociological and instrumentalist trends, "A better way to conceptualize the Bible's narrative coherence is to see creation as forming the backdrop for God's elective grace and covenant relationship rather than vice versa. God created the world in order that he might enter into covenant relationship with humankind."[38] Here, the church is viewed as being logically prior to creation, "chosen in Christ before the creation of the world." Thus, declares Chan, "God made the world in order to make the church, not vice versa."[39] Creation is the means by which grace is realized, and the destiny of human beings is to be more than simply creatures but "God's people, living in full knowledge of and relationship with God as Father, Son and Holy Spirit."[40]

Prioritizing the church over creation has two implications for Chan. First, the church "does not have a purely creaturely existence, and second, its basic identity is to be found not in what it *does* but in what it *is*."[41] In other words, the emphasis is not on ecclesial function but *ontology*—the church possesses a unique spiritual identity. Says Chan:

> It is, according to Sergius Bulgakov, a "divine-humanity" because of its organic link with its Head, Christ. This organic unity between Christ, the Head, with his Body, the Church, is usually designated by the term *totus Christus* (the total Christ). The Church is prior to creation precisely because it is the Body of *Christ*, the second person of the Trinity, and its *historical* existence is brought about by the action of the Holy Spirit. The Spirit's presence in the Church is by virtue of the latter being a divine-humanity.[42]

This "ontological status" means for Chan that the church should be viewed as "Mother church";[43] it "owes its existence to the action of the

---

38. Chan, *Liturgical Theology*, 22.

39. Ibid., 23.

40. Ibid., 22–23. Here Chan adopts the Eastern Orthodox view that Jesus' assumption was not simply for the purpose of eradicating sin; rather, the Incarnation was always planned to enable true communion between humanity and Trinity. Sin is overcome for the church to come into existence, but sin is not the reason for the church's existence.

41. Ibid., 23 (italics original). Chan cites Robert Jenson, seeing creation as the "raw material" God uses to "bring the church to perfection in Christ. The church is not an entity within the larger culture but *is* a culture" (italics original).

42. Chan, "Church and the Development," 63 (italics original). Cf. Chan, *Liturgical Theology*, 23; and Chan, "Mother Church," 177–78.

43. Chan, *Liturgical Theology*, 24. Elsewhere Chan states, the church is "a spiritual, transcendent and organic reality (mother church) . . ." (Chan, "Mother Church," 179).

triune God," and is therefore the creation of God, not humans.[44] Therefore, "We are not saved as individuals first and then incorporated into the church; rather to be a Christian is to be incorporated into the church by baptism and merged with the spiritual food of the body and blood of Christ in the Eucharist."[45] This concept of the church has implications that Chan hopes "will significantly shape Pentecostal spirituality."[46] In brief, it will entail that Pentecostals (and Protestants) adopt an "*ecclesial pneumatology rather than an individual pneumatology. . . . That is to say, the primary locus of the work of the Spirit is not the individual Christian but in the church.*"[47] To further explain the church's ontological status as "divine-humanity," Chan utilizes the three principal biblical images for the church: the people of God, body of Christ, and temple of the Spirit.

As the people of God, states Chan, the church shares continuity with the people of Israel; the church does not supersede Israel, nor will it be superseded—it is not merely a useful instrument for the restoration of creation. Of course, Chan admits, the church is a people with a "history of up's and downs, of successes and failures"; it is "a pilgrim church, a church on the way, a church that has not quite arrived." As a visible reality, it "is always a mixed body . . . made up of genuine believers and unbelievers until the final Eschaton."[48] But what distinguishes the people of God are its "core practices," the "marks of the church. . . . In sum, the people of God are distinguished by their faith in Jesus Christ, and the unique quality of their community by faithfulness to that gospel."[49]

44. Chan, "Mother Church," 178.

45. Chan, *Liturgical Theology*, 24.

46. Chan, "Mother Church," 179.

47. Chan, *Pentecostal Theology*, 99 (italics original). Chan states elsewhere, "A basic problem in Pentecostalism is that it is hardly aware of this communal context of Spirit baptism. The Pentecostal reality has tended to be understood as individualized experiences. My relationship with God is primary, while my relationship with others is secondary. But the truth of the matter is that we cannot conceive of fellowship with God apart from fellowship in God through the Spirit. There is no question of priority. Our relationship with the triune God at once brings us into the fellowship with the saints, since no real communion with God as possible without our being baptized into the body of Christ, the church. Yet all too often Pentecostals are more concerned with their 'personal Pentecost' than with the corporate reality of which each person has his share" (Chan, "Mother Church," 180–81).

48. Chan, *Liturgical Theology*, 26, cf. 24–26. Contrary to a Free Church model that assumes a "pure church," Chan adopts the idea of a "remnant" operating within the visible church. On this also see Chan, *Spiritual Theology*, 105–7.

49. Chan, *Liturgical Theology*, 26–27.

The ontological reality of the church as divine-humanity is best exemplified, however, by the image of the body of Christ, which is no mere metaphor for Chan. The church "is an ontological reality, as Christ is ontologically real."[50] During Christ's absence, between the ascension and parousia, "The church could therefore be said to be an extension of Christ, the way, the truth and the life, on earth."[51] Viewing the church as *totus Christus* has significant implications. It means communion is based on incorporation into the body by the Spirit, through which the church "becomes one body of Christ by eating and drinking the body and blood of Christ." This accent on "ecclesial communion [as] first and foremost an essentially eucharistic communion," implies that church hierarchy (oft feared by Protestants) is subsumed to shared koinonia.[52] Chan does believe that hierarchical structure is what most effectively traditions Christian identity,[53] but "the primary focus of the collegial life is not church hierarchy but *koinonia* characterized by *agape*."[54]

The image of temple of the Spirit, says Chan, highlights the church's connection to Christ by the Spirit, and participation in the history of the Trinitarian economy. "If the church is the body of Christ, the divine-humanity grounded in the narrative of the triune God, the Spirit's relation to the church explains how this body is constituted as a vibrant communion. It is the Spirit that links the church to Christ its Head, making it the body of Christ, the *totus Christus*." As temple of the Spirit, the church is a living tradition "moving inexorably toward its appointed End."[55] The Spirit constitutes the church, but also grants its dynamic, ongoing eschatological character. Further for Chan, that the Spirit is the eschatological Spirit (given from the future) is significant not only for the character of the church, but also because it is precisely in the Spirit's being poured out at Pentecost that its identity as "Third Person of the Trinity," is made

50. Ibid., 27.

51. Ibid., 28. Chan qualifies that the church is also distinct from Christ. Here he draws on Jenson's distinction between the church as Christ's "community" (accenting identity) and "association" (accenting distinction).

52. Ibid., 29.

53. Chan, "Mother Church," 181–84.

54. Chan, *Liturgical Theology*, 29 (italics original). Chan quotes Bulgakov in this regard, affirming, "First the church then the hierarchy, not vice versa" (cf. Bulgakov, *Bride of the Lamb*, 281). Being Christ's body also has implications concerning how Christian tradition is to be understood, and this will be explored in more detail shortly.

55. Chan, *Liturgical Theology*, 32 (italics original), cf. 31–32.

clear.[56] "Pentecost is the birth of the church not as the people of God but as the body of Christ and temple of the Spirit."[57] Pentecost, then, becomes (should be understood as) a defining event in the triune economy.

The Spirit is thus the gift of the Father, but "also the *giver* of gifts," making "the whole church a charismatic community"—a point that Pentecostals have helped the church more fully appreciate.[58] Pentecost further emphasizes the church's catholicity, uniting diverse people into one body, overcoming social, cultural, and racial barriers, while yet affirming plurality. States Chan, "real diversity exists side-by-side with real unity" in a body with many parts.[59] Further, this "catholicity has to do *primarily* with the wholeness of the local congregation that gathers together to share the one loaf regardless of race, culture or sex."[60] The church needs, then, to be visible; and this was something appreciated in the ecumenical impulse of early Pentecostals, but later quickly abandoned (especially as Pentecostals aligned themselves with fundamentalists).[61] There is, however, another significant implication to Pentecost that helps explain the nature of traditioning within the church. The Spirit not only constitutes the church, says Chan, but "the action of the Spirit in the church is ongoing and dynamic."[62] This point warrants further exploration.

56. Ibid., 32, 33; cf. Chan, "Mother Church," 184.

57. Chan, *Liturgical Theology*, 33. Again, it is Jenson, notes Chan, who concurs with Eastern Orthodoxy in viewing Pentecost as an intervention of the Trinity against the resurrection, thus giving the Spirit its own identity.

58. Ibid., 34 (italics original). Chan notes that even prior to the Roman Catholic charismatic renewal in 1967, some within that tradition, such as Congar and Rahner, were already emphasizing the church as "the *charismatic* body of Christ" (Chan, "Mother Church," 179; italics original).

59. Chan, *Liturgical Theology*, 34.

60. Chan, "Mother Church," 185 (italics original).

61. Ibid., 185–86. Chan observes that this ecumenical impulse was especially evident in William Seymour, who viewed glossolalia as not simply a sign of having had a specific spiritual experience, but as "a symbol of God bringing together into one body people from every conceivable background" (ibid., 186). Chan suggests that white Pentecostals later downplayed the contribution of black Pentecostals in the formation of the movement, which may be related to the loss of some of these types of emphases (ibid., 186–87).

62. Ibid., 184.

The Spirit, Pentecost, and Traditioning

For Chan, that Pentecost historically constituted the church means the church is, consequentially, an extension of Christ the "Truth";[63] and the Spirit operating in and through the church effects a dynamic "Truth-traditioning community."[64]

> [T]he action of the Spirit not only constitutes the church dynamically, it also makes the church the place where truth exists dynamically. This means the connection between Christ the Truth, the Head of the church, and the tradition of the church is far more profound than is usually acknowledged in Protestantism. Christ who is the truth is not just an individual, historical person, but is also the truth in relation to the church as his body. The church is therefore an extension of Christ the truth. The ongoing traditioning in the church of Christ the truth is made possible by the action of the Spirit.[65]

The Spirit in the church subjectively embodies the "way, the truth and the life in the church which is the embodied Christ."[66] Thus, the church experiences the Spirit tacitly or implicitly. Writes Chan, "There is a 'givenness' in her experience of God. Or to put it in the more familiar Barthian terms: the Church's experience arises from the givenness of revelation."[67] So, experience of God should not be understood individualistically (as in Free Church traditions, including Pentecostalism), but ecclesially.[68] This "ecclesial experience" is more than the sum of individual experiences of God and community. "It is the experience of being the Body of Christ, the Temple of the Spirit, the divine humanity or, to use an earlier phrase, the Church as *totus Christus*. In other words, because the Church is the body of Christ, it is the place in which truth exists dynamically as the Church at worship addresses God through Jesus Christ in the Spirit. Ecclesial experience refers to the Church's engagement with the gospel narrative which reveals the essential identities of the triune God."[69]

---

63. Chan, *Liturgical Theology*, 35.

64. Chan, "Mother Church," 190–93; Chan, *Pentecostal Theology*, 106–8.

65. Chan, *Pentecostal Theology*, 106; cf. Chan, "Mother Church," 190.

66. Chan, *Liturgical Theology*, 35.

67. Chan, "Church and the Development," 64.

68. Ibid., 66; cf. Chan, "Mother Church," 190.

69. Chan, "Church and the Development," 66 (italics original).

This ecclesial experience of the Spirit, Chan argues, is lived out historically, beginning at Pentecost and embodied in the tradition. Since the church is divine-humanity by the Spirit, this history includes a "vertical," supernatural dimension,[70] and the Spirit's operation in the church means the church produces "spiritual effects," one of which is the development of doctrine.[71] Doctrines, however, are not the result of the church reflecting on its own experience. Rather, the church, as the Spirit-vivified "Tradition *embodies* a living developing dogma."[72] Chan summarizes, "The presence of the Spirit makes ecclesial experience a truly living tradition. The living tradition of the Church may be defined as the transmission and development of the gospel of Jesus Christ in the on-going practices of the Church through the power of the Spirit."[73]

The above definition contains three components, each of which merits some discussion. First, Chan states that the gospel is the "content of the living tradition";[74] it does not exist merely as a "static deposit or timeless propositions" to which the church bears witness, but needs to be viewed "*as* the living Tradition."[75] The gospel *continues* "into ecclesiology and pneumatology."[76] So, "The Rule of Faith is not a formalized creed of the doctrinal corpus that faithfully preserves the apostolic preaching concerning Jesus Christ. The Rule embodies the authoritative content of the gospel of Jesus Christ. That is what makes it authoritative."[77] Further, reasons Chan, the Rule of Faith bears its authority precisely because "it is in *historic* continuity with the apostles."[78] Even the teaching of Scripture must be verified by "being shown to be historically transmitted from the apostles to the Church and subsequent generations, in short, the tradition."[79] The Rule of Faith as part of the dynamic ongoing life of the

---

70. Ibid., 67; Chan, "Mother Church," 192.

71. Chan, "Church and the Development," 64.

72. Chan, *Liturgical Theology*, 35 (italics added).

73. Chan, "Church and the Development," 67.

74. Ibid., 67–69.

75. Chan, *Liturgical Theology*, 35 (italics added).

76. Ibid., 36.

77. Chan, "Church and the Development," 67.

78. Ibid., 67 (italics original).

79. Ibid., 68, cf. 69. Chan realizes that this is not likely to be palatable to Protestants, since it implies an apostolic succession of sorts. He insists, however, that the link to the apostles must be historic, and not merely spiritual (ahistorical), which he considers to be a form of Gnosticism. Further, he notes that even evangelicals, when faced with chal-

church implies that it continues to develop—the Christian theological and spiritual tradition is living, not dead.[80] The church, then, by virtue of its link to the apostles, embodies the gospel.

Second, Chan argues, the gospel (as content of the living tradition) is preserved through the church's "Core Practices."[81] This view finds support in the phrase "*lex orandi est lex credendi*" (the rule of prayer is the rule of faith), which emphasizes the dynamic relationship existing between worship and dogma.[82] While doctrine does influence worship, this is not a one-way relationship (as Protestants might assume); rather, a dialectical rapport exists between liturgy and dogma.[83] In worship the church practices "primary theology," the liturgy tacitly expressing communal beliefs.[84] Thus, the liturgy, properly enacted through the "core practices,"[85] is the "equivalent of the apostolic witness to the paradigmatic encounter with Jesus Christ and is the basis of all subsequent belief."[86] It is a concrete means of expressing the gospel,[87] which responds to and reveals "*God's total character*,"[88] and has historically affected the shape of Christian doctrine.[89] Chan writes, "In this sense the rule of prayer *is* the rule of belief. The theology that is embodied in the *ordo* is called primary

---

lenging issues concerning doctrine, appeal to early church dogma, thus tacitly admitting to a form of apostolic succession.

80. Chan believes Pentecostals need especially to heed this point, since of late they have begun to "canonize" certain points in their own history, which are in danger of "fossilization" (Chan, "Encountering the Triune," 221).

81. Chan, "Church and the Development," 69, cf. 69–72.

82. Chan, *Liturgical Theology*, 48 (italics original), cf. 49; cf. Chan, "Church and the Development," 66.

83. Chan, "Church and the Development," 66; Chan, *Liturgical Theology*, 48, cf. 49.

84. Chan, *Liturgical Theology*, 48, 50; Chan, "Church and the Development," 69.

85. Chan, "Church and the Development," 69. It is important to note that for Chan not just any order of service can qualify as the rule of prayer (authentic Christian worship): "There are certain constitutive marks that make the Church the Church." Through these the Spirit concretely works to fulfill its own "sanctifying mission in the triune economy of salvation." Chan spends considerable space in *Liturgical Theology* outlining what true worship should look like (Chan, *Liturgical Theology*, 62–84).

86. Chan, *Liturgical Theology*, 49.

87. Chan, "Church and the Development," 69; Chan, *Liturgical Theology*, 48.

88. Chan, *Liturgical Theology*, 56 (italics original), cf. 52–61.

89. Ibid., 49. Here Chan cites the example of the doctrine of the Trinity, which "emerged from the early church's experience of worship and the Persons' distinct roles were expressed in its doxology: to the Father, through the Son and in the Holy Spirit."

theology because it is immediate to the divine-human encounter, an integrated or personal knowledge—the knowledge of God."[90]

At the same time, asserts Chan, primary theology elicits and requires critical reflection (secondary theology); doctrines do, in fact, help shape, regulate, and preserve the practices of the church.[91] "One could say that critical reflection arises ineluctably from the experience and, in a very decisive way, is determined by the experience. Yet it is only when the experience is reflected upon and made explicit that it can function effectively as a norm, that is, become liturgical *theology*. . . . Secondary liturgical theology seeks to explain as fully as possible this primary experience of the church in its encounter with God which is expressed in its public act of worship . . . [making] explicit what worshipers know mostly in an implicit or tacit way."[92]

Primary theology, then, depends upon secondary theology for articulating (explaining) the practices, creating a norm in order to preserve the church, and keeping her from false practice.[93] Yet, believes Chan, right worship must always and ultimately be the focus of secondary theology to avoid substituting right doctrines for right practice, leading to the abstraction of belief and potentially leading the church into error.[94] Doctrine and worship must be held together. Worship is not to be merely preliminary to the preaching of the Word (as often in evangelicalism). Nor is the emphasis to be simply on creating a worshipful atmosphere (as often in Pentecostal-charismatic services), since unregulated worship will eventually produce unorthodox belief. Therefore, says Chan, "Right belief and right practice (*orthopraxis*) can only come from right worship (*orthodoxia*), and vice versa."[95]

Third, reasons Chan, because the gospel (as content of the living tradition) is transmitted in and through the worship and dogma of the church, this implies there is a continuing and necessary "development of

---

90. Ibid., 50 (italics original).

91. Chan, "Church and the Development," 69; Chan, *Liturgical Theology*, 49, 50.

92. Chan, *Liturgical Theology*, 51 (italics original).

93. Ibid., 61. For example, worship constructed simply to meet human need is a "primary theology. But it is a false theology, because it distorts our vision of the divine glory."

94. Ibid., 51. This interconnection between worship and doctrine means that secondary theology should not be done outside of the worshipping community. The work of the theologian is to be done for and within the church (see Chan, "Church and the Development," 70–72).

95. Chan, *Liturgical Theology*, 52 (italics original).

doctrine in the power of the Spirit."[96] Recalling that Pentecost shapes the church's ontology, the church, then, by the Spirit, is included in and the location of the ongoing triune life of the Godhead; for it is only within the church that Christ is present eucharistically until the parousia.[97] "The story of the Church, therefore, could be said to be the story of the Spirit in the Church. In this sense, the Church could be called 'the polity of the Spirit.' That is why Pentecost is so vital to the continuing development of the Christian story."[98] The gospel does not end with the resurrection and ascension (a typical Protestant and evangelical emphasis), states Chan, but rather continues "into ecclesiology and pneumatology."[99] Hence, "the Church is not just an agent of the gospel, but also *part of the gospel story itself*. If this is the case, then the very life of the church on earth as it moves toward the eschaton is the continuation of the gospel story."[100]

Because the Spirit's work in the church is ongoing, the doctrines of the living tradition continue to develop, akin to the progression of a narrative.[101] Explains Chan, "The progress of dogma has the character of a plot, the ongoing story of God's action in the world, and the story of the church is part of the development."[102] Within this plot the Spirit guides the church into truth and preserves her from error, her story being historically continuous with the gospel of the apostles.[103] The "development of dogma does not lead the church astray," since it is not determined by the contingencies of history.[104] Rather, the development of doctrine "follows the trajectory of the Gospel events: Christ's life → death → resurrection → ascension → Pentecost → parousia."[105] The dogma of the church is thus preserved by the "Spirit of the Eschaton, the one who anticipates the End, who reveals something of the end to us, and who guarantees the Church's fulfillment of its intended end."[106]

96. Chan, "Church and the Development," 72, cf. 72–75.

97. Ibid., 72.

98. Ibid., 73; cf. Chan, *Liturgical Theology*, 35.

99. Chan, *Liturgical Theology*, 36; cf. Chan, "Church and the Development," 73.

100. Chan, "Church and the Development," 72 (italics original).

101. Ibid., 72–73.

102. Chan, *Liturgical Theology*, 35; cf. Chan, "Church and the Development," 73.

103. Chan, "Church and the Development," 74.

104. Chan, *Liturgical Theology*, 35; cf. Chan, "Church and the Development," 73. Chan cites Jenson in this regard.

105. Chan, *Liturgical Theology*, 35.

106. Chan, "Church and the Development," 72. In regard to the Spirit as an escha-

The above discussion strongly implies that experience of the Spirit must be understood in relation to ecclesiology. For Chan, the church's formation on Pentecost explicitly reveals the "distinctive role of the Spirit in the triune economy of salvation"; but conversely, the church is given identity by the Spirit. This relationship can be described as "pneumatological ecclesiology (when the Church is viewed as the Spirit-filled Church) and as ecclesiological pneumatology (when the Spirit is seen as taking an ecclesial shape and function)."[107] Only when ecclesiology and pneumatology are thus held together can the living tradition be preserved, and the church continue to grow into fullness as the body of Christ.[108] The church's mission, then, is simply an extension of the mission of the Trinity.[109] Chan states, this mission "could be summed up as nothing but the mission of the Spirit in the church. The church's very existence could be described as the Spirit's constantly pushing the body of Christ forward toward the parousia, the final fulfillment."[110] The church does not exist, then, for "soul-winning," or to fulfill some other goal for creation. Rather, "The goal is to be the church as the full people of God . . . uniting all in Christ," realized through the ongoing practice of a Eucharist-centered liturgy, and shaped by the nature of the Trinitarian economy.[111]

tological presence in the church see Chan, *Liturgical Theology*, 36–39; Chan, "Mother Church," 193–96; and Chan, *Pentecostal Theology*, 108–16.

107. Chan, "Church and the Development," 74. Here writes Chan, "Pentecost is all about the third person of the Godhead taking on ecclesial form and being revealed as the third person." Thus, "There is no ecclesiology without pneumatology, and there is no *proper* pneumatology without ecclesiology" (italics original). Elsewhere Chan states there is a sense in which the church as "temple gives shape to the Spirit" (Chan, "Mother Church," 182).

108. Chan, "Church and the Development," 75. Chan states, "The Church in its worship, or practices, and reflection, will continue to grow in the grace and knowledge of her Lord and Savior Jesus Christ. The articulation of that knowledge constitutes the development of doctrine."

109. Crouch, "Mission of the Trinity."

110. Chan, *Liturgical Theology*, 39.

111. Ibid., 40, cf. 39–40. Creation is consummated, then, in the church, when the people of God enjoy "deification," communion with the Trinity. Space does not permit further discussion on the mission of the church and the Eucharist. It is clear, however, that Chan views the church's mission as simply consisting in growing into its ontology (so to speak). For example, he states, "The essential nature of mission is for the church to be the *body* of Christ. . . . We can be available to other persons only as embodied beings, and the church as *totus Christus* is the embodied Christ made available to the world" (ibid., 39; italics original). Also, "The church's primary mission, then, is to be

We noted earlier that Chan believes Pentecostalism's future depends on satisfying three interrelated conditions: integrating their theology and spirituality within the larger dogmatic and spiritual tradition, recognizing the integral link between Spirit and church (including the Spirit's ongoing work in doctrinal development), and reconsidering the nature of worship within a liturgical framework. In short, since experience of the Spirit is mediated through the living Christian tradition, Pentecostals must become more "catholic."[112] "Thus," states Chan, "Pentecostal spirituality is best understood within and sustained by the church catholic (or universal), since it is the distinctive task of the third person of the Trinity to realize the church."[113] Pentecostals, then, must locate themselves within the "Great Tradition," for only by doing so will Pentecostal identity (the "Pentecostal reality") be preserved. So far, this survey has demonstrated *why* Chan believes such a move is necessary (and possible). What still remains to be seen is *how* Chan believes Pentecostalism will be practically and positively affected by doing so, and he provides several examples to this end.

Pentecostals and Ongoing Revelation

The first example will be brief, but it is important. The idea that the Spirit continues to speak in and through the tradition of the church is, argues Chan, congruent with what Pentecostals already intuitively believe concerning the ongoing revelatory work of the Spirit. Pentecostals insist that the truth the Spirit brings (through Scripture, charismatic speech, and such) is "supernatural," meaning that God's Word cannot be "relativized" to history or human reason.[114] Further, the Spirit continues to speak to

---

itself, which is to be "Christ" for the world" (ibid., 40). Concerning the centrality of worship toward the fulfilling of the church's mission, as well as the shape of the liturgy around the Eucharist, see *Liturgical Theology*, 41–61, 62–84 respectively.

112. Chan, "Church and the Development," 76–77.

113. Chan, "Encountering the Triune," 222. Chan believes this is possible due to the early Pentecostal ecumenical impulse, but this is not without challenges. He states here, "This catholic tendency, however, is being threatened from two opposite directions. One is to subsume the Pentecostal Movement under a narrowly defined evangelicalism; the other is to diffuse the Spirit into the world. The first undermines the ecumenical breath of the Pentecostal Movement; the second undermines its dogmatic specificity."

114. Chan, "Mother Church," 192. Chan believes this is why early Pentecostals sided with fundamentalists over Protestant liberals, the latter of which had "de-supernaturalized truth," which "would have completely undermined the fundamental structure of

believers, and is thus not limited to merely illuminating Scripture, "although what the Spirit says is always based on the truth of Scripture." So, reasons Chan, "Pentecostals who have a far more dynamic view of the Spirit's work in the church than their Protestant counterparts *could* develop a closer relationship between Truth and tradition."[115]

At least two factors, however, hinder Pentecostals from embracing this concept, both tied to a deficient understanding of Pentecost. First, writes Chan, "Their strong sense of the Spirit's action has tended to lead them toward an 'over-supernaturalized' concept of truth,"[116] divorced from history. They fail to recognize that "History is the avenue through which the Pentecostal event takes place. . . . Herein lies the Achilles' heel of Pentecostalism: by freeing the Pentecostal event from its historical moorings, it has considerably weakened its capacity for traditioning. If truth can come directly from the Spirit, what need is there to check it against the historical Christian tradition?"[117]

Secondly, related to this, Chan asserts, "The possibility of evolving a dynamic tradition . . . is hampered by the individualistic conception among Pentecostals of the Pentecost event."[118] This is why some Pentecostals over-emphasize personal (and private) illumination, while others, concerned to preserve orthodoxy, opt for a more "wooden doctrine of Scripture inherited from evangelicalism in which illumination refers solely to the Spirit's work of applying the Scripture to personal life. This 'safe' approach limits the normative traditioning of truth to the first century."[119] This latter approach, however, also conflicts with what Pentecostals believe about the Spirit's ongoing revelatory activity and their actual use of Scripture in practice.[120]

The solution to this, submits Chan, is also two-fold. Pentecostals need to recognize that in the Pentecost event "the Spirit 'transfigures' history, turning it into a charismatic-Pentecostal event," meaning "history is important, otherwise there would be nothing to transfigure."[121] Further,

---

Pentecostal experience."

115. Ibid., 190 (italics original); cf. Chan, *Pentecostal Theology*, 106.

116. Chan, "Mother Church," 192.

117. Ibid., 192–93.

118. Ibid., 190.

119. Ibid., 190–91.

120. Chan, *Pentecostal Theology*, 21.

121. Chan, "Mother Church," 192. Chan is here drawing on Eastern Orthodox theo-

Pentecostals need to prioritize the communal activity of the Spirit over the personal. "A more adequate approach would be to locate the Spirit-Word within the ecclesial community and the eucharistic event. Only within their ecclesial location can Spirit and Word retain their dynamism and continuity."[122] The eucharistic focus also overcomes the ahistorical deficiency, Chan believes, since "the context of the eucharistic worship [is] where the ordinary things are 'transfigured.'"[123]

The Spirit's ongoing revelatory activity, then, is logically inferred from the Pentecost event. So, Chan states, "Pentecostal spirituality as the experience of the third person in the church implies that *to be truly Pentecostal* is to be open to the continuation of the gospel, and this means the development of doctrine."[124] For Chan, belief in the ongoing development of doctrine is more harmonious with the "Pentecostal reality" than limiting the Spirit's revelatory work to the first century.

Tradition and the Pentecostal Doctrines of Initial Evidence and Spirit Baptism

Chan also believes that appreciation for the Christian dogmatic and spiritual tradition can help Pentecostals preserve the doctrine of initial evidence (albeit redefined) and the experience of Spirit baptism in a way truer to early Pentecostal experience than what has been developed by ignoring the theological resources of tradition.[125] The initial evidence doctrine, for want of "strong theological underpinning" is lacking sustainability, evidenced by its "practical abandonment" in many Pentecostal churches.[126] There is, however, something intuitively right, believes Chan, about this doctrine; although inadequately explained, it

---

logian, John Zizioulas, for the emphasis on the Spirit's truth being both supernatural and historical.

122. Ibid., 191. Chan continues, "Christ as the truth in the church is realised in the eucharist where he is sacramentally present. Christ the Truth is made present in the church by the action of the Spirit in the preaching of the Word and in the sacrament. This is not just a truth of history, subject to its relativities, but, because it is by the action of the Spirit, the truth of history, the Gospel story, comes to us vertically and drives us forward into the future."

123. Ibid., 193.

124. Chan, "Encountering the Triune," 221 (italics added).

125. Chan, *Pentecostal Theology*, 40–42.

126. Ibid., 40.

"rings true"[127] to Pentecostal experience and needs to be preserved.[128] To do this, he argues that a robust connection between glossolalia and Spirit baptism is needed, requiring a pneumatology that is able to integrate both the charismatic and soteriological dimensions of the Spirit's work. Such an "integrated pneumatology" can show "that Spirit-baptism is better understood primarily in terms of revelation and personal intimacy and only derivatively, as empowerment for mission." It is in this more personal and relational context that "Pentecostals seek to capture a unique reality with a unique sign: they see glossolalia as an appropriate symbol of the spiritual reality."[129]

In conveying this, however, traditional Pentecostal (naïve) biblicism has proven inadequate, and so too have the more sophisticated exegetical approaches of Stronstad and Menzies (utilizing redaction criticism).[130] Instead Chan sees promise in a canonical theological approach that looks for the larger patterns of meaning within the whole of Scripture, and in which "meaning arises from the interaction of Scripture and the interpretive community."[131] Inclusion of the interpretive community (the broader Christian theological and spiritual tradition) can help Pentecostals better discern the logic of why glossolalia might have "a necessary relationship to Spirit-baptism," and in doing so help expand the meaning of Spirit baptism to be understood as "experience involving a special kind of relationship with God," and not simply as empowerment for mission.[132]

127. Chan, "Language Game," 81.

128. Chan, *Pentecostal Theology*, 40.

129. Ibid., 41.

130. Ibid., 42–43.

131. Ibid., 43. Here Chan is drawing on the canonical theology of Brevard Childs. A canonical approach assumes a fundamental unity to Scripture, and so is less reductive than historical-critical methods, or seeking authorial intent (ibid., 50). This approach seeks, in Chan's words, "spiritual knowledge," not dividing head and heart, and leading to the discovery of larger Scriptural patterns. He explains, "Like the ancient study of Scripture, canonical hermeneutics seeks to discover the biblical message from the Canon as it now stands rather than from the historical construction of the biblical texts—a construction which is often based on very slender historical evidence" (ibid., 28). He suggests a similar approach allowed the historic church to derive the doctrine of the Trinity from Scripture (as opposed to proof-texting) (ibid., 29, cf. 24–31; also see Chan, *Spiritual Theology*, 158–63).

132. Chan, *Pentecostal Theology*, 45. "Relationship is a more basic category for understanding the nature of the work of the Spirit than mission. We can understand mission in terms of relationship but not vice versa" (ibid., 45–46). It should be noted that the

When the entire canon is taken into account (and not simply texts mentioning glossolalia), states Chan, we discover that Luke provides only one angle (i.e., charismatic, prophetic) for understanding Spirit baptism. Other texts highlight the soteriological and revelational dimensions of the Spirit's work, and so a "doctrine of Spirit-baptism" must primarily be understood as involving "relationship with the God who reveals himself in Jesus Christ through the illumination of the Spirit. Power is only the result of that revelational encounter with the triune God."[133]

This relational emphasis is further confirmed, for Chan, when the doctrines of initial evidence and Spirit baptism are brought into conversation with other theological symbols.[134] Since glossolalia is a language gift, its "logical function" should be viewed in the context of personal relationship—"*theologically* tongues are best understood as denoting a certain *kind* of personal relationship that believers have with God."[135] Spirit baptism, then, needs to be understood as a revelational encounter with the personal presence of Jesus, bringing transformation and eliciting a glossolalic response (as well as activating other charisms within the recipient's life).[136] Pentecostal experience of the Spirit, explains Chan, is "a kind of direct spiritual operation which has the character of a miracle in contradistinction to the working of divine providence," and phenomenologically is "understood in the context of personal relationships" with varying degrees of intimacy. Such experience (i.e., Spirit baptism) is a highly intimate and personal encounter, bringing with it a sense of familiarity with the person of the Spirit.[137]

In further developing this idea, Chan draws on Roman Catholic charismatic theologian Simon Tugwell, who suggests that glossolalia

---

method adopted here by Chan redefines Spirit baptism based on the experience of glossolalia (as initial evidence), as opposed to defining the significance of glossolalia based on Spirit baptism (e.g., as an evidence of a spiritual experience, or, as early Pentecostals thought, a xenolalic gift to assist in missionary work). This demonstrates the weight Chan grants to Pentecostal experience (see Chan, "Language Game," 93).

133. Chan, *Pentecostal Theology*, 49, cf. 46–49.

134. Ibid., 49–57; cf. Chan, "Language Game," 83.

135. Chan, "Language Game," 84 (italics original).

136. Chan, *Pentecostal Theology*, 51, 54–55.

137. Chan, "Asian Review," 35. Chan notes this does not necessarily imply these experiences can serve as indicators of maturity. Rather, "it simply means that they have a more focused and distinct awareness of divine presence, even to the point of familiarity (compare the familiarity of a child with its parents)." Also see Chan, "Language Game," 86, 95.

bears structural similarity to sacramental theology, one that also finds parallels in the Roman Catholic contemplative tradition.[138] A sacrament, in this understanding, is a "passive" act, received in response to divine initiative, the revelation of God's presence,[139] and "God's action in human acts."[140] As such, sacraments are not arbitrary, but necessary signs of the one being encountered. Viewed sacramentally, then, "a connection can be made between tongues as a sign and the presence of the Spirit as the thing signified."[141] Thus glossolalia symbolizes, not simply "power for service," but something deeper—a "basic relationship" with God, characterized by an "active passivity" in which "we speak, yet it is a speech that comes from a yieldedness and surrender to the will of God."[142] For this reason, Chan believes that sacramental traditions (those linking water baptism and confirmation) hold more promise than non-sacramental ones (e.g., evangelical) for understanding the meaning of Spirit baptism, which is not simply an intensification or refreshing of the Spirit received at conversion-initiation,[143] but a revelational, theophanic encounter with God, more congruent with the concept of the "actualization" of the Spirit in confirmation.[144] The notion of "intensification of a pre-existing reality" (advocated by some evangelicals open to the charismatic dimension) does not "ring true," he asserts, with Pentecostal experience. The "Pentecostal reality" views Spirit baptism as something more significantly unique.[145] Theologically, glossolalia indicates that Spirit baptism is a transformative, revelational experience with God.

138. Chan, *Pentecostal Theology*, 51, 50.

139. Ibid., 51.

140. Ibid., 57.

141. Chan, "Language Game," 86. Chan finds Macchia's emphasis in this regard to be helpful. Also see Chan, *Pentecostal Theology*, 52–53.

142. Chan, *Pentecostal Theology*, 51. Chan sees this basic yieldedness modeled theologically in the Trinitarian life of God, in which the Son submits to the Father's will, and they are bonded by the Spirit. The Spirit also bonds the church to the triune life, producing this same yieldedness (passivity).

143. Ibid., 54, cf. 63–64. Chan identifies James D. G. Dunn and Max B. Turner as proponents of this approach.

144. Ibid., 54–55.

145. Ibid., 56, cf. 53, 62–64. Chan believes one reason that Roman Catholic charismatics have been more open to an initial evidence doctrine (as opposed to evangelicals) is due to their previous exposure to the mystical stream within their own tradition (ibid., 63).

This viewpoint, Chan argues, is further supported from a cultural-linguistic perspective.[146] In the context of an individual's initial experience of Spirit-baptism, Pentecostals have understood "evidential tongues as God's action to which the believer simply yields."[147] Tongues-speech functions, then, as a spontaneous response to God's overwhelming presence,[148] akin to the "sign" of tears accompanying sadness. Tears are not sought to verify sadness (much less in order to cause sadness!); nevertheless, a "connaturality" exists "between tears and sadness."[149] Similarly, glossolalia is not so much a proof of Spirit baptism as it is the "most natural and regular concomitant of Spirit-filling involving an invasive or interruptive manifestation of the Spirit in which one's relationship to Jesus Christ is radically and significantly altered."[150] It is this type of "necessary" relationship that Chan believes the term "initial evidence" was originally intended to capture, and so the doctrine makes sense in that subcultural-linguistic context.[151]

Chan also believes that other parallels to "passivity" in Pentecostal experience may be seen in the "phases of contemplative prayer in the Christian mystical tradition."[152] For example, Teresa of Avila's "fourth 'mansion'" (level) of prayer exemplifies this sort of passivity—expressed in silence, since the joy being experienced is inexpressible.[153] One can only prepare for, but not cause such responses.[154] Viewed as "passive prayer," then, both glossolalia and silence may be understood as "functionally equivalent . . . Both symbolize a response from the depth of the human spirit to the reality of God felt as immediate presence.

146. Ibid., 57–62.

147. Ibid., 57.

148. Chan, "Language Game," 87. Chan also refers to this function of tongues as "the enthusiastic component," in contrast to the ascetical use of tongues, to be explored below.

149. Chan, *Pentecostal Theology*, 58.

150. Ibid.

151. Ibid., 57–58; cf. Chan, "Language Game," 90.

152. Chan, *Pentecostal Theology*, 58. Says Chan, "What Pentecostals experience in glossolalia is nothing more or less than what has always been seen as something utterly basic and essential to prayer itself" (ibid., 57).

153. Ibid., 59, cf. 58.

154. Ibid., 58–60. Chan states, "The main difference between the Pentecostal and the mystic is that the former's receptivity is signalled predominately by glossolalia while the latter's is signalled by a wider variety of responses, including silence and some form of ecstatic utterances of praise" (ibid., 60).

Such a response reveals the limits of human rationality and the need to transcend it." These two traditions, then, bear similarities, while yet employing different "sub-dialects"; or, in Lindbeck's nomenclature, utilizing unique cultural-linguistic "grammars."[155] In any case, "by locating glossolalia within the larger context of the mystical tradition, it makes perfectly good sense to say that glossolalia is the initial evidence or concomitant of Spirit-baptism."[156]

The Spiritual Tradition and Pentecostal Asceticism

Bolstering the "Pentecostal reality," however, will require more than identifying aspects of convergence between Pentecostal experience of Spirit baptism and the larger Christian spiritual tradition. Spirit baptism must, Chan affirms, also be integrated into the entire life of faith. But traditional Pentecostal methods for doing so, such as a two-stage model (new birth and empowerment for mission), have proved too anemic, and tend to bifurcate power and holiness. What is needed, rather, is for Spirit baptism (with glossolalia) to "be shown to constitute an essential part of a coherent schema of spiritual development in which one experiences growing intimacy with God and holiness of life. In short, without this final correlation between glossolalia and holiness, I doubt if the Pentecostal reality could be sustainable."[157]

Chan finds promise for sustaining the "Pentecostal reality" in both Scripture and the Christian tradition, which have always closely linked power and holiness. For example, he suggests that the "theology of miracles," developed by John Cassian and Thomas Aquinas, stressed a natural connection between power and holiness,[158] which might serve well as a corrective for Pentecostals overly enamored with extraordinary

155. Ibid., 61. Chan accounts for the differences between the Christian mystical tradition and Pentecostalism (concerning their expressions of silence and tongues respectively) as being due to the "complex relationship between an experiential reality and theological framework which shapes it and which in turn is shaped by it. In brief, Pentecostals had already inherited a framework which inevitably led them to support their experience from historical precedents in Acts" (Chan, "Language Game," 90n.35).

156. Chan, *Pentecostal Theology*, 61–62.

157. Ibid., 64, cf. 62–64.

158. Ibid., 64–66. Both Cassian and Aquinas, states Chan, distinguished between miracles of power (serving as a sign) and miracles attesting to an individual's holiness. Both, however, also emphasized the holiness/power connection as being more natural. Chan also notes that desert fathers taught humility in the exercise of spiritual gifts.

charismata.[159] Further, early Pentecostalism more naturally expressed the integral association between empowerment and broader soteriology with a three-stage model (new birth → sanctification → Spirit baptism), and a more holistic pneumatology, centered on Christ and the fivefold gospel.[160] If Spirit baptism and sanctification can be reconnected, proposes Chan, it will allow the "Pentecostal reality" to be viewed not as "just one component in the Christian life," but as "a perspective with which to view the whole of the Christian life. The Christian life can be seen in terms of the distinctive work of the Spirit in the Trinitarian relationship. The Spirit indwells believers, prompting and goading them to pray to the Father as the children of God through their union with the Son . . ."[161]

Pentecostal spirituality, then, is "distinguished by the emphasis it gives to the affective dimension of the Christian life."[162] While this early Pentecostal emphasis is promising, however, Chan believes linear stage models of spiritual development to be inadequate for sustaining the "Pentecostal reality" as a perspective for Christian life; and he again mines the Christian spiritual tradition for resources in this regard. Chan notices structural parallels between the early Pentecostal three-stage model and the "Three Ways" of spiritual progress found in the Christian ascetical tradition: the "purgative way" being akin to new birth, the "illuminative way" to sanctification, and the "unitive way" to Spirit baptism.[163] The "three ways" schema has an advantage in helping Pentecostals locate and chart their spiritual development, since it views spiritual progression as a "spiral development" as opposed to a "unilinear path," and as involving an ongoing oscillation between "consolation and

---

159. Ibid., 63–64, cf. 75. Chan views the Third Wave movement as being especially prone in this regard, largely due to an inadequate evangelical schema for spiritual progression. Elsewhere he utilizes Jonathan Edwards as a resource for discernment of supernatural manifestations (Chan, *Spiritual Theology*, 213–24).

160. Chan, *Pentecostal Theology*, 67–69. This refers to Pentecostalism prior to the 1910 "Finished Work" controversy.

161. Ibid., 70.

162. Ibid. Chan concurs with Steven Land, seeing the affections as core to Pentecostal spirituality. We will recall Yun's criticism of Chan (and Land) precisely on this point in chapter 1. Yun believes that Chan's emphasis on Pentecostalism being centered on the affections does not sufficiently acknowledge the existence of a pragmatic element from the beginning of the movement.

163. Ibid., 73.

desolation," experiences of joy as well as spiritual dryness (e.g., the "dark night of the soul") throughout each of the three phases.[164]

The "three ways," then, can help Pentecostals overcome some weaknesses in their own tradition, believes Chan. First, while Pentecostals have always advocated successive fillings with the Spirit (subsequent to initial Spirit baptism), the linear spiritual model has actually discouraged this in practice.[165] Second, separating sanctification and empowerment into linear stages has also sometimes inclined Pentecostals toward an over-realized eschatology, exemplified in fascination with extraordinary signs and wonders, while leaving little room in Christian experience for seasons of spiritual "aridity" or "desolation."[166] The "three ways" spiral phase model helps overcome both of these deficiencies, encouraging repeated experiential fillings with the Spirit, and integrating spiritual dryness as part of spiritual progress.

The "three ways" not only provides a better model, but Chan also believes that Pentecostalism already bears similarities to the Christian spiritual tradition, demonstrating the ascetical dimension in two ways. First, the traditional Pentecostal practice of "tarrying" in prayer (for sanctification and/or Spirit baptism) indicates they intuitively viewed asceticism as a way forward in spiritual life.[167] Second, Pentecostals have also used glossolalia as a form of ascetical prayer. Here Chan distinguishes between two functions of tongues: the enthusiastic or "passive" (evidential) function (noted earlier), and the ascetic function, when tongues are actively practiced as a form of prayer.[168] The former may be viewed as a *response to* grace, the latter as a *means to* grace (emphasizing the sacramental dimension) leading again to more "passive" experiences.[169] Glossolalia as ascetical practice allows Spirit baptism to be integrated into the whole of spiritual life (not simply "some initial experience of ecstasy"), meaning "The Pentecostal reality is not just the beginning but also the goal of Christian life."[170] Further, this approach helps the broader

---

164. Ibid., 71, 73, 74.

165. Ibid., 74–75, 77.

166. Ibid., 76, cf. 75–77.

167. Ibid., 77. Elsewhere Chan explains, "To describe spiritual theology as ascetical implies the systematic and disciplined spiritual exercises constitute the primary means of spiritual development" (Chan, *Spiritual Theology*, 19).

168. Chan, "Language Game," 87–88, 94; Chan, *Pentecostal Theology*, 78, 81.

169. Chan, *Pentecostal Theology*, 78, 81.

170. Ibid., 80. Chan states, "Baptism in the Holy Spirit, therefore, is initiation into a

Christian spiritual tradition to better appreciate the role of tongues in spiritual development. As "passive," glossolalia introduces the unexpected in prayer, and playfulness into the life of worship; as "active" (ascetical) it may be viewed as analogous to silence or repetitive prayers used in other traditions (such as the Jesus Prayer used in Eastern Orthodoxy).[171] Thus, "Pentecostalism cannot be regarded as a marginal movement, much less an aberration; it is a spiritual movement that matches in every way the time-tested method of spiritual development in the Christian tradition."[172]

Finally, to preserve the "Pentecostal reality," Chan contends that some form of the doctrine of subsequence (accenting a distinct experience of Spirit baptism) does need to be sustained, but located "within the conversion-initiation complex" to avoid bifurcating sanctification and empowerment.[173] The evangelical approach, based on a linear crisis model that collapses Spirit baptism into conversion-initiation, is inadequate, since it does not naturally lead believers into a course of spiritual progression.[174] Instead, conversion-initiation needs to be viewed "as a process of development rather than just a crisis experience."[175] Here, Chan believes that the sacramental tradition provides a more fruitful way forward, since it distinguishes water baptism and confirmation as two distinct experiences in Christian life, while locating both within the conversion-initiation complex.[176] Confirmation therefore marks a particular work of the Spirit, preserving the idea of a distinct experience of Spirit baptism, while also carefully situating this within a broader conversion-initiation framework—Spirit baptism being seen as an outworking

---

life-long and on-going life of prayer where tongues are freely spoken as part of the total life of prayer. . . . Glossolalia symbolizes both initiation and goal, a way of life oriented around 'the surprising works of God.'"

171. Ibid., 81–82; cf. Chan, "Language Game," 88; Chan, *Spiritual Theology*, 145–46. The "ideal" Pentecostal ascetic is portrayed in Chan, *Pentecostal Theology*, 82–85. For a broader discussion of prayer see Chan, *Spiritual Theology*, 125–40.

172. Chan, *Pentecostal Theology*, 71.

173. Ibid., 87.

174. Ibid., 88–89. Chan is quite critical of evangelical spirituality in this regard. He states, "Evangelicals tend to see the Christian life as one big indistinct blob. One is expected to grow, but what is the expected pattern of development remains at best a hazy notion" (ibid., 88).

175. Ibid., 87.

176. Ibid., 89–93.

("actualization") of the Spirit "objectively given at baptism."[177] So, in this way, sacramental theology is able to benefit Pentecostalism; and Pentecostalism already exhibits a sacramentality of sorts, demonstrated in its non-Western holistic spirituality.[178]

Traditioning through Liturgical Worship: Boundaries for Play

Even if Pentecostals begin to see themselves as existing in historical continuity with the Christian tradition (including being "open to doctrinal development"),[179] and adopt a more sacramental spirituality, this will only preserve the "Pentecostal reality" if it is also "sustained by a living liturgy."[180] For, says Chan, "what truly unites the people of God is not merely a set of beliefs professed, but the lived faith actualized in liturgical celebration." So, rather than modeling their worship after "the world of entertainment," Pentecostals need to develop a "liturgical spirituality."[181] Chan advocates liturgy as necessarily being Eucharist-centered, and proposes an order of service quite structured in comparison to typical Pentecostal worship.[182] Is such structure compatible with Pentecostal emphasis on the Spirit's spontaneity? Chan believes so: "freedom of the Spirit is not opposed to form. It is entirely possible for a service to have both."[183]

Chan offers several practical suggestions in this regard. First, certain more overt Pentecostal expressions of corporate spirituality may be practiced in gatherings other than the Sunday liturgy (e.g., a midweek

177. Ibid., 90. Chan cites Congar, who suggests that confirmation distinguishes Spirit from Word.

178. See Chan, "Encountering the Triune," 223–24. This holistic spirituality was highlighted in chapter 2. There are dangers here, admits Chan. Sacramental worldviews tend to be more given to attempting to manipulate spirituality and power by "magic" (e.g., prayer techniques, etc.), which he sees as exemplified in the Third Wave movement.

179. Ibid., 226, cf. 222–26.

180. Ibid., 225. Asserts Chan here, "If Pentecostal spirituality is to remain vibrant, be self-corrective and see healthy development, it needs a sound traditioning structure; and this means coming to terms with the dogma of the Church, with its sacraments and authority."

181. Ibid., 226.

182. On Eucharist as the focus of liturgy, and the structure of Sunday liturgy see Chan, *Liturgical Theology*, 70–78, 126–46.

183. Ibid., 126.

healing service). Second, it needs to be acknowledged that "genuinely unpredictable elements even in the charismatic worship service are quite rare." The so-called spontaneous elements most often actually fall within "an unwritten structure," meaning that Pentecostals should not be so resistant to more systematized forms of worship. "Third, many of the essential elements of Pentecostal faith and practice, such as praying for the sick and the altar call, can be incorporated within a formal liturgy without compromising their integrity. In short, a normative liturgy is large enough to incorporate the charismatic dimensions of worship."[184]

But beyond this, Pentecostals need to appreciate the necessity of locating the spontaneous work of the Spirit within structured communal liturgy. Drawing on the work of Jean-Jacques Suurmond, Chan concurs that Pentecostal worship has "the same logical function as play," and believes this can help Pentecostals understand how the "extraordinary" can be tied to the mundane of everyday life.[185] Play has both freedom and order, and so too does worship—theologically, Word representing structure and the Spirit spontaneity.[186] Thus, "The work of the Spirit always has a form: the Christ pattern."[187] Pentecostal worship accents the Spirit and therefore the spontaneous; and it recognizes that, in essence, worship does not exist for pragmatic purposes, but is its own end.[188] Pentecostal worship, however, has tended to focus too much on the individual, and needs to affirm the structure of the Christian community and its tradition. So, reminds Chan, while Pentecostal worship emphasizes the spontaneity and playfulness of worship, "yet, like play, the Pentecostal reality cannot properly function apart from the larger context of the 'ordinary' Christian life. This is why it must always be interpreted within the larger Christian spiritual tradition where the ordinary and extraordinary, the predictable and unpredictable are woven together to form a coherent and rich tapestry of life with God the Father, in Christ through the Spirit."[189]

---

184. Ibid., 127. Chan sees a healthy implementation of the charismatic elements within a formal liturgy exemplified in the International Communion of the Charismatic Episcopal Church (see Chan, "Encountering the Triune," 225).

185. Chan, *Pentecostal Theology*, 116, cf. 56, 80, 92.

186. Ibid., 117.

187. Chan, *Liturgical Theology*, 126.

188. Chan, *Pentecostal Theology*, 118. Chan decries "purpose-driven" worship, in which it becomes a means to an end. Here he particularly has in mind worship functioning as "magic," manipulating divine powers to human ends.

189. Ibid., 119, cf. 118.

Summary

In the above survey, we have observed that Chan argues strongly that the "Pentecostal reality" (Pentecostal experiential spirituality) is not an aberration, but an important component of Christian spirituality in general. He also, perhaps with even greater emphasis, advocates that Pentecostalism needs to more intentionally locate itself firmly within the historic Christian spiritual, dogmatic, and liturgical tradition, since *the Spirit is mediated through tradition*. Only by doing so will Pentecostalism be able to tradition (pass on) its own values and spirituality, and contribute to the larger ecumenical fellowship. Chan further contends that such a move may not be as awkward as might be assumed, since elements of Pentecostal spirituality appear to already be congruent with the broader Christian spiritual tradition. At the same time, Pentecostal linear stage models for understanding experience of the Spirit (whether two or three stages) are inadequate for promoting ongoing experiences with the Spirit or integrating these into the broader dimensions of Christian spirituality, and so alternative models are required.

On Schner's continuum, then, Chan, like Macchia, may be located at the "appeal constructive." Chan is obviously an advocate of the church's "confession"; however, his appeal is not naïve, or static. He is committed to the Spirit's ongoing revelatory activity, both through continuing doctrinal development and the Pentecostal-charismatic dimension in which the Spirit, through the charismata (e.g., prophecy), may speak and introduce change in surprising ways. Chan, then, also serves as an example of how Pentecostal theology is maturing, demonstrating a willingness to examine his own Pentecostal tradition critically, as well as being able to draw on, and interact with the broader Christian tradition.

Chan in Dialogue with Christian Theological Traditions

We noted at the outset that Chan's broader concern is not simply the preservation of the "Pentecostal reality," but rather for a more robust Christian spirituality, in which believers demonstrate spiritual progress in the journey toward union with God. To this end, he advocates a "spiritual theology" involving three criteria (or components): the "Pentecostal-charismatic" (discussed above), "global-contextual," and "evangelical." The latter two require further elaboration at this point. The "global-contextual" criterion acknowledges that spirituality is always worked out in a particular historical context, and is influenced by a variety of cultural, social, and political realities. These concrete realities shape the way that Scripture and the Christian tradition is understood in a given situation, and so, reasons Chan, it is necessary to recognize the contextual relativity of any theology to avoid universalizing one's own cultural and historical perspective.[190]

Concerning the "evangelical" criterion, Chan explains that this does not refer to Western evangelicalism, but more broadly to the idea that "truth is contained in the evangel; the preaching of the evangel mediates the experience of that truth." This criterion, then, grounds the global-contextual and Pentecostal-charismatic components, so as to avoid either ahistoricism or the baptizing of certain historical sociopolitical processes. Christian conversion is not, for example, to a "cosmic Christ" idea, but to a specific person, "the risen Jesus of Nazareth . . . Each conversion experience involves a living contact with the transcendent person of Christ in a concrete historical context."[191] For Chan, the person of Christ is located, as we have seen, in a unique way in the visible church. Important here, however, is that the evangelical criterion provides a way to transcend the variety of "evangelical conversion experiences" (shaped by cultures and personalities), and unite them as being conversion to the person of Christ, revealed in and through "the historical medium."[192] Put another way, this criterion emphasizes the historical objectivity of the person with whom Christians identify themselves—namely, Jesus.

A healthy Christian spirituality, then, necessitates the inclusion and integration of these three criteria. Such, states Chan, is also an ascetical spirituality (a spirituality of "small steps"), worked out in relation to the body of Christ, enabling believers corporately and individually to fill their divine call and the mission of the church.[193] Identifying these components of spiritual theology, however, also helps situate our ecumenical dialogue, since a number of the issues to be discussed are directly related to the evangelical, global-contextual and Pentecostal-charismatic criteria raised by Chan.

190. Chan, *Spiritual Theology*, 25–34.
191. Ibid., 34, cf. 34–37.
192. Ibid., 35.
193. Ibid., 11, 239.

The Identity of the Spirit

As we have seen, Chan clearly delineates the identity of the Spirit by emphasizing it as having been revealed in the story of the Trinity.[194] This story continues through Pentecost, through which the Spirit constitutes the church as body of Christ and Temple of the Spirit (a point to which we will return). Here we can note considerable convergence with Jenson's emphases on the Spirit's identity. Jenson clearly distinguishes between two appeals to experience of "spirit," one being rather vacuous, and the other more phenomenological, linked to the identity of a person (as opposed to simply an ambiguous 'presence').[195] Jenson's point is that the triune Godhead is only identifiable historically, within the temporal, and thus we should not think of God needing to be mediated temporally (as if God were timeless and impassible); there is no such metaphysical distance from God. What hides God is human sinfulness, not ontology.[196]

Chan's close proximity to Jenson here is expressed in his statement that "Trinity" is simply "shorthand" for describing how God works in the world as revealed in Scripture.[197] Also, the Spirit can clearly be identified within history now, located within Christ's body the church. It is, therefore, within the church that encounter with (experience of) the Spirit occurs. The church is where the Spirit's activity may be discerned, and the presence of the Spirit frees the church from historical determination alone.[198]

Chan cites Jenson several times on issues concerning the church as unique locus and identifier of the Spirit, as well as creation existing for the fulfillment of the church (and not vice versa). Again, this indicates considerable convergence between Chan and a Protestant high church theologian—perhaps an unexpected place for a Pentecostal to end up, considering their history of emphasizing the Spirit's freedom over against "dead tradition." But Chan's reason for advocating a position close to that of Jenson is precisely to preserve the Spirit's freedom

194. Chan, "Church and the Development," 72.

195. It should be recalled that Jenson does tend to lump Pentecostalism in with the former definition, along with contextual theologies (Jenson, *Systematic Theology: Triune,* 12).

196. Jenson, *Systematic Theology: Works,* 161–62; cf. Jenson, *Systematic Theology: Triune,* 233.

197. Chan, *Spiritual Theology,* 41.

198. Chan, "Church and the Development," 73.

(Pentecostal-charismatic spirituality). Whether Jenson is reciprocally open to integrating this "Pentecostal reality" into his theology remains to be seen; but perhaps Chan provides a way forward in this regard, demonstrating the congruency between Pentecostal-charismatic spirituality and the historical spiritual tradition.

Highlighting this particular convergence also helps to accent Chan's divergence from at least three of our dialogue partners concerning the identity of the Spirit, namely, Moltmann, Cone, and Johnson (and probably Bulgakov). Moltmann in particular is a significant voice here, since Chan is one of the Pentecostals with whom he interacted in the 1994 dialogue concerning his book, *The Spirit of Life*. In that dialogue Chan did affirm aspects of Moltmann's theology, particularly those elements conducive to a more holistic spirituality (to be discussed later).[199] Chan, however, is quite critical of Moltmann's immanent-transcendence emphasis, which (he believes) diffuses the Spirit into the world.[200] Macchia was also concerned with this element, believing it would not allow for the truly interruptive work of the Spirit. Chan's motive for doing so, however, is tied to his conviction that this will result in a loss of emphasis on the personhood and identity of the Spirit, leaving only a rather indistinct presence. This, he believes, is particularly dangerous in an animistic Asian context, in which "Spirit" can easily become confused with any number of "spirits." Holding God's transcendence and immanence in tension (rather than collapsing the former into the latter), he believes, is vital for Christian theology and spirituality in general, but especially in Asian culture (a point to which we will return).[201]

Moltmann's rejoinder to Chan is brief. He believes that he has sufficiently emphasized the Spirit's personhood in *The Spirit of Life* (using the metaphors of "Liberator," "Comforter," and "Judge" for the Spirit). But he also contends that the concept of Spirit as "an energy field and a space for life 'in' which believers live and develop," is necessary as well.[202] Further, Moltmann believes the question of spiritual discernment is addressed through his positing the person of the crucified Christ as a sufficient criterion for discerning the Spirit's activity. He explains,

---

199. Chan, "Asian Review," 36–38.
200. Ibid., 38–39.
201. Ibid., 39–40.
202. Moltmann, "A Response," 65.

Whatever can endure when it is confronted with the Crucified is Spirit from his Spirit; whatever cannot endure his presence is anti-Christian and demonic. In the struggle to which we are led in following Jesus we experience precisely what the Spirit of Christ is and what is the spirit of the Antichrist; we see who gives strength to live and who are the gods of death. Nor can a cosmic doctrine of the Holy Spirit become animistic or pay homage to New Age pantheism or Buddhism: Jesus makes the difference. I have never placed this at all in question. If anyone sees or has another criterion for discerning between spirits, it cannot be—in my opinion—Christian: *solus Christus.*[203]

That Chan is not convinced by Moltmann is evidenced in several of his later publications, in which he continues to highlight Moltmann as an example of one who has failed to preserve the identity of the Spirit. Chan also notes that Moltmann has had a strong influence among liberation theologians with his political theology, and for this reason Chan's critique may be viewed as applicable to Cone and Johnson as well. In brief, he argues that Moltmann and liberation theologies (of all stripes, but particularly from the West) are deficient in two of the criteria outlined earlier—the "evangelical" (preserving the Spirit's identity), and, perhaps ironically, the "global-contextual." It is worth exploring how Chan addresses Moltmann and liberation theologies, bearing these criteria in mind.

The neglect of attention to the Spirit's identity comes from what Chan considers to be a faulty understanding of *Creator Spiritus*, an attempt to comprehend the Spirit's work in the world "apart from creation's fulfillment in the church."[204] Chan believes that not only does the Spirit give the church its unique identity, but the church as constituted "gives to the Spirit his distinctive character as the church-located and church-shaped Spirit. . . . Pentecostals must continue to affirm this aspect of pneumatology especially against a growing tendency to 'free' the Spirit from his ecclesial location and release him into the world as Moltmann and the liberation theologians have done."[205]

203. Ibid., 67 (italics original).

204. Chan, "Church and the Development," 74, cf. 71–75. Cf. Chan, *Pentecostal Theology*, 110–16; Chan, "Mother Church," 196–208; and Chan, "Encountering the Triune," 215–26.

205. Chan, *Pentecostal Theology*, 111.

The implications of such misunderstanding of *Creator Spiritus* are multiplex for Chan, negatively affecting conceptions of God, the church and its mission, and spirituality in general—all of these related to the question of discerning the Spirit's identity. Chan is emphatic: "The one great difficulty with this concept is that we cannot adequately safeguard the Holy Spirit's identity unless the Spirit is understood in the context of an explicit Trinitarian relationship. That means postulating special revelation and ecclesiological pneumatology, without which how can we tell apart the work of the Spirit of God from that of a shaman or a Taoist medium? How can we tell that attractive liberation movement is a sign of the Spirit and not merely impelled by human ideology?"[206]

It is not, argues Chan, that the Christian tradition has failed to acknowledge God's broader providential work in creation, but it "has for the most part understood the goodness in creation as belonging not to the cosmic Christ or *Creator Spiritus* but to the *vestigia dei* (literally, the footprints of God)."[207] Any doctrine of *Creator Spiritus*, then, requires careful qualification. Creation can be viewed as an avenue of grace, but only through the perspective of the faith community, in which the Spirit cannot be identified apart from the Father and Son.[208] Chan even challenges the assumption that Scripture emphasizes a concept of a cosmic Spirit (contra Moltmann and Johnson). The Spirit's activity in creation is only noted, he states, at the beginning and end of the Bible, possibly implying that the Spirit's presence cannot be properly or sufficiently discerned in the midst of the broken and sinful world.[209] Chan's solution is, with Jenson, to locate the Spirit in the visible church, the body of Christ.

In contrast, Johnson, Cone, and Moltmann all locate the Spirit immanently within historical processes. Johnson, for example, views God's hiddenness as being not as a result of sin (contra Jenson and Chan), but due simply to divine incomprehensibility (perhaps sharing some affinity with Lossky here).[210] She then infers that only analogical language is appropriate for speaking of God, and therefore, other metaphors (outside those found in Scripture and tradition) may serve this purpose

---

206. Ibid., 112.

207. Ibid., 113 (italics original).

208. Ibid., 114.

209. Ibid., 114–15.

210. Johnson, *She Who Is*, 105–7.

equally well;[211] hence, her proposal for the Trinity as Spirit-, Jesus-, and Mother-Sophia.

It should be noted that Chan is not necessarily opposed to feminine imagery being applied to God. For example, he cites Gelpi's reference to Spirit as "Mother" as helpful for emphasizing the relational elements of spiritual life—the maternal image reminds believers that they participate in a "spirituality of the family."[212] Johnson, however, goes further with this, proposing that there is no special zone or realm of the Spirit's activity; rather, all history is sacramental, with the Spirit operating immanently within.[213] The Spirit is identified, then, not with the ecclesia (where Johnson believes women have often experienced the absence of the Spirit). Rather, the Spirit is discovered in women's experience, in particular where the flourishing of women and humanity in general can be found. Thus, experience of the Spirit is concrete and historical, but not in the same sense Chan and Jenson take this to mean. Johnson emphasizes the Spirit experienced in concrete historical realities and events, whereas Chan (and Jenson) emphasize the identity of the Spirit as being historically connected to and identified with the ongoing life of the ecclesia.

Cone shares similarities with Johnson's approach, identifying experience of the Spirit immanently in history in the context of the oppressed. He reaches this conclusion based on the story of enslaved Israel, and (even more so) the story of Jesus, the oppressed Jewish man. The presence of the resurrected Jesus (by the Spirit) is found in, and indeed cannot be understood apart from, the experience of the oppressed (blacks). This is why, again, the ecclesia, where Word is rightly preached and sacraments rightly administered, is no guarantee of the Spirit's presence. Discerning the Spirit's presence, for Cone, is a far more subjective process—positive identification being possible only where tangible liberative results are manifest.

There is obvious divergence here with Chan's insistence on identifying the Spirit through historical continuity with the ecclesia (implying the necessity of a visible church for the transmission of Christianity). Nevertheless, Chan, aware of sin's presence within Christ's body, argues the church is "on the way," and therefore imperfect.[214] In this

---

211. Lossky, of course, takes another tact, emphasizing an apophatic approach.

212. Chan, *Spiritual Theology*, 54.

213. Johnson, *She Who Is*, 124.

214. Chan, *Liturgical Theology*, 26.

manner he can account for the presence of sin and brokenness in the ecclesia—manifest, for example, in the marginalization of certain groups (e.g., blacks and women)—and aim to correct this as being incompatible with the gospel. Johnson's and Cone's response to brokenness within the ecclesia is to try to locate the Spirit's presence outside the church in the world.[215] Chan, however, finds this unacceptable, since it does not adequately protect the personhood of the Spirit, leaving only a more ambiguous notion of "presence."[216] His solution is to see the visible church as a "mixed body," within which exists a smaller "remnant," faithful to the gospel.[217] He is unconvinced by Free Church ecclesiologies that imagine some sort of "pure church," since this does not sufficiently acknowledge the ubiquity of sin, even among believers. Further, argues Chan, even liberation movements are not immune from sin's influence, and often themselves become oppressive over time.[218]

Other issues remain to be discussed concerning Moltmann, Johnson, and Cone, particularly regarding their emphasis on contextual theology. At this point, however, we are able to bring Bulgakov into the discussion. It will be recalled that Bulgakov was concerned with what he perceived as an over-emphasis on ecclesiasticism within Eastern Orthodoxy to the neglect of involvement in the world.[219] This motivated him to rethink the divine essence (Ousia) and develop his sophiology. Bulgakov does identify the church as "divine-humanity" by the Spirit given at Pentecost, and as the place in which deification can occur (via synergistic participation between God and humans). At times, however, he blurs the boundaries between church and world—Sophia's kenosis with creation means that the Spirit is not restricted to the church.[220]

215. Moltmann also, of course, views the Spirit as working in history. Our point here, however, is simply to acknowledge in particular Johnson and Cone's uneasy relationship with the church and the dogmatic tradition, since they view it as having directly contributed to the oppression of the communities of which they are a part—namely, women and blacks respectively.

216. Chan, "Encountering the Triune," 218; Chan, *Liturgical Theology*, 32.

217. Chan, *Liturgical Theology*, 26.

218. Chan, "Mother Church," 201–2. Chan states, "The fact that so many liberation movements in history that were confidently hailed as signs of the Spirit turned out later to be just as oppressive and constrictive as systems they replaced shows that discerning the Spirit in the world is not as easy as it is often made out to be. The reason is that the Spirit is not explicitly revealed in the world as in the church."

219. Bulgakov, *Sophia*, 20.

220. Bulgakov, *Comforter*, 220–21, cf. 219–27.

Although Bulgakov does distinguish the Spirit's work in the world and among pagan religions from the Spirit's more focused (explicit) activity in the church, nevertheless, his panentheism allows for the Spirit's immanent involvement within history and social evolutionary processes.[221]

Chan does appreciate Bulgakov's emphasis on the church as "divine-humanity" (a point to which we will return),[222] but would likely have difficulty with Bulgakov's emphasis on the Spirit's immanent work in historical processes. For Chan, the Spirit is the eschatological Spirit of the new creation, and thus, "The presence of the Spirit now is to serve as the foretaste of the new creation rather than gradually to transform the old creation (*by some sort of evolutionary process?*) into the new creation. This fact is further reinforced by the scriptural account of the role and identity of the Spirit as the Spirit of Christ. . . . Only at the parousia will the new creation be truly revealed for what it is."[223] That said, the above discussion simply illustrates Chan's strong conviction that the identity of the Spirit needs to be preserved, and that the way to do so is to locate the Spirit's presence in the church.

Global-Contextuality and Spirituality

Closely related to the issue of identity is that of contextuality. Identity corresponds to Chan's "evangelical" criterion for spirituality, whereas the focus here pertains to his "global-contextual" criterion. Johnson, Cone, and Moltmann once again become key participants in this particular conversation, since they associate the Spirit's presence, in one way or another, with the manifestation of tangible liberative activity within history. Related here is also the idea that the Spirit is mediated through the experiences of those living in particular historical and cultural contexts. Contextual theology, then, should be broadly understood as the unique perspective of a particular group (e.g., women, blacks, etc.) as being experience of the Spirit, and thus as serving as a resource for theological construction.

Johnson, for example, draws attention to the general global oppression of women due to overwhelming androcentrism (including in the field of theology). But since the Spirit works immanently within history,

---

221. Bulgakov, *Sophia*, 143.

222. Chan, *Liturgical Theology*, 23.

223. Chan, "Mother Church," 200–201 (italics added).

women's experience can be viewed as a potential theological resource—women's experience being experience of the divine. Theology has been, contextually, male-dominated; but now many women are experiencing an "awakening," or "conversion," and recognizing their own dignity and human worth. Of course Johnson acknowledges that there exists a plurality of feminisms globally, but this general awakening among women worldwide can be viewed as evidence of the Spirit's liberative activity.[224] Acknowledging women's experience as being the Spirit's work allows Johnson to revision various aspects of theology, including the way in which the Trinity is understood. She advocates, for example, a social Trinitarian model (i.e., a feminist relational model) in contrast to a traditional hierarchical Trinitarian model.[225]

We have also earlier noted Cone's contextual emphasis.[226] For Cone, all theological language is interested and political (power) language. There are, then, no universals, only contextual and particular theology. Black experience, then, is a legitimate place to discern the immanent Spirit at work, and moreover is a privileged context from which to hear the Spirit—black experience being closer to that found among the oppressed of Scripture.

Moltmann too promotes a hermeneutic emphasizing the Spirit's immanent operation in the *sitz im leben*, life's historical particularities.[227] Like Cone, he believes Scripture needs to operate dialectically with the experience of the church, allowing the uniqueness of culture, race, gender, and socio-political perspectives to help identify what elements of the Bible should be viewed to be "life-giving." In any case, what is being advocated in each of these voices is the importance of historical contextual particularity for constructing theology.

Chan also advocates a "global-contextual" criterion as necessary for healthy Christian spirituality. This contextuality, however, is not based on emphasizing the Spirit's historical involvement in a way that "collapse[s] transcendence into immanence." "Historical theologies," he asserts, not only fall short in properly accenting the Spirit's personhood (with Father and Son within the ecclesia), but also fail to take the

---

224. Johnson, *She Who Is*, 61–62.

225. Ibid., 207–22.

226. Along with chapter 1, also see Cone's dialogue with Macchia in chapter 3.

227. Moltmann, *Experiences in Theology*, 3.

Asian context seriously.[228] Chan does admit, "Historical consciousness has become a deeply ingrained modern habit"; but the resulting problem is that the "historical consciousness itself is taken to be a universal consciousness—a normative principle by which all contextual theologies must be judged. Sometimes even more audaciously, a particular stance within the Western liberal tradition is assumed to be valid for the rest of the world."[229]

Chan specifically targets Moltmann as an example of a Western theologian who is unaware of the degree to which he has been influenced by his own culture.

> For instance, Moltmann's main study on pneumatology, *The Spirit of Life*, is pretentiously subtitled *A Universal Affirmation*. His assertion is based on the doctrine of God as "immanent transcendence," that is, a God who reveals himself wholly within the historical processes, and on the belief that the modern historical consciousness is universal. And since the Spirit is a "cosmic Spirit," he can be experienced everywhere in the same way. But this is by no means the case. Can we simply assume that the Spirit that indwells the church also indwells a benevolent Taoist medium?[230]

Chan states that "Moltmann's 'cosmic Spirit,' upon close scrutiny, turns out to be just a religious version of Western liberal egalitarianism which owes more to the Enlightenment than to Christianity."[231] By way of example, Chan points to the trend among Western theologians of accenting God's vulnerability, grounded in a penchant for liberation movements and a general skepticism of power (also notable in Cone and Johnson). This trend applies a particular form of egalitarianism to the Trinity that attempts to avoid any hint of hierarchy (or, in Moltmann's nomenclature, "monotheism"), and is exemplified in social Trinitarian models.[232] Chan, however, views such approaches as potentially dangerous, and insufficient for emphasizing God's transcendent otherness. Declares Chan, "Moltmann represents just this sort of distortion when he equates monotheism with the structure of political and

228. Chan, *Spiritual Theology*, 10.

229. Ibid., 25, 26.

230. Ibid., 27.

231. Chan, *Pentecostal Theology*, 112.

232. Chan, *Spiritual Theology*, 26, 42.

clerical domination."[233] It is not that Chan outright opposes the use of such models contextually; he simply does not want these to be viewed as universally applicable. He advocates, then, distinguishing between primary and secondary symbols for God—primary being the triune identity of God, which is "shorthand" for describing the story of God as outlined in Scripture. "The threeness of God makes sense only in the context of his revelation as the supremely personal being as Father, Son and Holy Spirit."[234]

Asian theologians, Chan argues, in contrast to their Western counterparts, would not tend to reach the same conclusions regarding God's vulnerability from their reading of Scripture. They would more likely emphasize God's transcendence, God as "*invulnerable*," by which the church is led to "triumph against incalculable odds."[235] Chan qualifies this triumphalism as not being of the sort Western theologians fear; nevertheless, this helps reveal that the vulnerability of God emphasized by Western liberation theologies emerges from a particular socio-political cultural context.[236] He singles out feminist approaches by way of illustration: "For one thing, feminist individualistic egalitarianism itself is derived from the Western liberal tradition, which many people from traditional societies outside the West do not share. The hierarchical, communal and consensual ordering of life in Asia, for example, is inherently incompatible with modernist feminist assumptions."[237]

Chan also suggests that in Asia there is a tendency to accent the theological category of the eternal as opposed to the historical in many of the indigenous religions. So, Asians may find it easier to draw on Christian theology that emphasizes God's transcendence.[238] This has its dangers, admits Chan. Asians can sometimes tend to downplay Jesus'

---

233. Ibid., 28.

234. Ibid., 41.

235. Ibid., 26 (italics original).

236. Ibid., 27. Chan includes Korean Minjung theology as an example of a Western import into an Asian context (ibid., 44).

237. Ibid., 31, cf. 30–31.

238. Ibid., 27–28. The Christian spiritual tradition has generally accented God's transcendence over immanence. Writes Chan, "Christian progress is not just a forward movement into God's historical future, as Moltmann or Pannenberg envisions it, but also an upward movement on Jacob's ladder, as the Christian spiritual tradition has consistently affirmed. Although the Christian life is firmly grounded in history, it certainly is not confined to it" (ibid., 10).

historical life, death and resurrection, turning Christ into a cosmic salvific principle of sorts.[239] But more so (as noted earlier), a concept of *Creator Spiritus* that collapses transcendence into immanence holds great potential for confusion in Asia, where a Christian universe (worldview) cannot be assumed and in which animism abounds.[240]

Chan argues, then, that a paradox must be maintained, in which God's transcendence and immanence are held in tension.[241] This is necessary not only for an Asian context (in which failure to do so has immediate doctrinal implications), but also for a healthy Christian spirituality in general. In particular, first, this tension preserves the idea that God is related to, yet distinct from creation.[242] Hiding the Spirit immanently within history, says Chan, simply clouds issues such as the problem of sin and evil, and human responsibility in this regard.[243] Second, he argues, maintaining this tension preserves God's freedom, whereas Moltmann's approach tends to make God dependent on creation, and downplays the Spirit's spontaneity (the "Pentecostal-charismatic" criterion). Third, (as discussed) God's otherness needs to be emphasized in order to help discern what is, or is not of God. Reducing "spirit" to sociological concepts and dynamics overlooks important discernment questions in an Asian context, such as the relation of the Holy Spirit to, say, spirits of the dead.[244]

To preserve the polarities of God's immanence and transcendence, Chan therefore advocates a "Trinitarian spirituality" connected to the gospel narrative. God is not simply "wholly other" but also immanent, "not only the one who unifies all things but also the source of all real diversity in creation."[245] "In other words," states Chan, "contra Moltmann" (and, we might add, Johnson and Cone),

> monotheism should not be seen as a non-Christian accretion
> from Platonic metaphysics but as a true part of the Christian

---

239. Ibid., 31.

240. Chan, "Asian Review," 40. Cf. Chan, *Pentecostal Theology*, 113; and Chan, *Spiritual Theology*, 44.

241. Chan, *Spiritual Theology*, 45–50.

242. Ibid., 43.

243. Ibid., 42. "It is this otherness that Moltmann's doctrine has virtually eliminated," states Chan (ibid., 43).

244. Ibid., 44.

245. Ibid., 41.

understanding of God. Because God is the *one* God who is above all, transcendence can be a source of the Christian's deepest assurance that there is nothing that is not ultimately related to God. Because God is the *triune* God who is intimately related to each other and to the world and love, God's transcendence is an open transcendence that fills us with a sense of purpose rather than meaninglessness and despair.[246]

In sum, Chan would view Moltmann, Johnson, and Cone as having not sufficiently integrated the "evangelical" and "global-contextual" criteria for spirituality, largely due to their diffusion of the Spirit into the world, and their universalizing of Western egalitarianism. The "Pentecostal-charismatic" component is acknowledged by Moltmann (although less so by Johnson and Cone), but Chan would likely have doubts as to whether this could be sustained without a stronger "evangelical" component, linked to a robust ecclesiology—for it is in the historically continuous worshipping community that the triune God is encountered concretely and contextually.[247]

The Church as Locus of Experience of the Spirit

With regard to the church being the locus of experience of the Spirit, considerable convergence is noticeable between Chan and several of our dialogue partners. These include Jenson, Lossky, Congar, Bulgakov, and Gelpi—perhaps with some qualification in the case of the latter two.[248] Among the issues associated with this topic, Chan emphasizes the church as the *totus Christus* (implying a "pneumatological ecclesiology" and "ecclesiological pneumatology"), the reality of ongoing doctrinal development (ongoing revelation), and the need for "Pentecostal-charismatic" spirituality to be expressed within the church (including among the laity).

Concerning the church as the *totus Christus*, Chan cites Bulgakov on more than one occasion to emphasize the church's spiritual ontology as "divine-humanity." The church, writes Chan, "is a divine-humanity

246. Ibid., 45 (italics original), cf. 45–55.

247. Ibid., 45.

248. Moltmann also sees the church as the special place of the Spirit's operation, but not in the same way that Chan does, as we have already observed. For this reason, and because he has already been predominant in our dialogue, Moltmann will not be factored into this particular discussion.

because of its organic link with its Head, Christ."[249] Bulgakov also emphasizes this "mystical essence" (spiritual reality) of the church, "the body of Christ animated by the Holy Spirit, as his temple, and as the bride of Christ."[250] Further, because of this divine-creaturely "union" or "synergism," the church can be viewed not only as the location of the reception of grace, but also the place through which spiritual life is given to her members.[251] This latter point appears congruent with Chan's emphasis on Eucharistic liturgy as central to Christian spiritual sustenance. Bulgakov also finds convergence with Chan concerning the idea that creation exists for the church: "the Church is the very foundation of creation, its inner entelechy."[252]

It also should be noted, however, that Bulgakov's reason for viewing the church as "divine-humanity" rests not solely in the Pentecost event, but is grounded, firstly, in the fact that the church participates in Sophia, the divine essence. The church, then, can be considered "eternal," in some sense, "for it is the Divine Sophia herself."[253] But the church also shares in the creaturely Sophia by virtue of the Incarnation (uniting divine and creaturely worlds) and Pentecost (elevating humanity's ability to participate toward sophianization).[254] Chan does not utilize Bulgakov's sophiology, which, as noted earlier, allows Bulgakov to sometimes blur the boundaries of the Spirit's activity in the world and church (and which may prove to be a stumbling block to Chan).

That said, we do find considerable convergence between Chan and Bulgakov with regard to the Spirit's ongoing ecclesial activity. First, Bulgakov sees the church as an ongoing tradition, similar to Chan's portrayal. It is not simply "primitive Christianity" or the present "hierarchical Church" that bears the Spirit's truth, says Bulgakov; rather, these together exist as one "historical reality," as "the same apostolic Church."[255] The church as divine-humanity, for Bulgakov, allows for both historical continuity, and, it appears, the possibility of ongoing

---

249. Chan, *Liturgical Theology*, 23. Cf. Chan, "Church and the Development," 63; and Bulgakov, *Bride of the Lamb*, 253.

250. Bulgakov, *Bride of the Lamb*, 255.

251. Ibid., 253, 255.

252. Ibid., 253, cf. 254.

253. Ibid., 254.

254. Ibid., 300.

255. Ibid., 270, 271.

doctrinal development. This reading of Bulgakov is based, secondly, on his idea that the church is the "all-sacrament" in which all other sacraments are received.[256] Bulgakov acknowledges that the early church did not celebrate all the sacraments currently enjoyed; some were instituted later in history.[257] This implies, thirdly, "that the hierarchical-sacramental organization is not the adequate or absolute manifestation of the Church, that this organization therefore has a certain relative character."[258] This permits considerable room, fourthly, for the Spirit to effect sophianization within the church, not simply through the sacraments but *also through the charismata*.[259] This unregulated, prophetic working of the "breath of the Spirit" has been part of Christian history, asceticism, and teaching from the beginning, and needs to be preserved alongside the hierarchy. States Bulgakov, "Prophecy is dynamics, movement in the life of the church, whereas hierarchism is its statics, its backbone."[260] The similarities to Chan on all of these points are noteworthy, and indicate that he may find a resource in Bulgakov for more than simply church ontology.

Jenson, Congar, and Lossky are also very careful to locate the Spirit's presence in the church. Jenson does so in order to preserve the Spirit's identity, emphasizing the historical continuity of the church as *totus Christus* in doing so.[261] Chan would find convergence here, and actually cites Jenson often on this subject. For example: "[the] Spirit frees an actual human community from the merely historical determinisms, to be apt to be united to the Son and thus be the gateway of creation's translation into God."[262] Congruence between this emphasis of both Chan and Jenson, concerning creation existing for, and the preservation of, the gospel in the church could hardly be more apparent here.

A possible divergence, however, may occur with Chan's insistence on the "Pentecostal-charismatic" dimension as necessary for a

256. Ibid., 272, 273.

257. Ibid., 273–74.. He thus distinguishes between "evangelical" and "nonevangelical" sacraments, the former being baptism and the Lord's Supper.

258. Ibid., 274.

259. Ibid., 274, 290–93.

260. Ibid., 292.

261. Chan, "Church and the Development," 63; Jenson, *Systematic Theology: Works*, 167.

262. Chan, "Church and the Development," 73 (quoting Jenson, *Systematic Theology: Works*, 179).

well-balanced Christian spirituality, which is not really emphasized by Jenson. Chan believes this dimension is part of the Christian tradition—not an aberration. Jenson, on the other hand, tends to limit the Spirit's activity almost solely to mediating the Word preached, and sustaining the liturgy and tradition through the teaching office.[263] The Word may surprise the church at times,[264] but the prophetic dimension appears to be subsumed to an ecclesiastical function (the church as interpreter of Scripture is what makes it 'prophetic'),[265] as opposed to the more charismatic sort of prophecy allowed by Chan (and Bulgakov, Congar, and Gelpi). Chan has profited much from Jenson's emphasis on the Spirit's identity being localized in the church. It may be, however, that Jenson could reciprocally benefit by recognizing that not all charismatic movements in history were attempting to "free" themselves from the historical church, as Chan has attempted to demonstrate. Indeed, Chan's emphasis on "Pentecostal-charismatic" spirituality functioning (metaphorically) as "play," requiring both structure and spontaneity, may serve as a point of challenge to Jenson who appears reticent to make much room for this dimension.

Among our other dialogue partners, Lossky clearly locates the Spirit in the church, which is the "sphere of the Spirit." Having noted this, however, we will defer further conversation with him to the next subsection concerning ascetical and charismatic spirituality. Congar likewise views the church as the locus of the Spirit—there is no "free sector" of the Spirit—and here it seems appropriate to highlight some convergences and divergences with Chan.[266] We will recall that Congar's "Christological pneumatology" and "pneumatological Christology" allows him to view Word as not only the form and structure of the church, but also as being a product of the Spirit.[267] In this way Word and Spirit co-institute the church. The Spirit (as with Jenson) enables the spoken and written word to be received, and enables the church to bear prophetic witness to the world. At times Congar appears to relativize Spirit

---

263. Jenson, *Systematic Theology: Triune*, 228–29.

264. Ibid., 198.

265. Jenson, *Systematic Theology: Works*, 276.

266. Congar, *Word and the Spirit*, 61.

267. Chan draws attention to Congar concerning this emphasis. See Chan, *Spiritual Theology*, 49.

to Word, but at others presents a far more dynamic view of this relationship, therefore converging here with Chan in a number of respects.

Congar speaks, for example, of Word as form and Spirit as the more
spontaneous "breath,"[268] congruent with Chan's discussion of charismatic
worship as liturgical "play." Further, Congar challenges the Magisterium
and ordained clergy to recognize the "fullness of spiritual gifts" operating
among God's people, including the laity.[269] This means that believers' private revelations may speak prophetically to the body, challenging institution and traditions. Allowing more "immediate" charismatic experiences
also means the Spirit is not only experienced through the sacraments.[270]
With regard to sacramental structure, Chan notably finds a resource in
Congar's emphasis on confirmation as being the act that distinguishes
Spirit from Word. This enables Spirit baptism to be viewed as more than
merely an "intensification" of spiritual life—"we are baptized into Christ,
confirmed by the Spirit."[271] In short, Congar, by retaining emphasis on
church institution and sacraments, while also permitting (and encouraging) spontaneous experiences and manifestations of the Spirit, provides
the structure Chan believes is necessary to sustain the "Pentecostal reality," and links spiritual experiences (e.g., Spirit baptism) to the broader
conversion-initiation complex. It may very well be that Congar and
Chan bear the most similarities in this dialogue overall, theologically,
spiritually, and practically.

Gelpi is rather unique partner in this discussion due to his project
being a triadic construct that accounts for experience in general, and
the possibility of charismatic encounters within the church in particular.
Concerning the church, Gelpi believes that his metaphysics provides a
way to understand the mystery of the Spirit indwelling the church (as
well as that of the Trinity and Incarnation)[272] by highlighting a fundamental "inexistence" between God and the world—the latter panentheistically existing in the mind (*nous*) of God, the "Holy Breath."[273] The
church likewise subsists "inexistently" by and with the Spirit. Spirit (as

---

268. Congar, *I Believe*, 2:34–35.

269. Congar, *Word and the Spirit*, 33, 34–35.

270. Ibid., 52–58.

271. Chan, *Pentecostal Theology*, 90; cf. Congar, *I Believe*, 1:106.

272. Gelpi, *Turn to Experience*, 149ff.

273. Gelpi, *Divine Mother*, 45. Chan seems to prefer a similar psychological model
of the Spirit's relationship as love bond between the Father and Son (Chan, *Pentecostal
Theology*, 51).

divine mind) is bound to Son and Father, and therefore the church may be viewed as the special location of the Spirit.[274]

Gelpi's triadic construct also has implications for spirituality, which we will address shortly. There is reason, however, to believe that Chan might be uncomfortable with some elements of Gelpi's project, despite the latter's being open to the "Pentecostal-charismatic" dimensions of spirituality. In Chan's essay, "Encountering the Triune God," he critiques Yong's theology (the focus of chapter 5) for its diffusion of the Spirit into the world in hopes of providing ground for dialogue between Christianity and other faiths, as well as with the sciences. The problem, as Chan sees it, is that Yong has not grounded his theology in

> the concrete narrative of the triune God; rather, what we see is a Trinitarian *pattern* of working expressed in terms of metaphysical principles as a way of finding common ground with other religions. For example, Word and Spirit are understood as poles of concreteness and dynamism that are necessary for discerning the divine presence and activity (the pneumatological) in other religions. While Yong does not deny the status of the Spirit as the third person of the Trinity, his pneumatological approach to the religions tends to treat the Spirit modalistically, largely as God's action in the world. This is manifestly inadequate.[275]

In other words, we have again returned to the issue of the Spirit's identity as related to ecclesiology. While Chan is not addressing Gelpi in the above quotation, the parallels between Yong and Gelpi's projects are notably substantial (as will be seen). Both strongly employ metaphysics in developing their respective theological work, and so Chan's critique of Yong may very well apply to Gelpi as well.[276]

Ascetical, Pentecostal-Charismatic Spirituality

Our final area of dialogue in this chapter pertains to Chan's conviction that spiritual life must be undergirded by a basic ascetical structure.[277] Of course Chan believes the "Pentecostal-charismatic" dimension is a

274. Gelpi does suggest, however, the Spirit may have had other missions prior to the Incarnation (see Gelpi, *The Divine Mother*, 70).

275. Chan, "Encountering the Triune," 218 (italics original), cf. 217–18.

276. We will more closely compare Yong and Gelpi's work in the next chapter.

277. For more on Chan's Trinitarian structure of spirituality see Chan, *Spiritual Theology*, 50–55.

significant (but oft-neglected) component of the Christian spiritual tradition, but ideally "every Christian should be both charismatic and an
ascetic."[278] So, "Pentecostal-charismatic" spirituality must be connected
to the broader Christian tradition as well as a basic ascetical structure.
Asserts Chan, "An enthusiastic spirituality that is developed in isolation
from an ascetical spirituality cannot be sustainable for long, nor can it
have universal applicability."[279] For this reason, Chan attempts to demonstrate how "Pentecostal-charismatic" spirituality (in particular, the
Spirit baptism experience) can be placed within an ascetical structure,
such as the traditional "three ways." Several of our dialogue partners
demonstrate elements that converge with Chan's convictions in this regard, including Lossky, Bulgakov, Gelpi, and Moltmann. While all have
something to contribute, our primary focus here will be Lossky, since the
others have already had significant involvement in the discourse thus far.

Lossky especially converges with Chan with regard to the conviction that spiritual life ought to involve progress—it is an ascetical
way of small steps, involving cooperation with God along the journey.
Lossky insists that the way of union with God *assumes a simultaneous
cooperation* of the human will and divine grace, the operation of which
is an apophatic mystery.[280] Turning to Bulgakov for a moment, he also
views grace as already operative (due to creation being open to grace by
Sophia), and so a synergy is always assumed and expected in progress
toward divinization (sophianization). He highlights the importance of
the Incarnation and Pentecost as well in this regard, uniting the divine
and creaturely, and elevating human capacity to grow in grace. In this
respect, Bulgakov states Pentecost does not so much introduce grace as
a "what" (not acting coercively on the will), but as a "how," a means by
which to work out one's spiritual progress in the church.[281]

Returning to Lossky, following the Eastern ascetic tradition, he
views the "heart" as the human intellect and will, which, as it is filled by
grace, will transform the rest of the person's nature. The human "spirit"

---

278. Ibid., 39, cf. 38.

279. Ibid., 39, cf. 49–50.

280. Lossky, *Mystical Theology*, 196–98. Lossky differentiates the Eastern tradition
from the West in this regard. Western debates over the necessity of grace acting upon the
human will (Augustine) in opposition to the Pelagian emphasis on free will as being able
to merit grace are trapped, Lossky believes, in an unresolvable dilemma. The operation
of grace should be viewed as a "synergy of the two wills," divine and human (ibid., 198).

281. Bulgakov, *Bride of the Lamb*, 305, cf. 303–5.

(*nous*) is the seat of human personhood, through which God communicates his grace (beginning at baptism).[282] Thus, the heart must (consciously) cooperate with the spirit toward unification, the process toward which requires both action (praxis) and contemplation.[283] The way of union involves three "stages," says Lossky: "penitence, purification, and perfection—that is to say, conversion of the will, liberation from the passions, and the acquisition of that perfect love which is the fullness of grace." Lossky is also clear to define what he means by "stage." It is not "a passing moment, a stage to be left behind. It is in fact not a stage but a condition which must continue permanently, the constant attitude of those who truly aspire to union with God."[284] Lossky further describes these "stages," emphasizing the need for repentance and especially the need for personal, conscious prayer, which if actively practiced will often result in moments of (passive) ecstasy, including silence.[285] The ultimate fruit of prayer, however, is a growing consciousness of divine love being appropriated into the depths of the human being, and spilling out in love for others.[286]

The above summary has been necessarily brief, but the parallels with Chan's ascetical spirituality are considerable. Both Chan and Lossky draw on the "three ways" model, emphasizing not a linear but (in Chan's words) "spiral" progression. Like Lossky, Chan emphasizes the interrelatedness of the dogmatic and spiritual (Lossky's "mystical") traditions—experience and dogma dialectically informing one another.[287] Both also view ascetical prayer as necessary to spiritual progress and as leading to "passive" experiences of ecstasy, whether in silence (Lossky) or glossolalia (Chan). They both also agree that the experience of divine love should overflow into love of others.[288]

A couple points of divergence are also notable, however. Lossky views ecstatic experiences as being more common in the earlier stages of mysticism, and as occurring less frequently as the mystic matures,

---

282. Lossky, *Mystical Theology*, 200–201.

283. Ibid., 201–3.

284. Ibid., 204.

285. Ibid., 205–9.

286. Ibid., 209–15.

287. Ibid., 226.

288. Chan, *Spiritual Theology*, 101.

becoming more accustomed to the divine reality.[289] Chan, on the other hand, accents recurrence of the enthusiastic dimension—ever opening new awareness of God's presence, despite the maturity level of the ascetic. Lossky also views experiences of spiritual aridity as anomalies in spiritual progress,[290] whereas Chan (following more so the Western tradition) views such experiences as necessary to the journey. In any case, the overwhelming congruency between Chan and Lossky is very evident, perhaps indicating that further dialogue between these two, at least in the above areas, would be fruitful.

Returning to ecstatic experiences, we may again bring Gelpi into the conversation. One application of Gelpi's triadic construct of experience is that it helps him understand charismatic experiences with God, introducing the "radically new" into the life of faith.[291] Because experience of God is "inexistently" relational, it means that encounters with God can occur sacramentally (mediated through the created realm, including other people), as well as more directly in depth experiences.[292] God can be experienced in nonrational, intuitive ways (not simply through intellect and will),[293] and introduce radical religious "conversion" experiences, including manifestations of prophetic empowerment and other charismata.[294] Despite our previous speculative caution concerning Chan's attitude toward Gelpi's metaphysics, on this subject Chan explicitly cites Gelpi positively.[295] This is likely due, in part, to Gelpi's locating the charismatic dimension within a broader relational complex, which is, of course, something Chan believes essential to sustaining the "Pentecostal reality."

Finally, a few observations are in order concerning the implications of Moltmann's theology of experience for ascetic spirituality. Concerning this particular issue, Chan is generally positive towards Moltmann, complimenting his linking of pneumatology to the elements of the *ordo salutis* (including justification, regeneration, and

---

289. Lossky, *Mystical Theology*, 208–9.

290. Ibid., 225.

291. Chan, *Spiritual Theology*, 37–38.

292. Gelpi, *Divine Mother*, 94.

293. Chan, *Spiritual Theology*, 38.

294. Gelpi, *Divine Mother*, 73–74, 198–202.

295. Chan, *Spiritual Theology*, 37–38.

sanctification),[296] since this leads more naturally into a "spiritual theology."[297] Concerning the charismata, Moltmann's involving the Spirit in everyday existence means he sees no dichotomy between so-called "natural" and "supernatural" gifts—something Chan believes to be a helpful corrective to Pentecostals, who tend to equate the latter with "greater spirituality."[298] Chan also appreciates Moltmann's schema of mystical theology, suggesting Pentecostals (and Protestants) consider such a model for their own spiritual development, among other things because it does not avoid the practical implications of discipleship, including "martyrdom" (political involvement).[299]

This latter point highlights a possible convergence between Moltmann and Chan that we otherwise might not expect. Chan does, in fact, advocate a "spirituality of social involvement" (with the Asian context in mind).[300] In doing so he reaffirms his skepticism of "theologies of hope," including Moltmann's "political theology," which, despite producing considerable commitment to social issues, is unable to distinguish the Spirit from any popular "current ideology, be it liberal democracy, feminism or green politics."[301] In contrast to political theology, then, Chan advocates a "theological politics," which views the church as influencing the world only in so far as it (the church) preserves its own distinctiveness.[302] Despite this, however, Christian spirituality entails an "asceticism of social engagement"[303] that includes social and political action, and which may work itself out differently depending on the context. Writes Chan, "Even though the spirituality of social engagement takes on many forms (black, feminist) and methods (confrontational, consensual, critical cooperation) depending on the differing contexts, it must be impelled by the same Spirit of God who guides the Church aright in these different situations as it prays.

---

296. See Moltmann, *Spirit of Life*, 123–79.

297. Chan, "Asian Review," 36.

298. Ibid., 38.

299. Ibid., 37; cf. Moltmann, *Spirit of Life*, 208–11.

300. Chan, *Spiritual Theology*, 185–89.

301. Ibid., 186. Chan claims that in Moltmann's political theology, "One is spiritual by being full of spirit, not necessarily by being full of the Holy Spirit."

302. Ibid., 186–87; cf. Chan, *Pentecostal Theology*, 115–16. Here Chan draws on John Howard Yoder and Stanley Hauerwas.

303. Chan, *Spiritual Theology*, 187–89.

Only then is spirituality authentically Christian."[304] So, while Chan accents the preservation of Christian identity by locating the Spirit in the ecclesia, he does demonstrate appreciation for the practical trajectory of Moltmann's mystical theology.

Conclusion

The ecumenical dialogue in this chapter has exemplified Chan's conviction that the Christian tradition needs to be upheld as a means through which the Spirit is mediated to the church and world. For Chan, the identity of the Spirit is tied to the identity of the church, and vice versa. This placed him in considerable disagreement with several of our dialogue partners, but also demonstrated that he has much in common with a number of others—in particular those advocating a high ecclesiology. It is possible that Chan's openness to tradition may serve to bring greater appreciation of the "Pentecostal reality" to the broader ecumenical community, while at the same time challenging Pentecostals to recover their earlier ecumenical impulse. In doing so Chan exemplifies theologically that qualities of adulthood are certainly present and growing within Pentecostalism.

---

304. Ibid., 189. As an example, Chan highlights Vishal Mangalwadi of India, who has combined evangelism and social involvement, utilizing elements of both Moltmann's and Hauerwas' seemingly contradictory approaches to politics (ibid., 187).

5

Amos Yong

Experiencing the Spirit through Reason

IN THIS STUDY OVERALL, "REASON" HAS BEEN DEFINED MORE BROADLY TO
mean the "context" in which humans find themselves reflecting theologically (as opposed to any narrower technical philosophical use of the term).[1]
This chapter, then, will explore how Amos Yong's Pentecostal theology of
experience accents the Spirit's mediation through reason—in the particular contexts of life, and universally so.[2] His theological work is considerably
expansive,[3] a significant amount of attention being given to the theology of
religions (including interfaith dialogue),[4] the interrelation between theology and the sciences,[5] political theology,[6] and most broadly to developing

1. The reader is referred to this book's introduction, where this definition of "reason"
was discussed in more detail.

2. Yong is a Pentecostal theologian, licensed with the Assemblies of God (USA), and
is currently the J. Rodham Williams Professor of Theology at Regent University School
of Divinity in Virginia. He was born into a Malaysian home of a Pentecostal pastor, and
his family later moved to California as missionaries to Chinese speaking congregations.

3. Yong is the most prolific writer of the three Pentecostals in this project, having
authored and edited numerous books and articles. The reader is referred to the bibliography for a fuller listing.

4. See Yong, *Discerning the Spirit(s)*; Yong, *Beyond the Impasse*; Yong, *Hospitality and
the Other*; Yong, *Spirit Poured Out*, ch. 6; and Yong, "'Not Knowing Where,'" 1–21.

5. See Yong, *Spirit of Creation*; Yong, *Theology and Down Syndrome*; Yong, *Spirit-Word-
Community*, 297–300; Yong, "Discerning the Spirit(s) in the Natural World," 315–29; Yong,
"God and the Evangelical," 203–21; Yong, "'Tongues,' Theology,"; Yong, *Spirit Poured Out*,
ch. 7; and Yong, *Beyond the Impasse*, 68, 76–77. Yong and James K. A. Smith also directed
the Research Initiative entitled, "Science and the Spirit: Pentecostal Perspectives on the
Science/Religion Dialogue" from 2005–2009 (Smith and Yong, *Science and the Spirit*, vii).

6. See Yong, *In the Days*.

a general theological hermeneutic—all of which involves giving significant attention to issues of metaphysics and epistemology.[7] Methodologically, this chapter will follow the previous two; an exposition of Yong's theology will be followed by dialogue with our other partners, with a view toward demonstrating the maturation of Pentecostal theology.

Amos Yong and Pentecostal Experience of the Spirit

Pentecostal-Charismatic Experience as Point of Departure

Yong approaches his work largely from the starting point of pneumatology, specifically from an epistemological perspective based in "Pentecostal-charismatic" (henceforth PC in this chapter) experience.[8] Through an empirically-grounded understanding of PC experience a particular lens for viewing reality emerges that holds promise for theological construction. Yong calls this lens the "pneumatological imagination," which, he explains, is "a way of seeing God, self and world that is inspired by the Pentecostal-charismatic experience of the Spirit."[9] PC experience, then, generates a perspective of reality, which simultaneously informs PC experience in dialectical relationship.[10]

A sketch of PC experience is appropriate at the outset, so as to better appreciate how it informs the "pneumatological imagination" (to be explored in more detail later in this chapter) and theology in general. Yong sets out his description of PC experience most significantly in *Discerning the Spirit(s)* and *The Spirit Poured Out on All Flesh* (arguably his most comprehensive effort at a systematic theology to date).[11] In the latter

---

7. See especially Yong, *Spirit-Word-Community*.

8. Yong does not limit PC experience to classical Pentecostalism, but supplements this with insights from the charismatic movement (including those of the "third wave") to be explored below. See Yong, *Spirit Poured Out*, 18–20; Yong, *Discerning the Spirit(s)*, 151–57; and Yong, *Beyond the Impasse*, 75, cf. 74–81.

9. Yong, *Discerning the Spirit(s)*, 102. Elsewhere Yong expands this to "Christian" imagination (Yong, *Beyond the Impasse*, 64).

10. Yong, *Discerning the Spirit(s)*, 171, cf. 181. Yong writes, "The thesis I am suggesting is that the experience of the Spirit informs the pneumatological imagination of the Pentecostal or charismatic and vice versa." This is why Yong can speak at times of the pneumatological imagination enabling Pentecostal-charismatic experience (ibid., 168), and other times of Pentecostal-charismatic experience shaping the pneumatological imagination.

11. Ibid., 149–82; Yong, *Spirit Poured Out*, 17–80. Also see Yong, "Pentecostalism

work, he proposes a "world theology," based in PC experience, which is particularly suited for this theological undertaking.[12] PC experience has manifested itself globally in a multitude of cultural expressions,[13] and is able to contribute positively to three contemporary theological challenges: ecumenical fellowship, interreligious dialogue, and the religion/science interchange.[14]

Yong's distinctive PC approach to theology involves three elements. First, it is biblically-rooted in a Lukan hermeneutic. Second, it is theologically shaped by a pneumatological "orienting dynamic" (the "pneumatological imagination"), but also simultaneously by Christology (as its "thematic focus")—neither Spirit nor Christ is to be subordinated to the other. Yong's goal, then, is a "robustly Trinitarian theology of mutuality, reciprocity, and perichoresis." Third, this approach is "confessionally located in the sense of emerging from the matrix of Pentecostal experience of the Spirit of God."[15]

Using the third element as a point of departure, Yong provides a broad empirical case study of sorts, sketching the practices of PCs in Latin America, Asia, and Africa.[16] He observes that PCs worldwide are wrestling with a multitude of issues (in a variety of contexts and ways), including: socio-political involvement and women's liberation (Latin America), the influence of ancient established religions upon Pentecostalism (Asia), and racial equality and ecological concerns (Africa). Four general observations from his survey factor into Yong's theology. First, Pentecostalism is diversely expressed. Second, it tends to be more concrete as opposed to abstract (rooted in the experience of

---

and the Theological," 244–50; and Yong, *Beyond the Impasse*, 74–81.

12. This is opposed to a "global theology" that might impose a particular theology universally. A "world theology" attempts to preserve the particulars of theology and practice as it is worked out on the ground, so to speak.

13. Yong, *Spirit Poured Out*, 18; cf. Yong, "Whose Tongues," 1–21.

14. Yong, *Spirit Poured Out*, 22, cf. 22–24. Here Yong does note that Classical Pentecostalism in particular faces internal challenges in addressing each of these issues, having been reticent to involve themselves ecumenically, and even more so interreligiously. Pentecostals have also been ambiguous with regard to science—at times siding with evangelical fundamentalist suspicions, while at the same time pragmatically embracing technology (for use in all sorts of Christian ministries, evangelism in particular).

15. Ibid., 28, 29, cf. 30.

16. Ibid., 31–80; cf. Yong, *Discerning the Spirit(s)*, 158–61.

worship in community). Third, it is soteriologically holistic. Fourth, it easily connects with the poor and marginalized.[17]

It is in *Discerning the Spirit(s)*, however, where Yong provides more explicit grounds for connecting these various global experiences and grouping Pentecostals and charismatics: "it is the experiences of the Spirit—what is often referred as, but not limited to, the charismata—that links Pentecostals and charismatics together." He demonstrates this through a brief phenomenological survey of Pentecostal and charismatic ritual, which provides a framework for understanding experience of the Spirit.[18] Here Yong draws on Hollenweger, concerning the holistic emphases of Pentecostal spirituality and worship,[19] and Albrecht's characterization of PC ritual as "holistic involvement and engagement with the divine presence in anticipation of receiving something transformative from a new work of the Holy Spirit in the ritual process." The PC worship service engenders both expectancy, and active cultivation, of encounter with God.[20]

Thus the Spirit's presence and activity is fundamental to PC spirituality, says Yong, and the symbol of "Spirit-baptism" best typifies the PC "imagination" in this regard.[21] In short, "Spirit-baptism for Pentecostals and charismatics points to an encounter with the divine (Spirit) such as that experienced when one undergoes a deluge or is swept by a whirlwind (baptism)."[22] Despite theological differences, Yong argues, for both Pentecostals and charismatics the Spirit serves as a symbol of God's immanent presence, confirmed in "manifold expressions" of Spirit baptism.[23]

---

17. Yong, *Spirit Poured Out*, 79–80.

18. Yong, *Discerning the Spirit(s)*, 161.

19. Ibid., 162, cf. 163. These include: "democratic (read oral) participation in ritual" and the bringing together of the public/private, and mind/body, in general enabling "engagement with the world on the one hand, and . . . pursuit of the Spirit on the other." This characterization is strongly congruent with Wacker's "heaven below" characterization of Pentecostals.

20. Ibid., 164, 165.

21. Ibid., 169–70, cf. 165–70.

22. Ibid., 168.

23. Ibid., 168, 171. Thus "Spirit-baptism" can serve as the primary metaphor for what is the essence of PC experience. "The point is that there is sufficient evidence for a convergent understanding of Spirit-baptism as the 'essence' of what it means to be Pentecostal or charismatic even if we do recognize, as indeed we should, the diversity of its manifestations" (ibid., 169–70).

So, encounters with the Spirit shape the PC pneumatological imagination and "vice versa."[24]

We have so far briefly surveyed two elements of Yong's distinctive approach to PC theology; the remaining element is the PC Lukan hermeneutic. Not only is Luke-Acts a legitimate theological resource, he argues, but it also provides an essential lens by which to approach theology as a whole.[25] This is because Luke accents a "Spirit christology," not opposed, but complementary to dominant "Logos christology"—Jesus is the Spirit-anointed man.[26] Further, Luke demonstrates that the Spirit's work through Jesus is broadly soteriological, expressed in several dimensions, including: forgiveness of sin, deliverance from demons, healing of the sick, liberation of the poor, and eschatologically as salvation realized both now and not yet. This salvific work continues through Jesus' followers, anointed with the Spirit at Pentecost.[27]

Yong views PC experience, then, as a key resource for revisioning theology, and uses it to construct a pneumatological soteriology that appreciates the "multidimensionality of salvation,"[28] and helps overcome numerous theological impasses related to ecclesiology, ecumenical fellowship, and Trinitarian theology (particularly with regard to Oneness Pentecostalism).[29] Yong also believes that the PC "pneumatological

24. Ibid., 171, cf. 172–77. Yong believes that Pentecostal theology is undergoing considerable revision as it dialogues with charismatics. He notes three areas of development in particular. First, the doctrine of "subsequence" has been broadened to be understood as being the idea of "more"—accenting the process of human experience and relationship with God, including expectation of the continuing work of the Spirit in one's life in new "transformative" and "reorienting" ways. (Yong identifies Gelpi's work as having been influential in this regard.) Second, the tendency for Pentecostals to posit a dualism between the natural and supernatural realms is being redeveloped in light of sacramental interpretations. Third, the traditional Pentecostal reductive understanding of Spirit baptism as power for witness is being expanded to recognize various "levels of functionality" of the manifestations of charisms, including: "fruit-bearing" in the life of the individual, the building up of the congregation at a corporate level, drawing unbelievers into the body of Christ, and possibly even manifestations in the lives of those not associated with the Christian faith.

25. Yong, *Spirit Poured Out*, 83–86. It seems on this point that Yong is exhibiting more of a Classical Pentecostal approach than that of charismatics, who might prefer to begin with a Pauline lens. A similar approach is used in Yong's development of a Pentecostal approach to political theology (Yong, *In the Days*, 99–117).

26. Yong, *Spirit Poured Out*, 86–88.

27. Ibid., 88–91.

28. Ibid., 91, cf. 91–109.

29. Ibid., 121–234; cf. Yong, "Oneness and the Trinity," 81–107.

imagination" is able to provide a way forward with regard to dialogue between religions and with the sciences (to be discussed later).[30] In short, the PC "pneumatological imagination," informed by and informing PC experience of the Spirit, provides a robust means by which to construct a pneumatological Christian theology, one that is able not only to speak to its own tradition(s), but also better communicate in public arenas of life. At risk of getting ahead of ourselves, Yong's summary of PC experience and the "pneumatological imagination" is helpful here:

> Living in the world by way of a pneumatological imagination simply means participating in the fields of force generated by the Spirit's presence and activity. We do not own the Spirit, but simply comply with what the Spirit is doing in the world. The Pentecostal-charismatic experience of the Spirit is thus a vivid and intensified form of this encounter and cooperation because it grasps the individual in the totality of his or her being and moves that person into a public force field, even while that field, the larger whole, is effectively transformed by the newly located presence of the Spirit-filled individual.[31]

Several concepts here will be clarified later in our discussion. At this point, however, we simply note that, for Yong, PC experience of the Spirit can serve as a theological point of departure,[32] and holds resources for enabling believers to converse in the public realm. This is because Yong understands the Spirit to be already present and active in the public dimension. Put another way, the Spirit can be (and is already) experienced in general life *contexts*, enabling truth about God, oneself, others and the cosmos to be discerned ("all truth is God's truth").[33] But how or why should we believe this to be so? To answer such questions and better appreciate Yong's optimism in this regard, we need to examine his "foundational pneumatology" as well as further elucidate the meaning of "pneumatological imagination."

---

30. Yong, *Spirit Poured Out*, 235–302; cf. Yong, *Spirit of Creation*, 11–12.

31. Yong, *Discerning the Spirit(s)*, 177.

32. Yong, *Spirit-Word-Community*, 7.

33. Ibid., 306; Yong, *Spirit Poured Out*, 283.

The Metaphysical Basis of a Foundational Pneumatology

Yong's "foundational pneumatology" and "pneumatological imagination" are intricately related, the former emphasizing a particular metaphysical construct, the latter the accompanying epistemology emerging from, and feeding into this metaphysic. However, "foundational," here, does not simply refer to metaphysics, but also epistemology. He wants to demonstrate how the resources for theologizing can be "public"—accessible to all interested inquirers—since this provides the grounds for any number of opportunities for dialogue (including interfaith and with the sciences). Yong dedicates considerable space to articulating his foundational pneumatology and pneumatological imagination in various forms in several of his works.[34] So, this and the next subsection will necessarily be limited to sketching out his major points in this regard.

Yong constructs a foundational pneumatology in order to account for the Spirit's universal presence and activity in creation.[35] His attempt is not the first, and he readily acknowledges building on the metaphysical and epistemological work of Gelpi, as well as that of American pragmatic philosopher, Charles Sanders Peirce (to whom we will return shortly).[36] Yong's foundational pneumatology is highly complex, constructed using pneumatology as a point of departure, and weaving together a number of biblical, theological, and philosophical strands.

Biblically, for example, Yong observes that the Spirit is portrayed as "God present and active, the power of God in creation, re-creation, and final creation."[37] Because Scripture indicates that all things are created by Word and Spirit, this implies that the Spirit is universally present; and it is through the Spirit that God has knowledge of creation. In short, "the Spirit's universality is intimately connected with God's knowledge of and activity in the world of human beings."[38] Further, all human life

---

34. This is done in most detail in *Spirit-Word-Community*, which aims at developing a theological hermeneutic in general. Also see Yong, "On Divine Presence," 1–19; Yong, *Beyond the Impasse*, chs. 3, 6; Yong, *Discerning the Spirit(s)*, ch. 4; and Yong, *Spirit Poured Out*, chs. 6–7.

35. Yong, *Discerning the Spirit(s)*, 99.

36. Yong, *Beyond the Impasse*, 58, cf. 58–66. Gelpi is repeatedly used as a dialogue partner in Yong's work. See for example, Yong, *Discerning the Spirit(s)*, 99–104, 111–22; and Yong, *Spirit-Word-Community*, 91–96, 101–5, 222–23, 246.

37. Yong, *Beyond the Impasse*, 36, cf. 35–42; cf. *Spirit Poured Out*, 280–83.

38. Yong, *Beyond the Impasse*, 37.

"is animated by the presence and activity of God by and through the divine Spirit."[39] The Spirit's "re-creational" activity is exemplified in the Incarnation and Pentecost narratives in Scripture, highlighting the "pneumatological character" of soteriology.[40] The Pentecost event also accents the "eschatological character of the Spirit's activity," which extends to the final creation, the new heaven and earth. Further, the diversity of those present at Pentecost not only represents the church's catholicity, "but also anticipates the scope of the kingdom of God."[41] Thus, says Yong, Pentecost has implications for all people, and for all creation.[42] In sum, "The Spirit is thereby the universal presence and activity of God. He is a universality that permeates both the external structures of the natural and human world and the internal realms of human hearts. He is also a universality that spans the entirety of God's work from original creation, to re-creation, to final creation."[43]

Elsewhere, Yong identifies several biblical motifs associated with and helpful for understanding the Spirit's activity. First, from the Spirit's involvement in the Incarnation, Pentecost and the formation of the Christian community can be inferred the Spirit's "relationality."[44] Second, the Spirit is associated with being the source and communicator of "rationality."[45] Word and Spirit are necessary to make the world intelligible, but accent is on the latter, who "mediates and communicates" the revelation of God to creation.[46] He writes, "That divinely originated meaning and the mind of God can be grasped by human beings presupposes some sort of point of contact between the divine and human. The mediating key, it should now be clear, is pneumatological."[47] Thus, Spirit

---

39. Ibid., 38.

40. Ibid., 39, cf. 38–40.

41. Ibid., 40.

42. Ibid., 41.

43. Ibid., 42.

44. Yong, *Spirit-Word-Community*, 28, cf. 28–34.

45. Ibid., 35, cf. 35–43.

46. Ibid., 35–37, 39.

47. Ibid., 41. Yong states, Spirit "communicates rationality to the created order and is the condition of human rationality, but also provides the guiding soteriological rationale for human existence vis-à-vis the purposes and intentions of the creator. Thus the category of 'spirit' [is] intimately related to the question of meaning and truth . . ." (ibid., 42). Further, "Theological rationality and intelligibility is therefore pneumatological through and through" (ibid., 43).

is also understood to be the "mind of God." Yong explains, "She is the presupposition undergirding the intelligibility of divinity, our understanding of the same, and the interpretation of the divine life, meant in the twofold sense of our interpreting theologically the divine life, and the divine life's interpreting itself and its activity—the created order."[48] Third, the Spirit may also be discerned as the "*dunamis*" ("dynamic power") of life itself, emphasizing the communal dimension of the Spirit's activity.[49] The Spirit brings life to creation itself, to human life in particular, and is the guiding (purposeful) dynamic power in history and the cosmos—the Spirit breathed life, is breathing (renewing) creation now, and will bring creation to completeness.[50]

With regard to creation, Yong elsewhere draws on Robert Cummings Neville's philosophical theology of creation *ex nihilo*.[51] God is the "indeterminate, or transcendent, Creator of all things *ex nihilo*"; God is not dependent on creation, but free.[52] The act of creating has carved out, Yong believes, a "context of mutual relevance," enabling all created things to relate to one another—a place in which things may be determined.[53] What everyone (and all things) holds in common, then, is "createdness—our dependence on something other than ourselves."[54]

More significantly, however, creation *ex nihilo* implies for Yong "the trinitarian character of the creative act. An analysis of the creative act itself reveals creator, created, and the power of creating that mediates between the two." In this schema, God (Father) can be identified as "the aboriginal source, the Logos as the norm, and the Spirit as the power of the eternal creative act, each relative to the created order." Thus, there are "trinitarian features immanent within the act itself. From what is created, we see things that are a harmonious configuration of pluralities

---

48. Ibid., 42.

49. Ibid., 43 (italics original), cf. 43–48.

50. Ibid., 47. Explains Yong, "Creation can thereby be imaged as the product of the breath going forth and returning to the Godhead. History is the realm of this going forth and returning specifically vis-à-vis the affairs of humankind. Together, creation and history can be considered as the 'playing field' on which the dramatic works of God are manifest."

51. Yong, *Discerning the Spirit(s)*, 105, cf. 105–11. Yong identifies Neville as his *doctorvater*.

52. Ibid., 106, 107 (italics original).

53. Ibid., 106, 105.

54. Ibid., 105.

bound together by norms of determinateness." So, there are Trinitarian elements immanent within creation, the Spirit serving to mediate God and creation.[55] Yong affirms, "*Ruach/pneuma* thus calls attention to the dynamism at the heart not only of the divine life but also of the natural and human spheres of the created order."[56]

This connection between the Trinity and creation is further elucidated by Yong, utilizing the metaphysics and semiotic theory of Peirce and Gelpi.[57] Peirce, says Yong, proposes that

> all reality exhibits phenomenological features of *firstness*, *secondness*, and *thirdness*. *Firstness* is pure potentiality, the simple quality of feeling, that which makes a thing what it is in itself and impresses itself as itself upon our perception.... *Secondness* is the element of struggle or a brute, resistant fact. It is that by which a thing is related to others.... *Thirdness* is what mediates between firstness and secondness, on the one hand, and between that and others, on the other. *Thirdness* is the universals, laws, generalities, or habits that ensure the continuity of the process of reality.[58]

Reality consists, then, of a basic triadic structure that finds parallels with the life of the Trinity (by virtue of God being Creator). Yong explains that Peirce's categorical schema helps expound the nature of all things:

> in theological terms, all things in their suchness (firstness) consist of both Word and Spirit, or *logos* and *pneuma*. By "thing," I am referring to the essential complex determinations of being of which all reality consists.... [Each thing] has both concrete

55. Ibid., 108, cf. 108–11. Yong mentions two points here worth noting. First, Neville identifies the Logos as the "indeterminate norm," which Yong believes subordinates Spirit to Word—something he attempts to correct. Second, Yong is more comfortable speaking of the Trinity as immanent in creation, as opposed to speculating concerning the "Immanent Trinity" (divine life *ad intra*). He is cautious about Rahner's axiom concerning the "Economic Trinity" being the "Immanent Trinity" and vice versa. More recently, however, he has conceded that there is perhaps reason for viewing this axiom as at least helpful in moving in one direction—economic to immanent—but not necessarily vice versa. See Yong, *Spirit-Word-Community*, 73n.10, 78.

56. Yong, *Spirit-Word-Community*, 48 (italics original).

57. There are other voices feeding into Yong's foundational pneumatology (particularly as applied to theology of religions), including: Paul Tillich, Karl Rahner, and Michael Lodahl (Yong, *Discerning the Spirit(s)*, 71–95; on Rahner also see Yong, *Spirit-Word-Community*, 198–202).

58. Yong, *Beyond the Impasse*, 133 (italics original). Cf. Yong, *Discerning the Spirit(s)*, 112; Yong, *Spirit Poured Out*, 287–89; and Yong, *Spirit-Word-Community*, 92–93, 100.

form and inner spirit. A thing's concrete form is that which is manipulable, sensible, perceptible, and phenomenologically encounterable. A thing's inner spirit is the laws, habits, tendencies, and energetic force that shape its process of actuality and direct its temporal trajectory. My proposal is that any reality is what it is by virtue of having both form and spirit and that nothing can be apart from having both form and spirit (in addition, of course, to its simple self qualities, its firstness).[59]

This construal of reality also has epistemic implications and parallels, found in Peirce's semiotic theory. Reality's very nature suggests, for Yong, the means by which we come to understand reality.[60] In contrast to dyadic sign-object relations found in linguistic theory, Peirce posited a triadic sign theory in which a sign (*"representamen"*) addresses somebody (*"interpretant"*) and stands for something (*"object"*).[61] Important here, says Yong, is "the *irreducibility of the triadic relation* of representamen, object, and interpretant. Signs are not just things but *relational functions*. Smoke in the distance, for example, is a representamen, grounded in fire which creates in human minds any number of interpretants . . ."[62] Perception of reality, then, is by way of sign; however, sign is grounded in an object, as well as (subjectively) interpreted in the mind of the perceiver. Since we only perceive signs, the object is never directly or immediately perceived—it is always *mediated* by sign, and means the interpretant may be mistaken. At the same time, neither is interpretation merely subjective, existing only in the mind of the perceiver, since it exists only in relation to a sign connected to an object outside the mind. "For these reasons," states Yong, "Peirce's semiotic avoids the fallacies of rationalisms that ignore the groundedness of ideas in real objects, and of empiricisms that ignore the open-endedness of interpretants in the signifying process. It emphasizes a contrite fallibilism over and against either a positivistic objectivism, . . . or a relativistic subjectivism . . ."[63]

59. Yong, *Beyond the Impasse*, 134 (italics original).

60. In *Spirit Poured Out* (as well as in *Beyond the Impasse*) Yong actually approaches this in reverse order—Peirce's epistemology leading into his metaphysics, whereas in other works (*Discerning the Spirit(s)* and *Spirit-Word-Community*) he moves from metaphysics to epistemology. This demonstrates the intricate relationship between the two categories, each informing the other.

61. Yong, *Spirit Poured Out*, 285 (italics original).

62. Ibid., 285 (italics added).

63. Ibid., 286.

Interpretants are able to recognize errors in interpretations when these fail to lead to predicted or expected behaviors or events (the pragmatic dimension of interpretation), which allows for further (ongoing) reinterpretation.[64] Especially significant for our purposes in this book is that, for Yong, human epistemic activity "is set within the broader framework of interpretation in general. Indeed, *interpretation is central to creation's or nature's processes.*"[65] So, among other things, "Peirce's semiotic metaphysics . . . provides an account for the causal interface between human mentality and the orders of creation. Things become present to us through their signifying qualities, resistances, and lawful effects."[66] What this means is that while knowledge derives from our experience of reality, it is "semiotically mediated" and therefore fallible.[67] Yong then draws on Gelpi to demonstrate the connection between this semiotic metaphysic and experience of the Spirit.

Gelpi himself builds on Peirce's triadic categories and semiotic theory to construct a foundational pneumatology that explains how humans experience God. He utilizes the concept of "conversion" (in all its dimensions, but especially "religious conversion") as a methodological foundation for Christian theology.[68] Experience of God, then, is the assumed foundation of theologizing,[69] because "conversion" is "a subset of the category of experience."[70] Reality can thus be construed as "an experiential process";[71] further, this metaphysics of experience "is

---

64. Ibid. In this view, writes Yong, "each interpretant becomes another representamen grounded in the original interpretant." Thus, human knowledge "proceeds according to inferential hypotheses, deductive clarifications, and inductive confirmation or falsification and back again (Peirce's version of the hermeneutical circle)" (ibid., 292). This also entails a "turn to the community"—the process of inquiry must be shared and demands engagement with the world. With regard to the 'pragmatic dimension' of interpretation, this simply means, "We interpret to answer questions or to get things done" (ibid., 289).

65. Ibid., 287 (italics added). Elsewhere Yong states, "interpretation is an essential component of human life. What we experience is understood with greater and greater precision as we continuously interpret our experience" (Yong, *Discerning the Spirit(s)*, 113).

66. Yong, *Spirit Poured Out*, 288.

67. Yong, *Spirit-Word-Community*, 208, cf. 151–64, 207–11.

68. Yong, *Beyond the Impasse*, 59.

69. Yong, *Discerning the Spirit(s)*, 100.

70. Yong, *Beyond the Impasse*, 59.

71. Yong, *Discerning the Spirit(s)*, 117.

potentially universal in scope and applicable not only to human beings but also to God."[72]

Yong believes this semiotic experiential metaphysical framework to be very helpful in explaining how humans relate to the world, to God, and vice versa, since "experience" defines all human and sentient beings, including God.[73] Within this construct, Gelpi's concept of the Spirit as the mind of God is applied by Yong—Spirit occupies the role of interpretant: "As the divine wisdom or the mind of God, the Spirit can be said to interpret the Father and the Son."[74] In a parallel way, further, "Spirit interprets the creator to creation (and vice versa). In other words, our experience of the world and the emerging interpretations thereof point to the creator."[75] All reality is, by the Spirit, relational to the core,[76] and thus all experience and knowledge is "semiotically mediated" by the Spirit.[77] Moreover, the way in which humans experience the world is akin to the way in which they experience God, since both are by the Spirit. Explains Yong,

> Following Peirce and Gelpi, all experience can be understood as mediatedness and is, theologically, essentially of the Spirit. Our experience of God is not qualitatively different from our experience of anything else . . . All come through via perception and suggests to us, in a series of intuitions, that there is something there, not ourselves, that demands our understanding. We go about a process of inquiry to appease our curiosity (or surprise, or anger, as the case may be). What is different about our experience of God is that it relates us to a dimension of being that includes but is not exhausted by normal experience. This is a dimension in which there is a heightened sense of truth, beauty, excellence, goodness, and reality as it was and is meant to be. I

72. Yong, *Beyond the Impasse*, 59; cf. Yong, *Spirit Poured Out*, 291–92.

73. Yong, *Beyond the Impasse*, 61–62. Yong states, "People do not have experiences; rather, experiences are what people consist of. Used in this broad sense, experience refers to the complex integration of perception, mentality, affectivity, and volitionality involved in the human being-in-the-world" (ibid., 62).

74. Yong, *Discerning the Spirit(s)*, 113, cf. 117.

75. Ibid., 114.

76. Ibid., 115. "In short," says Yong, "relationality is at the heart of reality, and Peirce's triadic construct is suggestive of how nature and grace can each retain the integrity of their essential character even while being mutually related."

77. Yong, *Spirit-Word-Community*, 208, cf. 7–11, 102.

therefore prefer to speak of a *religious dimension of experience* rather than of "religious experience" itself . . .[78]

For Yong, then, God is experienced in the *context* of the world (for our purposes, through "reason"), through perceptions and interpretations made possible by the Spirit. This epistemic foundationalism is made possible by the Spirit's universal presence and activity, and implies the possibility of public (universal) access to truth (about God and all things). This epistemology, argues Yong, is not relativized by postmodern coherence truth theories, but yet is tempered by recognizing the fallibility of human knowing.[79] When it comes to perceiving (experiencing) God, like any other perception of reality, all humans comprehend reality (object), albeit symbolically (via sign). So, experience and knowledge of God is "real"; but this is not a naïve realism—human knowledge is fallible, built on "shifting foundations."[80] Experience (and knowledge) of God by the Spirit, then, is never direct, but always hidden in some respect, mediated through creation. Yong writes, "In light of the triadic structure of experience proffered by Peirce, we cannot but *shy away from claims regarding direct, unmediated experiences of the divine.* All religious experience is symbolically structured. Our experience of God takes place through an inferential perception of the Spirit's legal and habitual endowment of the world which enables human understanding."[81]

To this point we have explored in Yong's work the *possibility* of public knowledge of God (via Spirit) built upon certain pneumatological biblical themes, triadic metaphysics and semiotic epistemology. What yet remains to be established is how experience of the Spirit (and theological knowledge) is possible distinct from and yet related to Word in order for this to be truly a Christian (and PC) foundational (public) pneumatology.

---

78. Yong, *Discerning the Spirit(s)*, 122 (italics original).

79. Ibid., 101. We will address this further in an upcoming subsection.

80. Ibid., 103.

81. Ibid., 114–15 (italics added). Yong adds, "the Spirit is the supreme relation between us as knowers and the self-revealing God. As supreme relation, the Spirit is also non-objectifiable and therefore only accessible symbolically. . . . The world is therefore symbolic of the divine which we experience and interpret, always partially, by the presence and activity of (what we symbolize as) the Holy Spirit" (ibid., 114).

The "Two Hands" of God and
the Pneumatological Imagination

A pneumatological approach to theology, proposes Yong, leads to a "robust trinitarianism," which allows Spirit to be experienced publicly while still being identified as the Spirit of the Trinity.[82] In building this case, Yong employs Irenaeus' metaphor of Word and Spirit as the "two hands" of the Father—the "Father's direct and immediate agents of creation."[83] The "two hands" metaphor is significant (for Yong and for our purposes) in at least three respects. First, it emphasizes that the divine economies of Word and Spirit are "mutually related, and should not be subordinated either to the other."[84] Each "hand" is an equal and necessary agent demonstrating God's immanence in the world.[85] Yong supplements this point by drawing on Eastern Orthodox theologians Georg Khodr and Lossky, who reject the filioque in order to emphasize the divine mission as occurring through two distinct economies.[86] Lossky, in particular, Yong observes, rejects the filioque, since it tends to make Spirit subordinate to Word, and consequently, to ecclesiastical hierarchy. He also emphasizes Pentecost as not simply a continuation of the Incarnation, but as a distinct event—a "sequel"—accenting the unique contribution of the Spirit to the divine mission.[87]

Second, the "two hands" model implies Spirit and Word's ontological equality with the Father. Yong states, "insofar as Spirit and Word are truly God's personal activity in creation, neither is subordinate to the

82. Yong, *Beyond the Impasse*, 43.

83. Yong, *Spirit-Word-Community*, 50, 52, cf. 50–59. Cf. Yong, *Discerning the Spirit(s)*, 60–70, 116, 174, 226, 311; Yong, *Beyond the Impasse*, 42–44, 69, 130, 170, 186; and Yong, *Spirit Poured Out*, 216.

84. Yong, *Discerning the Spirit(s)*, 69.

85. Yong, *Spirit-Word-Community*, 52–53.

86. Yong, *Beyond the Impasse*, 87, cf. 86–91. On Eastern Orthodoxy and the filioque, also see Yong, *Discerning the Spirit(s)*, 65–77; Yong, *Spirit Poured Out*, 214–16; Yong, "Turn to Pneumatology," 437–54; and Yong, *Spirit-Word-Community*, 63–67. In this latter work, Yong also briefly utilizes Bulgakov's emphasis on the Spirit as having a mission preceding the Incarnation, and sees promise in Bulgakov for bringing together the Latin and Eastern traditions under a relational framework for the Trinity (ibid., 72). The interaction here is indirect, however, since Yong is using a third party source on Bulgakov: Graves, *Holy Spirit*.

87. Yong, *Spirit Poured Out*, 216, cf. 214–16; cf. Yong, *Discerning the Spirit(s)*, 65–66. Lossky also rejects Augustine's model of the Spirit as "love bond" between Father and Son.

Father ontologically. To put it crassly, without his hands, the Father is impotent and therefore neither creator nor divine; but it is precisely in and through the work of his two hands that the divinity of the Father is established as both creator and redeemer."[88]

Third, Yong believes that the "two hands" metaphor "connotes the *interdependence* of Spirit and Word in the work of creation and redemption," and further, an "an intratrinitarian egalitarianism" or "radically relational trinitarianism."[89] The "two hands" model both assumes and leads to a doctrine of "coinherence" (*perichoresis*) in which there is a "unity of the two hands with the Father."[90] Yong also acknowledges appreciation of Augustine's model of the Spirit as love bond (between Father and Son), since it emphasizes the Spirit as the relational key to the divine life.[91] But his accent clearly falls upon the "two hands" model, which Yong observes has served to evoke contemporary theological emphases on social and relational concepts of the Trinity. There is, states Yong, a "relational logic of pneumatology [that] translates into a relational trinitarianism."[92] This is because we cannot speak of the Spirit "apart from either the First or the Second Persons of the Triune God. The Spirit is the supremely mediational and relational symbol."[93]

The relationality of the Trinity extends by the Spirit to creation as well. Citing Elizabeth A. Johnson, Yong emphasizes that just as the Spirit is relationally connected to the Father and Son, so too, by virtue of the creative act, Spirit is intricately linked to creation.[94] Pneumatology is

---

88. Yong, *Spirit-Word-Community*, 52.

89. Ibid., 52 (italics added).

90. Ibid., 53, cf. 53–56. Emphasized here is the mutual indwelling of the divine persons, with relationship being that which defines and distinguishes the members of the Trinity *ad intra*.

91. Ibid., 59–72. Yong believes there may be value in affirming the filioque, insofar as it emphasizes the consubstantiality of Father and Son, and therefore (with the "two hands") of Spirit. He even suggests that Bulgakov's idea of the Son sending the Spirit (post-Incarnation), may serve as an "economic" filioque of sorts. Yong cautiously proposes that the Latin and Eastern emphases on "begottenness and spiration" (respectively) may perhaps be brought together under a "different frame of reference, that of relations, and if the framework was enlarged eschatologically to include return alongside procession, then the Eastern emphasis on the perichoretic interrelationality of the divine persons can be seen to complement the Latin doctrine of the filioque" (ibid., 72).

92. Ibid., 57, cf. 56–59.

93. Yong, *Beyond the Impasse*, 42.

94. Yong, *Spirit-Word-Community*, 58; cf. Johnson, *She Who Is*, 148.

the key, then, to both Trinitarian theology and the God-world relation-ship, and not only concerns the "divine vertically, but also a vast web of interconnectedness horizontally." All created things exist in symbiotic relationship, states Yong, "Symbiotic relationality . . . thus characterizes both the divine reality and the creation itself as well as the togetherness of the two."[95] This is why Spirit and Word (as the "two hands") can be viewed (metaphysically) as constituting all things—Word representing "concreteness" and Spirit the "dynamism" in all things.[96] Expounds Yong:

> My argument proceeds from the theological notion that Word and Spirit are the 'two hands of the Father.' As such, they are *both* present universally and particularly in creation . . . By doing so, I not only second what has been generally affirmed about the historical particularity of the incarnation of the Logos and the cosmic universality of the Spirit, but also lift up the contrasting terms somewhat neglected by each of the traditions. There is a universal dimension to the Logos; thus the fecundity of the doc-trine of the cosmic Christ. But there is also the particular dimen-sion of the Spirit . . . The dimension of the Word is the thisness and whatness of things . . . ; that of the Spirit is the howness and relatedness of things—their continuity and significance. Both Word in Spirit are universally present and active because they are at the heart of every particular determination of being, albeit in different ways.[97]

In this way, then, Yong reasons, Trinitarian theology bridges "the du-alism between Word and Spirit"; and conversely, through pneumatology

---

95. Yong, *Spirit-Word-Community*, 59, cf. 58. Again, Yong states, "The logic of pneu-matology is the connection, however obscure it may be at times, of the two orders" (ibid., 77).

96. Yong, *Beyond the Impasse*, 130.

97. Yong, *Discerning the Spirit(s)*, 116 (italics original), cf. 115–22. Elsewhere Yong states, "Word represents concreteness—as in, for example, Jesus of Nazareth and the written Scriptures—historical particularity, and the human experience of objectivity; the Spirit represents the dynamism of the Anointed One—as in, for example, the Christ and the living, inspired, and illuminating word of God—cosmic relationality, and the human experience of subjectivity. . . . God works all things with the divine hands: by and through *both* Word and Spirit. . . . Word and Spirit are inseparable features of all things. Thus, there is the universality of Word (e.g., the cosmic Christ) as well as a particularity of Spirit (e.g., that accentuates and values the differentiated order of determinate things) precisely because both aspects inhere—as in the patristic notion of *circumincessio* and the Greek notion of *perichoresis*—and inform each other" (Yong, *Beyond the Impasse*, 43 [italics original]; cf. Yong, *Spirit-Word-Community*, 84–96).

we arrive at a "robust trinitarianism."[98] On this basis there is a "pneumatological rationality,"[99] a "pneumatological imagination," that undergirds Christian theology—a point that begs further explanation.[100] While Yong appeals to the pneumatological imagination throughout his works, the fullest discussion of this concept is found in *Spirit-Word-Community*.[101] "Imagination" is used in its technical sense by Yong, meaning that rational and relational aspect of the human mind that allows us to engage and interpret (and therefore know) reality. Historically (philosophically and theologically), Yong notes, three conclusions concerning imagination have emerged: "the imagination as a synthesis of passive and active components (being functionally relational); the imagination as a cognitive blend of the affective and spiritual aspects of the human being (being functionally integrative); and, the imagination as valuational (being functionally normative)."[102]

Expanding on the first element, Yong writes, "imagination functions relationally, at least at three levels. First, the imagination mediates the human engagement with the external world through the recording of images derived from experience. Second, the imagination enables human beings to actively construct the world. Finally, the imagination holds both of these activities—of reproduction and production—together coherently such that one and the same person moves from one to the other subconsciously and fluidly.[103]

The second (functionally integrative) element emphasizes imagination's inclination to bring together head and heart in understanding reality.[104] The normative element, thirdly, highlights imagination's continual interpretive, evaluative and discerning activity. This element is closely tied to the idea of active "world-making," highlighting why it is that

---

98. Yong, *Beyond the Impasse*, 44, 43.

99. Yong, *Spirit-Word-Community*, 105.

100. Ibid., 76. Yong prefers the concept of pneumatological imagination to Gelpi's "conversion" for providing a broader lens to view self, the world and God (see Yong, *Beyond the Impasse*, 64, 72; and cf. Yong, *Discerning the Spirit(s)*, 102).

101. In particular, Yong, *Spirit-Word-Community*, chs. 4–6. Also see Yong, "'Life in the Spirit,'" 1–39.

102. Yong, *Spirit-Word-Community*, 123, cf. 123–32. Yong traces the concept of imagination from Plato and Aristotle, through Enlightenment philosophers and theologians (e.g., Kant and Schleiermacher) to postmodern conceptions.

103. Ibid., 128–29.

104. Ibid., 129–30.

imagination views some experiences (perceptions) as more significant than others.[105] Imagination has a *telos*, a goal toward which it works, explains Yong: "the imagination shapes and is shaped by the pragmatic orientation of thinking in the sense that it seeks to carry over the values of the objects of experience into the mind so as to enable more effective human engagement with the world."[106]

For Yong, the *pneumatological* dimension of imagination includes the above three elements, but is informed both by encounters with the divine (in general and religious aspects of experiences, in particular, PC encounters with God)[107] as well as certain "root metaphors," namely, those derived from Scripture and the Christian tradition.[108] There is, then, he reasons, a dialectic at work between "the experiential and the metaphoric," informing and being informed by the pneumatological imagination.[109] Thus, the pneumatological imagination involves both "passive reception" and active "worldmaking"; it includes the affective and spiritual dimensions (the "charismatic and dynamic dimensions of the Spirit" and the "formal and material content of the Word"), and the "valuational," enabling discernment of the powers at work within the world.[110]

It is the pneumatological imagination, then, that leads to Yong's foundational (epistemologically public) pneumatology discussed earlier, meaning that we have come full circle in our exploration of Yong's theology of experience. This began, it will be recalled, with PC experience of the Spirit,[111] which enabled a particular lens for viewing

105. Ibid., 131–32. States Yong, "The imagination is therefore world-making in the sense that it sorts out the experiential data and yields the limits of possibilities for human existence. These possibilities, however, are neither completely arbitrary nor are they completely indeterminate because imagination is selective, dividing what is trivial from what is important among experiential inputs in order for humans to engage the world evaluatively."

106. Ibid., 132, cf. 236–44.

107. Ibid., 77. Theological conceptions arise from "our human experience of and situatedness in the world."

108. These include concepts and metaphors already explored, such as, the Spirit's presence and activity in creation, and the "two hands" model, which allows the Spirit to be discerned in ways "not strictly christological" (Yong, *Discerning the Spirit(s)*, 122).

109. Yong, *Spirit-Word-Community*, 133, cf. 133–41.

110. Ibid., 134. We will return to the issue of discernment in an upcoming subsection.

111. See Yong, *Discerning the Spirit(s)*, 171. Yong states, "The thesis I am suggesting is that the experience of the Spirit informs the pneumatological imagination of the

the world as triadically constructed, and in which all things are constituted by Word and Spirit.[112] These observations (made within a faith community) both confirm and challenge experience and theology,[113] enabling further (more accurate) understanding of God and the world in a hermeneutical spiral, and leading to the establishment of certain "foundational categories" concerning the nature of reality and experience of God in the world.[114] In sum, writes Yong, a foundational pneumatology arises from the "dialectical interplay between personal (including my own) experiences of the Holy Spirit and reflection on this experience from within the broader Christian community of faith. I therefore propose the metaphor of *'shifting foundations'* to underscore the dialectic of Scripture and experience, of thought and praxis, of theology and doxology, of reason and narrative, of object and subject, of a priori rationality and a posteriori empiricism, of the self and its sociohistoric location in community, in all knowledge."[115]

What are the foundational categories that emerge for Yong from the process outlined above? Two have been mentioned—namely, the universal *presence* and *activity* of the Spirit (the latter being descriptive of the Spirit's work in and through relationships of all sorts), which enable and inform our knowledge of God.[116] This in turn evokes experience of the Spirit's presence and activity "in more precise, intense, and true ways."[117] The pneumatological imagination (particularly one informed

---

Pentecostal or charismatic and vice versa. Such an experiential vision is a holistic one which is integrative and transformative not only for individuals but also for whole communities. This holism can be explicated for individuals as a relationship between the cognitive, emotive and bodily components of Spirit-baptism; and can be understood on the communal level as in the charismatic relationship between individuals and the body of Christ." Also see Yong, *Beyond the Impasse*, 78–81.

112. Yong, *Beyond the Impasse*, 73, cf. 78–79; Yong, *Spirit-Word-Community*, 43.

113. Yong, *Beyond the Impasse*, 78–79. He states, "Experience and interpretation are mutually informing and correcting elements in any community of knowers."

114. Ibid., 65. Yong's theological hermeneutics, including the communal dimension, are worked out in most detail in Yong, *Spirit-Word-Community*, chs. 7–9.

115. Yong, *Beyond the Impasse*, 64–65 (italics added). Thus, this epistemological and metaphysical process "both envisions the foundational categories and is shaped by them" (ibid., 65).

116. Yong, *Discerning the Spirit(s)*, 123, cf. 123–36; Yong, *Beyond the Impasse*, 42, cf. 36–38. We will return to the issue of the Spirit's activity in "fields of force" shortly.

117. Yong, *Beyond the Impasse*, 65; cf. Yong, *Discerning the Spirit(s)*, 103.

by PC experience),[118] however, also introduces a third category—"*divine absence.*"[119] Yong proposes that while the Spirit is metaphysically present in all things, not all phenomena are congruent with the Spirit's presence and activity; room needs to be made for the *absence* of the Spirit, the "demonic."[120] The Spirit is mediated through the *contexts* of life (reason), but this does not mean for Yong that every theology or experience is of the Spirit. What is necessary in such a schema is a robust process of *discernment.* Yong believes the PC pneumatological imagination (linked to a foundational pneumatology) is especially capable of informing such discernment—in life in general and in particular within religions (and the sciences). At this point, then, it would be appropriate to explore how Yong applies the concept of the PC pneumatological imagination to further support his idea of a public theology, and to the discernment of the Spirit/spirits within the religions.

Overcoming the Postmodern/Cultural-Linguistic Impasse

Several times in this book it has been noted that a number of Pentecostal theologians (including Macchia and Chan) are attracted to elements of Lindbeck's cultural-linguistic theory of doctrine. This theory accents the coherence of doctrinal truth: that doctrine finds it meaning within a particular cultural-linguistic framework, which tends to shape experience of God, and not (so much) vice versa. Yong too values elements of the cultural-linguistic model, but also knows that such postmodern epistemological approaches are suspicious of appeals to universal knowledge or experience, which would include his own foundational pneumatology.[121] He is convinced, however, that the PC pneumatological imagination can support a foundational (public) pneumatology, while at

118. Yong readily acknowledges that PCs do not have exclusive claim to the pneumatological imagination, and that alternative forms have developed in other Christian traditions. He identifies Moltmann, among others, as having developed an alternative (but complementary) pneumatological imagination (see Yong, *Discerning the Spirit(s)*, 148n.70; and cf. Yong *Beyond the Impasse*, 79–80n.33).

119. Yong, *Discerning the Spirit(s)*, 125ff. (italics added).

120. Ibid., 127.

121. Yong, *Beyond the Impasse*, 67. Yong admits elsewhere that it was Lindbeck's "functional understanding of doctrine" that enabled him to affirm the doctrine of initial evidence. While such a move allows tongues to be affirmed as a normative sign, however, the "trade-off" is that it can no longer be considered normative for other Christian traditions (Yong, *Discerning the Spirit(s)*, 96–97; cf. Yong, *Hospitality and the Other*, 50–53).

the same time affirm aspects of cultural-linguistic theory, holding these together in tension.

On the one hand, Yong affirms the mediated nature of experience of God as being shaped by theological (communal) "root metaphors." In response to the question as to whether there can be "direct experience of the divine apart from our experiences of and with each other and the world," Yong explicitly appeals to Lindbeck's theory for understanding the mediated quality of Pentecostal and other appeals to experience of God.[122] He examines two biblical mediations of the divine, the Incarnation and Pentecost, observing that even face-to-face encounters with the incarnate Christ were always "perceptually mediated"; Jesus' identity was hidden apart from the Spirit's revelation. [123] Concerning Pentecost, "the first Christians experienced the Spirit through the violent rushing wind, through the tongues of fire which alighted on each of them, through stammering lips and strange tongues, all of which were interpreted or understood, at least in part, through the sacred writings . . ." Further, theologically, Christians experience Jesus through the Spirit-constituted body of Christ. So, concludes Yong, Pentecostal (and other) claims to "direct encounters with God" need to be qualified considerably. Any claims to theological knowledge based on such encounters are always grounded within a semiotic epistemology.[124]

This mediated view of experience of God implies for Yong that all theological knowledge is communicated analogically (using symbols of "similarities-in-differences"),[125] and all experience and knowledge of God is always partial and incomplete, due to human fallenness and embodiedness. "God is thereby always both disclosed and hidden, and theological semiotics is both cataphatic and apophatic."[126] In any case, Yong's (qualified) acceptance of Lindbeck's affirmation of experience of God as communally mediated means (for him) that appeals to experi-

122. Yong, *Spirit-Word-Community*, 208, cf. n.7.

123. Ibid., 207, 208, cf. 207–11.

124. Ibid., 208. Yong states, "The important point to register here is that the emergent epistemology of the divine—how human beings can experience and come to know divinity—can be conceived as a theological semiotic which would include within its compass a symbolics of human community and a symbolics of nature. And insofar as knowledge of the divine is conveyed semiotically, it provides a norm by which to gauge claims regarding the human encounter with an experience of God" (ibid., 209).

125. Ibid., 209.

126. Ibid., 210, 211.

ence of God and theological knowledge must be evaluated *empirically*. Each cultural-linguistic community, Christian or otherwise, must be understood on its own terms, and not through a priori abstract theories or claims.[127]

On the other hand, Yong's project is a foundational pneumatology. Further, it is based in PC experience of the Spirit, which has "little difficulty in granting that the Holy Spirit is indicative of divine presence and agency in the world."[128] He knows that this proposal will evoke postmodern skepticism concerning "the possibility of a universal rationality and grammar."[129] But there is also another issue here (noted also in chapter 2), namely, how can cultural-linguistic theory (at least in strong forms) account for the PC sense that (seemingly direct or immediate) encounters with the Spirit can be radically disruptive and transformative to a faith community? Would Pentecostals be satisfied to simply affirm that the Spirit is experienced in a particular way within their own community, but not available (in the same way) to a broader public audience, and in a way that could possibly radically reshape cultural-linguistic frameworks?[130] Within Yong's work at least a fourfold response to this apparent cultural-linguistic/foundational pneumatology impasse may be discerned.[131]

First, Yong argues that although his PC-inspired foundational pneumatology holds the potential to account for experience of the Spirit "regardless of cultural-linguistic-religious background,"[132] nevertheless, this involves a "'chastised optimism' that is painfully aware of the postmodern critique."[133] It is a "pneumatology of quest" that aims to provide sufficiently universal abstract categories (i.e., the Spirit's presence, activity and absence), while yet being empirically testable in the particulars.

127. Yong, *Beyond the Impasse*, 175–76, cf. 35, 81, 107, 121–22, 185, 188, 191.

128. Ibid., 67. He adds it is no coincidence that Gelpi, who advocates universal experience of the Spirit, is involved in the Catholic charismatic movement.

129. Ibid., 66, cf. 67 (also see n.17).

130. See Yong, *Spirit Poured Out*, 297. Yong argues that while it is possible to preserve their doctrines through a cultural-linguistic model, this may really restrict what Pentecostals want to affirm regarding experience of the Spirit.

131. Cf. Yong, "A P(new)matological Paradigm," 179–81.

132. Yong, *Beyond the Impasse*, 67. Yong states, "a pneumatological imagination—especially one cultivated within the Pentecostal-charismatic community—is uniquely suited to undertake the task of developing a foundational pneumatology . . ."

133. Ibid., 66.

It is thus fallible, continually open to correction and revision (both from voices within and outside the PC community), and only fully realized eschatologically.[134] Anti-foundationalist critique only applies, says Yong, to its Cartesian manifestations; "it does not mean that there are no 'foundations' at all or that all knowledge sits on thin air."[135] A universal foundational pneumatology is legitimated if based upon empirical discovery and in dialogue with other cultural-linguistic traditions.[136]

Second, Yong believes there is good reason to accept PC encounters with the Spirit as a suitable resource for theological reflection. This is because there is a sense in which experience functions "both phenomenologically and logically prior to reflection and the second-order activity of theologizing. As such, the norms emerging from our experiences operate powerfully, most often underneath our full consciousness."[137] It is impossible, asserts Yong, *not* to be influenced by experience of the world and others when it comes to theological reflection—"we all exegete our experiences (or lack of them, as the case may be) whether consciously or not." Thus, experiences "function as objects for theological interpretation."[138] As noted, humans selectively choose (consciously or not) certain experiences over others to inform theological reflection. Thoughts "are always-already semiotic interpretations of perceptual experience from the start. It follows then that aspects of our experiences emerge as objects for theological reflection precisely as interpretations from the beginning." Yong is explicit: "it should be clear that our 'pure

134. Ibid., 71, 78–81.

135. Ibid., 80.

136. Ibid., 81.

137. Yong, *Spirit-Word-Community*, 246, cf. 245–53, 253–73. Yong reviews Gelpi's various uses of the term "experience" (see chapter 1 of this book) and is here intentionally narrowing "experience" to mean "all uncritical or pre-reflective cognition; . . . [and] the entire spectrum of human evaluative responses" (i.e., perceptual experience). This is in contrast to his broader use of Gelpi's metaphysical category of "experience" elsewhere. Yong introduces this narrower definition of experience under a discussion of how "Word" functions in the theological hermeneutical process. So, "experience" here functions as one form of objective "Word," alongside Scripture and tradition. Because Logos is in all things, perceptual experience (encounters with the world and others) serves to inform understanding of self, God and the world. Thus careful empirical observation is essential for informing theology.

138. Ibid., 246. Yong adds, "thinking is a second-order activity that grasps by way of abstractions our experiences which are continuous and dynamic. All thought and reflection, in a sense, emerge out of experience."

experiences' are unavailable for reflection. *Thinking involves interpretation all the way down.*"[139]

For Yong, then, experience is simply that which "mediates and relates self and other," meaning "our access to the other is therefore through the experience of the self."[140] But given that all experience is interpreted experience, the point being emphasized here is that experience functions normatively as a universal "Word" of sorts for all humans.[141] Applying this to theology, Yong explores the "experiential objects" of "enthusiasm," "ritual," and "mystical encounter" to demonstrate how experience impacts theological reflection.[142] Since he closely associates "enthusiasm" with Pentecostal encounters with the Spirit, it is worth exploring this briefly.

Certain experiences with God can be identified with "enthusiasm"—being "of God (*en*-theos) . . . the in-breaking of the Spirit's presence," such as the Apostle Paul's encounter with Christ on the road to Damascus.[143] Such encounters inevitably evoke re-readings of Scripture and tradition, and therefore need to be taken into account for understanding any theological position. So, observes Yong, the experience of certain charismatic gifts (e.g., glossolalia) did cause early Pentecostals to (re)read Scripture in order to account for such phenomena. But in the same way, a "lack of experience of [such] phenomena" also led Reformers to develop the unscriptural doctrine of cessationism.[144] In both cases, experience impacted and shaped theological reflection. Thus, deduces Yong, "Christian experience of God, whether breaking upon the believer as radically other or mediated liturgically, ritually, mystically or otherwise, is fundamental to the data of theological interpretation."[145]

139. Ibid., 247 (italics added), cf. 246. Even interpretation of Scripture and tradition comes via "interpreted experience," says Yong. Thus, Christians do not interpret these directly "but rather interpret our experience of reading Scripture and tradition."

140. Ibid., 247.

141. Ibid., 253.

142. Ibid., 247, cf. 247–53.

143. Ibid., 247, 248 (italics original). Yong also mentions Augustine and Luther as having had such experiences.

144. Ibid., 248–49. Yong states, "In either case, God was experienced concretely in certain ways and not others, resulting in emphasis on certain points, neglect of others, and polemics against doctrines and positions which ran counter to one's experiential horizons" (ibid., 249).

145. Ibid., 252, cf. 249–53. Yong is quick to add that not all such experiences are of the divine and so discernment is required, a point to which we will return.

The above observation legitimates Yong's view that PC encounters with God may serve as a valid resource for theological reflection, which (in dialogue with Scripture and tradition) may develop into theological norms, and perhaps bring correction to current theological standards. He states, "In this sense, experience serves as a set of formal norms for theological understanding that in turn brings about novel or creative ways of being-in-the-world."[146] So, PC experience (among others) is a legitimate source for theological reflection; however, Pentecostals (in particular) need to also acknowledge the mediated quality of encounters with God—theological frameworks already shape the way such experiences are interpreted. Such experience cannot be (and is not) a normative source independent of Scripture and tradition, and always requires discernment to avoid the dangers of naïve subjectivity.[147] But PC experience, albeit fallible, is also valuable for developing a pneumatological imagination that facilitates discernment of the Spirit's presence, activity and absence in the world. Yong writes, "I do, however, think that any foundational categories generated from our interpretation of the PC experience will be correct in their general features, in large part because they will be pneumatological features that are intrinsic to human processes of engaging divine presence and agency in the world. There is a hermeneutical spiral in this process whereby the Spirit illuminates our experiences, which in turn reveal to us more about who the Spirit is."[148]

A third resource Yong provides for overcoming the apparent cultural-linguistic/foundational pneumatology impasse is through his suggestion that the PC-inspired pneumatological imagination helps explain the emergence of novel theological interpretations within cultural-linguistic frameworks. Yong reiterates, imagination is not only "world-affirming (re-productive) but also world-making (creative)."[149] In other words, the

146. Ibid., 253. Yong states, "How else would norms arise (even scriptural ones) if not out of experience . . . ? [I]t seems to me impossible to deny that they function normatively—in the formal sense—as general constraints on our capacity to understand." Thus, experience is an inescapable component of theological interpretation. "This is in part because experience serves as both the medium and as object of interpretation. As medium, experience is normative with regard to how we interpret. As object, experience is abstracted as a semiotic datum for interpretation."

147. Yong, *Beyond the Impasse*, 77–78. Yong notes that PCs often speak of exercising discernment, but have not developed a sufficient theology of discernment—something he hopes to correct.

148. Ibid., 79.

149. Yong, *Spirit-Word-Community*, 222; cf. Yong, *Beyond the Impasse*, 80.

Spirit, inspiring the faculty of imagination, enables new experiences with the world, others *and God*, disrupting theological norms and creating tensions within ecclesial traditions. Imagination "bridges the gap between the self and the other, [and] is therefore well suited to mediate the creative human engagement with the transcendent."[150] This is why, observes Yong, encounter with the (transcendent) Spirit is often described in terms of "irruption, interruption, and disruption"—introducing discontinuity within a cultural-linguistic framework.[151]

Fourth, Yong argues that cultural-linguistic communities are not as isolated as might be supposed. The boundaries of these communities are porous, so to speak, permeated by (and permeating) broader culture—or *context*—through which the Spirit also speaks. Theology cannot be merely "communitarian," Yong asserts, but must, and in fact already does, interact with broader culture (including the theologies of other faiths).[152] In an important summary, Yong explains, "This is why Wittgenstein and Lindbeck are so right and yet so wrong. Yes, cultures and theological traditions operate according to certain grammars, narratives, and assumptions. . . . Yet such otherness is never completely other; otherness can be bridged through encounter. Further, cultural and religious grammars are never pure or homogenous, but always exist in a complex togetherness of multiple histories, traditions, sources and experiences . . ."[153]

A "cross-fertilization" exists between language and culture, which means that "theology that intends its claims to be universally applicable needs to be fully public theology."[154] Public context (reason) is therefore a theological resource, implying that dialogue with other faiths and the sciences is necessary for informing Christian theology. PCs should, Yong reasons, be especially receptive to this possibility, since Luke's story of Pentecost affirms diversity of languages, and by implication cultures, which are not separable from religions.[155] In sum, this fourfold response

150. Yong, *Spirit-Word-Community*, 224. Yong elsewhere identifies the pneumatological imagination as being that which enables one to experience other religions and cultures without actually having to fully enter (assimilate) into these other cultural-linguistic frameworks, thus enabling interreligious (and other) dialogue (Yong, "P(new)matological Paradigm," 180–81).

151. Yong, *Spirit-Word-Community*, 224.

152. Ibid., 301.

153. Ibid., 302; cf. Yong, *Hospitality and the Other*, 53.

154. Yong, *Spirit-Word-Community*, 304; cf. Yong, *In the Days*, 93.

155. Yong, *Spirit Poured Out*, 195–202, 237–40; cf. Yong, *Beyond the Impasse*, 15–20;

discerned within Yong's work demonstrates his capacity to overcome the cultural-linguistic impasse toward developing a public theology.

The Discernment of Spirit(s) in the Religions

Yong's theology of religions[156] provides perhaps his most explicit encouragement for Pentecostals to adopt a more mediated concept of the experience of God, hoping they (and Christians in general) will be open to discerning the Spirit in dialogue with other faiths.[157] Yong's work is not limited to this application; more broadly he is seeking to develop a theological "hermeneutics of life,"[158] which is why, in recent years, he has also turned his attention to investigating ways in which the Spirit may be revealed through the sciences and in the political realm. The focus here, however, will be to explore how the PC pneumatological imagination informs discernment of the Spirit with regard to religions. Two issues in particular will be addressed: 1) the Pentecostal need to accept the possibility of the Spirit as present and active in non-Christian religions, and 2) how a PC pneumatological imagination might actually provide a way forward beyond the "Christological impasse" toward discerning the Spirit in other faiths.[159]

Concerning the first issue, Yong admits that Pentecostals (less so charismatics)[160] have tended to adopt an exclusivist position with regard

---

Yong, "P(new)matological Paradigm," 176–77; and Yong, *Hospitality and the Other*, 112–14.

156. See Yong, *Discerning the Spirit(s)*, 23–24. He focuses on "religions" not "religion," since the latter assumes an a priori assumption of an *essence* of religion, which Yong does not believe exists. A theology of religions attempts to provide a perspective that is sufficiently abstract to encompass all religions while also being true to the particularities (the empirical reality) of each religion.

157. Yong highlights the importance of interfaith dialogue repeatedly. See Yong, "Inviting Spirit," 29–45; Yong, *Discerning the Spirit(s)*, 24–25, 141, 206–19, 222–43; Yong, *Beyond the Impasse*, 19, 52–53, 114–15; Yong, *Spirit Poured Out*, 257–66; and Yong, *Hospitality and the Other*. The latter work is Yong's most comprehensive attempt to date in addressing the practical means by which to undertake interfaith dialogue.

158. Yong, *Beyond the Impasse*, 149, cf. 149–61, 165.

159. Yong, *Discerning the Spirit(s)*, 33ff.

160. Ibid., 27, 197–206. Yong acknowledges charismatics' (of various traditions) openness to exploring a theology of religions, including Yeow Choo Lak, Clark Pinnock, and Ralph Del Colle. A more detailed survey of Pinnock's theology of religions is found in Yong, *Beyond the Impasse*, 105–28.

to revelation.[161] In this view, non-Christian religions are often portrayed as revelationally void at best, and the realm of the demonic at worst.[162] This approach, however, overlooks the interrelated nature of language, religion, and culture (discussed earlier).[163] Further, the Pentecost event itself affirms cultural plurality, which opens the door to viewing interconnected religious expressions as holding revelational potential.[164] Writes Yong, "Language, culture, and religion must all be discerned, even as each is potentially a vehicle for mediating the presence of God. Acceptance of this possibility establishes the Day of Pentecost as the narrative 'ground' for understanding the world of religions in pneumatological perspective."[165] Since, argues Yong, the Spirit has been poured out on "all flesh" (Acts 2:17) including those of other religions, therefore, the Spirit is already present and active in, and can speak through other religions—all religions are, in this sense, potentially redeemable.[166] Interfaith dialogue, then, needs to be viewed as also being part and parcel of the Christian mission.[167]

The above assumes, of course, a PC-inspired foundational pneumatology and pneumatological imagination. It is on this basis that Yong suggests three hypotheses as providing the framework for his pneumatological theology of religions:

161. Yong, "Inviting Spirit," 29–33; Yong, *Discerning the Spirit(s)*, 185–86. Here Pentecostals are following certain evangelical fundamentalist influences. The primary, if not sole, acknowledged source of revelation, in this case, being the Bible.

162. Yong, *Discerning the Spirit(s)*, 21–22, 185–86, cf. 187–97. Cf. Yong, "Inviting Spirit," 33–37; and Yong, *Hospitality and the Other*, 15–29. Yong does, however, see evidence of this attitude changing among Pentecostal theologians, and even suggests that at a grassroots level Pentecostals have been willing to work with those from other faiths. He references Allan H. Anderson, Samuel Solivan, Cornelia Scott Cree and Veli-Matti Kärkkäinen by way of example.

163. Yong, *Discerning the Spirit(s)*, 209–11; Yong, *Spirit Poured Out*, 195–202, 238–40, 251–52. In the latter work Yong states, the gospel "always comes in cultural dress. Even Jesus came as a first-century male carpenter" (ibid., 240).

164. Yong, *Spirit Poured Out*, 240.

165. Yong, "P(new)matological Paradigm," 177.

166. Yong, *Spirit Poured Out*, 246–47. In response to whether seeing the Spirit active within other religions would potentially undermine motivation for Christian mission, Yong responds that the Lukan narrative emphasizes Christian mission as being motivated by the Spirit's empowerment, and not fear over eternal destinies (ibid., 244–45). Also see Yong, "P(new)matological Paradigm," 176–84.

167. Yong, *Discerning the Spirit(s)*, 213–15; cf. Yong, *Hospitality and the Other*, 130–39.

(1) Granted that God is universally present by the Spirit, God in this sense sustains even the religions for divine purposes. (2) Granted that the Spirit's work is to usher in the kingdom of God, the Spirit is active in and through various aspects of the religions insofar as the signs of the kingdom are manifest. (3) Granted that the Spirit's universal presence and activity presume a resistant and retarding presence and activity that work against the kingdom of God, Spirit is also absent from the religions to the extent either that the signs of the kingdom are absent or that they are being prohibited from being manifest.[168]

Yong's first point simply affirms God's omnipresence. It does not imply that just any religion is fully revelational, but that no religion (or culture, etc.) is entirely without the *presence* of the Spirit. The second point goes further, asserting the Spirit's *activity* in other religions. The Spirit is active in human culture and society, bringing in God's kingdom, emphasized by the Spirit's outpouring at Pentecost.[169] Concerning the third point, Yong states, "although the Spirit is God present and active in the world, this presence and activity are still eschatological—not yet fully experienced but punctuated here and now by the Spirit. This points to our human experience of God's hiddenness or God's *absence*. Using religious parlance, I identify this with the demonic in order to reserve some means to retrieve and reappropriate the traditional claim that the religions are bearers not only of the divine but also of the demonic."[170]

So, in this way Yong's three elements (categories) of foundational pneumatology—the Spirit's presence, activity and absence—are applied to his theology of religions. This, then, brings us to the second issue mentioned earlier: the reality of the Spirit's absence requires, for Yong,

168. Yong, *Spirit Poured Out*, 250, cf. n.25. This summary combines (and distils) elements of his previous works, Yong, *Discerning the Spirit(s)*, 122–32; and Yong, *Beyond the Impasse*, 44–46.

169. Yong, *Spirit Poured Out*, 251–52. Writes Yong, "Consider the nature of human religiosity (dependent, of course, on world religious traditions) and its mediation through the material, social, cultural, political, economic, and other spheres of human existence. Human religiousness is not an accidental feature of human life that can be put on and taken off at will. Rather, it informs these spheres even as it is formed in and through them. Thus religion is resolutely intertwined with the human condition and with human hopes and aspirations and is only arbitrarily divorced from individual and communal identities. So the Christian claim that the kingdom of God is now coming (even if also not yet) cannot be limited only to any one sphere (e.g., the social, political, or economic) and detached from any other (e.g., the religious)."

170. Ibid., 252 (italics added).

the exercise of discernment, which is a complex and ongoing process.[171] Discernment applies to all areas of life, contends Yong, and not simply to other religions, since the Spirit's absence may in fact occur in any human realm, including within Christianity itself.[172] The PC pneumatological imagination not only discloses the above three foundational categories, but also uniquely provides a means by which the Spirit (or spirits) may be correctly discerned in any *context* (including religious). It is important to understand here that Yong is constructing a *pneumatological* theology of religions, which uses the Spirit as a point of departure to provide a way forward beyond the "christological impasse" that has been reached in Christian theology of religions.[173] In this regard, Yong sees more promise in exploring the question of the Spirit's revelation in and through the religions, temporarily "bracketing" out issues of Christology and soteriology.[174]

171. Yong, *Beyond the Impasse*, 164–65.

172. Yong, *Spirit Poured Out*, 253. He cites, for example, racism, sexism and classism as evidences of the Spirit's absence (the demonic) within Christianity. Elsewhere he expands on this, and also suggests some guidelines for discernment in general, viewing it as both a divine gift as well as an ability to be cultivated (Yong, *Beyond the Impasse*, ch. 6).

173. Yong, "P(new)matological Paradigm," 175. Discussion of this issue is given considerable attention in Yong's work, and space does not permit a detailed exposition here. In brief, however, he believes that debates among Christians concerning other religions have too quickly focused on the soteriological question; i.e., whether other religions are salvific. The traditional categories of response (exclusivism, inclusivism and pluralism) have proven inadequate for understanding the religions and their relationship to Christianity due to a focus on the soteriological question. Yong surveys several approaches to the religions by those from various Christian traditions (including, Yves Congar, Karl Rahner, John Hick, Paul Knitter, Aloysius Pieris, Georg Khodr, Stanley Samartha, Jacques Dupuis, and Clark Pinnock). While he finds value in their insights, ultimately Yong believes that there is a general tendency to return too quickly to evaluating the religions based on a Christological criterion, which tends to emphasize Christ's particularity. Emphasis on particularity (even in inclusivist approaches) ultimately introduces an impasse for interreligious dialogue. See Yong, *Beyond the Impasse*, 22–29, 83–128; Yong, *Discerning the Spirit(s)*, 33–58; and Yong, *Hospitality and the Other*, 65–98. In the latter work Yong suggests that perhaps the approaches of exclusivism, inclusivism and pluralism may all be appropriate, depending on the context. Also see Yong, "Can We Get," 28–32.

174. Yong, *Beyond the Impasse*, 170, 22, 29. Thus, Yong attempts to transcend exclusivism/inclusivism/pluralism categories, although he (cautiously) admits that he can probably be considered an inclusivist (ibid., 27). On the challenge of temporarily bracketing out Christ to focus on pneumatology, see also Yong et al., "Christ and Spirit," 18, 61–63; and Olson, "Wind That Swirls," 52–55.

Why this is possible has already been discussed previously—Word and Spirit are metaphysically *present and experienced* in all things; they are distinct but interrelated.[175] Yong states, "All determinate things consist of both *logos* and *pneuma*, metaphysically understood—having both forms of concretions and dynamic vectoral trajectories. The *pneuma*, or spirit, of any 'thing' is the complex of habits, tendencies, and laws that shape, guide, and in some way manifest and/or determine its phenomenal or concrete behavior."[176]

This means it is possible (relying on the "two hands" model) to in some sense measure the Spirit's activity apart from the Word.[177] To this end, Yong proposes that while all things exist relationally in the Spirit's presence through the act of creation,[178] the Spirit's outpouring at Pentecost (as well as previous outpourings) introduces "force fields" (relational vectors), able to move humans beings towards healing and salvation (depending on human cooperation and participation). This is, for Yong, what is understood as the Spirit's *activity*, linked to the realm of ethics. All things are created with a divinely intended purpose, he argues, and will be measured (judged) eschatologically by how well this purpose (the norms for which they were created) is fulfilled. These ethical norms are, further, established by the "norms, ideals and values" of Christ.[179] Claims Yong, "The *activity* of the Spirit in this is to integrate a thing into its environment in a way such that it can be *authentically itself* and of service in its relationships with others."[180] It is through participation within the Spirit's fields of force that things (including corporate entities/institutions) are glorifying to God. Movement toward harmony

---

175. Yong, *Discerning the Spirit(s)*, 179.

176. Yong, *Beyond the Impasse*, 129–30.

177. Yong, *Discerning the Spirit(s)*, 122, 136.

178. Ibid., 125–27. Yong, using Neville, differentiates between "ontological and cosmological causation." God ontologically causes the universe to exist, within which freedom (the spontaneity of "spirit") exists in all things. Within the created universe, cosmologically, the freedom granted by the Spirit can be used in (causal) ways that go against the intended purpose of any given thing (individual or corporate), thus allowing for the possibility of creaturely rebellion from God's purposes and the Spirit's absence (demonic).

179. Ibid., 124.

180. Ibid., 125 (italics added).

and authenticity with regard to God's intended purposes, then, serves to indicate the Spirit's activity.[181]

At the same time, reasons Yong, the Spirit, while ontologically present, can be "impotent" or "absent" in contexts in which creaturely freedom and spontaneity are used to pervert divine intention, introducing destructive, demonic "force fields."[182] He explains,

> Whereas the Holy Spirit works to constitute each thing in its own normative integrity within the broader harmony of relations, the demonic strives towards maximizing inauthenticity and estrangement in the world. It does so through force fields that tempt each thing to overestimate its significance and purpose, and to overreach its sphere of influence . . . This results in a distortion of a thing's identity and the disruption of its network of relations. Relationships infected by the demonic are no longer mutually supporting and reinforcing but rather self-seeking and destructive. This is especially the case when the demonic is incarnated in persons.[183]

The Spirit's absence may therefore be concretely manifest (the logos element) in persons, relationships, and corporate institutions, such as political or religious systems.[184] When it comes to any given religion (with its texts, rituals, etc.), what needs to be discerned, argues Yong, is whether its inner dynamics evidence movement toward harmony and authenticity (defined by God's purposes) or not, thus tentatively indicating either the Spirit's activity or absence respectively.[185] Concrete forms,

181. Ibid., 125, cf. 134–36. States Yong, "Pneumatological norms are satisfied to the extent that determinations of being brought about by the Spirit are authentically themselves (i.e. not perverted) and do fill their created purpose (i.e. serving others rather than being destructive). To the extent that the world is being transformed from a place with lesser degrees of harmony to one in which the harmonies of things are heightened and intensified in their interrelatedness, to that extent we can say that the Spirit is at work in the world" (ibid., 125; cf. Yong, *Beyond the Impasse*, 165).

182. Yong, *Discerning the Spirit(s)*, 127, 129.

183. Ibid., 130, cf. 131; cf. Yong, *Beyond the Impasse*, 137–39.

184. Yong, *Discerning the Spirit(s)*, 128–29. Elsewhere he states, the "inner spirit or force field of any corporate entity is what determines its shape, personality, and activities vis-à-vis its relationship with other things and entities" (Yong, *Beyond the Impasse*, 137, cf. 136).

185. Yong, *Discerning the Spirit(s)*, 133–36. The reintroduction of "norms, ideals and values" (logos) indicates that ultimately pneumatology at some point must acknowledge its connection to Christology, says Yong (ibid., 136).

then, need to be penetrated to disclose the inner spirit at work,[186] and the PC pneumatological imagination is uniquely postured to facilitate this in what Yong proposes as a three-tiered process.[187]

First, Yong observes that PCs are open to viewing concrete phenomena in human religious activity as (potentially) signs of the Spirit's presence. Such phenomena can broadly include all sorts of symbols, such as rituals and texts, but also so-called "religious experiences," manifest in glossolalia, clapping, dance, dreams, visions, and so forth.[188] The Spirit, in other words, leaves an impression on the senses, difficult to ignore or deny, which is why PC experiences of the Spirit are understood in terms of encounter.[189] On the basis of the Spirit's universal presence, Yong suggests that such phenomena may empirically be compared; and this is the first step of discernment—the finite symbols pointing (potentially) to transcendent reality.[190] Such observation must be done carefully, cautions Yong. Religious phenomena need to be understood within the theological context in which they occur, each religion being allowed to speak on its own terms in order for the theological meaning of its symbols to be rightly understood.[191] The goal, then, is a "comparative

---

186. Yong, *Beyond the Impasse*, 129–30.

187. Yong, *Discerning the Spirit(s)*, 250. Yong outlines this process of discernment (enabling and encouraging interreligious dialogue) in different ways in his works; but the ways in which the PC experience informing this process arguably becomes most explicit is in *Discerning the Spirit(s)*. So, the points discussed here will be derived primarily from that source (see Yong, *Discerning the Spirit(s)*, ch. 7). Cf. Yong, *Beyond the Impasse*, chs. 6–7; and Yong, *Spirit Poured Out*, ch. 6.

188. Yong, *Discerning the Spirit(s)*, 224, 250–51, cf. 223–27. The three tiers in this process ("religious experience," "religious utility" and "religious cosmology") are all expanded modifications of Cox's three categories (outlined in *Fire From Heaven*) for understanding PC experience: "primal speech," "primal piety" and "primal hope" (ibid., 222–43).

189. Ibid., 225.

190. Ibid., 251, 225–26. We should begin, states Yong, not by invoking Christological criteria, but by exploring "phenomenological commonalities (divine presence) and the other's understanding of these phenomena." See also Yong, *Beyond the Impasse*, 150–51, 175–76.

191. Yong, *Discerning the Spirit(s)*, 226, cf. 142. Yong states that "religious experience" is a vacuous term, since experience is always "'of something' and shaped by social, cultural and linguistic forces." Further, such encounters need to be considered not as disconnected from broader human experience, but as being of the "religious dimension of human experience" (ibid., 225). Also see Yong, *Beyond the Impasse*, 176–83.

theology," and not a comparing of religions, as if they all shared a common worldview.[192]

This "comparative theology" necessitates the second step in Yong's discernment process: evaluating the symbols of a given religion on the basis of "religious utility."[193] PCs expect not only sovereign divine encounters, Yong observes, but also value the human response to such for assessing whether the Spirit has truly been active. PCs, in other words, are universally pragmatists; they expect what is truly a "move of God" to have "cash value," to elicit positive, liberative results ethically and morally.[194] Thus, discernment must involve this utilitarian element, and religious symbols should be examined to determine what outcomes these are intended to elicit, as defined by the practitioners of the given religious community.[195] Yong writes:

> In short, the issue here is pragmatic: do the symbols work? If they do, two further questions arise: how do they work and what is accomplished by practicing with the religious symbols over time? . . . Is there, in short, evidence of the Spirit's activity in the non-Christian faiths whereby lives are made whole and communal relationships are continually mended, formed and strengthened? If yes, let the Christian say a tentative and hearty "Amen"; if no, so much the worse for the other tradition and let the Christian then be led by the Spirit in developing further strategies for witness.[196]

Ethical criteria are not definitive, however, in the discernment process. There is, according to Yong, still need to determine the transcendental references, or "content meaning," to which religious symbols refer.[197] Here he draws on the early Pentecostal experience of marginalization, which helped shape their eschatological framework. They hoped for Jesus' return with heightened existential awareness of the Spirit's absence in the world around them. Thus, PCs "religious cosmology" makes

192. Yong, *Beyond the Impasse*, 174–83.

193. Yong, *Discerning the Spirit(s)*, 227–34, 251–53.

194. Ibid., 234, cf. 228–34; cf. Yong, *Spirit of Creation*, 11.

195. Yong, *Discerning the Spirit(s)*, 252–53. Yong differentiates here between the "network and content meaning" of symbols. The former refers to the "extensional references" within a cultural-linguistic community, the latter to transcendental referents, which cannot fully be determined at this stage.

196. Ibid.

197. Ibid., 253.

room for the Spirit's absence, and such a category may provide a means of comparison with other religions, all of which have some sort of cosmology (many including spiritual beings, such as the demonic). Careful discernment, then, includes openness to evidence of the existence of destructive force fields within a religion and its practices.[198] Yong also adds that since the inner workings of any given religion (or thing) are dynamic, and because we can only observe concrete manifestations, the process of discernment needs to be ongoing, and conclusions always provisional.[199] He believes, however, that "religious experience," "religious utility," and "religious cosmology" are "sufficiently vague" categories for enabling interreligious dialogue and discernment of the Spirit or spirits—and all of these have been derived from PC experience of the Spirit.[200]

Summary

Our exploration of Yong's contribution to Pentecostal theology has highlighted his foundational pneumatology, which simultaneously emerges from and informs a PC pneumatological imagination. On this basis, Yong believes that Pentecostals (and Christians) should be open to recognizing *the Spirit's mediation through reason*—i.e., outside Scripture and tradition in the context(s) of human society, culture, religion, politics, sciences, and so forth. So, where might Yong be found on Schner's continuum? Since his project shares so many similarities with Gelpi's, we can likewise locate Yong at the "appeal constructive." Scripture and tradition inform his theological reflection, yet he also strongly urges Christians to discern the Spirit outside of these realms, and proposes ample criteria for doing so. Once the Spirit is (provisionally) discerned dialogically in any given context (e.g., science, religion, etc.), then any associated knowledge gleaned from that resource may be utilized in Christian theological construction. There is arguably, however, also a "transcendental" element in Yong's work; he accentuates the Spirit's presence as universal in all things (further stressed by his temporary "bracketing" of Christology from the discernment process). But his

---

198. Ibid., 234–43, 253–55.

199. Ibid., 255; cf. Yong, *Beyond the Impasse*, 151–53, 164–67.

200. Yong, *Discerning the Spirit(s)*, 221, cf. 143; Yong, *Beyond the Impasse*, 176–79. Yong puts his criteria to the test in *Discerning the Spirit(s)* by examining the Afro-Brazilian Umbanda religion (ibid., 256–309).

foundational pneumatology is quite empirical and provisional, and he adamantly emphasizes the necessity of careful observation and discernment (e.g., advocating "comparative theology" rather than comparative religion). So, his appeal to experience of God is hardly of one that is universal or transcendental in an Enlightenment sense. For this reason, the "appeal constructive" best describes Yong's position. He exemplifies a maturation within Pentecostalism, utilizing Pentecostal experience to inform Christian theology in ways that are both innovative and challenging to Pentecostal and broader Christian tradition.

Yong in Dialogue with the Christian Theological Traditions

The previous section attempted to demonstrate Yong's affirmation of the Spirit's mediation through reason. In doing so, various metaphysical, epistemological and hermeneutical themes emerged, and will be used to guide our dialogue here. These themes also have further implications for Pentecostal spirituality, and so these will be addressed as well.

Metaphysics, the "Two Hands," and the Spirit's Universal Presence

When it comes to metaphysical issues, the nature of reality, the most obvious dialogue partner for Yong is Gelpi. Since, however, we have already surveyed Yong's use of Gelpi's triadic metaphysics of experience in the first part of this chapter, there seems little reason to reiterate that material here. Instead, we will reserve further dialogue with Gelpi until later, when we explore some ways he has influenced Yong's soteriology and charismology (theology of spiritual gifts). That said, Yong's reliance on Gelpi's triadic construct (via Peirce) should be kept in mind. This allowed Yong to suggest that all things are constituted of "spirit" and "logos," reflecting the interconnection of Spirit and Word with creation. At the same time, he also gleaned the "two hands" model to propose a distinction of the Spirit's presence and activity from that of Word.

This leads us to consider the first category of Yong's foundational pneumatology, namely, the Spirit's presence.[201] The Spirit, for Yong, is

---

201. We must somewhat awkwardly attempt to bracket aside issues of the Spirit's activity and absence until later in our dialogue, in the next subsection.

universally and identifiably present (tied to the metaphysical concept of "firstness"), and this belief can find both supporters and detractors among our dialogue partners. Of course, this is not a simple either/ or matter; qualification is required on both sides. But in general those who would likely find significant convergence with Yong here (leaving aside Gelpi for the time being) would be Moltmann, Johnson, Cone, and Bulgakov. Those diverging more so in this respect would be Congar, Jenson, and Lossky.

Moltmann's pneumatological doctrine of creation, in which creation is viewed as God's dwelling place (albeit, eschatologically not yet fully realized), may share considerable affinity with Yong's concept of the Spirit's universal presence.[202] This is not to say that Yong embraces Moltmann's doctrine of creation wholeheartedly. Yong has questioned Moltmann's speculative idea of God's contraction of God's self to create the nihil, and further suggests (more critically) that Moltmann has collapsed the immanent Trinity into the economic through an emphasis on the crucifixion event having caused the Father "infinite pain."[203] Nevertheless, considerable convergence remains. Yong speaks affirmatively regarding Moltmann's Trinitarian *perichoresis*, which provides considerable basis for Moltmann to posit a mutual indwelling of God and creation.[204] More explicitly, Yong endorses Moltmann's emphasis on the world being taken up into the triune life through the Incarnation and Pentecost, as well as Moltmann's eschatology, which links the unity of the Godhead as being only ultimately and fully realized (historically) in the eschaton.[205] Congruence is also noticeable

202. References to Moltmann are not infrequent in Yong's work. In particular, Yong appreciates elements of Moltmann's doctrine of Social Trinity and pneumatology. See Yong, "On Divine Presence," 20n.32; Yong, *Spirit-Word-Community*, 43, 73, 86–87, 90, 306; and Yong, *Discerning the Spirit(s)*, 148n.70.

203. Yong, "Oneness and the Trinity," 94–96, cf. 81–107; cf. Moltmann, *Trinity and the Kingdom*, 160. Yong believes that if the doctrine of creation *ex nihilo* is taken seriously, any attempt to distinguish the economic from the immanent Trinity will inevitably lead to the "dissolution" of the one into the other. Moltmann suggests this very point, but then continues to maintain this distinction. Yong is reluctant to speculate on the immanent Trinity apart from creation. He also argues similarly elsewhere in hopes of demonstrating potential convergence in dialogue with Oneness Pentecostals (Yong, *Spirit Poured Out*, 203–34).

204. Yong, *Theology and Down Syndrome*, 158.

205. Yong, *Spirit-Word-Community*, 306; Yong, "Oneness and the Trinity," 106–7n.87; cf. Moltmann, *Experiences in Theology*, 134–50.

with Moltmann's assertion of creation being animated and empowered by the energy field of the Spirit.[206] Moltmann also affirms the Spirit's presence (immanence) in every creature,[207] which may well correspond to Yong's concept of "firstness"—the Spirit's presence enabling freedom and spontaneity in every created thing. Especially important for our purposes, because Moltmann views Spirit as animating all things, he is able to connect revelation and experience, meaning there is no dualism between theology and (historical) experience; and this is a point with which Yong would strongly concur.[208]

Johnson and (tacitly) Cone also affirm the Spirit's universal presence, advocating the Spirit's presence in human experience outside ecclesial boundaries. Spirit is by no means bound by Word, in this sense. Significantly, in *Spirit-Word-Community* Yong quotes Johnson at length concerning the Spirit as both the relational factor within the Godhead, and also between God and the world. In doing so Yong affirms, with Johnson, that the relationship of creation to the Trinity is (as far as creation is concerned) a necessary one. The Spirit is the one who not only relates the divine to creation, but also serves to establish a horizontal symbiotic interconnectedness within creation between all things. On this point, Yong appears to come very close to advocating a panentheism similar to Johnson's, although in his work he does not appear to apply that specific term to himself.[209] Affirmation of the Spirit's universal presence inevitably also raises issues of discernment, and so we will return to Johnson (and Cone) concerning this in the next subsection.

Bulgakov may also find convergence with Yong concerning the Spirit's universal presence. Bulgakov, it will be recalled, found motivation for his sophiology in his desire to overcome the poles of otherworldliness and secularism. Thus, his theological and philosophical speculation concerning the nature of reality helped bridge the God/world relationship,

206. Moltmann, "A Response," 65.

207. Moltmann, "The Scope of Renewal," 104.

208. Moltmann, *Spirit of Life*, 39–57.

209. Yong, *Spirit-Word-Community*, 58–59; cf. Johnson, *She Who Is*, 148. Yong sees panentheism (and pantheism) as stronger forms of emphasis on the Spirit's relationship to the world; and doctrines of creation, Incarnation and Pentecost as being weaker forms of this emphasis. He also speaks of the Incarnation and Pentecost as being the events that draw the world into the divine life (Yong, *Spirit-Word-Community*, 306), and so, it is difficult to pin Yong down on this particular point. It would not be a stretch, however, to associate Yong with a relational panentheism such as found with Gelpi.

avoiding certain metaphysical dualisms. Yong's foundational pneumatology and metaphysics arguably helps overcome similar dualisms,[210] and also demonstrates how the various contexts of the world (e.g., cultures, religions, sciences, etc.), when viewed through the pneumatological imagination, hold potential as resources for theological reflection.

Bulgakov arrives at his position by rethinking the meaning of God's essence. He identifies the biblical concept of Wisdom, usually associated with Word or Spirit (or both), with Sophia (God's Ousia). In this schema, Word and Spirit serve to reveal Sophia.[211] Creation is constituted and energized by Wisdom (Sophia), and exists in panentheistic relationship to God; thus the world of creation mirrors the divine world.[212] Because of its sophianic constitution, creation does not exist in dichotomy with the divine world, but is characterized by "becoming, emergence, development, [and] fulfillment."[213] Creation is, then, naturally receptive to the workings of grace toward deification.

Yong, while not utilizing Bulgakov's sophiology, does propose that the created realm reflects, or echoes, the nature of its triune Creator in its very constitution—all things are constituted by logos and spirit, and Word and Spirit are both operative in the divine economy (based on the "two hands" model). Further, Yong's identification of the Spirit as relationality, not only within the Godhead but also between God and creation, accents Spirit as universally present, enabling life, and providing the potential for spontaneity and freedom among all creatures. Yong does not, it would seem, advocate the participation of creation in the divine essence; however, his description of the Spirit's universal presence (with all its complex implications) appears to *function* in ways similar to Bulgakov's Sophia—both attempting to provide a metaphysical foundation that will allow experience of God to be connected more readily to life and knowledge of the world in general.

The metaphysics of Yong and Bulgakov, while different, sometimes elicit similar theological effects. For example, Bulgakov indicates that the Incarnation and Pentecost are possible due to creation's sophianic nature.[214] For Yong, Pentecost and other prior "outpourings" are identi-

---

210. Yong, *Spirit Poured Out*, 291–92; cf. Bulgakov, *Sophia*, 14–15.

211. Bulgakov, *Orthodox Church*, 25–30; Bulgakov, *Sophia*, 69.

212. Bulgakov, *Sophia*, 65.

213. Ibid., 75.

214. Ibid., 88–96.

fied as vectors, or force fields, of the Spirit's activity, enabled on the basis of the Spirit's ubiquitous presence (providing metaphysical "firstness"). Because of creaturely Sophia's universality, Bulgakov can view the Spirit's outpouring on all flesh at Pentecost as also applying to all humanity (not confined to the ecclesia).[215] Yong likewise broadens "all flesh" to a scope beyond the church.

Further, for Bulgakov, not only may all people experience Sophia's life force, but existing in all is also a *"natural grace of inspiration."* This, while not coming *"directly* from the Holy Spirit," is "implanted" by the Spirit into creaturely Sophia, thus universalizing inspiration potential.[216] So, in "pagan" religions, there is a "natural revelation, although one that is distorted and beclouded"; and yet these "religions are not empty *sophianically."*[217] Such revelation can become quite distorted—"demonic or luciferian," as Bulgakov puts it—and so discernment is needed.[218] Nevertheless, natural revelation can serve as precondition for true Christian revelation. Yong not only bears similarities with this trajectory, but would appear far more optimistic regarding the quality of revelation occurring within other religions (or other realms of human society and culture). In sum, while Yong and Bulgakov differ in the construction of their metaphysics, nevertheless, both of their systems emphasize the universality of the divine presence (whether by Sophia or Spirit), the intricate relationship between God and the created world, and the possibility of theological revelation outside the church.

Conversely, Congar, Lossky, and Jenson would likely be less apt to endorse Yong's portrayal of the Spirit's universal presence, tending to accent more so the Spirit's association with Word and the church (Christ's

---

215. Bulgakov, *Bride of the Lamb*, 313.

216. Bulgakov, *Comforter*, 213 (italics original). Bulgakov here states, "it would be correct to say that in the creaturely Sophia, in creaturely being itself, the Holy Spirit has implanted the force of life and inspiration as the sophianic foundation of this being. And inspiration is real in man because he has something to reveal and something to be awakened to."

217. Ibid., 214 (italics original).

218. Ibid., 214, 225. Later, Bulgakov states that since Christianity's emergence, pagan religions have tended to take on a "negative, demonic coefficient," becoming "anti-Christian in proportion to their conscious rejection of and opposition to Christianity." Nevertheless, *"all* true religions, all religions that contain the experience of the Divinity, necessarily have a ray of Divinity, the breath of the Spirit." And so, "it is possible to have toward paganism a non-pedagogical attitude, which, in the light of the Christian revelation distinguishes its light side from its dark side" (ibid., 241; italics original).

body). It is not that these three deny any element of the Spirit's broader work in the world, but it is doubtful they would share Yong's optimism concerning the possibility of identifying the Spirit apart from the Word (even if only for a temporary "bracketing"). We will postpone dialogue with Jenson to the next subsection, and here focus on Congar and Lossky.

Congar does emphasize the Spirit, demonstrated in his pneumatological Christology, and advocacy for recognition of the Spirit's work among Church laity (in various forms of charismatic expression). He even utilizes the "two hands" model to emphasize that Word and Spirit are interconnected yet distinct. The Spirit is not to be subsumed to Word (or, within the ecclesial context, to clergy)—Word and Spirit together constitute the church.[219] Here it is notable that while both Congar and Yong appeal to the "two hands" model, they do not necessarily draw from it the same implications. For Yong, this model supports his attempt to discern the Spirit's work distinct from (yet interconnected to) Word. Congar exhibits less confidence concerning the identification of the Spirit outside the body of Christ. While he does suggest the possibility of the Spirit's work in the world, he more so stresses there is no "free sector" of the Spirit outside the ecclesia; the Spirit may be present in the world, but not discernably so outside the church.[220] Thus Congar emphasizes distinction between Word and Spirit, but still views Spirit as primarily aiding reception of Word within the church.[221]

It will be recalled that Yong utilized Lossky's "two hands" emphasis in building his own case for distinguishing the missions of Spirit and Word. In this respect (and some others) Yong and Lossky share commonalities. For example, Yong echoes some of Lossky's preference for an apophatic approach to the divine mystery, although Yong is not as closed to the cataphatic approach, and does engage in considerable speculation with regard to metaphysics (as we have seen).[222] Yong also concurred with Lossky's rejection of the filioque, at least in his earlier work. More recently, Yong admits to new appreciation for the filioque in

---

219. Congar, *Word and the Spirit*, 58–62, 78–84; Congar, *I Believe*, 2:7–12. With regard to ecclesiology, Yong does dialogue with Congar considerably concerning the marks of the church (one, holy, catholic, and apostolic), but that discussion falls outside of our scope here. See Yong, *Spirit Poured Out*, 134–51.

220. Congar, *Word and the Spirit*, 61, 126.

221. Ibid., 25.

222. Yong, *Spirit-Word-Community*, 210–11, cf. 73 n. 10; Yong, *Discerning the Spirit(s)*, 69.

certain theological contexts, largely in an effort to include the experience of Oneness Pentecostals (with their emphasis on divine unity) as a valid theological resource.[223] Lossky's theology of the divine energies may also hold potential congruence with aspects of Yong's theology, namely, the latter's concept of the Spirit's activity as field of force. The extent of convergence here is, however, difficult to surmise. Lossky does posit that the energies are distinct from the divine essence and hypostases, and that these energies are more fully released at Pentecost, enabling greater potential for deification.[224] This bears some resemblance to Yong's concept of Pentecost creating a (new) force field of the Spirit's activity, although Yong does not adopt a theology of energies.

This also means, however, that there is likely less congruency between Lossky's divine energies and Yong's category of universal divine presence, identified with one of the hypostases (Spirit).[225] Lossky's carefulness to avoid any idea of direct human participation in the divine hypostases and essence (hence the appeal to energies) would likely make it difficult for him to accept Yong's metaphysical categories in this regard. Conversely, at one point Yong comments that the Eastern Orthodox approach to the Trinity can tend to "produce a modalistic notion of divine energies in the economy of God's work on the one hand, and a frozen and static conception of the divine essence on the other."[226]

Further, while Lossky does appeal to the "two hands" model to distinguish the Spirit and Word's missions, he does so to counter issues of ecclesial hierarchy rather than to "free" the Spirit into the world in general (in this way bearing some resemblance to Congar). Lossky is quite clear on this—the divine energies and the Spirit's activity are located in the ecclesia. The Spirit may be present in some way in creation, but the activity of the Spirit, that which enables deification, is found within ecclesial boundaries.[227] Yong, of course, does not restrict the Spirit's activity to the church. Although he attempts to avoid discussion as to whether salvation is found outside the church (e.g., in other religions),

223. Yong, *Spirit Poured Out*, 203–34. Oneness Pentecostals (as their name implies) would be more apt to accent the unity of the Godhead as opposed to threeness.

224. Lossky, *Mystical Theology*, 133, cf. 73.

225. The Word could likely be included here as well, since Yong sees all things as constituted by logos and spirit.

226. Yong, *Spirit-Word-Community*, 65. Yong likely has Lossky in mind here, since he cites him earlier in the same paragraph.

227. Lossky, *Mystical Theology*, 171.

he advocates that revelation of the Spirit is more widely available than Lossky would likely allow.

One other point is worth mentioning here (anticipating upcoming discussion concerning soteriology and spirituality). Yong's category of "firstness" helps him explain human spontaneity and freedom, allowing for and necessitating human participation with God toward deification. While Lossky would concur with this synergistic emphasis, he simply assumes human freedom and participation as being (yet) another theological mystery, without speculating as to the metaphysics that might make such possible. On the other hand, Yong (and Bulgakov) has entered into speculation as to how this might be the case. In sum, while Lossky and Yong do share some theological affinities, it is likely Lossky would diverge from Yong's particular construal of the Spirit's universal presence (and activity).

Identifying the Spirit's Activity:
Hermeneutics and Discernment

Closely associated with the issue of the Spirit's presence is that of discerning the Spirit's activity and absence. These latter two categories will be our focus here (although they have already intruded into our above discussion). Yong is quite optimistic concerning the possibility of discerning the Spirit's activity or absence based on particular criteria. The Spirit may be discerned in the multifaceted contexts of life, provided an appropriate interpretive (hermeneutical) framework is utilized. In this regard, Jenson would likely view Yong's approach with considerable skepticism, while others like Johnson, Cone, and Moltmann, with their emphasis on contextual hermeneutics, may find in Yong an ally (albeit with qualification).

We bring Jenson into the dialogue at this point due to his emphasis on the necessity of appropriate criteria for discerning the Spirit's presence and activity.[228] Jenson contends that "spirit" has come to be defined in two ways—either of a vacuous sort, or a spirit of someone. It is the latter of these definitions that he is convinced the biblical revelation demands. The Spirit's identity in the Bible is revealed historically as being

---

228. Jenson could have factored into the previous subsection, but it seemed more appropriate to introduce him here.

the Spirit of Jesus (and of Israel's God).[229] God and creation, in this view, are related through time, meaning there is no metaphysical distance between God and the world.[230] Both Yong and Jenson agree in some sense concerning God's presence in creation, but they appear to differ considerably as to the "how." For Jenson, God's speech occurs via the Logos, embodied in creation.[231] Revelation (and experience) of God occurs by hearing the Word, enabled by the Spirit.[232] The Spirit is presently localized in the church, which is Christ's body. This means that the identity of the Spirit is tied up with the Word and located in the ecclesia,[233] which is why Jenson is suspicious of any notion of a cosmic Spirit.

Yong is not unaware of Jenson's concerns with regard to the Spirit's identity. At one point, in describing the metaphysical basis for his foundational pneumatology (and thus the possibilities of a "universal rationality"), Yong acknowledges the potential pitfalls in such an undertaking, citing Jenson explicitly: "Note, however, the warning of Robert Jenson that the tension in pneumatology between the particularity of the Spirit in Jesus and in the Church and the universality of the Spirit as a cosmic reality 'strains Western intellectual tradition to breaking. . . . [T]hose who have ventured cosmic pneumatology have not always been able to avoid producing nonsense or myth.' It is therefore with fear and trembling that I set us forth on this path of exploring the implications of the claim that reality is relational, rational, and dynamic."[234]

So, Yong shares some of Jenson's concerns regarding over-speculation concerning the immanent Trinity, and the Spirit not calling attention to "herself."[235] The above quote, however, indicates that Yong is knowingly moving in a direction antithetical to that of Jenson. It is likely that Jenson would concur here with Chan's criticism of Yong (see chapter 4), namely, that Yong ends up defining Spirit not by the biblical narrative,

229. Jenson, *Triune Identity*, 7–8.

230. Ibid., 107.

231. Ibid., 140.

232. Jenson, *Systematic Theology: Triune*, 109–10.

233. Jenson, *Systematic Theology: Works*, 271.

234. Yong, *Spirit-Word-Community*, 84 (brackets original); citing Robert W. Jenson, "The Holy Spirit" in *Christian Dogmatics*, Vol. 2, ed. Carl Braaten and Robert W. Jenson (Philadelphia: Fortress Press, 1984), 165.

235. Yong, *Spirit-Word-Community*, 64–65; cf. Jenson, *Systematic Theology: Triune*, 152–53. Yong's earlier noted criticism of the Eastern Orthodox tendency to end up with a static concept of divine essence is also an insight he gleans from Jenson.

but by using late-modern philosophical categories.[236] In other words, Jenson would probably view Yong's "Spirit" as being of the vacuous sort, without historical identity. Yong may not agree with this assessment (if I am applying it accurately here), but the task at hand is only to identify the likelihood of divergence on this point.[237]

When it comes to contextual/liberation theologians, such as Johnson and Cone (and Moltmann), there are a number of areas of possible convergence with Yong concerning his category of the Spirit's activity. But Yong also offers contextual theologians a potential way forward with regard to theological construction, as well as perhaps recovering an appreciation for the historical Christian tradition. For Johnson and Cone, experience of the Spirit occurs most acutely through the historical experience of women and blacks respectively—the Christian tradition, up through the modern era, having marginalized these and other oppressed groups. Experience of the Spirit, then, is not restricted to traditional ecclesial boundaries, but is found in the concrete, historical experience(s) of the oppressed. For Cone, association with the traditional church is hardly an adequate criterion by which to locate the Spirit's activity; and in fact he implies the marked *absence* of the Spirit in "white" theology.[238] Both Cone and Johnson reject modernist foundational (universal) epistemology, since they view it as culturally arrogant, and as leading to the oppression and marginalization of particular groups. Thus, because all theology is interested theology (Cone), a strong hermeneutics of suspicion is employed. Experience of the Spirit is understood not through universal abstract categories, but in the context of daily life, in particular within the experience of oppressed groups. For this reason, Johnson speaks of the "field of the Spirit" operating (active) outside the church as a universal presence.[239]

Both Johnson and Cone do realize, of course, that any appeal to experience of the Spirit by any particular group cannot be taken at face

236. Chan, "Encountering the Triune," 217–18.

237. Cf. Yong, *Spirit-Word-Community*, 106–7. Here Yong also briefly dialogues with Jenson regarding the difficult issues concerning God's sovereignty and predestination, which he attempts to resolve by an emphasis on the Spirit as the eschatological power of the future. This discussion, however, lies beyond our scope of interest.

238. Cone, *God of the Oppressed*, 42. Cone here states, "For black and red peoples in North America, the spirit of the Enlightenment was socially and politically demonic, becoming a pseudo-intellectual basis for their enslavement or extermination."

239. Johnson, *She Who Is*, 122.

value. Criteria for discernment must be offered, sufficient to identify the Spirit's activity. They discount, as noted, association with an ecclesial tradition as guarantee of the Spirit's activity. Further, they exhibit discomfort with subjective, ecstatic (charismatic) religious experiences as a criterion, although neither do they entirely disregard these as being of the Spirit.[240] Such experiences are simply considered less than reliable indicators of the Spirit's activity, and may in fact serve as a distraction (Cone). So, what criteria might serve to identify the Spirit's activity? Johnson speaks of human flourishing (especially among women) as one such indicator, related to the idea that the Spirit works against injustice in its various forms (with gender inequality predominantly in view).[241] Cone echoes similar criteria, emphasizing God as liberator of the oppressed; therefore, tangible (pragmatic) outcomes serve to indicate the Spirit's activity.[242] Cone admits that discernment is a somewhat subjective process, allowing only for "existential certainty" in distinguishing the Spirit from a given ideology.[243] But he is fairly confident that transformation (conversion) evidenced in taking the side of the oppressed largely serves to indicate the Spirit's activity.[244] He is also optimistic that the Spirit will enable the ability to perceive the limitations of one's own perspective, so as to become less ideological in the discernment process.[245]

Yong's theology converges with contextual/liberation theologies in a number of respects. He exemplifies numerous times, for example, his willingness to listen to the voices of the marginalized, and even more so champions this as a PC theological necessity. The outpouring of the Spirit on "all flesh" is a recurring theme in Yong's work,[246] meaning that all peoples, cultures, genders, and languages are participants in the Spirit's outpouring and (therefore) activity. Yong's presentation of PC experience explicitly incorporates a global perspective, including marginalized voices of blacks and women.[247] Further, his soteriology includes a social

240. Ibid., 129; Cone, *Black Theology*, 57–58.

241. Johnson, *She Who Is*, 30.

242. Cone, *God of the Oppressed*, 189.

243. Cone, *Black Theology*, 60.

244. Cone, *God of the Oppressed*, 189.

245. Ibid., 93–98.

246. This is especially the case in *Spirit Poured Out*. Also see Yong, "Poured out on All Flesh," 16–46.

247. On the contribution of black Pentecostalism see Yong, "Justice Deprived," 127–47.

dimension in which race, class, and gender are moved toward reconciliation by the activity of the Spirit, which involves hearing the voices of the marginalized.[248] But perhaps the most unique evidence in his work of his desire to give a voice to the marginalized (as well as demonstrating dialogue with the sciences) is found in his book, *Theology and Down Syndrome*, in which he utilizes the experience of the cognitively disabled as a resource for revisioning theology in such areas as creation, ecclesiology, soteriology, and eschatology.[249]

Yong also applauds the ethical prophetic witness against injustice, with a view toward liberation, found among contextual theologians.[250] Moreover, he would likely resonate with Cone's pragmatic emphasis on discerning the Spirit's activity through empirical examination of observable action and outcomes. Yong's criterion of the Spirit's activity discerned by whether things are being moved toward (or away from) their divinely intended purpose might find considerable convergence with the liberation praxis criteria adopted by Cone and Johnson. Finally, there may also be some practical parallels between Yong's pneumatological imagination and Cone's idea that the Spirit enables discernment concerning the limitations of one's own perspective. Both, in other words, count on the Spirit to be active in shaping one's perspectives (and interpretations), although Yong develops this idea in a far more sophisticated way.[251]

In sum, Yong would find convergence with the idea of the Spirit's mediation in all sorts of *contexts*, and certainly not limited to Western European theological traditions. Yong does, however, indicate some divergence from liberation theologies, at one point stating that such need to develop a more "global view of God."[252] In other words, liberation/contextual theologies can demonstrate a tendency to locate the Spirit's activity almost exclusively within certain marginalized groups (e.g., women, blacks, etc.), inadvertently excluding other voices through

248. Yong, *Spirit Poured Out*, 93–95.

249. Yong, *Theology and Down Syndrome*, 151–292; also see Yong, "Disability, the Human Condition," 5–25.

250. Yong, *Spirit-Word-Community*, 279–81.

251. See Yong, "P(new)matological Paradigm," 180–81. Yong argues that the Spirit helps one enter into the perspective of the other, to bring about mutual appreciation and understanding. This is exemplified most practically in Yong, *Hospitality and the Other*, especially chs. 4 and 5.

252. Yong, *Spirit-Word-Community*, 281, cf. 279–82.

whom the Spirit is also able to speak. Yong's approach is to affirm contextual particularities, listening to voices through careful empirical observation, and with the global scope in view, since the Spirit has been poured out on "all flesh." There is perhaps considerable convergence here with Moltmann's hermeneutical approach in *Experiences in Theology*, in which he not only accents the Spirit operating in historical particulars, but also attempts to integrate insights from various forms of contextual theologies globally.[253]

While Johnson and Cone are, to varying degrees, also concerned with Yong's above critique (Cone perhaps less so), it may be that Yong is able to acknowledge the Spirit's global activity more eagerly, largely due to his PC (and Lukan) theological emphasis (with its global scope), and because he has developed a more sophisticated criteriology for doing so. This statement requires some elucidation. To reiterate, Yong's foundational pneumatological categories include not only the Spirit's presence and activity, but also the Spirit's absence. Every situation (context, theology, etc.), then, must be carefully scrutinized for signs of the Spirit's activity and/or absence; and further, this process must be ongoing, since reality is dynamic and discernment always revisable. Further, one must not be too quick to demonize other groups (or theologies), since one never quite knows at face value whether the Spirit is active in the inner workings of that context or not.[254]

So, while Yong might, for example, concur to some extent with Cone that "white" theology is marked by the Spirit's absence, he would perhaps qualify this as a *present possibility* as opposed to an ongoing given. At the same time, Yong may also want to look for evidence of the Spirit's activity within "white" theology, since it is unlikely that any theology is totally devoid of the Spirit's presence and activity—a point that Cone might not find as palatable. Moreover, if Yong is correct, Cone and Johnson would need to also scrutinize their own theologies for evidence of the demonic (Spirit's absence), since no system escapes this possibility this side of the eschaton.[255] In noting this, we would do well to again

253. Moltmann, *Experiences in Theology*, 183–299. While more could be said, discussion with Moltmann is being intentionally limited here since he has already factored considerably in our dialogues in this project so far.

254. Yong, "P(new)matological Paradigm," 176.

255. It should be noted that in different ways both Johnson and Cone acknowledge their theologies as provisional. Johnson, for example, argues that female imagery for God is helpful at this point in history, but that this by no means universalizes this ap-

bear in mind Yong's sensitivity to hearing the voices of the marginalized; there is little doubt that he is sympathetic with the concerns of Johnson and Cone. Yet, Yong's foundational pneumatology and robust theology of discernment enables him to more readily open the doors, so to speak, to a myriad of voices (contexts, languages, cultures, genders, etc.) as a resource for theology without discounting any too quickly.

Further, Yong may actually provide a potential means by which liberation theologies might recover (or grow in) appreciation for more traditional Christian theology (not to mention PC charismatic encounters!). The PC pneumatological imagination facilitates the possibility of discerning the Spirit's activity even within ecclesial traditions that have, at times, perhaps been oppressive. In short, for Yong, no voice should be excluded before careful discernment is applied, and this process is ongoing. Affirms Yong, "It is essential therefore that theological interpretation proceed via a pluralistic and dialogical hermeneutics that engages with any and all who are interested in the theological quest."[256]

Expanding the Boundaries of Pentecostal Spirituality: Soteriology and Charismology

The final topic of dialogue broadly concerns issues of Pentecostal spirituality, including soteriology and charismology. Our primary discourse partner here will be Gelpi, who has significantly influenced Yong's theological work. Yong readily acknowledges that his own work builds upon Gelpi's triadic metaphysics of experience; and while he develops this in new directions, there are few (if any) areas in which Yong and Gelpi seriously diverge. In Yong's earlier work he did question whether Gelpi's conversion theology could adequately serve as a foundation for interreligious dialogue, believing Gelpi's "religious conversion" referred only to Christian conversion. This implied that other religions were not experiencing the revelatory presence and activity of the Spirit, and is one reason that Yong advocated his pneumatological imagination as basis for a foundational pneumatology, as opposed to Gelpi's conversion theology.[257] More recently, however, Yong has acknowledged that he mis-

---

proach. Here, however, we are simply identifying theological emphases for the sake of contrast.

256. Yong, *Spirit-Word-Community*, 305, cf. 305–10.

257. Yong, *Discerning the Spirit(s)*, 101–2; Yong, *Beyond the Impasse*, 60–64.

read Gelpi on this point, which leaves little else to highlight as points of divergence.[258]

More significantly, Yong and Gelpi have published direct dialogue with each other, and Yong has further utilized Gelpi's work in *The Spirit Poured Out* in ways that merit attention. First, direct dialogue between Yong and Gelpi occurred most explicitly in two essays appearing in the *Journal of Pentecostal Theology* in 2002.[259] The self-identified purpose of Yong's essay was simply to review the "oeuvre" of Gelpi's work in order to raise awareness of its importance as a resource for Pentecostal theology and philosophy, and to demonstrate how Gelpi's work is connected to his personal Pentecostal experience and involvement with the Catholic charismatic movement.[260] Yong reviews Gelpi's fallibilistic foundational pneumatology and triadic metaphysics of experience, tracing his reliance on Charles Sanders Peirce, Josiah Royce, and Bernard Lonergan in his philosophical construction.[261] He highlights the application of Gelpi's work in two areas in particular: his "systematic theology of conversion" (to which we will return shortly) and the application of his metaphysics of experience and Peircian semiotic epistemology for analyzing, clarifying, and correcting doctrinal statements within Christian traditions.[262] Yong also includes a helpful survey of Gelpi's more recent contributions to systematic Christology.[263] Gelpi's work should be especially significant for Pentecostals, Yong argues, since it has largely been motivated by his "life-transforming encounter with Pentecost in 1968."[264] Yong's summary expresses his assessment of the value of Gelpi's work: "Let me now make what may be the bold claim that Pentecostals (and charismatics) should take Gelpi seriously because his *oeuvre* is, to date, not only the richest

258. Yong, *Spirit Poured Out*, 108n.78. The only other reference I could find to a possible divergence is a brief comment that Yong finds Gelpi's reference to a "tri-personal God" unappealing; but he does not expand on this point (see Yong, *Discerning the Spirit(s)*, 123n.33).

259. Yong, "In Search of Foundations," 3–26; Gelpi, "Response," 27–40. Portions of Yong's essay and Gelpi's response were originally presented at the 2002 Society for Pentecostal Studies annual meeting.

260. Yong, "In Search of Foundations," 4, 23–26. In particular, Yong identifies Gelpi's more recent work as emerging from his earlier theological reflections on his 'Pentecostal' experience.

261. Ibid., 7–19.

262. Ibid., 12, 16–19.

263. Ibid., 19–23.

264. Ibid., 23, cf. 23–26.

philosophical explication of Pentecostal-charismatic experience, but perhaps also the most original, penetrating, and systematic theological project to appear which is both deeply rooted in and pervasively imbued with intuitions derived from charismatic and renewal praxis."[265]

Gelpi's response to Yong's affirming review is reciprocally positive. In fact, Gelpi acknowledges he finds "nothing to fault in what [Yong] says." So, he simply confirms and expands on three themes raised by Yong's analysis of his own work. These include: "(1) the impact of Pentecostal/charismatic forms of prayer on my theology; (2) the centrality of the notion of christological knowing to my foundational Christology; and (3) the role of philosophy and metaphysics in theology."[266] The result, then, is not so much a dialogue with Yong, but rather an opportunity for Gelpi to highlight why these themes are important to him and for his work overall.

Gelpi's opinion of some specifics of Yong's work is perhaps best seen in his review of *Discerning the Spirit(s)*.[267] Here, Gelpi's comments are again overwhelmingly positive, with no real critique apparent. It is helpful, however, to highlight what Gelpi views as noteworthy in Yong's work. Gelpi concurs with Yong that interreligious dialogue will be prematurely hindered if Christians begin with christological issues, and so endorses Yong's PC-inspired pneumatological point of departure.[268] Gelpi also indicates his agreement with: 1) Yong's portrayal of Spirit and Word as having "different but inseparable roles in the economy of salvation"; 2) the necessity of pneumatological criteria for discernment, including the possibility of the Spirit's absence; 3) the idea that humans experience the Spirit as a field of force; and 4) the epistemological fallibility of human knowing.[269] He is also particularly impressed with Yong's articulation of how the pneumatological imagination enables discernment. States Gelpi, "That discernment engages the imagination makes eminently good sense to me, since the charism of discernment graces

---

265. Ibid., 24 (italics original).

266. Gelpi, "Response," 28 (on these three themes see ibid., 28–30, 31–36, and 36–40 respectively).

267. Gelpi, "Discerning the Spirit(s)," 98–101.

268. Ibid., 98.

269. Ibid., 99–100. He also believes Yong's application of his criteria to the Umbanda religion "passes the test with flying colors."

human prudential deliberation and since prudential deliberation helps give shape to intuitive and therefore to imaginative thinking."[270]

In sum, Gelpi believes that Yong's work "demonstrates that Pentecostal theology has indeed come of age."[271] So, Yong and Gelpi appear to be pretty much on the "same page" theologically and philosophically, with Yong building on Gelpi's work in new and creative ways, particularly with an eye toward helping Pentecostals develop more sophisticated theology (and philosophy) in general.[272] With that said, we can now summarize two more ways that Yong utilizes Gelpi's work specifically toward developing a more robust Pentecostal soteriology and charismology in *The Spirit Poured Out on All Flesh*.

To reiterate, in that work, Yong argues that PC experience impacts all areas of Christian theological reflection, including soteriology.[273] Specifically, he accents Lukan narratives for informing a pneumatological soteriology,[274] and suggests a "multidimensionality of salvation," identifying seven dimensions: personal, family, ecclesial, material, social, cosmic and eschatological.[275] It is worth highlighting, in view of our earlier dialogue with Johnson and Cone, that the social dimension refers "to the healing and reconciliation of interpersonal relationships . . . [and] to the redemption of the socioeconomic and political structures," which include racial, class, and gender reconciliation.[276]

Salvation also, argues Yong, needs to be viewed not only as a once-for-all crisis experience, but as a dynamic concept, allowing for subsequent experiences with the Spirit and a growing and conscious "deeper intimacy with Christ."[277] This dynamic soteriology is supported by four "steps," the first of which is to retrieve the patristic teaching concerning Christian rites of initiation—in particular, water baptism, which was associated with the reception of the Spirit. The second step (accent-

270. Ibid., 99.

271. Ibid., 100–101.

272. Yong acknowledges that while Pentecostals in times past would not have found Gelpi to be a helpful resource, they have grown in theological sophistication and are now able both to understand and utilize Gelpi's work (see Yong, "In Search of Foundations," 26).

273. Yong, *Spirit Poured Out*, 81–120.

274. Ibid., 83–90.

275. Ibid., 91, cf. 91–98.

276. Ibid., 93–95.

277. Ibid., 99, 98–103.

ing Lukan pneumatology) is to view Spirit baptism as neither simply
Christian initiation into the body of Christ, nor empowerment for service, but as encompassing both elements. Third, Yong utilizes Wesley's
notion of a *via salutis* (contra *ordo salutis*) based on an emphasis on the
prevenience of grace, and an expectation that real change (sanctification) should be observable in the lives of believers.[278] Thus, Spirit baptism can be used as a metaphor for Christian salvation accenting "the
process of humans experiencing the saving graces of God along with the
process of crisis moments when such grace is palpably felt as radically
transformative."[279]

Such a dynamic soteriology necessitates a robust theology of conversion that can account for "the complexity of the human encounter
with God"; and in this regard Yong believes Gelpi provides "just what
the doctor ordered." Here (citing Gelpi) conversion is defined as "a
turning from and a turning to. . . . One turns from irresponsible to
responsible living in some realm of experience."[280] There are (as noted
in chapter 1) "different domains wherein conversion is experienced besides the religious one, and these include the intellectual, the affective,
the moral and the sociopolitical."[281] Since each domain of conversion is
dynamically interrelated with the others, this means that "conversion
in one realm impacts conversion in the others"; likewise "the lack of
conversion in any one realm . . . negatively impacts, either by prohibit-
ing or distorting, conversion in the other realms." Religious conversion, or in this case, "Christian conversion[,] is the reorientation of
the totality of our intellectual, affective, moral and sociopolitical lives
according to the revelation of God in Jesus Christ as nurtured by our
participation in the sacraments . . ."[282] All this is facilitated by the dynamic working of the Spirit (the "divine Breath"); however, conversions

278. Ibid., 99–105. The third step includes healing as part of soteriology.

279. Ibid., 105, cf. 106. Yong then identifies "three logical moments" of Spirit baptism: the initial experience of reception of the Spirit ("I was saved"), ongoing experiences
of being filled ("I am being saved") and eschatological experience of "full baptism" ("I
will be saved").

280. Ibid., 106; citing Donald L. Gelpi, *The Conversion Experience: A Reflective
Process for RCIA Participants and Others* (New York: Paulist, 1998), 26.

281. Yong, *Spirit Poured Out*, 106.

282. Ibid., 107. This reorientation is also spoken of as "transvaluing" or "transmut-
ing" (ibid., 293–94). Moltmann also speaks of a religious dimension of experience that
operates tacitly below the others, which indicates considerable convergence on this particular point (Moltmann, *Spirit of Life*, 27).

in other realms, prior to Christian conversion, may actually be involved in "precipitating Christian conversion and giving it its distinctive and qualitative shape."[283]

How is this significant for Yong's dynamic pneumatological soteriology? Yong explains, "Gelpi's multidimensional and interactive theory of conversion (step four)" helps bring together the insights of the other three steps. "First, Gelpi's theory is able to account for the holistic nature of Christian conversion seen in the New Testament and captured in the gospel metaphor of baptism in the Holy Spirit." Second, Gelpi's theory is able to account for the complexities of conversion-initiation, allowing for crisis moments, "but set against a fluid backdrop of ecclesial, interpersonal, and sociopolitical relationships."[284] Third, the interactivity of the realms of conversion "resist[s] systematic definition," since "every conversion experience in any domain serves as a divinely gracious prompt for deeper conversions in other domains." This process is ongoing, and involves both divine and human participation along the way.[285] It is also worth noting that the above is coherent with Yong's categories of foundational pneumatology, in which all experience (including conversions) occurs within the Spirit's universal presence.

It is appropriate here to recall that Johnson and Cone also emphasize a conversion of sorts, associated with the Spirit's activity. Johnson suggests that while women's experience differs globally, it is linked by a common experience of "conversion" (or "awakening") to a new liberative experience and understanding of God (and women).[286] Cone similarly speaks of a "conversion" that takes place, in which one's mind and actions are transformed, enabling tangible participation toward the liberation of the oppressed and marginalized (blacks), and serving as a primary indicator of the Spirit's activity.[287] Yong identifies such conversion as "conscientization," which is a new awareness of the reality of one's own marginalization and oppression in view of God's liberative activity.[288] This type of conversion may roughly correspond to Gelpi's socio-political conversion. While Yong would certainly concur with the

283. Yong, *Spirit Poured Out*, 108.
284. Ibid.
285. Ibid., 108–9.
286. Johnson, *She Who Is*, 61–62.
287. Cone, *God of the Oppressed*, 89, 130.
288. Yong, *Spirit-Word-Community*, 282.

importance of this aspect of conversion, his multidimensional approach would seek to integrate this with the other elements of conversion in a more holistic manner.

One more application of Gelpi's work will be mentioned here. Yong believes that Gelpi's triadic metaphysics provides a way forward to a "pneumatological theology of creation" that is able to overcome the traditional dualisms of philosophy, including the rationalist/empiricist dichotomy, and the "ontological fallacies of idealism and (especially naïve) realism."[289] This has implications as to how Christian theology might better dialogue with the sciences—implications that Yong believes Pentecostals in particular need to appreciate.[290] He states, "If experiences are ultimately real things, then objects of experience lie within, not without, experience—hence objects of science lie within, not without the semiotic triad—and subjects and objects are mutually subsistent or in-existent. If this is the case, then mind is not opposed to nature, nor is spirit opposed to matter."[291]

Such an approach demands Pentecostals rethink the grace/nature, God/world relationship, and has implications for their theology of spiritual gifts (charismology). Gelpi, explains Yong, views the Incarnation and Pentecost as God's most explicit identification with creation—both very tangible, physical events. Gelpi's "Holy Breath" (Spirit), further, "is a life-force functioning in the midst of other vectoral feelings that shape experience."[292] Thus, within Gelpi's triadic metaphysical framework the Spirit is experienced in a number of ways, including various realms of conversion, and through the "concrete realities of the sacraments," among other things.[293]

---

289. Yong, *Spirit Poured Out*, 291–92.

290. See Yong, "Academic Glossolalia?," 61–80; and Yong, *Spirit of Creation*, 9–12.

291. Yong, *Spirit Poured Out*, 292.

292. Ibid., 293, cf. 293–96.

293. Ibid., 293–94. Yong here writes, "First, the Spirit's presence and activity transmute (set in a new framework) every other dimension of human experience, be it the affections, the intellect, the moral or the interpersonal. Second, divine grace is mediated through the concrete realities the sacraments, the communion of saints, or whatever other events are chosen by God. Third, the charisms reflect the increased sensitivity, receptivity, and docility of the human person to interpret the habitual activities of the Spirit. Fourth, the Spirit enables human freedom by gifting human experience with genuine opportunity to collaborate with the divine offer of grace; there can never be a simple dualistic opposition between divine and human willing in a triadic metaphysical framework. Finally, the Spirit personalizes human beings more and more fully (through

Important here is Gelpi's suggestion that "the charisms reflect the increased sensitivity, receptivity, and docility of the human person to interpret the habitual activities of the Spirit."[294] Such insights, Yong believes, are valuable toward developing a broader and more sophisticated PC charismology. A "pneumatological theology-of-creation framework" suggests, first, that the natural/supernatural dichotomy needs to be abandoned with regard to traditional Pentecostal categorization of some spiritual gifts as charismatic (cf. 1 Cor 12:4–11) and others as less so (cf. Rom 12:6–8; Eph 4:11).[295] Second, continues Yong, "the manifestation of the *charismata* is simply a more obvious sign of the interpenetration of the divine and the orders of creation."[296] This implies, thirdly, that spiritual gifts "can be cultivated and developed." Fourth, charismata are to be cultivated for "edification of others" and not for self-serving purposes. Finally, since the Spirit's presence is universally experienced (not only within the ecclesia), this means the gifts must "be discerned in all circumstances"; i.e., in all contexts of human life.[297] To summarize, then, Gelpi's metaphysics and theology of conversion are readily adopted by Yong in hopes of constructing a more dynamic and robust Pentecostal theology and spirituality. This spirituality, it should be noted, is not detached from, but is intricately entwined with the metaphysical issues with which we began this entire dialogue.

Conclusion

The above exposition examined Yong's attempt to utilize PC experience and theology toward the development of a foundational pneumatology, which, enabled by the pneumatological imagination, allows for the Spirit to be discerned in the multifaceted contexts of life. In other words, we have seen how "reason" can be accented as a means by which the Spirit is mediated. The ecumenical dialogue in the latter part of this chapter served to further underscore how Yong exemplifies a coming-of-age

---

the conversion process), orienting human experience toward the full assimilation of the image and life of Christ in their own lives."

294. Ibid.

295. Ibid., 294. Moltmann's view of the charisms, which avoids a natural/supernatural dichotomy, is congruent with Yong and Gelpi's view here.

296. Ibid., 295 (italics original).

297. Ibid., 295.

within Pentecostal theology through his ability not only to listen to other theological voices, but also contribute significantly to the discussion, suggesting fresh ways to address long-standing, yet ongoing issues.

Conclusion

AT THE OUTSET OF THIS STUDY WE NOTED THAT PENTECOSTALISM FINDS itself at a crucial juncture, needing to take conscious steps toward theological maturity in order to better establish and preserve its own identity, and to speak as an adult voice ecumenically among the Christian traditions. Our goal, then, has been to demonstrate evidence of a Pentecostal theological coming-of-age through an exploration of something near and dear to the heart of Pentecostals—experience of the Spirit. It is been argued that the maturation within Pentecostal theology can be observed in the adoption of a more mediated conception of experience of the Spirit, in particular in the works of three Pentecostals—Macchia, Chan, and Yong—with a focus on Word (Scripture), tradition, and reason as the media of the Spirit's revelation.

Along the way some discoveries were made. For one, the appeal to experience of the Spirit is an important topic in contemporary Christian theology in general; it is hardly simply a Pentecostal point of interest, which makes it such a useful subject of focus for dialogue between Pentecostals and other Christian traditions. We also confirmed, however, that experience of the Spirit is especially significant for Pentecostal identity and self-understanding. Pentecostalism cannot be rightly understood without an appreciation of the weight granted to encounters with the Spirit as a resource for theological reflection, even if this is not always being done self-consciously by Pentecostals.

Further, the appeal to experience for Pentecostals has always existed in somewhat awkward relationship with theological reflection and doctrine. For example, while a Pentecostal theology of experience is challenging to assess given the global diversity of Pentecostalism, nevertheless, Pentecostal experience of the Spirit is hardly of a vacuous sort. Put another way, experience of the Spirit would not be understood by Pentecostals simply to be a generic "religious experience." Rather,

Pentecostal experience of the Spirit is quite tied to the Jesus of Christian Scripture, which enables Pentecostals to clearly identify the Spirit being experienced, and furthermore is why the term "encounter" is an appropriate one for understanding Pentecostal experience of the Spirit. Indeed, for Pentecostals, the Spirit being encountered is quite personal, and such encounters are radically transformative, which feeds into the somewhat typical Pentecostal notion that such experiences are more or less direct or immediate. So, while Scripture (and other expressions of Word, e.g., prophetic utterance) may fit more naturally into this type of framework as mediation of the Spirit's revelation, the Christian theological (and liturgical) tradition(s), and "reason" have been customarily viewed by Pentecostals with varying degrees of suspicion.

At the same time, despite resistance to accepting the Spirit's mediation through the resources of tradition and reason, Pentecostals nevertheless have always adhered, at least tacitly, to particular theological and doctrinal confessions. This is why Althouse located Pentecostalism at the "appeal confessional" on Schner's continuum. But such a location does not always allow for growth and development, and may indeed lead to stagnation. For this reason there has been considerable movement among not a few Pentecostals away from a naïve form of the "appeal confessional," and it is my hope that this study will help persuade Pentecostals to progress even more so in this direction. There is, we have observed, growing openness to fresh (and arguably more Pentecostal) ways of reading Scripture, a clearer recognition and acknowledgment of the ways in which Pentecostalism has always relied on the Christian theological and spiritual tradition, as well as the influence of "context" (reason) in shaping its identity (e.g., modernism and pragmatism), and a deeper valuing of other Christian traditions as an ongoing resource for the construction and development of Pentecostal theology. In short, a growing appreciation for how Scripture (Word), and more particularly, tradition, and reason serve as means by which the Spirit is mediated is becoming more evident within Pentecostal theology.

Three Pentecostals theologians—Macchia, Chan, and Yong—were held up as case studies to demonstrate the ways in which they are revisioning Pentecostal theology. All explicitly acknowledge the importance and integration of Pentecostal experience of (encounter with) the Spirit, each working to preserve a sense of the directness of encounter with the Spirit. At the same time, they all exemplify an appreciation for the mediated quality of experience of the Spirit. Each utilizes, to varying degrees, elements of Lindbeck's cultural-linguistic theory of doctrine—qualifying this, of course, so as to allow for the sense of Pentecostal immediacy of the Spirit's presence and influence. In short, these theologians are wrestling to integrate their Pentecostal experience with a broader view of the Spirit's mediated activity in the world—and this approach is bearing fruit!

Openness to and integration of a more mediated view of experience of the Spirit allows Macchia, Chan, and Yong to utilize other theological voices in constructing their own work, developing new ways forward for Pentecostal theology. Specifically, it enables Macchia to revision the concept of Spirit baptism, as well as the understanding of the function of Scripture and glossolalia. It undergirds Chan's appeal for Pentecostals to embrace the Christian spiritual and liturgical tradition in order to better preserve and express their own identity. And it allows Yong to propose that Pentecostals can discern the Spirit speaking through reason—operating universally in the broader contexts of life, including through culture, religion, and the sciences. It also permits each of them to enter into dialogue with those of other Christian traditions as peers (rather than as adolescents) contributing to the discourse.

In sum, Macchia, Chan, and Yong each exemplify in their own way the maturation occurring within Pentecostal theology. Their integration of a mediated concept of experience of the Spirit allows them to demonstrate considerable self-awareness and understanding with regard to their own Pentecostal tradition, including the contextual and theological forces that shaped its development, not viewing such as antithetical to the Spirit's work. They also display an ability to identify both strengths and weaknesses within their tradition—perceiving areas within Pentecostalism that require renovation, and envisioning possible ways forward. But further, they are also able, utilizing their Pentecostal tradition, to both challenge and contribute to the theology of other Christian traditions. In short, these three theologians all demonstrate a move from a naïve "appeal confessional" to an "appeal constructive" with regard to experience of the Spirit, while preserving and utilizing core elements of Pentecostal theology and spirituality. With their integration of the mediated nature of experience of the Spirit through Word, tradition, and reason, these three serve as examples of how Pentecostal theology is emerging into adulthood.

This project also raises some questions and possibilities for further research. The first such possibility concerns the issue of defining Pentecostal experience in general. While chapter 2 attempts to provide a fairly detailed exposition of Pentecostal experience, it is certainly not exhaustive or the final word on the subject. The diverse expressions of Pentecostalism globally make defining Pentecostal experience quite challenging; yet experience of God appears to be a significant unifying factor among rather diverse Pentecostal and charismatic groups. This means that it might also serve as a potential resource for encouraging broader ecumenical conversations and relationships. Further study, then, of the nature of Pentecostal experience is worth the effort, and Pentecostal work on this issue is ongoing.[1]

A second and related area pertains to what might be referred to as intra-Pentecostal dialogue, and there are at least two sub-issues involved here. This book did not, it will be noted first of all, place Macchia, Chan, and Yong in any extensive dialogue with one another, or with other Pentecostal theologians for that matter. While all three value and draw on their own Pentecostal tradition in constructing their theology, this does not mean they see eye-to-eye on all things. The most obvious example of contrast in this regard is found between Chan and Yong, who, as we briefly noted in chapters 4 and 5, diverge considerably on their view of the Spirit's work in the world—Chan locates the Spirit firmly within the ecclesia, while Yong emphasizes the possibility of the Spirit's presence and activity universally. In any case, it would be worth comparing and contrasting the works of these three to explore at least some of the diverse directions in which Pentecostal theology may be evolving. It would also be valuable to explore how the works of these three are being received and integrated into the growing Pentecostal academy. I avoided venturing in this direction, however, since there were already a significant number of voices involved in the dialogue, and doing so would have expanded this already lengthy project considerably.[2]

1. This was the very recent topic of the 2009 Presidential address to the Society for Pentecostal Studies. See Cross, "Divine-Human Encounter," 3–34. I have also attempted to contribute to this theme at a more recent annual meeting of the Society for Pentecostal Studies (Neumann, "Whither Pentecostal Experience?," 1–32).

2. For example, Yong and Macchia have dialogued concerning glossolalia, and Dale Irvin has provided a helpful review of Yong's theology of religions. A four-way dialogue involving Yong, Macchia, Del Colle, and Irvin on the subject of Spirit and Word is also evidence of the potential for dialogue based on the works of these theologians.

Intra-Pentecostal dialogue also involves another important issue—namely, whether the revisionary Pentecostal theology of Macchia, Chan, and Yong will be embraced by Pentecostals at popular and denominational (institutional) levels. Put alternatively, in the form of a question: which of the three might find the least resistance to their theological proposals from within their own Pentecostal tradition at a grassroots level? This question assumes, of course, that there will be resistance; but this assumption seems appropriate given the history of Pentecostal suspicion concerning the discipline of theology in general and the fact that Macchia, Chan, and Yong each challenge Pentecostals to rethink their traditional doctrines and values in significant ways.

My hunch in this matter is that Chan and Yong will likely encounter more resistance from Pentecostals at grassroots levels, especially in North America. This is due to the fact that they challenge certain ingrained Pentecostal values more so than Macchia. Chan faces the task of overcoming a long-held (but thankfully subsiding) suspicion of the Christian theological and liturgical tradition as hindering the freedom of the Spirit, coupled with the Pentecostal pragmatic impulse that tends to look for immediate, rather than long-term results.[3] Yong, on the other hand, with his pneumatological theology of religions, challenges the traditional Pentecostal understanding of mission, that Christian believers are to witness to and convert, as opposed to dialogue with, those of other religions. In other words, Yong's work may be viewed by some Pentecostals as undermining Pentecostal mission—not a small obstacle to overcome![4] Further, Yong's (temporary) "bracketing out" of Christology for a pneumatological approach may also evoke wariness from Pentecostals who have traditionally been very Jesus-centered in their theology.[5] Macchia, while calling Pentecostals to expand their

---

Respectively, see Macchia, "Discerning the Truth," 67–71; Yong, "Truth of Tongues Speech," 107–15; Irvin, "Review," 277–80; Yong, "Beyond *Beyond the Impasse?*," 281–85; and Yong et al., "Christ and Spirit," 15–83. Also see Yong, "Radically Orthodox," 233–50; and Smith, "Spirit, Religions," 251–61.

3. R. Brian Robson echoes similar concerns. He finds Chan's ecclesiological proposals appealing, but has doubts as to whether they will be readily embraced in a North American context in which Pentecostalism has been greatly influenced by evangelical and Free Church theology (Robson, "Response to Simon Chan's," 1–4).

4. On several occasions over the past few years in personal conversations I have heard (or overheard!) a number of comments from PAOC denominational leaders and credential holders expressing suspicion concerning Yong's work for precisely this reason.

5. Yong is aware of this concern and is attempting to respond. See Yong, *Hospitality*

understanding of Spirit baptism, might also face challenges with regard to acceptance by Pentecostals.[6] But he will not likely be perceived as threatening the above-mentioned values to the same extent, and the fact that he is working to recover the Spirit baptism metaphor as central to understanding Pentecostalism may in fact help his work to be received more readily at a popular level.[7] In any case, the degree to which Macchia, Chan, or Yong's work will be received by Pentecostals at the grassroots remains to be seen.

The third area inviting further exploration concerns Christian ecumenical dialogue. Among other things, this book has served to demonstrate that Pentecostal theology is evidencing an ability to stand on its own and contribute to theological conversation with Christian traditions (even outside evangelicalism). On the one hand, it is hoped that the voices from other Christian traditions introduced in this project will pique the curiosity of Pentecostals in general to take a look at their work (and the theology of these other traditions overall) as potentially serving as a resource for Pentecostal theology. On the other hand, and more significantly at this point, it is also hoped that those from other Christian traditions (represented at least by our dialogue partners) will be able to recognize that indeed Pentecostal theology has come a long way, and that Pentecostals have something theologically and spiritually significant to contribute to the church globally. Yong's work, of course, also invites dialogue with other religious traditions as well as the sciences, and the response to his work from outside the theological community also holds potential for future analysis. My point here, however, is that the Christian traditions have much to gain by listening to the voices of Pentecostals such as Macchia, Chan, and Yong, among a growing number

---

and the Other, xiv.

6. This is true even within the Pentecostal academy, where there is greater awareness of the implications of Macchia's revisioning than at a popular level. During a round table discussion concerning Macchia's *Baptized in the Spirit* at the 2007 annual meeting of the Society for Pentecostal Studies, Mark Cartledge (one of two official respondents) suggested that Macchia had become "third wave" (in contrast to Classical Pentecostalism) based on his broadened definition of Spirit baptism. Another attendee publicly expressed that she was not quite willing to "sell the farm," to embrace Macchia's revisions in this regard.

7. This appeared to be the response at the McMaster Divinity College 2007 Pentecostal Forum to Macchia's original presentation of his essay "Baptized in the Spirit," in which a number PAOC credential holders were in attendance. Admittedly, this is based on informal observation only.

of others. It is my sincere hope that this book will help contribute to greater openness and dialogue between the various Christian traditions and Pentecostalism, and especially toward Pentecostal theology being recognized more broadly as a significant resource for those outside the Pentecostal tradition.

Bibliography

Albrecht, Daniel E. "An Anatomy of Worship: A Pentecostal Analysis." In *The Spirit and Spirituality: Essays in Honour of Russell P. Spittler*, edited by Wonsuk Ma and Robert P. Menzies, 70–82. Journal of Pentecostal Theology Supplemental Series 24. New York: T. & T. Clark, 2004.

———. "Pentecostal Spirituality: Ecumenical Potential and Challenge." *Cyberjournal for Pentecostal-Charismatic Research* 2 (1997). No pages. Online: http://www.pctii.org/cyberj/cyberj2/albrecht.html.

———. "Pentecostal Spirituality: Looking through the Lens of Ritual." *Pneuma* 14.2 (1992) 107–25.

———. *Rites in the Spirit: A Ritual Approach to Pentecostal/Charismatic Spirituality.* Journal of Pentecostal Theology Supplemental Series 17. Sheffield, UK: Sheffield Academic, 1999.

Alexander, Estrelda Y. "What Doth the Lord Require: Toward a Pentecostal Theology of Social Justice." Paper presented at the annual meeting of the Society for Pentecostal Studies, Wycliffe College, Toronto, March 7–9, 1996.

Althouse, Peter. *Spirit of the Last Days: Pentecostal Eschatology in Conversation with Jürgen Moltmann.* Journal of Pentecostal Theology Supplement Series 25. London: T. & T. Clark, 2003.

———. "Towards a Theological Understanding of the Pentecostal Appeal to Experience." Paper presented at the annual meeting of the Society for Pentecostal Studies, Tulsa, OK, March 8–10, 2001.

Ameriks, Karl. "Kant, Immanuel." In *The Cambridge Dictionary of Philosophy*, 2nd ed., edited by Robert Audi, 460–66. Cambridge: Cambridge University Press, 1999.

Anderson, Allan H. "Burning Its Way into Every Nation: The Experience of the Spirit in Early Pentecostal Missions." Paper presented at the annual meeting for the Society for Pentecostal Studies, Lee University, Cleveland, TN, March 8–10, 2007.

———. "Global Pentecostalism in the New Millennium." In *Pentecostals after a Century: Global Perspectives on a Movement in Transition*, edited by Allan H. Anderson and Walter J. Hollenweger, 209–23. Journal of Pentecostal Theology Supplemental Series 15. Sheffield, UK: Sheffield Academic, 1999.

———. *An Introduction to Pentecostalism: Global Charismatic Christianity.* Cambridge: Cambridge University Press, 2004.

———. "Introduction: World Pentecostalism at a Crossroads." In *Pentecostals after a Century: Global Perspectives on a Movement in Transition*, edited by Allan H. Anderson and Walter J. Hollenweger, 19–31. Journal of Pentecostal Theology Supplemental Series 15. Sheffield, UK: Sheffield Academic, 1999.

Anderson, Allan H., and Walter J. Hollenweger, eds. *Pentecostals after a Century: Global Perspectives on a Movement in Transition*. Journal of Pentecostal Theology Supplemental Series 15. Sheffield, UK: Sheffield Academic, 1999.

Anderson, Gordon L. "Pentecostals Believe in More than Tongues." In *Pentecostals from the Inside Out*, edited by Harold B. Smith, 53–64. The Christianity Today Series. Wheaton, IL: Victor, 1990.

Anderson, Robert Mapes. *Vision of the Disinherited: The Making of American Pentecostalism*. New York: Oxford University Press, 1979.

Archer, Kenneth J. "The 3-D View of Pentecostalism." Paper presented at the annual meeting of the Society for Pentecostal Studies, Southeastern University, Lakeland, FL, March 14–16, 2002.

———. "Early Pentecostal Biblical Interpretation." *Journal of Pentecostal Theology* 9.18 (2001) 32–70.

———. *A Pentecostal Hermeneutic for the Twenty-First Century: Spirit, Scripture and Community*. Journal of Pentecostal Theology Supplemental Series 28. London: T. & T. Clark, 2004.

———. "The Pentecostal Way of Doing Theology: Manner and Method." Paper presented at the annual meeting of the Society for Pentecostal Studies, Marquette University, Milwaukee, WI, March 11–13, 2004.

Armstrong, Chris. "Embrace Your Inner Pentecostal." *Christianity Today* 50.9 (October 2006). No pages. Online: http://www.christianitytoday.com/ct/2006/september/40.86.html.

Autry, Arden C. "Dimensions of Hermeneutics in Pentecostal Focus." *Journal of Pentecostal Theology* 1.3 (1993) 29–50.

Baker, Robert O. "Pentecostal Bible Reading: Toward a Model of Reading for the Formation of Christian Affections." *Journal of Pentecostal Theology* 3.7 (1995) 34–48.

Barnes, Roscoe, III. "Experience as a Catalyst for Healing Ministry: Historical Evidence and Implications from the Life of F. F. Bosworth." Paper presented at the annual meeting for the Society for Pentecostal Studies, Lee University, Cleveland, TN, March 8–10, 2007.

Barrett, David B. "The Worldwide Holy Spirit Renewal." In *The Century of the Holy Spirit: 100 Years of Pentecostal and Charismatic Renewal, 1901–2001*, edited by Vinson Synan, 381–414. Nashville, TN: Thomas Nelson, 2001.

Bauckham, Richard. *The Theology of Jürgen Moltmann*. Edinburgh: T. & T. Clark, 1995.

———. "Tradition in Relation to Scripture and Reason." In *Scripture, Tradition and Reason: A Study in the Criteria of Christian Doctrine: Essays in Honour of Richard P.C. Hanson*, edited by Richard Bauckham and Benjamin Drewery, 117–45. Edinburgh: T. & T. Clark, 1988.

Bauckham, Richard, and Benjamin Drewery, eds. *Scripture, Tradition and Reason: A Study in the Criteria of Christian Doctrine: Essays in Honour of Richard P. C. Hanson*. Edinburgh: T. & T. Clark, 1988.

Bevins, Winfield H. "A Pentecostal Appropriation of the Wesleyan Quadrilateral." Paper presented at the annual meeting for the Society for Pentecostal Studies, Regent University, Virginia Beach, VA, March 10–12, 2005.

Boeve, Lieven. "Theology and the Interruption of Experience." In *Encountering Transcendence: Contributions to a Theology of Christian Religious Experience*, edited by L. Boeve, Hans Geybels, and S. Van den Bossche, 11–40. Annua Nuntia Lovaniensia. Leuven: Peeters, 2005.

Boeve, Lieven, Hans Geybels, and S. Van den Bossche, eds. *Encountering Transcendence: Contributions to a Theology of Christian Religious Experience.* Annua Nuntia Lovaniensia. Leuven: Peeters, 2005.

Brown, David. "Experience Skewed." In *Transcending Boundaries in Philosophy and Theology: Reason, Meaning and Experience,* edited by Kevin J. Vanhoozer and Martin Warner, 159–75. Burlington, VT: Ashgate, 2007.

Bruce, Frederick F. "Scripture in Relation to Tradition and Reason." In *Scripture, Tradition and Reason: A Study in the Criteria of Christian Doctrine: Essays in Honour of Richard P. C. Hanson,* edited by Richard Bauckham and Benjamin Drewery, 35–64. Edinburgh: T. & T. Clark, 1988.

Bruner, Frederick Dale. *A Theology of the Holy Spirit: The Pentecostal Experience and the New Testament Witness.* Grand Rapids: Eerdmans, 1970.

"Bulgakov, Sergei Nikolaevich." In *Dictionary of Christian Biography,* edited by Michael Walsh, 237. Collegeville, MN: Liturgical, 2001.

Bulgakov, Sergius. *The Bride of the Lamb.* Translated by Boris Jakim. Grand Rapids: Eerdmans, 2002.

———. *The Comforter.* Translated by Boris Jakim. Grand Rapids: Eerdmans, 2004.

———. *The Orthodox Church.* Translated by Lydia Kesich. Crestwood, NY: St. Vladimir's Seminary Press, 1988.

———. *Sophia, the Wisdom of God: An Outline of Sophiology.* Rev. ed. of *The Wisdom of God: A Brief Summary of Sophiology.* Translated by Patrick Thompson et al. Library of Russian Philosophy. Hudson, NY: Lindisfarne, 1993.

Burhenn, Herbert. "Philosophy and Religious Experience." In *Handbook of Religious Experience,* edited by Ralph W. Hood, 144–60. Birmingham, AL: Religious Education, 1995.

Byrd, Joseph. "Paul Ricoeur's Hermeneutical Theory and Pentecostal Proclamation." *Pneuma* 15.2 (1993) 203–14.

Cargal, Timothy B. "Beyond the Fundamentalist-Modernist Controversy: Pentecostals and Hermeneutics in a Postmodern Age." *Pneuma* 15.2 (1993) 163–87.

Carpenter, John B. "Genuine Pentecostal Traditioning: Rooting Pentecostalism in Its Evangelical Soil: A Reply to Simon Chan." *Asian Journal of Pentecostal Studies* 6.2 (2003) 303–26.

Carson, D. A. *Becoming Conversant with the Emerging Church: Understanding a Movement and Its Implications.* Grand Rapids: Zondervan, 2005.

Cartledge, Mark J. "Attending to Experience in Pentecostal-Charismatic Theology: Disciplined Attentiveness, Evaluation and Practical-Theological Construction." Paper presented at the annual meeting for the Society for Pentecostal Studies, Lee University, Cleveland, TN, March 8–10, 2007.

———. "Empirical Theology: Towards an Evangelical-Charismatic Hermeneutic." *Journal of Pentecostal Theology* 4.9 (1996) 115–26.

———. *Encountering the Spirit: The Charismatic Tradition.* Traditions of Christian Spirituality. Maryknoll, NY: Orbis, 2007.

———. "Interpreting Charismatic Experience: Hypnosis, Altered States of Consciousness, and the Holy Spirit?" *Journal of Pentecostal Theology* 6.13 (1998) 117–32.

———. "Testimony to the Truth of Encounter: A Study of Pentecostal-Charismatic Epistemology." Paper presented at the annual meeting for the Society for Pentecostal Studies, Southeastern University, Lakeland, FL, March 14–16, 2002.

Chan, Simon K. H. "Asian Pentecostalism, Social Concern and the Ethics of Conformism." *Transformation* 11 (1994) 29–32.

———. "An Asian Review." *Journal of Pentecostal Theology* 2.4 (1994) 35–40.

———. "The Believing Heart: An Invitation to Story Theology." *Pneuma* 23.1 (2001) 159–61.

———. "The Church and the Development of Doctrine." *Journal of Pentecostal Theology* 13.1 (2004) 57–77.

———. "Encountering the Triune God: Spirituality since the Azusa Street Revival." In *The Azusa Street Revival and Its Legacy*, edited by Harold D. Hunter and Cecil M. Robeck, Jr., 215–26. Cleveland, TN: Pathway, 2006.

———. "Evidential Glossolalia and the Doctrine of Subsequence." *Asian Journal of Pentecostal Studies* 2.2 (1999) 195–211.

———. "The Language Game of Glossolalia, or Making Sense of the 'Initial Evidence.'" In *Pentecostalism in Context: Essays in Honor of William W. Menzies*, edited by Wonsuk Ma and Robert P. Menzies, 80–95. Journal of Pentecostal Theology Supplement Series 11. Sheffield, UK: Sheffield Academic, 1997.

———. *Liturgical Theology: The Church as Worshiping Community*. Downers Grove, IL: InterVarsity Academic, 2006.

———. "The Logic of Hell: A Response to Annihilationism." *Evangelical Review of Theology* 18.1 (1994) 20–32.

———. "Mother Church: Toward a Pentecostal Ecclesiology." *Pneuma* 22.2 (2000) 177–208.

———. *Pentecostal Theology and the Christian Spiritual Tradition*. Journal of Pentecostal Theology Supplemental Series 21. Sheffield, UK: Sheffield Academic, 2000.

———. "The Pneumatology of Paul Yonggi Cho." *Asian Journal of Pentecostal Studies* 7.1 (2004) 79–99.

———. "The Puritan Meditative Tradition, 1599–1691: A Study of Ascetical Piety." PhD diss., Cambridge University, 1986.

———. "The Renewal of Pentecostalism: A Response to John Carpenter." *Asian Journal of Pentecostal Studies* 7.2 (2004) 315–25.

———. "A Response to Max Turner." *Asian Journal of Pentecostal Studies* 2.2 (1999) 279–81.

———. "Second Thoughts on Contextualization." *Evangelical Review of Theology* 9.1 (1985) 50–54.

———. *Spiritual Theology: A Systematic Study of the Christian Life*. Downers Grove, IL: InterVarsity, 1998.

———. "'Whither Pentecostalism?'" In *Asian and Pentecostal: The Charismatic Face of Christianity in Asia*, edited by Allan Anderson and Edmond Tang, 575–86. Oxford, UK: Regnum, 2005.

Clark, Mathew S. "Pentecostalism's Anabaptist Roots: Hermeneutical Implications." In *The Spirit and Spirituality: Essays in Honour of Russell P. Spittler*, edited by Wonsuk Ma and Robert P. Menzies, 194–211. London: T. & T. Clark, 2004.

Clark, Mathew S., and Henry I. Lederle et al. *What Is Distinctive about Pentecostal Theology?* Pretoria: University of South Africa, 1989.

Clemmons, Ithiel. "True Koinonia: Pentecostal Hopes and Historical Realities." *Pneuma* 4.1 (1982) 46–56.

Cone, James H. *Black Theology and Black Power*. Maryknoll, NY: Orbis, 1997.

————. *God of the Oppressed*. Rev. ed. Maryknoll, NY: Orbis, 1997.

Congar, Yves. *I Believe in the Holy Spirit*. Translated by David Smith. Three-volume work in one volume. Milestones in Catholic Theology. New York: Crossroad, 1999.

————. *The Word and the Spirit*. Translated by David Smith. San Francisco: Harper and Row, 1986.

"Congar, Yves Marie-Joseph." In *Dictionary of Christian Biography*, edited by Michael Walsh, 327. Collegeville, MN: Liturgical, 2001.

Conyers, A. J. *God, Hope, and History: Jürgen Moltmann and the Christian Concept of History*. Macon, GA: Mercer, 1988.

Coulter, Dale M. "What Meaneth This? Pentecostals and Theological Inquiry." *Journal of Pentecostal Theology* 10.1 (2001) 38–64.

Cox, Harvey G. *Fire from Heaven: The Rise of Pentecostal Spirituality and the Reshaping of Religion in the Twenty-First Century*. Reading, MA: Addison-Wesley, 1995.

————. "Foreword." In *Pentecostals after a Century: Global Perspectives on a Movement in Transition*, edited by Allan H. Anderson and Walter J. Hollenweger, 7–12. Journal of Pentecostal Theology Supplemental Series 15. Sheffield, UK: Sheffield Academic, 1999.

————. "Some Personal Reflections on Pentecostalism." *Pneuma* 15.1 (1993) 29–34.

Crawford, Nathan. "The Role of Experience in the Religion-Science Conversation." Paper presented at the annual meeting of the Society for Pentecostal Studies, Duke University, Durham, NC, March 13–15, 2008.

Cross, Terry L. "Can There Be a Pentecostal Systematic Theology?: An Essay on Theological Method in a Postmodern World." Paper presented at the annual meeting of the Society for Pentecostal Studies, Oral Roberts University, Tulsa, OK, March 8–10, 2001.

————. "The Divine-Human Encounter: Towards a Pentecostal Theology of Experience." *Pneuma* 31.1 (2009) 3–34.

————. "The Rich Feast of Theology: Can Pentecostals Bring the Main Course or Only the Relish?" *Journal of Pentecostal Theology* 8.16 (2000) 27–47.

Crouch, Andy. "The Mission of the Trinity." *Christianity Today* (June 2007). No pages. Online: http://www.christianitytoday.com/ct/2007/june/11.48.html.

Crouter, Richard. "Introduction." In *On Religion: Speeches to Its Cultured Despisers*. Translated by Richard Crouter. Texts in German Philosophy. Cambridge: Cambridge University Press, 1988.

Dayton, Donald W. *Theological Roots of Pentecostalism*. Studies in Evangelicalism. Metuchen, NJ: Scarecrow, 1987.

Del Colle, Ralph. "Postmodernism and the Pentecostal-Charismatic Experience." *Journal of Pentecostal Theology* 8.17 (2000) 97–116.

Dempster, Murray W. "Issues Facing Pentecostalism in a Postmodern World: An Introductory Overview." In *The Globalization of Pentecostalism: A Religion Made to Travel*, edited by Murray W. Dempster et al., 261–67. Oxford: Regnum, 1999.

————. "Paradigm Shifts and Hermeneutics: Confronting Issues Old and New." *Pneuma* 15.2 (1993) 129–35.

————. "The Search for Pentecostal Identity." *Pneuma* 15.1 (1993) 1–8.

————. "The Structure of a Christian Ethic Informed by Pentecostal Experience: Soundings in the Moral Significance of Glossolalia." In *The Spirit and Spirituality: Essays in Honour of Russell P. Spittler*, edited by Wonsuk Ma and Robert P. Menzies, 108–40. Journal of Pentecostal Theology Supplemental Series 24. London: T. & T. Clark, 2004.

Dieter, Melvin E. "Wesleyan-Holiness Aspects of Pentecostal Origins: As Mediated through the Nineteenth-Century Holiness Revival." In *Aspects of Pentecostal-Charismatic Origins*, edited by Vinson Synan, 55–80. Plainfield, NJ: Logos International, 1975.

Donahue, Michael J. "Catholicism and Religious Experience." In *Handbook of Religious Experience*, edited by Ralph W. Hood, 30–48. Birmingham, AL: Religious Education Press, 1995.

"Donald L. Gelpi, S. J." No pages. Online: http://www.jstb.edu/faculty/bios/gelpi.html.

Dulles, Avery Robert. *Models of Revelation*. Maryknoll, NY: Orbis, 1992.

Dunn, James D. G. *Baptism in the Holy Spirit: A Re-Examination of the New Testament Teaching on the Gift of the Spirit in Relation to Pentecostalism Today*. Philadelphia: Westminster, 1970.

Ellington, Scott A. "Pentecostalism and the Authority of Scripture." *Journal of Pentecostal Theology* 4.9 (1996) 16–38.

Erickson, Douglas R. "Can We Believe in Miracles?: Charles Taylor as a Resource for Understanding Pentecostal Experience." Paper presented at the annual meeting for the Society for Pentecostal Studies, Lee University, Cleveland, TN, March 8–10, 2007.

Ervin, Howard M. *Conversion-Initiation and the Baptism in the Holy Spirit: A Critique of James D. G. Dunn, Baptism in the Holy Spirit*. Peabody, MA: Hendrickson, 1984.

————. "Hermeneutics: A Pentecostal Option." *Pneuma* 3.2 (1981) 11–25.

Faupel, D. William. "The Function of 'Models' in the Interpretation of Pentecostal Thought." *Pneuma* 2.1 (1980) 51–71.

————. "Whither Pentecostalism?" *Pneuma* 15.1 (1993) 9–27.

Fee, Gordon D. "Baptism in the Holy Spirit: The Issue of Separability and Subsequence." *Pneuma* 7.2 (1985) 87–99.

————. *Gospel and Spirit: Issues in New Testament Hermeneutics*. Peabody, MA: Hendrickson, 1991.

————. "Toward a Pauline Theology of Glossolalia." In *Listening to the Spirit in the Text*, 105–20. Grand Rapids: Eerdmans, 2000.

Fiorenza, Francis Schuessler. "The Experience of Transcendence or the Transcendence of Experience: Negotiating the Difference." In *Religious Experience and Contemporary Theological Epistemology*, edited by L. Boeve et al., 184–218. Bibliotheca Ephemeridum Theologicarum Lovaniensium 188. Leuven: Peeters, 2005.

Frei, Hans W. *The Eclipse of Biblical Narrative: A Study in Eighteenth- and Nineteenth-Century Hermeneutics*. New Haven: Yale University Press, 1974.

Galli, Mark. "Stopping Cultural Drift: An Asian Pentecostal Argues That We Need to Know What the Church Is before We Figure Out What the Church Does." *Christianity Today* 50.11 (November 2006) 66–69.

Gelpi, Donald L. *The Conversion Experience: A Reflective Process for RCIA Participants and Others*. New York: Paulist, 1998.

————. "Discerning the Spirit(s): A Pentecostal-Charismatic Contribution to Christian Theology of Religions." *Pneuma* 24.1 (2002) 98–101.

————. *The Divine Mother: A Trinitarian Theology of the Holy Spirit.* Lanham, MD: University Press of America, 1984.

————. *Experiencing God: A Theology of Human Experience.* New York: Paulist, 1978.

————. "A Response to Amos Yong." *Journal of Pentecostal Theology* 11.1 (2002) 27–40.

————. *The Turn to Experience in Contemporary Theology.* New York: Paulist, 1994.

Graves, Charles Lee. *The Holy Spirit in the Theology of Sergius Bulgakov.* Geneva: World Council of Churches, 1972.

Greer, Robert. *Mapping Postmodernism: A Survey of Christian Options.* Downers Grove, IL: InterVarsity, 2003.

Groupe des Dombes. *For the Conversion of the Churches.* Geneva: World Council of Churches, 1993.

Gunter, W. Stephen. *The Limits of "Love Divine": John Wesley's Response to Antinomianism and Enthusiasm.* Nashville, TN: Kingswood, 1989.

Hamilton, Barry W. "The Experiential Construction of Ordo Salutis in the Early Holiness and Pentecostal Movements: Foundations for Ecumenical Dialogue." Paper presented at the annual meeting for the Society for Pentecostal Studies, Church of God Theological Seminary, Cleveland, TN, March 12–14, 1998.

Harrington, Hannah K., and Rebecca Patten. "Pentecostal Hermeneutics and Postmodern Literary Theory." *Pneuma* 16.1 (1994) 109–14.

Hart, Kevin. "The Experience of the Kingdom of God." In *The Experience of God: A Postmodern Response,* edited by Kevin Hart and Barbara Eileen Wall, 71–86. Perspectives in Continental Philosophy 48. New York: Fordham University Press, 2005.

————. "Introduction." In *The Experience of God: A Postmodern Response,* edited by Kevin Hart and Barbara Eileen Wall, 1–19. Perspectives in Continental Philosophy 48. New York: Fordham University Press, 2005.

Hemming, Laurence Paul. "Are We Still in Time to Know God?: Apocalyptic, Sempiternity, and the Purposes of Experience." In *Religious Experience and Contemporary Theological Epistemology,* edited by L. Boeve et al., 159–75. Bibliotheca Ephemeridum Theologicarum Lovaniensium 188. Leuven: Peeters, 2005.

Hess, Diana. "Religious Experience and Theological Epistemology in Relation to the Doctrine of God and to the Concept of Reality Involved: Some Thoughts Developed in Connection with the Writings of Richard Swinburne." In *Encountering Transcendence: Contributions to a Theology of Christian Religious Experience,* edited by L. Boeve et al., 299–313. Annua Nuntia Lovaniensia 53. Leuven: Peeters, 2005.

Higgins, John R. "God's Inspired Word." In *Systematic Theology,* rev. ed., edited by Stanley M. Horton, 61–116. Springfield, MO: Logion, 1994.

Higgins, John R., et al. *An Introduction to Theology: A Classical Pentecostal Perspective.* Dubuque, IA: Kendall/Hunt, 1993.

Hill, W. J., and Berard L. Marthaler. "Experience, Religious." In *New Catholic Encyclopedia* 5:555–57. 2nd ed. Detroit: Gale, 2003.

Hocken, Peter. "The Meaning and Purpose of "Baptism in the Spirit."" *Pneuma* 7.2 (1985) 125–33.

Hollenweger, Walter J. "The Critical Tradition of Pentecostalism." *Journal of Pentecostal Theology* 1.1 (1992) 7–17.

———. *Pentecostalism: Origins and Developments Worldwide.* Peabody, MA: Hendrickson, 1997.

———. *The Pentecostals: The Charismatic Movement in the Churches.* Minneapolis: Augsburg, 1972.

———. "Rethinking Spirit Baptism: The Natural and the Supernatural." In *Pentecostals after a Century: Global Perspectives on a Movement in Transition,* edited by Allan H. Anderson and Walter J. Hollenweger, 164–72. Sheffield, UK: Sheffield Academic, 1999.

Hollenweger, Walter J., and Allan H. Anderson. "Crucial Issues for Pentecostals." In *Pentecostals after a Century: Global Perspectives on a Movement in Transition,* 176–91. Sheffield, UK: Sheffield Academic, 1999.

Holm, Randall. "A Paradigmatic Analysis of Authority within Pentecostalism." PhD diss., University of Laval, 1995.

———. "Varieties of Pentecostal Experience: Pragmatism and the Doctrinal Development of Pentecostalism." *Eastern Journal of Practical Theology* 10 (Fall 1996) 31–48.

Hopson, Ronald E., and Kurt Openlander. "Protestantism and Religious Experience." In *Handbook of Religious Experience,* edited by Ralph W. Hood, 49–71. Birmingham, AL: Religious Education, 1995.

Horton, Stanley M. *What the Bible Says About the Holy Spirit.* Springfield:, MO: Gospel, 1976.

Hudson, D. Neil. "Worship: Singing a New Song in a Strange Land." In *Pentecostal Perspectives,* edited by Keith Warrington, 177–203. Carlisle, UK: Paternoster, 1998.

Hunter, Harold D. "'Full Communion': A Pentecostal Model." Paper presented at the annual meeting of the Society for Pentecostal Studies, Lee University, Cleveland, TN, March 8–10, 2007.

Irvin, Dale T. "'Drawing All Together in One Bond of Love': The Ecumenical Vision of William J. Seymour and the Azusa Street Revival." *Journal of Pentecostal Theology* 3.6 (1995) 25–53.

———. Review of Amos Yong's *Beyond the Impasse. Journal of Pentecostal Theology* 12.2 (2004) 277–80.

Israel, Richard D., et al. "Pentecostals and Hermeneutics: Texts, Rituals and Community." *Pneuma* 15.2 (1993) 137–61.

Jacobsen, Douglas G. "Introduction: The History and Significance of Early Pentecostal Theology." In *A Reader in Pentecostal Theology: Voices from the First Generation,* edited by Douglas G. Jacobsen, 1–18. Bloomington, IN: Indiana University Press, 2006.

———. *Thinking in the Spirit: Theologies of the Early Pentecostal Movement.* Bloomington, IN: Indiana University Press, 2003.

"James H. Cone." No pages. Online: http://www.utsnyc.edu/Page.aspx?pid=353.

Jay, Martin. *Songs of Experience: Modern American and European Variations on a Universal Theme.* Berkeley: University of California Press, 2005.

Jenson, Robert W. "An Interview with Robert W. Jenson." No pages. Online: http://www.religion-online.org/showarticle.asp?title=3405.

———. *Systematic Theology: The Triune God*, Vol. 1. Oxford: Oxford University Press, 1997.

———. *Systematic Theology: The Works of God*, Vol. 2. Oxford: Oxford University Press, 1999.

———. *The Triune Identity: God according to the Gospel*. Reprint, Eugene, OR: Wipf and Stock, 2002.

Johannesen, Stanley. "Remembering and Observing: Modes of Interpreting Pentecostal Experience and Language." Paper presented at the annual meeting for the Society for Pentecostal Studies, Christ for the Nations Institute, Dallas, TX, November 8–10, 1990.

Johns, Cheryl Bridges. "The Adolescence of Pentecostalism: In Search of a Legitimate Sectarian Identity." *Pneuma* 17.1 (1995) 3–17.

Johns, Donald A. "Some New Directions in the Hermeneutics of Classical Pentecostalism's Doctrine of Initial Evidence." In *Initial Evidence: Historical and Biblical Perspectives on the Pentecostal Doctrine of Spirit Baptism*, edited by Gary B. McGee, 145–67. Peabody, MA: Hendrickson, 1991.

Johns, Jackie David. "Pentecostalism and the Postmodern Worldview." *Journal of Pentecostal Theology* 3.7 (1995) 73–96.

Johnson, Elizabeth A. *She Who Is: The Mystery of God in Feminist Theological Discourse*. Tenth Anniversary ed. New York: Crossroad, 2002.

———. *Women, Earth, and Creator Spirit*. New York: Paulist, 1993.

Jones, Richard R. "Culture, Context, Pentecostal Experience, and Knowing God." Paper presented at the annual meeting for the Society for Pentecostal Studies, Lee University, Cleveland, TN, March 8–10, 2007.

Jongeneel, Jan A. B. "Preface." In *Experiences of the Spirit: Conference on Pentecostal and Charismatic Research in Europe at Utrecht University, 1989*, edited by Jan A. B. Jongeneel, ix–xi. New York: Lang, 1991.

Kärkkäinen, Veli-Matti. "Authority, Revelation, and Interpretation in the Roman Catholic-Pentecostal Dialogue." *Pneuma* 21.1 (1999) 89–114.

———. *An Introduction to Ecclesiology: Ecumenical, Historical & Global Perspectives*. Downers Grove, IL: InterVarsity, 2002.

———. "Pentecostals as 'Anonymous Ecumenists'?" In *Toward a Pneumatological Theology: Pentecostal and Ecumenical Perspectives on Ecclesiology, Soteriology, and Theology of Mission*, edited by Amos Yong, 39–51. Lanham, MD: University Press of America, 2002.

———. *Pneumatology: The Holy Spirit in Ecumenical, International, and Contextual Perspective*. Grand Rapids: Baker Academic, 2002.

———. "Trinity as Communion in the Spirit: Koinonia, Trinity, and Filioque in the Roman Catholic-Pentecostal Dialogue." *Pneuma* 22.2 (2000) 209–30.

Kay, William K. "Pentecostal Experiences: Type, Prevalence and Meaning." Paper presented at the annual meeting for the Society for Pentecostal Studies, Lee University, Cleveland, TN, March 8–10, 2007.

Kelly, Thomas M. "Not One without the Other: Conceptions of 'Language' and 'Religious Experience.'" In *Encountering Transcendence: Contributions to a Theology of Christian Religious Experience*, edited by L. Boeve et al., 143–63. Annua Nuntia Lovaniensia 53. Leuven: Peeters, 2005.

King, Paul L. "Searching for Genuine Gold: Discerning Spirit, Flesh, and Demonic in Pentecostal Experiences." Paper presented at the annual meeting for the Society for Pentecostal Studies, Lee University, Cleveland, TN, March 8–10, 2007.

Klaus, Byron D. "Pentecostalism as a Global Culture: An Introductory Overview." In *The Globalization of Pentecostalism: A Religion Made to Travel*, edited by Murray W. Dempster and Douglas Petersen, 127–30. Oxford: Regnum, 1999.

Kuzmic, Peter. "A Croatian War-Time Reading." *Journal of Pentecostal Theology* 2.4 (1994) 17–24.

Kydd, Ronald R. N. "'Better Felt Than Telt.'" *Eastern Journal of Practical Theology* 4 (Spring 1990) 30–34.

———. *Charismatic Gifts in the Early Church*. Peabody, MA: Hendrickson, 1984.

Land, Steven J. "A Passion for the Kingdom: Revisioning Pentecostal Spirituality." *Journal of Pentecostal Theology* 1.1 (1992) 19–46.

———. *Pentecostal Spirituality: A Passion for the Kingdom*. Journal of Pentecostal Theology Supplemental Series 1. Sheffield, UK: Sheffield Academic, 2001.

———. "Praying in the Spirit: A Pentecostal Perspective." In *Pentecostal Movements as an Ecumenical Challenge*, edited by Jürgen Moltmann and Karl-Josef Kuschel, 85–93. Concilium. Maryknoll, NY: Orbis, 1996.

Land, Steven J., et al. "Editorial." *Journal of Pentecostal Theology* 1.1 (1992) 3–5.

Lane, Dermot A. *The Experience of God: An Invitation to Do Theology*. New York: Paulist, 1981.

Lederle, Henry I. *Treasures Old and New: Interpretations of "Spirit-Baptism" in the Charismatic Renewal Movement*. Peabody, MA: Hendrickson, 1988.

Leggett, Dennis. "The Assemblies of God Statement on Sanctification (a Brief Review by Calvin and Wesley)." *Pneuma* 11.2 (1989) 113–22.

Lewis, Paul W. "Reflections of a Hundred Years of Pentecostal Theology." *Cyberjournal for Pentecostal-Charismatic Research* 12 (2003). No pages. Online: http://www.pctii.org/cyberj/cyberj12/lewis.html.

———. "Towards a Pentecostal Epistemology: The Role of Experience in Pentecostal Hermeneutics." Paper presented at the annual meeting for the Society for Pentecostal Studies, Church of God Theological Seminary, Cleveland, TN, March 12–14, 1998.

Lindbeck, George A. *The Nature of Doctrine: Religion and Theology in a Postliberal Age*. Philadelphia: Westminster, 1984.

Lord, Andrew M. "The Pentecostal-Moltmann Dialogue: Implications for Mission." *Journal of Pentecostal Theology* 11.2 (2003) 271–87.

Lossky, Vladimir. *The Mystical Theology of the Eastern Church*. 1957. Reprint, Crestwood, NY: St. Vladimir's Seminary Press, 1976.

———. *The Vision of God*. Translated by Asheleigh Moorhouse. Wingroad, UK: Faith, 1973.

"Lossky, Vladimir Nikolaevich." In *Dictionary of Christian Biography*, edited by Michael Walsh, 787. Collegeville, MN: Liturgical, 2001.

Lyon, David. *Postmodernity*. Concepts in Social Thought. Minneapolis: University of Minnesota Press, 1994.

Ma, Wonsuk. "Biblical Studies in the Pentecostal Tradition: Yesterday, Today, and Tomorrow." In *The Globalization of Pentecostalism: A Religion Made to Travel*, edited by Murray W. Dempster et al., 52–69. Oxford: Regnum, 1999.

Macchia, Frank D. "African Enacting Theology: A Rediscovery of an Ancient Tradition?" *Pneuma* 24.2 (2002) 105–9.

———. "Astonished by Faithfulness to God: A Reflection on Karl Barth's Understanding of Spirit Baptism." In *The Spirit and Spirituality: Essays in Honor of Russell P. Spittler*, edited by Wonsuk Ma and Robert P. Menzies, 164–76. London: T. & T. Clark, 2004.

———. "The Azusa Street Mission and Revival: The Birth of the Global Pentecostal Movement." *Worship* 81.2 (2007) 190–91.

———. "B. B. Warfield and Karl Barth: Another Look at a Classical Evangelical Divide." In *From the Margins: A Celebration of the Theological Work of Donald W. Dayton*, edited by Christian T. Collins Winn, 207–19. Eugene, OR: Pickwick, 2007.

———. "Babel and the Tongues of Pentecost: Reversal or Fulfilment?—A Theological Perspective." In *Speaking in Tongues: Multi-Disciplinary Perspectives*, edited by Mark J. Cartledge, 34–51. Studies in Pentecostal and Charismatic Issues. Milton Keynes, UK: Paternoster, 2006.

———. *Baptized in the Spirit: A Global Pentecostal Theology*. Grand Rapids: Zondervan, 2006.

———. "Baptized in the Spirit: Towards a Global Pentecostal Theology." In *Defining Issues in Pentecostalism: Classical and Emergent*, edited by Steven M. Studebaker, 13–28. McMaster Theological Studies Series 1. Eugene, OR: Pickwick, 2008.

———. "Beyond Word and Sacrament: Rediscovering the Church's Charismatic Structure." *Living Pulpit* 9.4 (2000) 28–29.

———. "Christian Experience and Authority in the World: A Pentecostal Viewpoint." *Ecumenical Trends* 31.8 (2002) 122–26.

———. "The Covenant of the Lamb's Bride: A Subversive Paradigm." *Living Pulpit* 14.3 (2005) 14–15.

———. "Democrat or Republican? Theological Reflection on Party Loyalty." *Pneuma* 26.2 (2004) 177–81.

———. "Discerning the Spirit in Life: A Review of God the Spirit by Michael Welker." *Journal of Pentecostal Theology* 5.10 (1997) 3–28.

———. "Discerning the Truth of Tongues Speech: A Response to Amos Yong." *Journal of Pentecostal Theology* 6.12 (1998) 67–71.

———. "Dominus Iesus: A Pentecostal Perspective." *Pneuma* 22.2 (2000) 169–75.

———. "Editorial: Terrorists, Security, and the Risk of Peace: Toward a Moral Vision." *Pneuma* 26.1 (2004) 1–3.

———. "Finitum Capax Infiniti: A Pentecostal Distinctive?" *Pneuma* 29.2 (2007) 185–87.

———. "From Azusa to Memphis: Evaluating the Racial Reconciliation Dialogue among Pentecostals." *Pneuma* 17.2 (1995) 203–18.

———. "From Azusa to Memphis: Where Do We Go from Here? Roundtable Discussions on the Memphis Colloquy." *Pneuma* 18.1 (1996) 113–40.

———. "God Present in a Confused Situation: The Mixed Influence of the Charismatic Movement on Classical Pentecostalism in the United States." *Pneuma* 18.1 (1996) 33–54.

———. "Groans Too Deep for Words: Towards a Theology of Tongues as Initial Evidence." *Asian Journal of Pentecostal Studies* 1.2 (1998) 149–73. Online: http://www.apts.edu/ajps/98-2/98-2-macchia.htm.

———. "'I Belong to Christ:' A Pentecostal Reflection on Paul's Passion for Unity." *Pneuma* 25.1 (2003) 1–6.

———. "Is Footwashing the Neglected Sacrament? A Theological Response to John Christopher Thomas." *Pneuma* 19.2 (1997) 239–49.

———. "Jan Milic Lochman: A Tribute to My Doktorvater." *Pneuma* 29.1 (2007) 1–3.

———. "Justification and the Spirit: A Pentecostal Reflection on the Doctrine by Which the Church Stands or Falls." *Pneuma* 22.1 (2000) 3–21.

———. "Justification through New Creation: The Holy Spirit and the Doctrine by Which the Church Stands or Falls." *Theology Today* 58.2 (2001) 202–17.

———. *Justified in the Spirit: Creation, Redemption, and the Triune God.* Pentecostal Manifestos. Grand Rapids: Eerdmans, 2010.

———. "Karl Barth Meets David Du Plessis: A New Pentecost or a Theater of the Absurd?" *Pneuma* 23.1 (2001) 5–8.

———. "The Kingdom and the Power: Spirit Baptism in Pentecostal and Ecumenical Perspective." In *The Work of the Spirit: Pneumatology and Pentecostalism,* edited by Michael Welker, 109–25. Grand Rapids: Eerdmans, 2006.

———. "The Nature and Purpose of the Church: A Pentecostal Response." Paper presented at the annual meeting of the Society for Pentecostal Studies, Regent University, Virginia Beach, VA, March 10–12, 2005.

———. "A North American Response." *Journal of Pentecostal Theology* 2.4 (1994) 25–33.

———. "Pinnock's Pneumatology: A Pentecostal Appreciation." *Journal of Pentecostal Theology* 14.2 (2006) 167–73.

———. "Praying for the Terrorists." *Pneuma* 23.2 (2001) 193–96.

———. "The Question of Tongues as Initial Evidence: A Review of *Initial Evidence,* Edited by Gary B. McGee." *Journal of Pentecostal Theology* 1.2 (1993) 117–27.

———. "Rediscovering the Church's Charismatic Structure." *Living Pulpit* 9.4 (2000) 28–29.

———. "A Reply to Rickie Moore." *Journal of Pentecostal Theology* 8.17 (2000) 15–19.

———. "A Response and Corresponding Request for Forgiveness." *Journal of Pentecostal Theology* 8.17 (2000) 22–23.

———. "Resurrection: A Dance of Life." *Pneuma* 27.2 (2005) 223–24.

———. "Revitalizing Theological Categories: A Classical Pentecostal Response to J. Rodman Williams's Renewal Theology." *Pneuma* 16.2 (1994) 293–304.

———. "The Secular and the Religious under the Shadow of the Cross: Implications in Christoph Blumhardt's Kingdom of Spirituality for a Christian Response to World Religions." In *Religion in a Secular City: Essays in Honor of Harvey Cox,* edited by Harvey G. Cox and Arvind Sharma, 59–77. Harrisburg, PA: Trinity, 2001.

———. "Sighs Too Deep for Words: Toward a Theology of Glossolalia." *Journal of Pentecostal Theology* 1.1 (1992) 47–73.

———. "Signs of Grace in a Graceless World: The Charismatic Structure of the Church in Trinitarian Perspective." In *The Azusa Street Revival and Its Legacy,* edited by Harold D. Hunter and Cecil M. Robeck, Jr., 205–14. Cleveland, TN: Pathway, 2006.

———. "The Spirit and Life: A Further Response to Jürgen Moltmann." *Journal of Pentecostal Theology* 2.5 (1994) 121–27.

———. "The Spirit and the Kingdom: Implications in the Message of the Blumhardts for a Pentecostal Social Spirituality." *Transformation* 11.1 (1994) 1–5, 32.

———. "The Spirit of God and the Spirit of Life: An Evangelical Response to Karl Barth's Pneumatology." In *Karl Barth and Evangelical Theology: Convergences and Divergences*, edited by Sung Wook Chung, 149–71. Grand Rapids: Baker Academic, 2006.

———. "Spirit, Word, and Kingdom: Theological Reflections on the Reformed/Pentecostal Dialogue." *Ecumenical Trends* 30.3 (2001) 1–7.

———. *Spirituality and Social Liberation: The Message of the Blumhardts in the Light of Wuerttemberg Pietism.* Metuchen, NJ: Scarecrow, 1993.

———. "The Struggle for Global Witness: Shifting Paradigms in Pentecostal Theology." In *The Globalization of Pentecostalism: A Religion Made to Travel*, edited by Murray W. Dempster et al., 8–29. Oxford: Regnum, 1999.

———. "Terrorists, Security, and the Risk of Peace: Toward a Moral Vision." *Pneuma* 26.1 (2004) 1–3.

———. "Theology, Pentecostal." In *The New International Dictionary of Pentecostal and Charismatic Movements*, revised and expanded ed., edited by Stanley M. Burgess, 1120–41. Grand Rapids: Zondervan, 2002.

———. "Tongues and Prophecy: A Pentecostal Perspective." In *Pentecostal Movements as an Ecumenical Challenge*, edited by Jürgen Moltmann and Karl-Josef Kuschel, 63–69. Concilium. Maryknoll, NY: Orbis, 1996.

———. "Tongues as a Sign: Towards a Sacramental Understanding of Pentecostal Experience." *Pneuma* 15.1 (1993) 61–76.

———. "The Tongues of Pentecost: A Pentecostal Perspective on the Promise and Challenge of Pentecostal/Roman Catholic Dialogue." *Journal of Ecumenical Studies* 35.1 (1998) 1–18.

———. "The 'Toronto Blessing': No Laughing Matter." *Journal of Pentecostal Theology* 4.8 (1996) 3–6.

———. "Tradition and the Novum of the Spirit: A Review of Clark Pinnock's *Flame of Love*." *Journal of Pentecostal Theology* 6.13 (1998) 31–48.

———. *The Trinity, Practically Speaking.* Colorado Springs: Biblica, 2010.

———. "Unity and Otherness: Lessons from Babel and Pentecost." *Living Pulpit* 13.4 (2004) 5–7.

———. "Waiting and Hurrying for the Healing of Creation: Implications in the Message of the Blumhardts for a Pentecostal Theology of Divine Healing." Paper presented at the annual meeting of the Society for Pentecostal Studies, Wycliffe College, Toronto, March 7–9, 1996.

———. "The Wrath of the Lamb: A Case of Cognitive Dissonance." *Living Pulpit* 8.1 (1999) 40–42.

Mackintosh, Hugh Ross. *Types of Modern Theology: Schleiermacher to Barth.* London: Nisbet, 1937.

Maddox, Randy L. "The Enriching Role of Experience." In *Wesley and the Quadrilateral: Renewing the Conversation*, edited by W. Stephen Gunter, 107–27. Nashville, TN: Abingdon, 1997.

———. *Responsible Grace: John Wesley's Practical Theology.* Nashville, TN: Kingswood, 1994.

Massey, Richard D. "The Word of God: 'Thus Saith the Lord.'" In *Pentecostal Perspectives*, edited by Keith Warrington, 64–79. Carlisle, UK: Paternoster, 1998.

McDonnell, Kilian, et al. "Confessions of a Catholic and a Pentecostal Ecumenist." *International Review of Mission* 89.355 (2000) 568–71.

McDonnell, Kilian, and Frank D. Macchia. "Confession of Sins." *Pneuma* 22.1 (2000) 23–25.

McGee, Gary B. "Early Pentecostal Hermeneutics: Tongues as Evidence." In *Initial Evidence: Historical and Biblical Perspectives on the Pentecostal Doctrine of Spirit Baptism*, edited by Gary B. McGee, 96–118. Peabody, MA: Hendrickson, 1991.

———. "Popular Expositions of Initial Evidence." In *Initial Evidence: Historical and Biblical Perspectives on the Pentecostal Doctrine of Spirit Baptism*, edited by Gary B. McGee, 119–30. Peabody, MA: Hendrickson, 1991.

McGee, Gary B., ed. *Initial Evidence: Historical and Biblical Perspectives on the Pentecostal Doctrine of Spirit Baptism*. Peabody, MA: Hendrickson, 1991.

McKay, John. "When the Veil Is Taken Away: The Impact of Prophetic Experience on Biblical Interpretation." *Journal of Pentecostal Theology* 2.5 (1994) 17–40.

Menzies, William W. "The Non-Wesleyan Origins of the Pentecostal Movement." In *Aspects of Pentecostal-Charismatic Origins*, edited by Vinson Synan, 81–98. Plainfield, NJ: Logos International, 1975.

Menzies, William W., and Robert P. Menzies. *Spirit and Power: Foundations of Pentecostal Experience: A Call to Evangelical Dialogue*. Grand Rapids: Zondervan, 2000.

Middleton, J. Richard, and Brian J. Walsh. *Truth Is Stranger Than It Used to Be: Biblical Faith in a Postmodern Age*. Downers Grove, IL: InterVarsity, 1995.

Miller, Donald E., and Tetsunao Yamamori. *Global Pentecostalism: The New Face of Christian Social Engagement*. Berkeley: University of California Press, 2007.

Moltmann, Jürgen. "An Autobiographical Note by Jürgen Moltmann." In *God, Hope, and History: Jürgen Moltmann and the Christian Concept of History*, edited by A. J. Conyers, 203–23. Macon, GA: Mercer, 1988.

———. *The Church in the Power of the Spirit: A Contribution to Messianic Ecclesiology*. Translated by Margaret Kohl. Minneapolis: Fortress, 1993.

———. "Come Holy Spirit—Renew the Whole of Creation." In *History and the Triune God: Contributions to Trinitarian Theology*, translated by John Bowden, 70–79. London: SCM, 1991.

———. *The Coming of God: Christian Eschatology*. Translated by Margaret Kohl. Minneapolis: Fortress, 1996.

———. "Creation and Redemption." In *Creation, Christ and Culture: Studies in Honour of T. F. Torrance*, edited by Richard W. A. McKinney, 119–34. Edinburgh: T. & T. Clark, 1976.

———. *The Crucified God: The Cross of Christ as the Foundation and Criticism of Christian Theology*. Translated by John Bowden and R. A. Wilson. Minneapolis: Fortress, 1993.

———. *Experiences in Theology: Ways and Forms of Christian Theology*. Translated by Margaret Kohl. Minneapolis: Fortress, 2000.

———. *Experiences of God*. Philadelphia: Fortress, 1980.

———. *God for a Secular Society: The Public Relevance of Theology*. Translated by Margaret Kohl. Minneapolis: Fortress, 1999.

———. *God in Creation: A New Theology of Creation and the Spirit of God*. Translated by Margaret Kohl. Minneapolis: Fortress, 1993.

—. "A Response to My Dialogue Partners." *Journal of Pentecostal Theology* 2.4 (1994) 59–70.

—. "The Scope of Renewal in the Spirit." *Ecumenical Review* 42.2 (1990) 98–106.

—. *The Spirit of Life: A Universal Affirmation.* Translated by Margaret Kohl. Minneapolis: Fortress, 1992.

—. *Theology of Hope: On the Ground and the Implications of a Christian Eschatology.* Translated by James W. Leitch. Minneapolis: Fortress, 1993.

—. "Theology of Mystical Experience." *Scottish Journal of Theology* 32.6 (1979) 501–20.

—. "Trinitarian History of God." *Theology* 78.666 (1975) 632–46.

—. *The Trinity and the Kingdom of God: The Doctrine of God.* Translated by Margaret Kohl. Minneapolis: Fortress, 1993.

—. "The Wealth of Gifts of the Spirit and Their Christian Identity." In *Unanswered Questions,* edited by Christoph Theobald and Dietmar Mieth, 30–35. Concilium 1. London: SCM, 1999.

Moltmann, Jürgen, and Karl-Josef Kuschel, eds. *Pentecostal Movements as an Ecumenical Challenge.* Concilium. Maryknoll, NY: Orbis, 1996.

Moore, Rickie D. "A Letter to Frank Macchia." *Journal of Pentecostal Theology* 8.17 (2000) 12–14.

Moore, Robert L. "Toward a Psychological Understanding of Pentecostal Phenomena." Paper presented at the annual meeting for the Society for Pentecostal Studies, Lee University, Cleveland, TN, March 8–10, 2007.

Neumann, Peter D. "Encountering the Spirit: Pentecostal Mediated Experience of the Spirit in Theological Context." PhD diss., University of St. Michael's College, Toronto School of Theology, 2010.

—. "Whither Pentecostal Experience?: Mediated Experience of God in Pentecostal Theology." Paper presented at the annual meeting for the Society for Pentecostal Studies, Memphis, TN, March 10–12, 2011.

Nichols, David R. "The Search for a Pentecostal Structure in Systematic Theology." *Pneuma* 6.2 (1984) 57–76.

Nieto, José C. *Religious Experience and Mysticism: Otherness as Experience of Transcendence.* Lanham, MD: University Press of America, 1997.

Noble, E. Myron, ed. *Like as of Fire: Newspapers from the Azusa Street World Wide Revival.* Washington, DC: Middle Atlantic Regional, 1994.

Oden, Thomas C. *John Wesley's Scriptural Christianity: A Plain Exposition of His Teaching on Christian Doctrine.* Grand Rapids: Zondervan, 1994.

Olson, Roger E. "A Wind That Swirls Everywhere: Pentecostal Scholar Amos Yong Thinks He Sees the Holy Spirit Working in Other Religions, Too." *Christianity Today* 50.3 (March 2006) 52(3)–55.

Pailin, David A. "Reason in Relation to Scripture and Tradition." In *Scripture, Tradition and Reason: A Study in the Criteria of Christian Doctrine: Essays in Honour of Richard P. C. Hanson,* edited by Richard Bauckham and Benjamin Drewery, 207–38. Edinburgh: T. & T. Clark, 1988.

Palma, Anthony D., and Stanley M. Horton. *The Holy Spirit: A Pentecostal Perspective.* Springfield, MO: Logion, 2001.

Parker, Stephen E. "Led by the Spirit: Toward a Practical Theology of Pentecostal Discernment and Decision Making." PhD diss., Emory University, 1992.

————. "Pentecostal Experience: Object Relations and the Work of the Holy Spirit." Paper presented at the annual meeting for the Society for Pentecostal Studies, Lee University, Cleveland, TN, March 8–10, 2007.

Pattison, George. "What to Say: Reflections on Mysticism after Modernity." In *Transcending Boundaries in Philosophy and Theology: Reason, Meaning and Experience*, edited by Kevin J. Vanhoozer and Martin Warner, 191–205. Aldershot, UK: Ashgate, 2007.

Pearlman, Myer. *Knowing the Doctrines of the Bible.* Springfield, MO: Gospel, 1939.

Pentecostal Assemblies of Canada. *Statement of Fundamental and Essential Truths.* Mississauga, ON: Pentecostal Assemblies of Canada, 1994.

Petts, David. "The Baptism in the Holy Spirit: The Theological Distinctive." In *Pentecostal Perspectives*, edited by Keith Warrington, 98–119. Carlisle, UK: Paternoster, 1998.

Pinnock, Clark. "A Bridge and Some Points of Growth: A Reply to Cross and Macchia." *Journal of Pentecostal Theology* 6.13 (1998) 49–54.

Plüss, Jean-Daniel. "The Frog King: Or the Coming of Age of Pentecostalism." *Cyberjournal for Pentecostal-Charismatic Research* 9 (2001). No pages. Online: http://www.pctii.org/cyberj/cyberj9/pluss.html.

————. "Religious Experience in Worship: A Pentecostal Perspective." *PentecoStudies* 2.1 (2003) 1–21. Online: http://www.glopent.net/pentecostudies/2003/pluess2003.pdf/view.

Poirier, John C., and B. Scott Lewis. "Pentecostal and Postmodernist Hermeneutics: A Critique of Three Conceits." *Journal of Pentecostal Theology* 15.1 (2006) 3–21.

Pojman, Louis P. *Philosophy: The Pursuit of Wisdom.* 4th ed. Belmont, CA: Thomson/Wadsworth, 2004.

Poloma, Margaret M. "The Sociological Context of Religious Experience." In *Handbook of Religious Experience*, edited by Ralph W. Hood, 161–82. Birmingham, AL: Religious Education, 1995.

Postlethwait, D. Michael. "The Soteriological Language and Experience of Luke's Gospel as They Relate to a Lukan Pneumatology and Its Impact on Pentecostal Theology." Paper presented at the annual meeting of the Society for Pentecostal Studies, Fuller Theological Seminary, Pasadena, CA, March 23–25, 2006.

Price, Matthew. "Why Experience Matters: What Pragmatists Teach Wesleyans About Educational Experience." Paper presented at the annual meeting for the Society for Pentecostal Studies, Asbury Theological Seminary, Wilmore, KY, March 20–22, 2003.

Railey James H., Jr., and Benny C. Aker. "Theological Foundations." In *Systematic Theology*, edited by Stanley M. Horton, 39–60. Rev. ed. Springfield, MO: Logion, 1994.

Reed, David A. *"In Jesus' Name": The History and Beliefs of Oneness Pentecostals.* Dorset, UK: Deo, 2008.

————. "Oneness Pentecostalism." In *The New International Dictionary of Pentecostal and Charismatic Movements*, edited by Stanley M. Burgess, 936–44. Revised and Expanded ed. Grand Rapids: Zondervan, 2002.

Robeck, Cecil M., Jr. "An Emerging Magisterium?: The Case of the Assemblies of God." In *The Spirit and Spirituality: Essays in Honour of Russell P. Spittler*, edited by Wonsuk Ma and Robert P. Menzies, 212–52. London: T. & T. Clark, 2004.

————. "Pentecostal Origins in Global Perspective." In *All Together in One Place*, edited by Harold D. Hunter and Peter D. Hocken, 166–80. Sheffield, UK: Sheffield Academic, 1993.

————. "Pentecostals and Ecumenism in a Pluralistic World." In *The Globalization of Pentecostalism: A Religion Made to Travel*, edited by Murray W. Dempster et al., 338–62. Oxford: Regnum, 1999.

————. "Taking Stock of Pentecostalism: The Personal Reflections of a Retiring Editor." *Pneuma* 15.1 (1993) 35–60.

Robinson, Brian. "A Pentecostal Hermeneutic of Religious Experience." Paper presented at the annual meeting for the Society for Pentecostal Studies, Assemblies of God Theological Seminary, Springfield, MO, Nov. 12–14, 1992.

Robinson, Martin. "David Du Plessis—A Promise Fulfilled." In *Pentecost, Mission, and Ecumenism: Essays on Intercultural Theology: Festschrift in Honour of Professor Walter J. Hollenweger*, edited by J. A. B. Jongeneel, 143–55. New York: Lang, 1992.

Robson, R. Brian. "A Response to Simon Chan's 'The Church and the Development of Doctrine.'" Paper presented at the conference: The Spirit in Tradition?, Wycliffe College, Toronto, March 3, 2003.

Rossi, Philip. "The Authority of Experience: What Counts as Experience?" In *Religious Experience and Contemporary Theological Epistemology* 188, edited by L. Boeve et al., 269–84. Bibliotheca Ephemeridum Theologicarum Lovaniensium. Leuven: Peeters, 2005.

Schleiermacher, Friedrich. *The Christian Faith*. Translated by Richard Crouter. Edited by H. R. Mackintosh and J. S. Stewart. Texts in German Philosophy. Edinburgh: T. & T. Clark, 1928.

Schlitt, Dale M. *Theology and the Experience of God*. American Liberal Religious Thought. New York: Lang, 2001.

Schner, George P. "The Appeal to Experience." *Theological Studies* 53.1 (1992) 40–59.

————. "'. . . New Ways of Speaking with Love and Mercy . . .': The Teaching Responsibility of the Church in Our Times." Paper presented at Villanova University, Feb. 10, 1994.

Sepúlveda, Juan. "The Perspective of Chilean Pentecostalism." *Journal of Pentecostal Theology* 2.4 (1994) 41–49.

Shaull, Richard, and Waldo A. Cesar. *Pentecostalism and the Future of the Christian Churches: Promises, Limitations, Challenges*. Grand Rapids: Eerdmans, 2000.

Sheppard, Gerald T. "Biblical Interpretation after Gadamer." *Pneuma* 16.1 (1994) 121–41.

————. "Pentecostals and the Hermeneutics of Dispensationalism: The Anatomy of an Uneasy Relationship." *Pneuma* 6.2 (1984) 5–33.

————. "Pentecostals, Globalization, and Postmodern Hermeneutics: Implications for the Politics of Scriptural Interpretation." In *The Globalization of Pentecostalism: A Religion Made to Travel*, edited by Murray W. Dempster, Byron D. Klaus, and Douglas Petersen, 289–312. Oxford: Regnum, 1999.

————. "The Seduction of Pentecostals within the Politics of Exegesis: The Nicene Creed, Filioque, and Pentecostal Ambivalence Regarding an Ecumenical Challenge of a Common Confession of Apostolic Faith." Paper presented at the annual meeting for the Society for Pentecostal Studies, Mother of God Community, Gaithersburg, MD, Nov. 14–16, 1985.

Shuman, Joel J. "Toward a Cultural-Linguistic Account of the Pentecostal Doctrine of the Baptism of the Holy Spirit." *Pneuma* 19.2 (1997) 207–23.

Sire, James W. *The Universe Next Door: A Basic Worldview Catalog.* 4th ed. Downers Grove, IL: InterVarsity, 2004.

Smith, Harold, ed. *Pentecostals from the Inside Out.* The Christianity Today Series. Wheaton, IL: Victor, 1990.

Smith, James K. A. "Advice to Pentecostal Philosophers." Paper presented at the annual meeting for the Society for Pentecostal Studies, Oral Roberts University, Tulsa, OK, March 8–10, 2001.

———. "The Closing of the Book: Pentecostals, Evangelicals, and the Sacred Writings." *Journal of Pentecostal Theology* 5.11 (1997) 49–71.

———. "Faith and the Conditions of Possibility of Experience: A Response to Kevin Hart." In *The Experience of God: A Postmodern Response*, edited by Kevin Hart and Barbara Eileen Wall, 87–92. Perspectives in Continental Philosophy 48. New York: Fordham University Press, 2005.

———. "The Spirit, Religions, and the World as Sacrament: A Response to Amos Yong's Pneumatological Assist." *Journal of Pentecostal Theology* 15.2 (2007) 251–61.

———. "Teaching a Calvinist to Dance." *Christianity Today* 52.5 (May 2008). No pages. Online: http://www.christianitytoday.com/ct/2008/may/25.42.html.

Smith, James K. A., and Amos Yong, eds. *Science and the Spirit: A Pentecostal Engagement with the Sciences.* Bloomington, IN: Indiana University Press, 2010.

Smith, Ken. "Spirit, Word, and Stream of Consciousness: Some Implications of Jamesian Pragmatist Theory for Pentecostal Thought and Practice." Paper presented at the annual meeting for the Society for Pentecostal Studies, Regent University, Virginia Beach, VA, March 10–12, 2005.

Spittler, Russell P. "Maintaining Distinctives: The Future of Pentecostalism." In *Pentecostals from the Inside Out*, edited by Harold Smith, 121–34. The Christianity Today Series. Wheaton, IL: Victor, 1990.

———. "Spirituality, Pentecostal and Charismatic." In *The New International Dictionary of Pentecostal and Charismatic Movements*, revised and expanded ed., edited by Stanley M. Burgess, 1096–1102. Grand Rapids: Zondervan, 2002.

Staples, Peter. "Ecumenical Theology and Pentecostalism." In *Pentecost, Mission, and Ecumenism: Essays on Intercultural Theology: Festschrift in Honour of Professor Walter J. Hollenweger*, edited by J. A. B. Jongeneel, 261–71. Studien Zur Interkulturellen Geschichte Des Christentums. New York: Lang, 1992.

Stephenson, Christopher A. "Epistemology and Pentecostal Systematic Theology: Myer Pearlman, E. S. Williams, and French L. Arrington." Paper presented at the annual meeting of the Society for Pentecostal Studies, Lee University, Cleveland, TN, March 8–10, 2007.

———. "The Rule of Spirituality and the Rule of Doctrine: A Necessary Relationship in Theological Method." *Journal of Pentecostal Theology* 15.1 (2006) 83–105.

Stibbe, Mark W. G. "A British Appraisal." *Journal of Pentecostal Theology* 2.4 (1994) 5–16.

Stoker, Wessel. "The Rationality of Religious Experience and the Accountability of Faith." In *Religious Experience and Contemporary Theological Epistemology*, edited by L. Boeve et al., 285–301. Bibliotheca Ephemeridum Theologicarum Lovaniensium 188. Leuven: Peeters, 2005.

Stronstad, Roger. *The Charismatic Theology of St. Luke.* Peabody, MA: Hendrickson, 1984.

———. *"The Charismatic Theology of St. Luke* Revisited (Special Emphasis Upon Being Baptized in the Holy Spirit)." In *Defining Issues in Pentecostalism: Classical and Emergent,* edited by Steven M. Studebaker, 101–22. McMaster Theological Studies Series 1. Eugene, OR: Pickwick, 2008.

———. "Pentecostalism, Experiential Presuppositions and Hermeneutics." Paper presented at the annual meeting for the Society for Pentecostal Studies, Christ for the Nations Institute, Dallas, TX, Nov. 8–10, 1990.

———. *The Prophethood of All Believers: A Study in Luke's Charismatic Theology.* Journal of Pentecostal Theology Supplement Series 16. Sheffield, UK: Sheffield Academic, 1999.

Suurmond, Jean-Jacques. *Word and Spirit at Play: Towards a Charismatic Theology.* Grand Rapids: Eerdmans, 1995.

Synan, Vinson, ed. *The Century of the Holy Spirit: 100 Years of Pentecostal and Charismatic Renewal, 1901–2001.* Nashville, TN: Thomas Nelson, 2001.

Tarr, Del. "Transcendence, Immanence, and the Emerging Pentecostal Academy." In *Pentecostalism in Context: Essays in Honor of William W. Menzies,* edited by Wonsuk Ma and Robert P. Menzies, 195–222. Journal of Pentecostal Theology Supplement Series 11. Sheffield, UK: Sheffield Academic, 1997.

Thomas, John Christopher. "Pentecostal Theology in the Twenty-First Century." *Pneuma* 20.1 (1998) 3–19.

Thorsen, Donald A. D. *The Wesleyan Quadrilateral: Scripture, Tradition, Reason & Experience as a Model of Evangelical Theology.* Lexington, KY: Emeth, 1990.

Turner, Max. *Power from on High: The Spirit in Israel's Restoration and Witness in Luke-Acts.* Journal of Pentecostal Theology Supplement Series 9. Sheffield, UK: Sheffield Academic, 1996.

"Vital Theology." No pages. Online: http://www.vitaltheology.com/advisory.shtml.

Vlach, Michael J. "Jürgen Moltmann." *TheologicalStudies.org* (November 2004). No pages. Online: http://theologicalstudies.org/resource-library/theologian-biographies/modernpostmodern-theologians/313-jurgen-moltmann-b-1926.

Voiss, James K. "Thought Forms and Theological Constructs: Toward Grounding the Appeal to Experience in Contemporary Theological Discourse." In *Encountering Transcendence: Contributions to a Theology of Christian Religious Experience,* edited by L. Boeve et al., 241–56. Annua Nuntia Lovaniensia 53. Leuven: Peeters, 2005.

Wacker, Grant. *Heaven Below: Early Pentecostals and American Culture.* Cambridge: Harvard University Press, 2001.

———. "Playing for Keeps: The Primitivist Impulse in Early Pentecostalism." In *The American Quest for the Primitive Church,* edited by Richard T. Hughes, 196–219. Urbana, IL: University of Illinois Press, 1988.

———. "'Wild Theories and Mad Excitement.'" In *Pentecostals from the Inside Out,* edited by Harold B. Smith, 19–28. The Christianity Today Series. Wheaton, IL: Victor, 1990.

Ward, Horace S. "The Anti-Pentecostal Argument." In *Aspects of Pentecostal-Charismatic Origins,* edited by Vinson Synan, 99–122. Plainfield, NJ: Logos International, 1975.

Warrington, Keith. "Experience: The Sina Qua Non of Pentecostalism." Paper presented at the annual meeting of the Society for Pentecostal Studies, Lee University, Cleveland, TN, March 8–10, 2007.

———. *Pentecostal Theology: A Theology of Encounter.* London: T. & T. Clark, 2008.

Wiebe, Phillip H. "Religious Experience, Cognitive Science, and the Future of Religion." Paper presented at the annual meeting for the Society for Pentecostal Studies, Lee University, Cleveland, TN, March 8–10, 2007.

Wulff, David M. "Phenomenological Psychology and Religious Experience." In *Handbook of Religious Experience*, edited by Ralph W. Hood, 183–99. Birmingham, AL: Religious Education, 1995.

Yong, Amos. "Academic Glossolalia? Pentecostal Scholarship, Multi-Disciplinarity, and the Science-Religion Conversation." *Journal of Pentecostal Theology* 14.1 (2005) 61–80.

———. "As the Spirit Gives Utterance: Pentecost, Intra-Christian Ecumenism and the Wider Oikoumene." *International Review of Mission* 92.366 (2003) 299–314.

———. "Asian American Religions." *Nova religio* 9.3 (2006) 92–107.

———. "Beyond *Beyond the Impasse*? Responding to Dale Irvin." *Journal of Pentecostal Theology* 12.2 (2004) 281–85.

———. *Beyond the Impasse: Toward a Pneumatological Theology of Religions.* Grand Rapids: Baker Academic, 2003.

———. "Beyond the Liberal-Conservative Divide: An Appreciative Rejoinder to Allan Anderson." *Journal of Pentecostal Theology* 16.1 (2007) 103–11.

———. "Can We Get 'Beyond the Paradigm'?—A Response to Terry Muck's Proposal in Theology of Religions." *Interpretation* 61.1 (2007) 28–32.

———. "Christian and Buddhist Perspectives on Neuropsychology and the Human Person: Pneuma and Pratityasamutpada." *Zygon* 40.1 (2005) 143–65.

———. "The Demise of Foundationalism and the Retention of Truth: What Evangelicals Can Learn from C. S. Peirce." *Christian Scholar's Review* 29.3 (2000) 563–88.

———. "Disability, the Human Condition, and the Spirit of the Eschatological Long Run." *Journal of Religion, Disability & Health* 11.1 (2007) 5–25.

———. *Discerning the Spirit(s): A Pentecostal-Charismatic Contribution to Christian Theology of Religions.* Journal of Pentecostal Theology Supplement Series 20. Sheffield, UK: Sheffield Academic, 2000.

———. "Discerning the Spirit(s) in the Natural World: Toward a Typology of 'Spirit' in the Religion and Science Conversation." *Theology and Science* 3.3 (2005) 315–29.

———. "Divine Omniscience and Future Contingents: Weighing the Presuppositional Issues in the Contemporary Debate." *Evangelical Review of Theology* 26.3 (2002) 240–64.

———. "God and the Evangelical Laboratory: Recent Conservative Protestant Thinking about Theology and Science." *Theology and Science* 5.2 (2007) 203–21.

———. "God in the Wasteland: The Reality of Truth in a World of Fading Dreams." *Pneuma* 18.2 (1996) 239–43.

———. "The Holy Spirit and World Religions: On the Christian Discernment of Spirit(S) "After" Buddhism." *Buddhist-Christian Studies* 24 (2004) 191–207.

———. *Hospitality and the Other: Pentecost, Christian Practices, and the Neighbor.* Faith Meets Faith. Maryknoll, NY: Orbis, 2008.

———. "In Search of Foundations: The Oeuvre of Donald L. Gelpi, S.J., and Its Significance for Pentecostal Theology and Philosophy." *Journal of Pentecostal Theology* 11.1 (2002) 3–26.

———. *In the Days of Caesar: Pentecostalism and Political Theology*. The Cadbury Lectures, 2009. Grand Rapids: Eerdmans, 2010.

———. "Interpreting Charismatic Experience: Hypnosis, Altered States of Consciousness and the Holy Spirit?" *Journal of Pentecostal Theology* 6.13 (1998) 117–32.

———. "The Inviting Spirit: Pentecostal Beliefs and Practices Regarding the Religions Today." In *Defining Issues in Pentecostalism: Classical and Emergent*, edited by Steven M. Studebaker, 29–45. McMaster Theological Studies Series 1. Eugene, OR: Pickwick, 2008.

———. "Justice Deprived, Justice Demanded: Afropentecostalisms and the Task of World Pentecostal Theology Today." *Journal of Pentecostal Theology* 15.1 (2006) 127–47.

———. "'Life in the Spirit': Pentecostal-Charismatic Life and the Dialectic of the Pneumatological Imagination." Paper presented at the annual meeting of the Society for Pentecostal Studies, Northwest College, Kirkland, WA, March 16–18, 2000.

———. "No Place for Truth, or Whatever Happened to Evangelical Theology." *Pneuma* 18.2 (1996) 239–43.

———. "'Not Knowing Where the Wind Blows . . .': On Envisioning a Pentecostal-Charismatic Theology of Religions." Paper presented at the annual meeting of the Society for Pentecostal Studies, Church of God Theological Seminary, Cleveland, TN, March 12–14, 1998.

———. "On Divine Presence and Divine Agency: Toward a Foundational Pneumatology." Paper presented at the annual meeting of the Society for Pentecostal Studies, Evangel University, Springfield, MO, March 11–13, 1999.

———. "Oneness and the Trinity: The Theological and Ecumenical Implications of Creation *Ex Nihilo* for an Intra-Pentecostal Dispute." *Pneuma* 19.1 (1997) 81–107.

———. "Pentecostalism and Ecumenism: Past, Present and Future." *Pneuma Review* 4.3 (2001). No pages. Online: http://www.pneumafoundation.com/article.jsp?article=article_ecum3.xml.

———. "Pentecostalism and the Theological Academy." *Theology Today* 64.2 (2007) 244–50.

———. "A P(new)matological Paradigm for Christian Mission in a Religiously Plural World." *Missiology* 33.2 (2005) 175–91.

———. "Poured out on All Flesh: The Spirit, World Pentecostalism, and the Renewal of Theology and Praxis in the 21st Century." *PentecoStudies* 6.1 (2007) 16–46. Online: http://www.glopent.net/pentecostudies/2007/yong-2007.pdf/view.

———. "Radically Orthodox, Reformed, and Pentecostal: Rethinking the Intersection of Post/Modernity and the Religions in Conversation with James K. A. Smith." *Journal of Pentecostal Theology* 15.2 (2007) 233–50.

———. "*Ruach*, the Primordial Chaos, and the Breath of Life: Emergence Theory and the Creation Narratives in Pneumatological Perspective." In *The Work of the Spirit: Pneumatology and Pentecostalism*, edited by Michael Welker, 183–204. Grand Rapids: Eerdmans, 2006.

—————. *The Spirit of Creation: Modern Science and Divine Action in the Pentecostal-Charismatic Imagination*. Pentecostal Manifestos. Grand Rapids: Eerdmans, 2011.

—————. *The Spirit Poured Out on All Flesh: Pentecostalism and the Possibility of Global Theology*. Grand Rapids: Baker Academic, 2005.

—————. *Spirit-Word-Community: Theological Hermeneutics in Trinitarian Perspective*. Burlington, VT: Ashgate, 2002.

—————. "Spiritual Discernment: A Biblical-Theological Reconsideration." In *The Spirit and Spirituality: Essays in Honor of Russell P. Spittler*, edited by Wonsuk Ma and Robert P. Menzies, 83–107. London: T. & T. Clark, 2004.

—————. *Theology and Down Syndrome: Reimagining Disability in Late Modernity*. Waco, TX: Baylor University Press, 2007.

—————. "'Tongues of Fire' in the Pentecostal Imagination: The Truth of Glossolalia in Light of R. C. Neville's Theory of Religious Symbolism." *Journal of Pentecostal Theology* 6.12 (1998) 39–65.

—————. "'Tongues,' Theology, and the Social Sciences: A Pentecostal-Theological Reading of Geertz's Interpretive Theory of Religion." *Cyberjournal for Pentecostal-Charismatic Research* 1 (1997). No pages. Online: http://www.pctii.org/cyberj/cyberj1/yong.html.

—————. "The Truth of Tongues Speech: A Rejoinder to Frank Macchia." *Journal of Pentecostal Theology* 6.13 (1998) 107–15.

—————. "The Turn to Pneumatology in Christian Theology of Religions: Conduit or Detour?" *Journal of Ecumenical Studies* 35.3–4 (1998) 437–38.

—————. "Whither Systematic Theology? A Systematician Chimes in on a Scandalous Conversation." *Pneuma* 20.1 (1998) 85–93.

—————. "Whither Theological Inclusivism? The Development and Critique of an Evangelical Theology of Religions." *Evangelical Quarterly* 71.4 (1999) 327–48.

—————. "Whose Tongues, Which Interpretations?: Pentecostalism and the Possibility of World Theology." Paper presented at the annual meeting of the Society for Pentecostal Studies, Marquette University, Milwaukee, WI, March 11–13, 2004.

—————. "The Word and the Spirit or the Spirit and the Word: Exploring the Boundaries of Evangelicalism in Relationship to Modern Pentecostalism." *Trinity Journal* 23.2 (2002) 235–52.

Yong, Amos, et al. "Christ and Spirit: Dogma, Discernment, and Dialogical Theology in a Religiously Plural World." *Journal of Pentecostal Theology* 12.1 (2003) 15–83.

Yun, Koo Dong. "A Metaphysical Construct of Experience: Concerning the Problematic Usage of 'Experience' within Pentecostal Horizons." Paper presented at the annual meeting for the Society for Pentecostal Studies, Lee University, Cleveland, TN, March 8–10, 2007.

Author Index

Subject Index